Language   S

William Downes has been lecturer in linguistics in the
School of English and American Studies, University
of East Anglia, since 1976. Born in Canada, he was
educated there at Queen's University and the
University of Toronto, before coming to England to
study at University College London. He taught
English and linguistics at York University, Toronto,
from 1966 to 1968, and at the London School of
Economics from 1972 to 1976, and has published
papers in the area of discourse and belief systems and
the relationship between syntax and pragmatics.

Fontana Linguistics

William Downes

Language and Society

Fontana Paperbacks

First published in 1984 by Fontana Paperbacks
8 Grafton Street, London W1X 3LA

Second impression August 1988

Copyright © William Downes 1984

Set in 10 on 11 point Times by Aylesbury Keyboarding

Printed and Bound in Great Britain by
Hartnolls Limited, Bodmin, Cornwall

Author's acknowledgements: I gratefully acknowledge all
those works which are referred to in this book, and the
scholars on whose research it depends. For permission to
quote from published works, thanks are due to Alan
Sillitoe, for passages from *Saturday Night and Sunday
Morning* © Alan Sillitoe; McGraw-Hill Ryerson Ltd,
Toronto, for stanza from 'Montreal' by A. M. Klein (1948);
Thames and Hudson for 'the Robeson text' (Bentley, 1972);
Cambridge University Press (Trudgill, 1974); Edward
Arnold, publishers of the series Social Psychology of
Language (Hughes and Trudgill, 1979; Ryan and Giles,
1982); Basil Blackwell (Boissevain, 1974; Milroy, 1980);
Adademic Press (Frake, 1975); Center for Applied
Linguistics (Wolfram, 1969; Wolfram and Chistian, 1976;
Labov, 1966); John Wiley and Sons (Lieberson, 1970); and
M. Laferriere whose work on the (or) variable and ethnicity
in Boston I have used (Laferriere, 1979). Full
bibliographical details of all works referred to are given in
the text and references. Particular thanks to Peter Trudgill
(or helping to correct Figure 6.3; and a special
acknowledgement to Professor William Labov on whom so
much of modern sociolinguistics depends, including this
book.

Contents

Introduction to Fontana Linguistics

In the past twenty-five years, linguistics – the systematic study of language – has come of age. It is a fast expanding and increasingly popular subject, which is now offered as a degree course at a number of universities. As a result of this expansion, psychologists, sociologists, philosophers, anthropologists, teachers, speech therapists and numerous others have realized that language is of crucial importance in their life and work. But when they tried to find out more about the subject, a major problem faced them – the technical and often narrow nature of much writing about linguistics.

The Fontana Linguistics series is an attempt to solve this problem by presenting current findings in a lucid and non-technical way, both for students of linguistics and other interested social scientists. Its object is twofold. First, it hopes to outline the 'state of play' in certain crucial areas of the subject, concentrating on what is happening now, rather than on surveying the past. Secondly, it aims to show how linguistics links up with other disciplines such as sociology, psychology, philosophy, speech therapy and language teaching.

The series will, we hope, give readers a fuller understanding of the relationship between language and other aspects of human behaviour, as well as equipping those who wish to find out more about the subject with a basis from which to read some of the more technical literature in textbooks and journals.

Jean Aitchison
London School of Economics

1. Linguistics and Sociolinguistics

> It is difficult to see adequately the functions of language, because it is so deeply rooted in the whole of human behaviour that it may be suspected that there is little in the functional side of our conscious behaviour in which language does not play its part.
>
> Sapir (1949)

Language is a complicated phenomenon. Consider the ways we use the word 'language' in our day-by-day conversation. We talk about how a child's 'language' is developing; how beautiful, or ugly, is the 'language' of a region or country. We read about political problems to do with 'language' in countries like Canada, Belgium or Wales. We comment on the obscure 'language' of legal documents and hear of calls for reform and simplification. People claim that problems of industrial relations are somehow fundamentally 'language' problems: "The trouble is," they note, "the two sides just do not speak the same 'language'." Teachers puzzle over their pupils' essays and conclude that "Johnny has no control over the English 'language'," and parents and politicians worry that there has been a decline in the standards of teaching English 'language' in schools.

At the same time, we talk of such things as 'body language', or the 'languages' of music, painting or dance. It is fairly clear that these various ordinary uses of the word refer to different aspects of language, and take different perspectives on the sort of thing language is. Or, alternatively, we have simply grouped together under the heading of 'language' a range of diverse phenomenon which are only partially related to each other.

In order to clarify our thoughts about language, let's look at some of the ways language is viewed by linguists. We can then give a precise statement of the specifically **sociolinguistic** view of language, and contrast it to other views of language assumed in **linguistics** proper.

The primary aim of all linguistic scholarship is to determine the properties of natural language, the features it has which distinguish it from any possible artificial language. This means that linguistics will be universalistic in its basic aims. It will examine individual natural languages in the course of constructing a theory of **universal grammar** that explains why the whole set of natural languages are the way they are. Natural languages, English, French and so on, are in fact the data for this theory of natural language. Artificial languages are of interest too since they can exhibit certain properties any language has, but they also have features that can sharply distinguish them from any naturally evolved language.

We will look at some artificial languages to illustrate this. The linguist Noam Chomsky, in his influential book *Syntactic Structures* (1957), employed the following languages in the course of his argument:

  (i) ab, aabb, aaabbb, ... and all sentences of the same type.
 (ii) aa, bb, abba, baab, aaaa, bbbb, aabbaa, abbbba, ... and all sentences of the same type.
(iii) aa, bb, abab, baba, aaaa, bbbb, aabaab, abbabb, ... and all sentences of the same type.

Why would we want to call (i), (ii) or (iii) languages? The answer is that they have certain properties of any language. They have a vocabulary of symbols, in this case two letters of the alphabet 'a' and 'b'. Also, they have a **syntax**. That is, each of the languages has specific rules for joining together their symbols to produce the sentences or strings of that language. If the rule of syntax is not followed, then the **string** or sentence produced is not a sentence of that language.

Consider the syntactic rules of the three languages. In language (i) the rule seems to be that for each sentence, whatever the number of occurrences of the first symbol, a, it is immediately followed by exactly the same number of occurrences of the second symbol, b. In language (ii), the rule is that, for each sentence, whatever the arrangement of a and b in the first half of that sentence, then that arrangement is repeated in reverse in the second half of the same sentence. I'll leave the reader to work out the equally simple syntax of language (iii).

Note that the output of the application of their respective

syntactic rules to the symbols of these languages is an *infinite set of strings* which are members of the language sharply distinguishable from another infinite set of strings which are not members of the language.

In brief, then, these artificial languages have vocabularies and syntactic rules for joining their symbols together. And, by following the rules of their syntax, an infinite set of strings can be produced. Natural languages can also be considered in this way. Thus, English can be viewed as a set of strings. And this infinite set is produced by the vocabulary and syntactic rules of English. If the linguist can construct a device, a **grammar**, which can specify the grammatical strings of English and separate them from the combinations of symbols which are not English, he has gone a considerable distance towards making explicit the syntactic properties of the language. And if the types of rule in that grammar are also necessary for the grammar of any natural language, then he might have discovered some of those universal properties of language which it is the aim of linguistics to discover. Chomsky, in fact, used languages (i), (ii) and (iii) to rule out a certain class of grammars as candidates for grammars of natural language.

Of course, the above artificial languages are also extremely unlike natural languages. The most noticeable difference is that the symbols and strings of the languages don't bear any relation to the world. The strings aren't true or false, for example. The languages have no **semantics**.

There are other man-made languages which have symbols referring to states of affairs and strings which can be true or false. An obvious example is mathematics. Consider a simple example from arithmetic:

$$(2 + 1) \times 3 = 9$$

This sum has a number of language-like properties. It has a vocabulary of symbols illustrated here by the numbers 2, 1, 3 and 9. It has rules for joining these numbers together to produce strings, for example, by the operations of 'addition' and 'multiplication' and the relationship of 'equals'. We know that the bracket means that the operation of addition precedes that of multiplication in that the sum of $2 + 1$ is to be multiplied by 3, rather than 2 be added to the multiplication of 3 by 1. But we also know that $(2 + 1) \times 3 = 9$ is true, as opposed to $(2 + 1) \times 3 = 12$, which we know is false.

For a sentence of any language to be true or false it must be able to pick out states of affairs in the world. And if we understand what the world must be like for the sentence to be true or false, then we must understand the mechanism by which the sentence 'picks out' those respective states of affairs. We understand the **meaning** of the sentences, the semantics of the language. Consider what you have to know about the world to know whether the sentence "Brenda is pregnant" is true or false. To start with, you would have to know that 'pregnant' means something like, "is going to have a baby", or that females normally give birth, and so on! What does the world have to be like if the sentence is to be true? That knowledge is equivalent to a knowledge of the meaning of the sentence.

So far, no social factors have been mentioned. How do social factors figure in the explanation of language? In the first artificial languages, of course, since the languages are used by Chomsky for the purposes of argument and not for communication with anyone else, social explanation is by definition excluded. In the case of the example from arithmetic, however, social factors are essential in explaining how the system is actually used. We can introduce society into our account in this way.

A fundamental factor making the arithmetical example work is **convention**. In the case, for example, of the symbols '2' or '9', we have confidence when we use them that our hearer or reader will understand that we intend to refer to sets of two or nine respectively. And our hearer and reader likewise has confidence, based on past experience, that in using '2' or '9' we intended to refer to sets of two or nine. This cooperative coordination is motivated by the fact that we both wish to convey our belief successfully. We could have used the symbols to refer to some other sets, or indeed to all birds and all crocodiles, but it wouldn't be in our interests to do so, since coordination with our hearers depends on their confidence that '2' is used to refer to two. Likewise with the syntactic symbols. So, via the notion of convention, social coordination underlies the mechanism of using a language to communicate.

Notice, however, that such conventions *do not explain* the particular properties of the language itself; the properties that characterize the set of strings. To say that '2' picks out all and only sets of two by convention, does not explain why the language has the symbol '2', or the symbol '4' and not some alternative symbols in some alternative arrangement. This is also true of natural language. The actual properties by virtue of which a set of strings are members of language appear to be **arbitrary**.

The obvious question now is: "Apart from convention, are there properties of natural language which *require* social explanation?" The answer is, "Yes, there are many such properties." We will now look at a typical example of one such property.

This property is called **variability**. Consider the English word 'butter'. On the levels of syntax, vocabulary and semantics, it is a single English item; a mass noun which means something like an edible, yellow, dairy product used in cooking and as a spread. Yet although it is one item, if I asked you to describe its pronunciation in English, you would not be able to give a single answer: there are various **phonetic** realizations of 'butter'.

In British English **Received Pronunciation** the *t* is made by putting the tongue tip on the ridge behind the teeth, and releasing the air in a small explosion without vibration of the vocal chords. The *r*, however, is not pronounced, although it is present in the written form. Instead, a vowel sound, schwa (phonetically transcribed as ə) follows the *t*. The schwa is the same sound that is normally final in the word *sofa*. Thus, the RP speaker and many other British English speakers say [bʌtə].

In Canadian and American accents there is a rule that when explosive sounds like *t* are made between two vowels, the vibration of the vocal chords, called **voice**, continues through the whole sequence. This has the effect of turning the [t], which is voiceless, into [d], which is its voiced counterpart. Thus, a Canadian saying 'butter' in fact pronounces it as if it were 'budder' (strictly speaking, this sound is not a normal [d] but a so-called 'flap' which involves a mere tap of the tongue). However, the Canadian and many of his American neighbours also have **r-full** accents (as do the Scots and Irish). This means that, unlike the RP British English speaker, he pronounces the written *r* in butter, giving us the final form [bʌdəʳ].

In many British English accents there is yet another variation in the pronunciation of *t* in this environment. The vocal chords themselves are closed tightly and then released abruptly, giving the impression that *t* is missing. In fact, the gap is filled by a so-called **glottal stop**, symbolized by ʔ. So 'butter' is pronounced [bʌʔə]. Such a pronunciation would typify London working-class speech, familiar to North Americans as a Cockney accent from films like *My Fair Lady*.

My Fair Lady, from George Bernard Shaw's *Pygmalion*, introduces another feature of the variability we have been describing. For Professor Higgins (modelled by Shaw on the famous phonetician, Henry Sweet) to take such pains to train Eliza Doolittle to pronounce words like 'butter' as [bʌtə], as opposed to [bʌʔə], indicates that the variation must mean something. There is no conceptual difference in the word-meaning itself. The meaning difference of the variation is socially significant and relates to those groups in a social structure who typically use one form rather than another. Such **social meanings** of variants can be further illustrated by looking at two other versions of 'butter'.

In the West Country of England there are some local accents which, like Canadian and some American accents, are *r*-full. Speakers would typically pronounce the *r* in 'butter'. And this can be combined with the use of the glottal stop to give the form [bʌʔəʳ]. Currently on British television an advertisement promoting butter uses this regional form, presumably because it has a social meaning to British audiences suggestive of honest West Country farmers genuinely in touch with real, non-synthetic cows.

In New York City a working-class accent will, in casual speech, be largely *r*-less like the British RP. But this would be combined with the voicing of the written 't' between vowels giving the form [bʌdə]. Followers of the *Kojak* detective series on television will recognize this form. Imagine, however, the different social meaning that would be conveyed if Lieutenant Kojak pronounced the word [bʌdəʳ] as might an upper-middle-class New Yorker, or [bʌtə] as might an upper-middle-class Englishman. It would not be the impression of the 'tough New York cop'.

The diagram opposite gives a summary of the various ways 'butter' can be pronounced which we have looked at. The actual situation is far more complex and interesting than I have indicated, but we will be studying this in more detail later in the book. The purpose here is to merely illustrate the property of variability which natural languages possess.

It is clear that this property requires social explanation. This is in contrast with the arbitrary property of language mentioned earlier. In characterizing the variant forms of 'butter', I needed to make reference to the geographical location in which the form was characteristically employed, and to the socio-economic class of the speaker. I also described the variants in terms of the

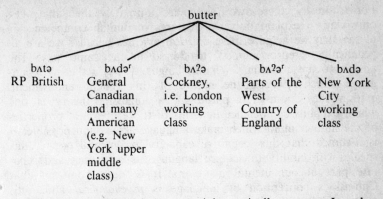

social meaning which their use might typically convey. In other words, I was explaining the variants in terms of social characteristics of their users.

So what is **sociolinguistics**? I will now propose a definition, in order to distinguish this branch of linguistic inquiry from other ways of approaching language, and also to try to unite the diverse kinds of inquiry which goes under this name:

> Sociolinguistics is that branch of linguistics which studies just those properties of language and languages which *require* reference to social, including contextual, factors in their explanation.

The term 'social' is to be contrasted with those explanations of language which either explain language without reference to factors outside the language faculty itself, or in terms of other psychological properties of humans, such as perception, memory, and so on.

We can also relate our definition of sociolinguistics to Chomsky's conception of linguistic theory. I said earlier that the aim of linguistics is universalistic. It sets out to explain why the whole set of natural languages are the way they are. For Chomsky, the basic answer to this question is that language has the properties it does because the human mind is constructed that way.

Every normal human being 'knows' his or her native tongue. He or she has linguistic **competence**. Every normal human being acquires this mature competence in the first few years of life. The linguist's first job is to develop a theory of language which can explain our 'knowledge of language' and how it is acquired.

For Chomsky, these two things are ultimately the same. The only way to explain universal features of human competence is to say that we acquire these uniform abilities because we are all genetically 'preprogrammed' to do so in the same way. The answer to the question, "What is language?", is a theory of language which specifies the nature of this genetic endowment. Within the Chomskyan paradigm, a linguistic theory is one which explains competence in terms of those invariant properties of the human mind which make language acquisition possible. It is assumed that this 'cognitive capacity' or 'mental organ', this species-wide ability to acquire language, is a distinct and separate part of our mental make up. It is clear from this that Chomsky's conception of language is *psychological* and, ultimately, *biological*.

So where do social explanations fit in? Social explanations will enter into an account of language at the places where we find patterns of language which can't be explained in psychological terms. Characteristically, these are patterns in the use of language. It is quite clear that there are properties of language which *must* be explained either in terms of large-scale social structure or in terms of how people use language to communicate with one another. Social explanations will be concerned with aggregate regularities in group performance and with the explication of acts of communication. Of course, these involve human mental abilities too. We exhibit psychological abilities in social life and action. However, these abilities, according to Chomsky, are not part of our specific linguistic ability, however much they may underlie our use of language. Our concern, by contrast, is precisely that use of language.

Just where the boundaries might be between properties of language which are psychological in Chomsky's sense and those which are socially or contextually explicable is not clear. Perhaps very few properties of language require social explanation. Alternatively, perhaps features which are derivable only from the social contexts in which people use language penetrate very deeply into the language system itself – into the very rules of grammar. In part, whether social features are visible or not depends on how the linguist approaches the subject of his investigation – how he generates his data. Within the Chomskyan paradigm the data is very idealized. Natural languages are viewed as sets of sentences about which native speakers can make certain judgements. Given this approach, it is hardly surprising that social explanation has a minimal role to play. In sociolinguistics, on the other hand, natural languages are viewed as the totality of utterances which speakers or hearers can make in context. This extension of the data, while it adds enormously to the complexity of what we must look at, raises the question of the extent to which the patterns of language on all levels can be socially explained. Like *all* kinds of explanation, social explanation is a problematic notion. In Chapter 11 we will be looking at this problem as it relates to the explanation of language. But we have already seen how we need to use social factors in accounting for variation in accents.

There are other features of language which require a different sort of social explanation. One such is the use of language in small-scale conversational settings. Consider the following exchange from the film *Saturday Night and Sunday Morning* (1961), written by Alan Sillitoe. We will be using excerpts from this film at various points in our discussion. Doreen is talking about a girl at the firm in Nottingham where she and Arthur work. They are sauntering together in a park, arm in arm.

DOREEN: She got married yesterday. She looked ever so nice.
ARTHUR: What was the bloke like, could yer smell the drink? He must have been drunk to get married.

After his utterance of the word 'drink', Arthur physically moves away from Doreen, losing her. Doreen has uttered two English sentences. We are in the same position as Arthur. We have to ask, 'What did she *intend* to convey?' This is the same as asking *why* she uttered it, to me, here and now, in this context. Consider this possible answer. She intended to convey that she believes that the **propositions** are true, namely that the girl in question got married yesterday and that she looked nice. We can say that Doreen *stated* this. She performed a statement. But now see how we are referring to Doreen's language. Words like 'intention', 'state', 'perform', mean that we are explaining Doreen's utterance as a kind of human action. She *did* something. She performed a **speech act**. This is a crucial concept in the study of discourse, the use of language in interaction.

But there are other possible answers to the 'why' question. Consider these possibilities. Let's first assume something about the context, namely that Doreen and Arthur are 'going together', part of a social institution which can lead to 'marriage'. They have the roles of boyfriend and girlfriend. If we assume this, then it is plausible that Doreen intends Arthur to understand that they also ought to get married. That's what she intended to convey. She performed not only a statement, but also a *request for action*. There are other possibilities. Perhaps she was only *suggesting* that they get married, or *broaching the topic* of marriage. Arthur's job is to construct an explanation of why she performed that particular utterance, to discern the intention behind her action.

Note that all these indirect interpretations would have to be reasoned out by Arthur. Overtly, all Doreen is doing is making a statement. Now consider the context, the sort of things Arthur would have to know, in order to do this reasoning. Much of the context of the reasoning is social, for example, about the institution of 'going together', as well as how their own roles and history together fit into this pattern.

The kind of reasoning involved in decoding conversational utterances is even better illustrated when we look at Arthur's *reply*. Ask yourself whether his reply is to her statement, or rather does it give us evidence that he took what she said as a request or suggestion. Is he rejecting or repudiating a perceived request? Or merely replying to a statement with a question? If he is repudiating her suggestion then try to work out the reasoning required to connect 'X married Y' and 'X is drunk'. We see at this stage how semantics enters into discourse. To do the reasoning, we have to know the conventional meanings of the words 'marry' and 'drunk' and their contributions to sentence-meaning. We also have to know the social background, knowledge without which we could not understand what Doreen and Arthur are doing.

There are three further points to note about this exchange. First, the meanings involved are specific to this particular context with these particular participants. If Doreen had been speaking to her mother, for example, she could not conceivably have intended to suggest or request they get married. She would have been intending something else. Second, note that the interpretations are indeterminate. She might have been only stating, or suggesting, or broaching the topic. She might have been requesting. Neither a hearer nor an analyst can say for sure. And she could always deny any interpretation we propose, saying: "Is *that* how you took it? I didn't mean that. You misunderstood my intention." In this, she could be lying or telling the truth. This property of indeterminacy is a major linguistic resource in negotiating our relationships.

Looking at language in such small-scale conversational settings is called **discourse analysis**.

In this chapter, then, we have defined sociolinguistics as that branch of linguistics which studies those properties of language which require social explanation. The social explanations are of two main types: first, they involve large-scale social settings. We attempt to correlate variation within a language with categories such as **class**, **sex**, **style**, **geography** and so on. Second, they involve small-scale conversational settings. We look at the use of language in everyday conversation and we ask how meaning depends on the actual situation of speech and on the belief-systems of speaker and hearer. We shall see that these two types of explanation, although they appear to be radically different, are not unconnected.

In this book, we shall begin by looking at language in large-scale social settings. Later on, we will change focus, and study the use of language in the setting of everyday conversation.

2. A Tapestry in Space and Time

> We must be careful not to overrate the uniformity of existing languages; it is far enough from being absolute. In a true and defensible sense, every individual speaks a language different from every other.
>
> Whitney (1875)

Sociolinguistics was defined in the last chapter as the branch of linguistics which studies the properties of language which require reference to social factors for their explanation. One such property is **variation**. We recognize many different 'ways of speaking' the same language; for example, speakers with different dialects or accents. Sometimes we get variation within the same community between two distinct languages; for example, between French and English. In this first part of the book, we shall examine such large-scale patterns of variation.

But first notice that both of these examples of variation presuppose that we know what *a* language is. This is not as easy a question as it sounds. In fact, the title of this chapter is not a bad metaphor for the sort of entity in question.

The question, 'What is a language?'

The question, 'What is *a* language?' is not the same as the question, 'What is language?' In the former case we are asking about the nature of particular languages, 'the English language' or 'the French language' etc. We shall see that in this case the answer proves, surprisingly, to be at least partially social. To the latter question, the answer is largely a psychological one. To the universalistic question, 'What is language?' the current best answer is Chomsky's: language is a set of very specific universal principles which are intrinsic properties of the human mind and part of our species' genetic endowment. Such principles are what permit any normal child to learn any natural language.

However, whenever we confront language we always confront such principles realized in a particular **variety** of language. A variety is a neutral term which simply means any particular 'way of speaking'; it is applicable to any linguistic phenomenon we want to treat as a single unit. Thus, when we observe an utterance it is always in a particular **language**, in a particular **dialect** of that language, and pronounced with a particular **accent**. Note that I am using the word 'dialect' here as a subdivision of a language; a 'dialect of a language'. A dialect varies from other dialects of the same language simultaneously on all three linguistic levels; phonologically, grammatically, and in terms of its vocabulary or lexically. An accent, by contrast, consists of phonetic variation on its own.

The problem is to explain these varieties and this variation. If, as some people suggest, there are universal principles at work in all human languages, why do we find in actuality so many varieties, and massive and seemingly random fluctuations? There are two answers to this.

One has to do with **typology**, or **language types**. In putting together a language, there must be a systematic way of relating a given meaning to the superficial arrangement of parts of a sentence. For example, there has to be a way of telling apart the subject and object of the sentence. It seems that there are only a limited number of logically possible ways to do this. Therefore, given the available psychological mechanisms we have for the production and interpretation of sentences, and the logical possibilities, it follows that there will only be a certain number of types of strategies which are possible. And these will be reflected in the structure of differing types of languages. Historically unrelated and widely geographical separated languages often are typologically similar in some respect. For example, Eskimo, most Australian aboriginal languages, and languages of the Caucasus in the Soviet Union all share a highly exotic type of case system, the way in which changes in the endings of words relate to who is doing what, and so forth.

But typology is only one reason why languages differ so much. The other reason is historical and social. Speech is always uttered by individuals who are members of social groups which are both separated from and related to other social groups in space and time. Space and time are both crucial. To begin tackling this, let's consider, in an idealized way, the nature and relationships of the dialects of a language.

The simplest way to consider a dialect is as a language variety associated with a particular place, or a geographical dialect. Indeed, our names for most dialects are geographical: Parisian, Lancashire, Liverpudlian and so on. If we imagine the area in which Figure 2.1 is printed as representing merely geographical

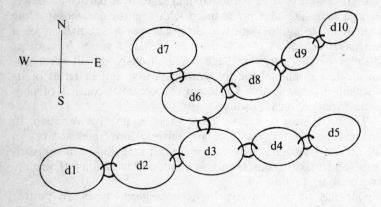

Figure 2.1 A dialect continuum

space, then the numbered dialects simply occupy different geographical regions. The numbers of the dialects represent the names speakers give to the way they speak, as distinguished from their neighbours.

In general, dialects differ from each other more radically the more remote they are from each other geographically. So, in our model, dialects 1 to 10 would be linguistically the most distinct from each other. The dialects in our model also form what is called a **dialect continuum**. This is a chain of dialects with the following property. Speakers of dialect 1 understand dialect 2 extremely well. The number of linguistic features differentiating the two regional varieties may be quite small. However, speakers of dialect 1 and dialect 3 understand each other rather less well, and speakers of dialect 1 and dialect 4 less well again. There comes a point, however, say at dialect 5, where dialect 1 is no longer intelligible to the local people and vice versa. That is, dialects more remote from each other fade into mutual unintelligibility, while adjacent dialects are mutually intelligible. This reflects the fact that the degree of geographical separation reflects the degree of linguistic difference between the dialects. There are some famous examples of such dialect continua. For example, the West Romance dialect continuum means that one can proceed through rural communities from the Atlantic coast of France through Italy, Spain and Portugal, never losing intelligibility between adjacent villages, although speakers of the standard languages, French, Italian, Spanish, Portuguese, find each other mutually unintelligible.

Separation and divergence

It seems, then, that sheer geographical separation is a causal factor in the differences between dialects. When the distribution of any given variant feature is independently plotted and its boundary, or isogloss, drawn on a map, it is often found that the boundaries of a number of features at least partially coincide forming **isogloss bundles**. These linguistic boundaries tend to coincide with major physical features, such as rivers and mountains, which separate one community from the other. The inference can then be drawn that geographical separation produces linguistic divergence, given time. This kind of conclusion reflects one type of model of the historical processes that lead to language differentiation and the existence of separate varieties. Dialects emerge through time by a process of **splitting** from a single parent variety.

But why should geographical separation lead to linguistic divergence? An obvious answer would lie in the idea of a **communication network**. Consider a population extended over geographical space. Any given person will communicate much more frequently and over a wider range of speech-event types with individuals who are adjacent to him, than with those who are more remote. This will produce a pattern of density of communication among those individuals who are immediately adjacent, in contrast to a much lesser density of talk between those who are not. Distinct groups will be nodes of very dense mutual interaction. Boundaries of less dense interaction will exist between distinct groups. Since people mutually affect each other's linguistic habits, there will be a tendency for such distinct groups to evolve away from each other in terms of the linguistic forms they normally employ. And one form of human group is obviously all those people who live in a given geographical locale, hence geographically based varieties of language.

Waves of change

But the picture of separation and divergence is far too simple to account for the facts by itself. Consider the linguistic data. It appears very messy indeed. Dialect continua show that the degree of divergence between the language or groups is relative to distance and accumulates gradually. Isogloss boundaries coincide only very roughly, and sometimes differ substantially for different variant features. Often, the occurrence of a feature spreads out from some centre. Other features radiating from the same centre spread out less far or perhaps farther. These meet and overlap with features radiating from other centres. Some features are intensely local, and others extend over large areas. Some **relic areas** suggest the preservation in a particular area of earlier forms. The situation becomes even less clear if one examines the linguistic variants in use in a given community. Imagine, for example, that there are different ways of producing the *same* speech sound. The *r* described in Chapter 1 could serve as an example. You will recall that variant pronunciations of English were *r*-full, pronouncing the *r* in words like 'car' or 'guard', while others were *r*-less, omitting it.

In fact, faced with a real community, one finds very great complexity. Speaker A, who is a middle-aged man, may produce *r*s, but only a certain fairly low percentage of the times when it would be possible for him to do so. Speaker B, another middle-aged man, may only produce a low percentage of *r*s in casual speech, but more in formal speech. Speaker C, a young woman, who appears to be middle-class, may produce a fairly high number of *r*s, but Speaker D, her grandmother, may produce none. Speaker E, who was not born in the locality, may have the highest *r*-score of all. Speaker D, a member of an ethnic minority, may have a different pattern.

We'll be looking in later chapters at how such recalcitrant kinds of data can be explained. At this stage, let's just take an overview. It's clear we're not observing any one relationship to the variants in the community. Its use of the form is not uniform. This lack of uniformity could be accounted for, if a change is in progress, and different individuals stand in different relationships to the change. There is clearly no sudden or abrupt division between those that have a variant and those that do not, as one might expect from a splitting theory.

A **wave theory** of linguistic change accounts for this. In this view, variant forms originate at some point. The variant then gradually spreads by diffusion. In geographical terms, the variant would move in time farther and farther from its point of origin, producing a pattern like a wave that spreads out when a stone is dropped in a pond. Other, later innovations would produce waves which, at any given point in time, are behind those caused by the spread of earlier innovations. Waves coming from different directions, that is, those that have different points of origin, will meet and overlap with these former waves. Some innovations, of course, might not spread at all beyond the immediate vicinity of their point of origin while others might be aborted almost as soon as they begin. Patterns of convergence as well as divergence could be accounted for by this kind of model.

But why do individuals stand in different relationships to the variants? This is because the community itself is not uniform with respect to the variant feature. Up to now, I have been considering space quite literally, in terms of the distribution of population between two points. What is needed is the notion of **social space**. Clearly, there will be weaknesses in density of communication between many different kinds of social group within a given community, and each group will thus form a communication network of its own.

Social space can be viewed as including the geographical distribution of a population. After all, where a person lives determines his membership in a social group by virtue of that fact alone. Thus urban and rural are important social dimensions in themselves. Relevant dimensions of social space are those that are needed to account for the distribution of linguistic variants. Thus, besides geographical factors, such dimensions as age, sex, ethnicity and social class place social groups in differing relationships to the variable features of language. There is a great deal more to it than this, but that will become clear in later chapters.

Changes propagate through communities in waves. Figure 2.2 displays this process schematically. There is an innovation at point O, adopted by various social groups successively. The change spreads by diffusion through social space. In Figure 2.2, then, points A, B, C, D could represent the fact that a given social group has adopted one variant over the other for any given variable feature. There will be a stage, however, when a given group uses both variants, when the change is passing through that social space. Observed at that time, the group will be distinguished statistically from other groups, in terms of its preference for one variant or the other. Changing features will

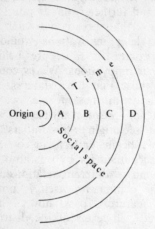

Figure 2.2 Waves of change

always be variable and statistical in the overall community, while unchanging features (for example, after a change has completed its propagation through a group) may be categorical in a given group.

But we are talking about time as well. Successiveness entails temporality – thus O, A, B, C and D also represent points in time. B could be the time when both features, but with different statistical preferences, first appear in group B, having crossed a boundary in social space, and so on for C and D. If we are studying a geographical diffusion, the points in time, marked by the successive waves, will coincide with the extension of the variability in literal space. They will be isoglosses drawn on a map.

There is a further subtlety and complication. Variant linguistic features usually have more than one environment in the linguistic system itself. For example, the (r) variable occurs in word-final position, as in 'car', or immediately following a vowel as in 'guard'. Linguistic changes in which variants occur characteristically move through the language system, environment by environment. The rate at which one variant is chosen also depends, therefore, on which environment the change has reached, as well as on social factors. This can also be represented by a wave diagram. The letters A through D could represent the propagation of the change through the environments in which the variable occurs within the language system itself.

Clusters of features

What then is a dialect? The processes of change explain the fact that any variety, including a geographical dialect, is part of a continuum in social space and time. *They are not absolutely discrete entities.* One can see, however, how complex boundaries, or discontinuities, can occur which would serve to distinguish one variety from another. These would predictably mirror boundaries in social space and run along lines of weakness of communication. Consider, too, a sort of 'metropolitanism' view of diffusion. Factors of prestige, that is, people's attitude to a variant and, more importantly, to the group with which it is associated, will lead to its propagation. This will produce similarities in the varieties spoken by those groups under the 'metropolitan' influence of another group. But such propagations will reach boundaries at the limits of that 'metropolitan' influence, where they meet waves from other centres of such influence or from local resistance to outside innovation. In other words, there are pressures towards both difference and similarity, and these together produce a continuum with internal boundaries which are 'more or less' statistical affairs. This reflects the groupings and processes in the social space in which the speakers are located.

In terms of its linguistic features, no variety of language is a discrete entity. What is true of dialects is true of any variety. We can thus define a variety more precisely. If there is a tendency for variable features to occur together in a cluster and if speakers utter given variants for a similar percentage of the time, and if this also correlates with some common social feature of the group of speakers, then this joint characteristic of speech and speaker is a variety. *A variety is a clustering together of linguistic features within a continuum which is explicable in terms of some dimension of social space.*

In the literature, besides geographical dialects, we find reference to ethnic varieties, mens' and womens' varieties, and **sociolects**, varieties which are based on features like social class. We can talk about the particular kind of speech which adults use to babies and very small children, or the speech of adolescent peer groups, as varieties. And there are **registers** of speech. These are varieties defined by the social **function** of language; for example, the linguistic choices which characterize advertising copy, scientific prose or sports commentary. And, of course, there are the recognized forms of literary language: poetry, the novel, drama and so forth.

Note that a variety is by definition a social entity. It is not just a type of language but a type of language that is socially definable and explicable. The linguistic side of any variety, however, is always problematical because it is a clustering tendency within a continuum. And any given utterance is multi-dimensional, exhibiting simultaneously the features which correlate with each of the dimensions of social space, and the point in time in which the speaker is located.

Interfaces

I have explained how it is we always confront a variety of language, and not Language, because of the social and historical processes of differentiation. Now consider again the original question, 'What is a language?', in the sense of the English language, the French language, the German language and so on. Let's try some definitions:

1. A language is an aggregate of related dialects.
2. A language is the aggregate of those dialects which are mutually intelligible.

But neither of these work. They are both refuted by the data of dialect continua. Linguistic relatedness and difference is a matter of degree. These definitions would have the West Romance or West Germanic dialect areas as single languages. I mentioned the West Romance area earlier. A similar situation exists between Holland and Germany. One could proceed, village by village, from the Dutch coast to Vienna and always find mutual intelligibility between adjacent communities, although unintelligibility obviously occurs when the varieties are remote from each other in the continuum. But the Dutch and Germans consider that they speak distinct languages.

Scandinavia, except for Finland, also forms a dialect continuum. In an article entitled 'Semicommunication: the language gap in Scandinavia' (1967), Einar Haugen found a considerable degree of mutual intelligibility between native speakers of Norwegian, Swedish and Danish. Figure 2.3 shows the percentage of informants from each country who claimed to understand their

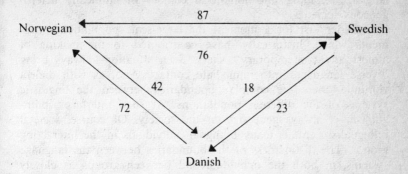

Figure 2.3 Semicommunication in Scandinavia (*from Haugen, 1967*)

neighbours' language fairly easily upon first encounter. This degree of mutual intelligibility is a matter of linguistic distance, but Haugen also found that it correlated closely with the informants' attitudes to the other groups and also with the degree of 'perceived beauty' of the language in question. The fact is that linguistic relatedness and mutual intelligibility between what are thought of as distinct languages is a matter of degree. One study of related dialects and languages from the Algonquin family of American Indian languages, that is, languages and dialects which have diverged from a single hypothetical parent language, found that the degree of mutual intelligibility was precisely related to the degree of linguistic distance. A degree of divergence which results in unintelligibility between dialects, on the other hand, is no guarantee that the dialects will be unambiguously promoted to the status of separate languages. This is the case of Chinese, which has a number of mutually unintelligible dialects.

All the above examples are drawn from clear dialect continua or involve historically related, and therefore similar, languages. (Historically related languages are divergent dialects of the parent.) But are there not clear situations where historically very remotely related languages have clear boundaries? One might expect such situations, for example, where Romance languages meet Germanic languages. It is indeed very often the case that distinct languages come into contact. This is usually the result of some historical process such as immigration, emigration, invasion, conquest or trade. Mass dislocations or movements of peoples, such as the mass enslavement and transportation of Africans to the Americas, often result in populations with different languages coming into long-term contact in ethnically heterogeneous societies.

Consider just for a moment the large-scale population movements which, historically, have contributed to the making of almost any contemporary society. Such situations always bring diverse languages into immediate contact. And, as with dialect continua, there are complex boundaries between the linguistic systems of the different populations. At such interfaces, bilingualism is always generated in the society. Of course, societal bilingualism entails many bilingual individuals in the interacting groups. The distinctness of the boundaries between the language systems, in both the individual and between groups, is closely related to the social processes that are taking place. It depends, for example, on the degree of segregation or assimilation between the groups. And there are always pressures working in both directions. In other words, the processes at the linguistic interface are both dynamic and social. In multilingual situations many varieties may be involved.

In a classic study, *Languages in Contact* (1964), Uriel Weinreich studied the social and individual factors involved in such interfaces, and examined mechanisms of **interference** between varieties on the lexical, phonetic and phonological levels. He noted that interference is not random, not merely a question of piecemeal borrowing, but was systematic. Systematic changes occurred in the speech of bilingual communities, as foreign elements on the various linguistic levels· were integrated into, and restructured, the tightly knit patterns of the interacting languages. Weinreich's analysis was of a situation which was stable, between Swiss German and Romansh, a Romance language spoken in Switzerland. In such contact situations, languages and dialects sometimes die. On the way to extinction, they are the mother tongue of gradually shrinking speech communities. Finally, they become no one's mother tongue, like a star blinking out.

Nancy Dorian (1973) made a study of the variation in grammar in a dialect of Scots Gaelic in the final stages of collapse. Three villages on the east coast of Scotland retained the language, in an area in which it had otherwise disappeared in the course of the last century and a half. The remaining Gaelic speakers, who ranged in age from eighty to only forty, were *all* bilingual in English. Bilingualism is, of course, a prerequisite for **language shift**.

The form of Gaelic spoken, compared with healthier dialects in the west of Scotland, was much reduced in grammatical and lexical alternatives. The verb class was lexically "extremely weak and showed borrowing from English on a truly massive scale". Since the community now lacked a monolingual Gaelic norm, the younger speakers, those in their forties, lacked confidence in the correctness of their speech and, Dorian noted, even those who claimed Gaelic as a mother tongue were often more competent in English than in the Gaelic language. There was much variation between the generations. Accelerated syntactic changes were occurring in the direction of simplification. Not much is known about what happens to the structure of a language in a terminal phase, but features such as this may be part of a regular process.

In contact situations, however, new languages are also born. This can happen if there is an urgent requirement for communication across sharp ethnic and linguistic boundaries and the social conditions are right. The process is called **creolization**. Bailey and Maroldt (1977) provide a useful and a general definition. Creolization is a "gradient mixture of two or more languages; in a narrow sense, a creole is the result of mixing which is substantial enough to result in a new system, a system that is separate from its antecedent parent systems." Creoles are widely distributed throughout the world. One inventory (Hancock, 1977) lists 127 varieties which have arisen through such interaction.

There is another, somewhat narrower, definition of a creole, based on one particular type of contact situation. Frequently, when peoples of very divergent tongues come together for specific purposes like trade, or under the conditions of slavery, a functionally specialized variety emerges called a **pidgin**. These are simplified but rule-governed varieties developed to facilitate the necessary communication. However, if a pidgin becomes the first language of a group and it is naturally acquired by the children as their mother tongue, a more fully developed new language emerges. Sometimes the term **creole** is restricted to a variety that emerges from a pidgin in this particular way.

The notion that a new linguistic system can emerge through the gradient mixing of languages contrasts with the view, which I have mentioned earlier, that new varieties emerge through separation and divergence. In the view of this latter type of theory, the reason that English differs from German or Dutch is that they are on different branches of a family tree which came about through divergence from a common ancestor. But just as a simple theory of divergence cannot account, at least by itself, for the complex patterns of sameness and difference between contemporary dialects, similarly divergence alone cannot account for inconsistencies in the patterns of relationship between historically related languages. The fact that creoles exist offers another model, to supplement simple divergence, to explain the emergence of very distinct varieties in contact situations, a theory of mixture and creolization.

Creolization processes, widely defined, may figure in the history of European languages. Bailey and Maroldt (1977), for example, have suggested that such an interpretation of the data is needed to account for many fundamental features of Middle English which differ radically from the antecedent Anglo-Saxon. Figures 2.4 and 2.5 contrast the family-tree and language-mix models as they might be applied to English. In Figure 2.4 the interaction is seen as a more fundamental one than simply interference or borrowing between otherwise closed systems. Similarly, it has been argued that Old French went through a creolization process in its emergence from vulgar Latin.

Standardization

We are confronted with continua in every dimension, including the historical, in our attempt to discover what sort of entity 'a language' is. Obviously, it is just simply wrong, on the linguistic level, to think of 'the English language', 'the French language', and so on, as discrete entities with clear boundaries, internal homogeneity, or invariant rules, either in space or time. All the processes we have discussed point towards variation and heterogeneity within a language. But there is an opposing process, working towards making a language *uniform*. And the fact of fundamental importance is that, just as the diversity was social, so are the processes that lead to uniformity. These lead to the evolution of **standard languages**.

There is an ambiguity in our use of the phrase 'a language', and this has been part of our problem with definition. Consider the following sentences. They illustrate, among other things, negation in English:

1. Im *duon* wier shuuz *nontaal*.
2. He *don't never* wear shoes.
3. He *never* wears shoes.

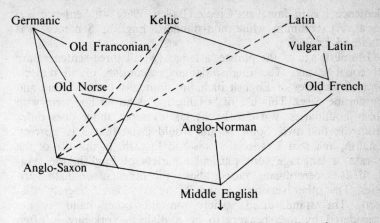

Figure 2.4 A language-mixture view of Middle English (*from Bailey and Maroldt, 1977*)

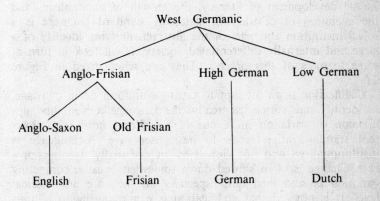

Figure 2.5 A family-tree view of English

Sentence 1 is in Jamaican Creole (Bailey, 1966:54); Sentence 2 is in a very common white non-standard English; Sentence 3 is standard English.

In one usage of the phrase 'a language', all three sentences are of equal status. 'The English language' consists of all dialects and all varieties of English including mutually unintelligible and borderline cases. This use of 'a language' is an ad hoc term with fuzzy boundaries. But clearly the last example above does differ from the first two. Some people would insist that 3 is 'correct' English, and that 2 especially was bad English. In this use of the phrase 'a language', one particular variety of English, the standard, is **superordinate**, raised above the other **subordinate** varieties. The other versions, 1 and 2, are considered 'merely' dialects. The standardized variety, on the other hand, is *not* considered by the speakers to be a dialect. Yorkshire is often regarded as a dialect of English, but standard English is not. Rather, it *is* English, to those who speak it.

Standardization is a complex of belief and behaviour towards language which evolves historically. It is a social behaviour towards language, deeply integrated into such historical factors as the development of literacy, the growth of nationalism, and the evolution of centralizing states. A standard language is a social institution and part of the abstract, unifying identity of a large and internally differentiated society. I will look in turn at some features of this process. They are schematized in Figure 2.6.

Codification is an attempt to create a uniform norm of usage, to identify one variety as 'really' the language. Given this suppression of variation in favour of a uniform norm, it follows that standardization tends to be conservative. A language is institutionalized and not viewed as an essentially dynamic process. Change is often slowed down somewhat because competing variation is smoothed out, especially on the core grammatical level. It is obvious that codification is a prerequisite to notions of correctness.

Standardization has an ideological dimension and is intimately related to the slow process of nation-building. The standard has more **prestige** than other varieties. One source of this prestige is related to its role in the symbolic integration of the larger national society. Not only does the standard language serve the actual purpose of internal integration and external segregation, it

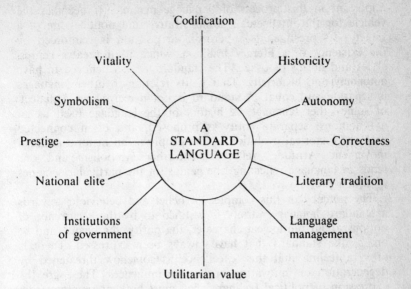

Figure 2.6 Standardization

does so **symbolically**. The language serves as a symbol of the society, a representation of its identity and unity. People feel 'language loyalty' reflecting their sense of national identity.

Another source of the prestige of the standard is derived from its use by the dominant groups within the society. To the degree that some regional or social elite was critical in the evolution of the national standard, as was the case in England, then its way of speaking, as it slowly developed, will have had a major influence in the formation of the norm. Thus, in most cases, the standard is associated with a **national elite**, the most powerful and prestigious group in the nation. The elite runs the major institutions of the society and the standard is central to the identity of the state. Accordingly, it is characteristically used in the **institutions of government**. Governments actively support its use.

There is **language management**. Those people within the society who are professionally involved with language, such as teachers, journalists, writers and so on, assist in both the creation and preservation of the standard. The codification is implemented through dictionaries, grammars and manuals of usage; standards of **correctness** evolve. The written language is very important in this process of 'language making'. It becomes the vehicle for the intellectual, administrative and political life of a society. Its prestige, its superordinate position is reinforced by the existence of a **literary tradition**, which itself creates genres, styles and norms of usage. The standard is also believed to have **autonomy** and **historicity**. That is, its relation to other languages is separate and equal. A standard is not perceived as 'a dialect' of some other language. A history of the language itself as an autonomous, separate entity is proposed, and often connected with the historical evolution of the people or an historic national movement. Attitudes reflect this further symbolism and one reads of language reflecting 'the genius' of the particular societies in which they evolved.

The potency of this complex of belief and behaviour towards a standard language variety is testified to by the recurrence of notions about the logical character, the purity, the beauty and so on, of the standard that have always been expressed. There is often a feeling that this 'excellence' is somehow threatened by degeneration or innovation or outside influences. These are the expression of political feelings. They must be kept separate from various levels of proficiency which people may have in actually using a language to convey their intentions competently, or write and speak via conventional styles.

The attitude of individuals to the group is encoded in their attitude to the language. In turn, attitudes to subordinate dialects and minority languages within a national society reflect the level of diversity which will be tolerated in a given society in particular historical periods. There may be **regional standards** or **minority languages**. There may be pressure towards assimilation and concomitant language shift among minorities and immigrants. But just as a national standard is symbolic of the overall nation, other varieties are symbolic of other groups within the larger whole. Attitudes to these varieties may conflict with attitudes to the larger whole, and the conflict will reflect social and political processes at work.

But standardization also has a very important practical dimension. It has a **utilitarian value** in allowing people to communicate with each other over the whole extent of the state without the impediment of divergent dialects. It facilitates internal communication networks too, such large-scale activities as trade, administration, and the dissemination of ideas. The practical and the symbolic meet, also, in the **vitality** of most standards, their use in the maximum of situations.

The utilitarian value of a standard language is so important in the process of nation-building, of unifying a state composed of many diverse groups, that many developing countries utilize the language of the former colonial power in this way. Obviously, however, this creates problems because the normal symbolic integrative function of a standard cannot operate fully. In other developing countries, creole varieties are beginning the process of standardization. They will eventually become the languages of national societies.

One word of warning which illustrates the complexities involved in the notion of varieties of a language. A standard variety need not be pronounced with any particular accent. You will recall that an accent involved purely phonetic variation. Standard English can be pronounced with any number of accents: British English Received Pronunciation, or different varieties of American, Canadian, South African, Irish pronunciation and so on. The grammatical and lexical variation between standard English as it is spoken in these communities is minimal, although there is significant variation in accent. We will be looking at phonetic variation in more detail later. It is now clear that the question, 'What is a language?' is answerable in more than one way. From one perspective, a language is a *dynamic process*, a continua in many dimensions. From another, it is an *institutionalized entity* deeply identified with the life of a society, and intricately involved in both its political and historical development and its social structure. In this view, the language is a codified set of norms in which the ongoing processes of variation and change are partially repressed from general social consciousness.

The nature of 'a language' will vary from the different perspectives. From the wider 'process' view, a language will have a great deal of variability. Consider English negation. A statement of the rules for this process will have to account for and interrelate variants. Variation due to ongoing processes of change, and the position of variants in social space, will be part of a study of English. From the narrower 'institutionalized entity' perspective, however, a language will appear to consist largely of invariant structures. Changes in progress will not be obvious. In this case, a statement of the rules will not refer to variants. The social explanation of linguistic structures would not be necessary.

In considering the question, 'What is a language?' we have examined the nature of relationships between languages, and the dialects of languages. We have suggested that differences between dialects or languages are not just a matter of geography, but that linguistic variation between communities, and inside a single community, requires social and temporal analysis.

But we have also considered a uniformity which is as complex as diversity. A standard variety has been described as an institutionalized form of language; a symbolic representation of a proposed national identity. It has an integrative function within a society, as well as a utilitarian value.

In the next few chapters, we will be looking at varieties and variation in more detail. Three perspectives will be taken into account: from the point of view of the society, from the point of view of the individual in that society, and from a purely linguistic point of view. In any given description, these three will be necessarily interrelated.

3. Language Varieties: Processes and Problems

Grand port of navigations, multiple
The lexicons uncargo'd at your quays,
Sonnant though strange to me; but chiefest, I,
Auditor of your music, cherish the
Joined double-melodied vocabulaire
Where English vocable and roll Ecossic,
Mollified by the parle of French
Bilinguefact your air!

From 'Montreal' by A.M. Klein (1948)

Let us now look at some of the differing ways in which linguistic varieties occur in speech communities, beginning with some large-scale variation and then working our way down to differences which occur on a smaller scale.

We will begin with societal bilingualism, the situation in which two or more distinct languages form the repertoire of a community. For this, Canada will be the example. We will then turn to those cases in which the society recognizes and names two distinct varieties of the *same* language as the repertoire, and speakers with more than one variety at their disposal switch or fluctuate between the alternatives. This leads us to the problem of relating the larger social pattern of the varieties to what individuals actually do in specific situations; and, even thornier, the problem of the actual linguistic relationship between varieties which people perceive as linguistically distinct.

Linguistic diversity in Canada

When one thinks of language in Canada, one thinks of the relationship between English and French. These are the languages of the two founding peoples and the two 'official languages'. But this relationship, though the central one, is part of a very much more diverse picture of languages in Canada.

The first source of linguistic diversity is the languages of Canada's native peoples. These have approximately 154,000 speakers. There are eleven indigeneous language families in Canada: Algonquian, Athapaskan (Northern), Eskimo-Aleut, Haida, Iroquoian, Kutenai, Salishan, Siouan, Tlingit, Tsimshian and Wakasham (Foster, 1982). These families of languages consist altogether of roughly fifty-three separate languages. Foster assesses their chances of survival. Some, like Tuscarora, with seven speakers, or Tagish, with five, are almost extinct. Others, like Cree, with fifty-five thousand speakers, or Chipewyan, with five thousand have better chances. But the survival of the native languages is threatened.

A second source of linguistic diversity in Canada is the existence of a multiplicity of languages spoken by immigrant groups. Here, the languages which contact each other are as diverse as Icelandic, Chinese and the Russian of the Doukhobors. Most European languages can be found in Canada. The central question for immigrant communities is their adaption to, and possible absorption within the host society. This is balanced against the need to preserve and redefine a distinct ethnic identity in the new context. Popularly, Canada is thought of as a 'mosaic' of ethnic identities, rather than as a 'melting pot' in which origins disappear or become irrelevant.

The greatest pressure is towards cultural assimilation and language shift. Almost all Canadians can speak either English or French, irrespective of their origin. Of the 1 per cent who do not, 34 per cent are urban Italians who have immigrated recently (Darnell, 1971). So the diversity we speak of takes place against a background of bilingualism. The overall pattern in Canada is towards the adoption of English by other groups. This theme will concern us when we look at the relationship of the official languages, English and French.

Of course, these two languages themselves exhibit internal diversity in Canada and in relation to the varieties spoken abroad. There has recently been much research into variation within Quebec French. Canadian English has been less systematically studied (Urion, 1971), but differences exist. For example, there is a distinct accent, itself with internal diversity, on the long-settled island of Newfoundland. This has affinities with English as it is spoken in Ireland and south-west England. In the 'broad' accent, 'think' and 'then' are pronounced as if they were 'tink' and 'den' – a familiar feature of some Irish speech (Wells, 1982). One suspects, however, that the surface has only been scratched in the study of the variation within Canadian English.

Demography

Against this background of diversity, let us now turn to the relationship of English and French in Canada. Most of what I am going to say is based on Stanley Lieberson's study, *Language and Ethnic Relations in Canada* (1970). Lieberson's initial concern is demographic. How much bilingualism is there in the society? Who exactly is bilingual? Is **language maintenance** or **language shift** going on between English and French?

In the Canadian case, the data was provided by the census. Lieberson used Canadian census information from 1931 to 1961. The results may be out of date today, over twenty years later, but his study provides clear pointers to the types of factors with which sociolinguists need to concern themselves. First we will use Lieberson's study to paint a picture of the Canadian scene up to 1961. Later in the chapter I will attempt to update this from more recent sources.

A number of notions are crucial for demographic studies of bilingual communities. The first is **ethnic origin**. This term explains itself: what 'descent group' does an individual belong to, British, French and so on? The second is **mother tongue**. In the Canada census the citizen is asked which was the first language he learned which he still understands. If a person has replied that his mother tongue is different from the language of his descent group, then we have evidence that language shift has occurred between generations somewhere in his family's history. Alternatively, if there is no divergence, then the language of his ethnic group has been maintained. Successive censuses will reveal the rate and location of language shift, if there is any.

The number of bilingual individuals in the society can be roughly measured by the 'official language question'. The census baldly asks, 'Can you speak English? French?' Note that this way of obtaining information requires self-assessment and this leaves open many thorny issues about what counts as bilingualism and how it might be objectively measured. This census data, therefore, is only what people *say* about which language is their mother tongue and their ability to speak the other official language. The degree of bilingualism in the community is relevant to the measurement of language maintenance and shift since it is the children of bilingual parents that are at risk in relation to intergenerational language shift.

Language maintenance and shift in Canada (1961)

The conclusions which can be drawn from the census data are extremely interesting. At first glance the official languages look remarkably stable. The percentage of people reporting themselves to be bilingual remained steady at 12 per cent from 1921 to 1961. If one looks at the percentages of persons in each ethnic group and compares them with the percentages of persons in each mother-tongue group for Canada as a whole, there seems to be little evidence of language shift relating to English and French:

	Canada as a whole (1961)		
	French	British	Other
Ethnic Origin (%)	30.37	43	27
Mother Tongue (%)	28.09	58.45	14

The major process is the large-scale language shift occurring between Other and English. Those of other ethnic origins prefer English, and assimilate into the Anglophone community in Canada.

But these figures concerning the relationship of the official languages are misleading. A clearer demographic picture emerges only when one examines what is happening in each province. Compare Ontario, the largest Anglophone province, and Quebec, the province where French ethnicity and mother tongue are overwhelmingly concentrated:

	Ontario (1961)			Quebec (1961)		
	French	British	Other	French	British	Other
Ethnic Origin (%)	10	59	31	80.64	10	10
Mother Tongue (%)	6.82	77.52	16.63	81.18	13.26	6

This reveals language shift occurring from French to English and from Other to English in Ontario, while in Quebec, although the Other have shifted principally to English, the French mother-tongue group is maintained and only very slightly strengthened.

The extent of language shift from French to English from 1931 to 1961 in all parts of Canada except Quebec, and adjacent New Brunswick, was very substantial indeed. The French-speaking people outside Quebec fall into two main groups. There are the Acadians, descendants of the first French colony established in 1605 on the Bay of Fundy in the Maritimes. And there are the Francophones west of Quebec, the Franco-Ontarians, and the Francophones of the Prairies. These are mainly the descendants of settlers from Quebec who were the first to colonize the north and west. In all, by 1971, there were 1,417,255 persons of French ethnic origin outside Quebec. Their communities have been deeply affected by assimilation. Figure 3.1 shows by province the percentage of those of French ethnic origin with French mother tongue in 1931 and again in 1961.

Province	PERCENTAGE OF FRENCH ETHNIC GROUP WITH FRENCH MOTHER TONGUE	
	(1931)	(1961)
Prince Edward Island	77.3	44.5
Nova Scotia	67.7	42.8
New Brunswick	94.9	87.6
Quebec	99.4	98.2
Ontario	77.4	61.4
Manitoba	86.0	67.2
Saskatchewan	78.5	54.4
Alberta	70.4	46.8
British Columbia	48.5	33.7

Figure 3.1 A pattern of language shift, 1931–61 (*from Arès, 1964, reprinted in Lieberson, 1970*)

The trend is sharply towards the loss of French as a mother tongue by those of French ethnic origin everywhere except in Quebec, and among the Acadians of New Brunswick.

Asymmetrical bilingualism

Can we relate these processes to the number of people who claim to be bilingual in the various provinces? Although the percentage of bilingual individuals had remained constant throughout Canada from 1921 to 1961, the concentration of that bilingualism was among the French ethnic group, and this was particularly marked outside Quebec. For example, in 1921, 86.8 per cent of those of French mother tongue in Ontario acquired English. In 1961, this was 77.3 per cent. In Alberta, far from the Francophone community of Quebec, 90.8 per cent of those with French mother tongue acquired English. Conversely, the number of people of British and Other mother tongues acquiring French in Quebec was surprisingly low considering the fact that they were a minority in that province. The figures for 1921 and 1961 are:

Quebec

	percentage learning French		percentage learning English	
	British	Other	French	Other
1921	29.8	38.8	41.1	84.7
1961	26.6	37.0	24.0	66.4

The percentage of British learning French is low. The Other also prefer to learn English. The percentage of French learning English, although declining, is very high given the overwhelming French majority. *It is clear that bilingualism in Canada is asymmetrical and is generated primarily in those of French mother tongue*. This occurs very markedly outside Quebec, but also significantly within that province. It is this asymmetric bilingualism that puts the French-mother-tongue group outside Quebec at risk to language shift.

There are some obvious questions. What factors lead to this asymmetric bilingualism? Why has widespread bilingualism among those of French ethnic origin and mother tongue outside Quebec led to language shift? Why has similar widespread bilingualism *not* led to language shift inside Quebec? Why had not the numerically small British ethnic group in Quebec become more bilingual up to 1961 and laid the basis for a language shift towards French in that province? In Quebec, both official languages are maintained. Elsewhere, French slowly disappears.

Montreal

To explore these questions, the best tactic is to look very closely at the interface, the place where the largest number of the two communities meet and where the largest number of bilingual individuals are concentrated. That is in the Montreal metropolitan area. Lieberson (1981: 131) writes:

> Montreal might be viewed as a battleground between the French language and culture of Quebec and the English-speaking Canadians and Americans who surround French Canada. This metropolitan area, containing more than 10 per cent of Canada's population, is incontestably the great centre of English–French contact in North America.... Perhaps 'battleground' is too dramatic a term for describing French –English relations in Montreal, although the occasional acts of violence, the more frequent verbal expressions of nationalism and the self-consciousness about language make our metaphor apt. If inherent in linguistic contact is the danger or possibility that one language will decline and the other expand, then, in this fundamental sense, Montreal, or any other multilingual setting, is a battleground.

The configuration of the varieties in the Montreal metropolitan area in 1961 as published by the *Royal Commission on Bilingualism and Biculturalism* is displayed below.

Montreal metropolitan area (1961)

	British	French	Other	Total
Population by ethnic origin	377,625	1,353,480	378,404	2,109,509
No. of bilinguals by ethnic origin	101,767	554,929	119,907	776,603
No. of individuals monolingual in each official language	462,260	826,333	....	1,288,593

The contact of the languages in the city shows some of the characteristics we noted at the provincial levels. There is a preference of the Other for English, as witnessed by the divergence between the number of those of British ethnic origin and the number of those who are monolingual in English. There is also an asymmetric generation of individual bilingualism in the majority community, and relatively little in the British minority. This is the opposite to the situation outside Quebec, where the British majority has virtually no bilingualism generated within it by the presence of a French minority. It is worth adding at this point that these figures show the very real distinction between societal and individual bilingualism. It seems on the face of it quite possible, at least in 1961, to be perfectly monolingual in the heart of the Montreal interface, as the majority of both ethnic groups are. However, one is more likely to be bilingual in Montreal, in 1961, if one is ethnically French.

The functions of the varieties in the city

Why do we get this imbalance? One possible explanation is that this asymmetrically distributed bilingualism results from the use of English in much of the city's economic life, a situation historically imposed on the French ethnic majority by the English-speaking minority. Lieberson's investigation into the uses of the two languages in Montreal corroborates this intuition. There are very marked occupational pressures generating bilingualism within the French majority. These are some of his findings.

The Yellow Pages. One method which Lieberson used to study the allocation of the two languages in the economic life of the city was to examine the distribution of entries for various activities under French and English rubrics in the Yellow Pages of the Montreal telephone directory. An entry might be under a French rubric, an English rubric, or both. One can infer from this which language would normally be used for the activity in question, or whether both languages would normally be used.

It was found that as one moved from retailing (activities which involve face-to-face contact at a local level) to manufacturing, industry and offices, the number of 'French only' entries markedly declined. This suggests that being able to speak only French would be a social disadvantage in these areas. But being a monolingual speaker of English would not be such a handicap.

Appointments columns. Lieberson examined the appointments advertised in the *Montreal Star* and *La Presse*. He noted that the jobs which required English, for example technicians, accountants, managers, clerk-typists and stenographers, were heavily white-collar. Such jobs, it followed, demanded individual bilingualism from members of the French-mother-tongue group, but not of the English. Labouring, sales and service jobs were over-represented in *La Presse*.

Status of occupation. Bilingualism correlated with the status of the French group, but not with the British one. The number of bilingual individuals of the French-mother-tongue group was 94 per cent for managerial positions, through 70 per cent to 80 per cent in sales positions, to 49 per cent for labourers. For the British group, there was no such correlation.

Income. These patterns were reflected in the average incomes of the two language groups. As a group, those monolingual in English had the highest average income of all. The French monolinguals were at the bottom of the pile. But even French bilinguals, although better off than their monolingual fellows, earned less than people of the British ethnic group, both those who spoke French and those who did not.

Such factors paint a picture of a city which is vertically stratified by income and occupation according to ethnic and mother-tongue group. In 1961, the allocation of English as the principal language of business and industry produced a high percentage of bilingualism among those of French mother tongue, but did not place a corresponding demand upon those of English mother tongue. This also explains the preference of Others for English, and not for French. When one further notes that the highest concentration of bilingualism is among French men of working age, the conclusion is clear that it is occupational pressure which, in general, motivates the individuals to become bilingual and, in turn, produces the pattern of societal bilingualism.

Residential segregation

Now, given this distribution of bilingualism, what factors lead simultaneously to French language maintenance within Quebec, and language shift from French to English elsewhere?

One factor which is very revealing of the interaction between the linguistic and ethnic groups in Montreal is their degree of

residential segregation, as explored in Lieberson (1965: 1970a). I must simplify his findings. Segregation was measured by an **index of dissimilarity**. The urban area was divided into tracts (the census tracts). The index was a measure of the number of individuals of each group in each tract. Complete segregation, in which there was no mix of groups at all, would be registered by an index of 100; complete integration, by an index of 0. This method was used to study both linguistic and ethnic segregation in Montreal.

	English monolingual		French monolingual	
French monolingual	Bilingual	Neither	Bilingual	Neither
64.3	43.4	61.9	24.6	59.4

Figure 3.2 Residential segregation by language, Montreal, 1961 (*from Lieberson, 1965*)

The first column, for example, illustrates a high degree of segregation between French monolinguals and English monolinguals (64.3), whereas the low index score (24.6) between French monolinguals and bilinguals reveals that segregation between these two groups is low. In fact, the bilinguals of both groups are more integrated with their respective monolingual 'cores' than they are with each other. This means that each group has a spatial 'homeland' where the chances of intelligible communication are higher (you are more likely to be proximate to someone who speaks your mother tongue) than for the city taken as a whole.

Such segregation suggests that the languages have specialized functions within the larger society. One imagines that the situations typical of a residential community (home, shopping, church and so forth) are enacted in the language of each relatively segregated community. But in the larger economic sphere, English is required for many occupations. If this is true, segregation is a measure of the existence of coherent communities based on language and ethnicity, and in which the functions of the languages are specialized.

It is interesting to note, by contrast, that the segregation indices are very low in those Anglophone cities where language shift has occurred from French to English. The indices are 21 for Toronto and only 12 for Calgary. This suggests that bilingualism, rather than residential segregation, has been the French ethnic minority's solution to language diversity in these cities. This, combined with low numbers and different attitudes, is leading to their assimilation within Anglophone Canada.

Domains of language use

It is clear that specialized uses for varieties is very important in bilingual and multilingual settings. I have talked of 'functional specialization', but so far the notion is very imprecise. Joshua Fishman, a major figure in the sociology of language, has developed the notion of a **domain of language use** (Fishman, 1971). This construct provides a way to study systematically the distribution of varieties within a speech community. The notion of a domain links the larger society-wide level to that of particular utterances in context. On the larger level, it gives us ways of studying 'the distribution of varieties in a society as a whole'. *A domain is a grouping together of recurring situation types in such a way that one of the languages or varieties in a repertoire, as opposed to the others, normally occurs in that class of situations. And members of the speech community judge that the use of that variety, and not the others, is appropriate to that domain.*

Examples of possible domains are the school, the family, employment, the playground and street, government administration and so on. There is no universal set applicable to all speech communities. The number and nature of the domains in any given society are determined by what is necessary for an account of the distribution of the varieties within the society. Now imagine an analyst who is observing individual interactions in some context. He notes that a certain participant switches between the varieties in the community's repertoire. The source of puzzlement is, 'Why did he switch?' If the classes of situation in which each variety normally appears, and is adjudged to be appropriate, is known, then individual switching is explicable and interpretable in these terms. The 'domains analysis' explains the individual switching in terms of the overall social distribution of the varieties.

It can be argued that the allocation of the varieties in a repertoire to separate domains is essential for language maintenance. For example, in the process of immigrant assimilation and adaption to a host society, large-scale societal bilingualism is gener-

ated in the immigrant group. The language shift that often ultimately occurs is made possible by the spread of the new
language into more and more domains. Figure 3.3, adapted from

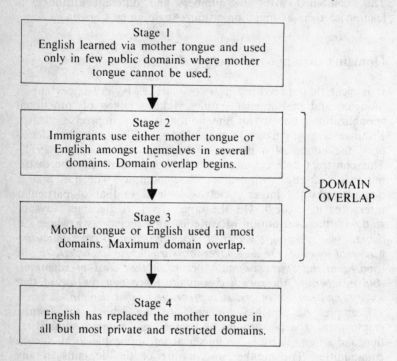

Stage 1
English learned via mother tongue and used
only in few public domains where mother
tongue cannot be used.

Stage 2
Immigrants use either mother tongue or
English amongst themselves in several
domains. Domain overlap begins.

Stage 3
Mother tongue or English used in most
domains. Maximum domain overlap.

DOMAIN
OVERLAP

Stage 4
English has replaced the mother tongue in
all but most private and restricted domains.

Figure 3.3 Domain overlap and language shift

Fishman, illustrates the relation of varieties to domains in the
successive stages of immigrant acculturation.

We can relate Fishman's theory to the situation in Montreal.
It would follow from his view that the existence of widespread
societal bilingualism combined with the maintenance of both English and French is the result of the stable allocation of both
languages to separate domains within the larger society.
Lieberson's analysis of the occupational pressures and the residential segregation is indirect evidence for this. More particularly, the existence of separate 'home' and 'neighbourhood'
domains for both languages, to which such segregation probably
testifies, would be a *sine qua non* for maintenance. Each lan-

guage has 'core' domains in which it is possible to live unil-ingually. The peculiarity of the Quebec situation in 1961 was the historic allocation of the minority language, English, to the 'eco-nomic' domains and the concomitant generation of asymmetric bilingualism among the Francophone majority.

By contrast, the evidence suggested that outside Quebec, French language and ethnicity underwent the process of assimi-lation typical of the Anglophone North American 'melting pot', involving as it does the disappearance of distinct domains for the minority tongue.

Social meaning

But the allocation of varieties to domains also involves the **social meaning** of the variety. This is the set of values which the variety itself encodes or symbolizes, and which its use communi-cates. The notion is very important in sociolinguistics, and we will be coming back to it again and again. Any human group or community can in one sense be defined as a communication network. It follows that the variety of languages employed by that network for its various functions will 'take on' and thus conventionally convey the meaning – X conveys the social iden-tity of the group. This identity also entails not only the 'who we are' of the group, but the system of values, beliefs and patterns of culture which are part of 'who we are'. To perform an utter-ance in French, for example, conveys something *by that very fact* apart from its cognitive content, when English is also a con-trasting variety in the repertoire.

We can ask why a given variety is allocated to given domains, or why a whole community tacitly agrees that a variety is appro-priate to a given domain. The answer will inevitably involve us in a circle. One answer will be in terms of the social meaning of the variety. It has a social meaning appropriate to that domain in the speech community. But why does it have that meaning? The answer will be historical: because a certain social group has used it and therefore it encodes both the identity and values of the representative users of the variety, and the values of typical situations in which they use it. A variety may also be seen as appropriate for certain functions of language, for example formal or public uses. This is usually derivable in the same way, via the representative groups who have used that variety in that way, and thus given it the social meaning which makes it appropriate.

Be that as it may, once that meaning is established, it is clear that both the allocation of varieties to domains, and the maintenance or decline of a variety, depends on it. To put this in another way, members of a speech community have an **attitude** towards the variety. They understand what it means to say something *in a given language*. And that fact is important in explaining both the existence of domains in which that variety is agreed, by convention, to be appropriate, and for its continued existence as a separate variety in the repertoire of the speech community. We will be seeing this later when we consider language varieties of many diverse kinds. And later on we will try to make the notion of social meaning more precise.

Canada: an update

The way in which the Canadian situation developed after 1961 allows us to see the political consequences of linguistic diversity in crisis and the ways in which **language legislation** can be used to plan linguistic developments. The sketch above added up to a political and demographic time-bomb, which duly exploded into a demand for change. One response to the perceived crisis has found political expression through successive Quebec governments, which have embarked, since 1960, on the wholesale modernization of the society. The concensus was that French-speaking Quebec no longer wished merely to survive (indeed, on the trends we described, it would decline), but it wished to build a Francophone society in which it would be possible to 'live in French' in all aspects of life. This would involve a new relationship with Anglophones. The powers, both symbolic and real, claimed by Quebec to achieve such aims provoked a continuing constitutional crisis in Canada as a whole.

The Quebec language laws of 1974 and 1977 are extremely interesting from the point of view of Lieberson's analysis in 1961. They are a programme for the 'francization' of Quebec society. There are two main practical thrusts behind these laws: the extension and specification of the domains where, by law, the French language must be used, and an attempt to ensure that immigrants whose mother tongue is neither English nor French become part of the Francophone community. To achieve the former aim, French is made the sole official language of Quebec, of the Assemblée Nationale, of the courts, and of civil administration, semi-public agencies, labour relations and, very significantly, commerce and business. Article 4 of Bill 101 states, 'workers have a right to carry on their activities in French.' To implement this, firms are required to obtain 'francization certificates' upon the submission of satisfactory plans. Education is the key to the aim of integrating the immigrant groups into Francophone society. The basic principle is established that French is to be the language of instruction in schools.

These laws, if successful in effecting social change, will have major consequences in exactly the areas Lieberson highlighted in 1961. The approach of the Federal government in Ottawa to language legislation and planning has been rather different. It has been concerned with protecting individual rights, promoting community development among minorities, and ensuring that Francophones, at least in their dealings with the Federal government, feel more 'at home' in all of Canada. The new Constitution of 1982 requires, for example, that its Charter of Rights 'be interpreted in a manner consistent with the preservation and enhancement of the multicultural heritage of Canadians'.

More specifically, the Official Languages Act of 1969 reaffirmed that both French and English were official languages of equal status not only in the Federal parliament but also in all Federal government activities. The principle was established that, where there was sufficient local demand, Canadians had a right to deal with their central government in either French or English. This led to intensive 'bilingualization' of the Federal civil service (creating opportunities for Francophones already bilingual for historical reasons), and to the extension of French services in areas such as broadcasting. Bilingualism was generally promoted – for example, assistance was provided to encourage educational opportunities for people to learn the second official language. A Commissioner of Official Languages was appointed to 'take all actions and measures within his authority with a view to ensuring recognition of the status of the official languages'; a sort if linguistic Ombudsman.

The Constitution Act of 1982, while incorporating these earlier language rights, goes further. French is established as the second official language on the provincial level in New Brunswick, where the Acadians are concentrated. But the new rights are in education; a mother-tongue group of the minority official language in any province has the right to have their children educated in that mother tongue where the number of children is sufficient to warrant it. Note that this will guarantee education in English for Quebecers of English mother tongue, for

Anglophone immigrants to Quebec, as well as for the Francophone minorities in other provinces.

The legislation by government at both levels is an attempt to shape linguistic and social trends to achieve political ends. Can any effects be seen at this early stage? Among the threatened Anglophones of Quebec, two things seem to be happening. There has been considerable migration into English Canada, both individual and corporate. This is reflected in a substantial decrease in the number of individuals claiming English mother tongue in Quebec, as is shown in Figure 3.4. The other trend seems to be

| | 1971 | | | | | |
| | *French* | | *English* | | *Other* | |
	Number	*%*	*Number*	*%*	*Number*	*%*
Province of Quebec	4,867,250	81	789,185	13	371,330	6
Montreal	1,819,640	66	595,395	22	328,180	12
Quebec City	458,435	95	18,035	4	4,030	1

| | 1976 | | | | | |
| | *French* | | *English* | | *Other* | |
	Number	*%*	*Number*	*%*	*Number*	*%*
Province of Quebec	4,989,245	80	800,680	13	444,525	7
Montreal	1,831,115	65	607,505	22	363,865	13
Quebec City	513,895	95	15,745	3	12,515	2

| | 1981 | | | | | |
| | *French* | | *English* | | *Other* | |
	Number	*%*	*Number*	*%*	*Number*	*%*
Province of Quebec	5,307,010	82	706,115	10.9	425,275	7
Montreal	1,936,215	68	520,490	18	371,635	13
Quebec City	554,775	96	15,585	3	5,720	1

Figure 3.4 Mother-tongue groups in Quebec, 1971–81 (from *Language and Society*, 8, 1982)

an increase in the bilingualism of Anglo-Quebec. In a recent assessment Caudwell (1982) writes,

> Our knowledge of the linguistic adaption of Quebec Anglophones – or at least those who are still in Quebec – is very imperfect. The best available estimates suggest that whereas in 1970 only a quarter of Quebec Anglophones could function socially in French, today the proportion has risen to two-thirds. As for integration, generally understood to mean

active participation in Francophone institutions as opposed to just linguistic accommodation, the situation is evolving very quickly. Bilingual Anglophone professionals and businessmen are now an everyday phenomenon.

There is evidence, too, that beginning in 1977, the majority of parents whose mother tongue was neither English nor French were enrolling their children in French schools. In other words, events in general are moving to reverse the historic situation.

The demands of the Quebec Francophones, the political representations and responses, and the ensuing social shift which is now in process represent exactly the nature of the complexity and symbolic potency of language when considered sociolinguistically.

Varieties of the 'same' language

Linguistic diversity occurs not only in strictly bilingual or multilingual settings, but where varieties are those within a single language. Indeed, Fishman has argued that distinct linguistic 'codes' emerge whenever there is any role differentiation in a human group at all. The linguistic variety signals and enacts the social distinction. Another important point is the relevance of notions we have used in describing societal bilingualism to the situation in which varieties of the 'same' language make up the repertoire.

In Chapter 2, we saw how standardized varieties, or standard languages, emerge. So one possible configuration within a repertoire would be a standard and various dialects, regional or otherwise. Another such configuration is Ferguson's **diglossia**. (This sounds like some kind of sociolinguistic disease; Haugen (1967) describes the preoccupation with 'correct' norms of usage, when faced with varieties of one's own language, as schizoglossia.)

Diglossia may be thought of as a kind of super-standardization. Ferguson (1959) defines it thus:

Diglossia is a relatively stable language situation in which, in addition to the primary dialects of the language (which may include a standard or regional standard), there is a very divergent, highly codified (often grammatically more complex) superimposed variety, the vehicle of a large and respected body of literature (written) either of an earlier period or in another speech community, which is learned largely by formal education and is used for most written and formal spoken purposes but is not used by any sector of the community for ordinary conversation.

The advantage of examining it at this point is that once again it is relatively easy to distinguish between the varieties. Ferguson examines four defining cases where diglossia obtains. In each case he calls the superordinate variety the High (H), and the colloquial variety, the Low (L). The four communities are Switzerland, Haiti, Greece and the Arab world. In the German-speaking parts of Switzerland, the H variety is standard German, while the L is Swiss German or Schweizerdeutsch. In Haiti, the L is the creole and the H is standard French. Two varieties of Greek are likewise in a diglossic relationship: the H, classical Greek or Katharévusa, and the L, Dhimotiki, or demotic contemporary Greek.

The nature of diglossic language can be seen if we look more closely at the Arabic case. Arabic is spoken over an enormous area, from the Persian Gulf to Morocco, and contains many varieties. The H is classical Arabic. Ferguson (1970) notes that this variety, in its written form, has been attested in literature for a millenium and a half, extending from pre-Islamic poetry to modern technical journals. The L is colloquial Arabic. But this general term covers many written varieties. There are the regional dialects which are the mother tongues of Arab speakers. Of these, some are regional standards: the speech of Cairo, Beirut-Damascus-Jerusalem, of Baghdad and of the northern Moroccan cities. Below these are the dialect continua. In other words, between classical and colloquial are many intermediate types: "shadings of 'middle language'", as Ferguson calls them.

An interesting feature of these four cases is that the linguistic nature of the H and L, their respective uses, their differing prestige and the manner in which they are acquired, all interact to create diglossia and maintain it as a stable system.

Linguistic features of H and L

In each case, the H is linguistically 'very divergent' from the L. Interestingly, the divergence is most marked in the grammar, rather than in the lexicon or phonology. In general, the H is more complex than the L. For example, the H may have more alternative grammatical categories and more exceptions to its rules. Stewart (1968) represents the linguistic relationship between French and Haitian creole in the following diagram:

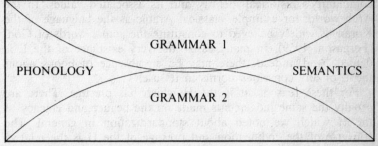

This linguistic pattern is a reflection of the social nature of diglossia. Sound and word meanings are characteristically the two levels of language which change and therefore diverge most rapidly. By contrast, the grammatical core of language is more resistant to change and evolves more slowly. Therefore, the normal pattern of relationships between dialects is that of considerable phonological and lexical differences and rather less grammatical ones. In diglossia, the normal pattern of divergence seems to be somewhat reversed. The H and L grammars have evolved apart while the other levels tend to be more alike. But consider that the H, a written variety, has been codified and thus 'fixed' and *self-consciously elaborated* over an extended time and over a wide area, and the local colloquial variants have not. The latter are thus relatively free to diverge. Also, since the H is *only* formally acquired, through education, those learning it must mediate it through their mother tongues, the L. This probably would tend to make the sounds and word meanings partially converge, as the H is successively relearned each generation by speakers of the evolving L. But there are systematic divergences in the lexicon and phonology as well. In the lexicon, Ferguson notes, there are very often lexical pairs in the H and L, synonyms which radically mark a text as belonging to one variety or the other.

The social meaning of the H

As we said, the divergence between H and L is probably partly related to the long period of standardization and codification which the H has undergone. It is the H which has been the object of scholarship and language management. It is the H which is the vehicle of the major religious and literary traditions of the community. It is the H, therefore, which symbolizes the community's historical identity and its associated values. In the Arab world, for example, classical Árabic as the language of the Koran 'is widely believed to constitute the actual words of God' (Ferguson, 1959). In many cases, the very existence of the L is denied. And, indeed, there may be an absence of books about the L or any conscious norms in its use.

For these reasons, it is the H which has prestige. There are usually the same judgements made on the beauty and efficacy of the H which we noted about standardization in general. The converse of the codification and prestige of the H is the relative absence of these in the L. The latter, therefore, is subject to variability and diversity in a way that the former is not.

Specialization of functions

The prestige of the H, in turn, is a major factor in the functional specialization of the two varieties. Figure 3.5 presents the characteristic uses to which H and L are put. Each variety is considered appropriate only to certain types of situation. For example, *the H is never used by any sector of the community for casual conversation*. It follows that it is not used in conversations between adults and children, and that, therefore, the H is no one's mother tongue. It has a distinctive pattern of acquisition which is a consequence of its functional specialization. It is largely acquired through formal education.

It is the interaction of these features which makes diglossia stable. The system which maintains it works like this. The historical prestige of the H and its current social meaning leads to its functional specialization. Simultaneously, of course, these formal and culturally significant functions reinforce its prestige and symbolic value. A variety symbolizing such values cannot appropriately be used in speaking to children. Therefore, it can only be acquired formally, along with literacy at school. Once acquired, it is used on those occasions when it is appropriate, but *not* to children, and so on. This system will last for as long as the social meaning of the H leads to functional specialization, and this is a reflection of the structure of the society itself. We noted the same kind of factors at work in Canada, maintaining

	High	Low
Sermon in church or mosque	x	
Instruction to servants, waiters, workmen, clerks		x
Personal letter	x	
Speech in parliament, political speech	x	
University lecture	x	
Conversation with family, friends, colleagues		x
News broadcast	x	
Radio soap opera		x
Newspaper editorial, news story, caption on picture	x	
Caption on political cartoon		x
Poetry	x	
Folk literature		x

Figure 3.5 Specialization of functions of H and L in diglossia (*from Ferguson, 1959*)

societal bilingualism. It would seem, then, that to account for the stable existence of language varieties, we need to use a system of four mutually defining terms thus:

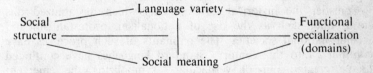

Diglossia, in Ferguson's sense, is one particular arrangement of varieties and relates to one particular configuration of social factors. Social changes could destabilize the system: changes such as the competing prestige of a local nationalism, loss of belief in the values which the H symbolizes, or loss of clearly defined domains which must be conducted in H. In diglossic situations, there is characteristically a sharp social stratification between an elite, who alone have access to literacy, and therefore can learn the H, and the bulk of the people who are only competent in L. The existence of H, therefore, simultaneously excludes most people from participation in key social functions (politics, law, the church, education) while at the same time symbolizing the unifying values of the society; for example, by alluding to the body of literature from the past or from a wider 'culture area' which encodes such values.

Note the very intimate relation between social structure and language structure. Compare diglossia, for example, with the relationship between a standard language and its dialects which we discussed in the last chapter. Diglossia seems to be an extreme case of standardization. Partly, this would be a reflex of the sharper social discontinuities in diglossic situations. Accordingly, the varieties are more sharply divergent. But the H also alludes to a historical 'culture area', and the identity of the society is at least partly defined outside itself, in space or time. The Hs are unifying in this sense. By contrast, the Standards of modern Europe are the linguistic side of the evolution of nation states and are the standardized 'local vernaculars' of societies. The Standards of Europe are part of the 'nationalisms' of Europe. However, at earlier stages in history diglossia was a characteristic European configuration. Thus, Latin would have been the H in those countries which have Romance vernaculars, which are modern dialects of Latin. The allusion encoded by the H's social meaning would be the values and identity of 'Christendom', and its continuity with the ancient world. The situation in the Germanic, Slavic and other areas of Europe would not have been strictly diglossic, by Ferguson's definition, but rather diglossia-like, with Latin as the H.

Consider the historical developments which destabilized this status quo, such as the rise of nationalism, protestantism and secular national societies. The remnants of such processes have continued into this century. Standard languages have continued to be created out of vernaculars, symbolizing the emergent nationalisms of Europe. (In a moment, we will be mentioning one such standard, in Norway.) On the other hand, Latin still retains some prestige today. Its social meaning seems still to be perceived. And, indeed, it has only very recently lost a remaining functional specialization, as the official language of the supernational Roman Catholic Church.

Diglossia describes only one particular configuration of varieties. It very closely reflects, because it is used to enact, a cluster of social properties. A typology of different linguistic repertoires, if it were to be complete, would presuppose a similar typology of societies. One factor of significance has emerged from our examples, and that is social differentiation, or the degree of discontinuity or continuity between social groups. In societal bilingualism and in diglossia we found both distinct language varieties and fairly sharp social boundaries. We will now look at an example, between a standard and a regional dialect in Norway, which involves mutually intelligible dialects of a language. There is much less social discontinuity and, correspondingly, much less 'separateness' of the varieties in linguistic terms. However, the four interrelated themes we diagrammed above are still involved, even in cases where the linguistic distinctions between varieties become problematic.

Code-switching

We will now change perspective slightly. The focus will shift to the question of **code-switching**. We have two mutually intelligible dialects of the same language. What factors are needed to account for speakers switching between one variety and the other? Can we relate the large-scale social patterning to individual choice of variety?

An important study of these issues was made by Blom and Gumperz (1972). They examined the small community of Hemnesberget in northern Norway. Its repertoire consists of two varieties of Norwegian: Bokmål, the form of standard Norwegian current in northern Norway, and Ranamål, the local dialect of the area. An important feature of Blom and Gumperz's analysis of Hemnesberget is its holistic approach. Besides studying the formal linguistic relationship of the two varieties, a subject to which we will return in a moment, they studied instances of code-switching in small groups and did this in the context of a detailed analysis of the local social system. This included the systems of values to which members of the community were oriented. Code-switching, they argued, was ultimately explicable in terms of the values which Ranamål and Bokmål encoded. In a community like Hemnesberget, where for all practical purposes everyone can speak both varieties, the most likely explanation for the maintenance of distinct codes is that each conveys particular social meanings.

There were two broad systems of values in the community. The first, local values, were beliefs concerning the solidarity, the unique identity and the egalitarian values of the local community. Contrasted to this were various sorts of non-local values.

Thus, there were the beliefs associated with pan-Norwegian activities, for example, nationwide political, cultural and economic concerns, and the values implicit in such activities. Blom and Gumperz were able to group members of the community, not only according to occupation, descent and patterns of interaction, but also in terms of the orientation of their values.

Within the community, Ranamål and Bokmål symbolized the local and non-local values respectively. The social meanings of the two varieties were readily explicable both in terms of their historical origins, and how they were acquired. Bokmål, one of the two forms of standard Norwegian, had first been introduced into the local area as the language of a now departed aristocracy, with its non-local and elitist values. Ranamål was indigenous in, and confined to the local community. The ways in which the two varieties were acquired parallel this historical contrast. Bokmål is acquired in school and church, where non-local values are involved, while Ranamål is acquired in the home.

In the community, then, there are contrasting systems of values. History and a pattern of acquisition associated the two linguistic varieties with those systems of values as their social meanings. The varieties can therefore be used to convey those values, or enact situations in which those values are taken for granted. In Hemnesberget, the existence of the two varieties serves to integrate the community in two directions, both locally and within the larger national society.

Situational code-switching

With such an analysis of the social meanings, the switching of an individual from one variety to the other becomes explicable. It is not random. The social meaning of the code is the link between the actual linguistic varieties, Bokmål and Ranamål, and the situations in which it is used. This meaning also connects the large-scale patterning – how the varieties are distributed within the community – with the individual's specific choice of variety. Given what we have said so far, Ranamål ought to occur in those types of situation in which local values predominate, and Bokmål ought to occur where non-local, pan-Norwegian values are most important.

We will expect **situational code-switching**. That is, the situation type will predict which variety a speaker will employ. However, in Hemnesberget, whether a speaker situationally code-switches or not further depends on the orientation of values of the particular sub-group of the community to which he belongs. For example, two groups, the artisans and the merchants and managers, are both strongly oriented towards local values, although with some conflict in the latter case. These groups code-switch by situation and use Bokmål, for example, in church, in school, or in speaking to an outsider, and Ranamål in local situations. Thus yet again we find the allocation of distinct linguistic varieties to distinct uses: what we have referred to earlier as 'functional specialization' or the existence of 'domains of language use'.

But since we have now introduced the dimension of the individual speaker and his choice of code, we can perhaps go further into the nature of these patterns. Since speakers regularly code-switch in the requisite situations, we might state this regularity as a causal generalization. In domain A, code A occurs; in domain B, code B occurs. On this basis, predictions could be made, deducing the occurrence of the code, given the generalization, the situation and the group membership of the speaker.

But there is a difficulty in applying this sort of explanation alone to social facts; for the collective phenomenon is made up of regularities which are individual choices. More on this later, but at this stage, it must be noted that 'a type of social situation' is a complex idea, and one part of it is that the choice of the variety is part of the definition of the situation itself. This means that in choosing a given code, a speaker can be enacting an intention to *redefine* the situation in which they are participating. He may be saying, "I want what we are doing to count as an instance of a given situation." In other words, the choice of code can be *tactical*. This depends, in turn, on the larger social norm of appropriateness of variety to situation type.

A very nice example of the use of situational code-switching to redefine the situation itself is provided by Denison (1972) in his study of language variety in Sauris, Italy. In this community, three varieties have a characteristic domain allocation: the local variety of German, in the home; Friulian, the regional dialect of Italian, in semi-public places such as the local bar; and standard Italian in church and school. Denison taped one instance, however, in which German was uncharacteristically employed in the bar. A local farmer, who was supposed to have been making cheese at the cooperative dairy, was in the bar when his wife burst in and harangued him in German for drinking when he should have been working. At one stage he briefly attempted to calm her in Friulian, but on the whole conducted the argument in German. Denison (1972: 71) interprets his utterances in Friulian (for example, *"ööö! No stà rabiàti, capis-tu!"* – 'Oh! Don't lose your temper, d'you understand!') as an attempt to redefine the situation by language choice. This example demonstrates a number of points: that locale alone is only a component of situation; that in using German with husband-wife roles in a domestic argument, a home situation has been created in an incongruent locale; that the farmer can *use* Friulian tactically to try to recreate a situation which is congruent with the semi-public locale of the bar. Thus, he can use the possibilities of the repertoire in this context to try to evade his wife's accusations, for specific conversational purposes.

Metaphorical code-switching

Situation alone is not sufficient to account for all instances of code-switching. Blom and Gumperz describe cases of **metaphorical code-switching**. In these cases, the use of the variety alludes to the social values it encodes, but is otherwise inappropriate to the situation in which it is uttered. This is familiar in those common cases in which speakers use a local variety humorously or ironically for a rhetorical effect in a discourse otherwise uttered in a standard. There is no attempt to change the situation itself, but merely to make a comment. In Hemnesberget, speakers from groups who owed allegiance both to local and to pan-Norwegian values (for example, students at home from university), code-switched into Bokmål if topics involving non-local values were introduced. The situation of casual conversation remained otherwise unchanged and Ranamål was clearly appropriate.

Bokmål was being used in these cases to convey specific meanings related to a speaker's attitude to the topic being discussed. The conventional social meaning is being used conversationally. So although the use seems inappropriate according to the norm of situational code-switching, it can be interpreted as meaningful against that background. In cases where this is done with communicative intent, code-switching connects the societal allocation of varieties, a society-wide fact, and individual intentionality. Intention presupposes convention.

The linguistics of code-switching

The notion of code-switching presupposes that there are codes to switch. The theory which we have developed thus far, which has largely originated in the studies of the anthropologists Gumperz and Dell Hymes, is a descriptive and predictive framework which goes like this. Speech communities have linguistic repertoires of varieties, each of which has a distinct social meaning. This meaning determines, and may have arisen from, the historical allocation of each variety to certain classes of situation within the society as a norm of behaviour. In general, code-switching is predictable using such a framework. However, metaphorical and tactical code-switching also occurs which is not always predictable, but is always interpretable. Note that its interpretation must be relative to the rules of appropriateness described by the theory. Furthermore, there is no difference in this phenomenon or its explanation between communities whose repertoires consist of distinct languages and whose repertoires consist of dialects of a language. Now let us consider what happens linguistically when speakers switch between codes.

Sankoff (1971) has pointed out difficulties in the linguistic interpretation of code-switching. There are two aspects of this problem. It is impossible to account for every switch in a text, certainly predictively and perhaps interpretatively. There is a residue of 'extremely frequent and rapid switching which, to put it bluntly, defies explanation, if by explanation one means accounting for every switch.' Secondly, there is often difficulty encountered in saying to which variety a given segment belongs. They can be so linguistically 'mixed' that it is hard to decide whether the text is an instance of variety A or variety B. Labov (1972: 189) has analysed a text in which a speaker has switched eighteen times in six lines. The italicized portions can be assigned to standard English and the rest to the black English vernacular:

> And den like *if you miss onesies*, de *oth*uh person shoot to skelly; ef he miss, den you go again. An' *if you get in, you shoot to twosies*. An' *if you get in twosies, you go to* threesies. An' *if you miss* threesies, *then the person tha*' miss skelly shoot *the skellies* an' shoot in *the onesies*: an' *if he miss, you go* f'om threesies to foursies.

As Labov says, there is no obvious motive for switching eighteen

times in such a short passage. He interprets this text as variation, not between distinct codes, but within a single system.
Sankoff herself produces a fairly short text in which twenty-nine
switches are identifiable between Buang, a language of New
Guinea, and Neo-Melanesian, an English-based pidgin language
used for specialized functions.

To account for such switching, in cases where it is between
separate languages, a common tactic has been to identify the
text as *basically* in language A, with an admixture from language
B, or vice versa. Sankoff uses this tactic to reduce the twenty-
nine switches in her text to five. Denison (1972: 67) terms the
basic language of a text its **macro-structure**, and the admixtures
its **micro-structure**. He writes that, 'in order to retain the concept
of separate languages . . ., the language of a text must be defined
as the language of its macro-structure.' Let us visualize this situation of fluctuation as in Figure 3.6, and then consider possible
ways in which we might be able to account for it.

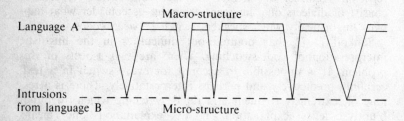

Figure 3.6 Intrusions from language B into a text which is basically
in language A

Assume that we are dealing with two distinct languages. The
theory of code-switching does not predict or explain such intrusions, although it can be used for the interpretation of switching
between macro-structures. Consider other ways in which we
could explain the intrusion of elements of language B into language A and supplement the code-switching theory with other
explanations.

Proficiency. Speakers in general may have differing proficiency in
the two languages. Denison notes uncertainty about German
words for activities in Italian domains. Similarly, in his study of
the Norwegian language in America, Haugen noted instances of
uncertainty about Norwegian words for objects from English

domains. Such uncertainties would produce fluctuations in a text, which would be especially sensitive to topic.

Language boundaries and borrowing. There may be cases in which one language is in the process of borrowing terms from another. Such words would be **incipient loans** as yet unassimilated into the sound structures of the borrowing language. This would be an especially active process in those situations in which the lending language had highly developed vocabulary in certain areas (for example, technology) in which the borrowing language was deficient. Large-scale borrowing would be convenient for talk on such topics in domains where the borrowing language was otherwise appropriate. If the loans were unassimilated, they would appear as intrusions from the lending language into a text basically in the borrowing language. One might expect the Low to be more open to borrowing terms from the High than vice versa, because of the prestige and standardization of the latter.

Bilingual interference. Bilingual individuals often have systematic interference between the two language systems on the phonological, grammatical and lexical levels. There is variation in the degree to which individuals can keep the systems separate. We might hypothesize that certain of the observed intrusions from one language into another in a given text might be cases of such interference. Again, the expectation would be that speakers would attempt to keep the High as free as possible from interference – from the Low rather than vice versa.

In these three cases – proficiency, borrowing and interference, the relation between the codes will relate in a complex way to the nature of the social boundaries that exist in the society. Sankoff (1971) suggests two further possibilities.

Both codes are appropriate. Perhaps there are situations in which both codes are appropriate in order to convey two distinct social meanings simultaneously. If this view is correct, then any attempt to explain individual switches in a text will fail. The use of *both* codes throughout a text conveys *both* social meanings in that situation.

Relative frequencies. Sankoff further advances the hypothesis that the relative frequency of the two codes in a text may itself be determined by social and situational factors. She writes, 'it is possible to show that the extent of the use of Neo-Melanesian ... forms a continuum which could be correlated with various social and situational variables, simply in terms of the relative proportion of Neo-Melanesian used. In terms of social stratification, for example, it seems clear that high status correlates with high frequency of use of Neo-Melanesian.'

In both these last explanations, although the fluctuation is explicable in the same social terms as code-switching in general, each individual switch or intrusion need not be explained. The mixture of the two codes is itself the realization of the speaker's intention to convey a social meaning.

The linguistic boundaries between codes in those cases where the codes are dialects of a language is also problematic. We saw in Chapter 2 that dialects are not discrete entities, that the relationship between dialects is a continuum. If we look for discrete codes in situations of switching between dialects, we are not likely to find them. What we will find is a 'more or less' situation.

This is clear from Blom and Gumperz's analysis of the two codes in Hemnesberget. The community recognizes the social reality of the two distinct varieties, Ranamål and Bokmål, and it is clear that the speech community has distinct attitudes to the varieties which therefore encode contrasting social meanings. But the linguistic relationship of the two socially distinct dialects is that of a continuum.

This is particularly marked on the phonological level, the level on which sounds of language are organized. Grammatically (for example, in the system of pronouns), the two dialects have distinct and contrasting pairs. But, consider the way in which the dialects are related with respect to their sounds. Ranamål is said to have a **palatalized** series of consonants. Bokmål is said not to have this feature. What this means is that Ranamål has versions of 't', 'd', 'n', 'l' which are pronounced so that the front of the tongue also articulates with the hard surface at the front of the roof of the mouth (the hard palate) making an 'i' sound of the sort found in the pronunciation of English words like 'Kew' or 'huge'. These sounds are used to distinguish words in Ranamål, but not in Bokmål. What Blom and Gumperz found, however, was not an absolute linguistic discontinuity between the two dialects, but rather that they differed in terms of degree of palatalization on a single scale. Similarly with vowel sounds: they sometimes varied on a continuous scale between the dialects, depending on the degree to which the tongue was lowered and retracted in their pronunciation.

	Palatalization	Height and retraction of tongue in pronunciation of [ae] and [a]	
Bokmål	zero	high	not retracted
continuous variation	weak	lower	some retraction
Ranamål	strong	lowest	quite retracted

The dialects, therefore, were at different ends of a single scale with respect to each of these variable features. Blom and Gumperz discovered that, linguistically at least, the variants which were sensitive to social factors were cases of continuous variation within a single system, not of switching between two discrete and discontinuous systems. When informants seemingly code-switched, what they really did was move in varying degrees up and down continua. Informants each moved *different* distances. However, they all agreed which end of the scale marked each of the two contrasting dialects.

How is it possible, then, to conceive of the dialects as entities in linguistic terms (they are clearly entities in social terms)? We must return to our definition of any variety as a clustering together of linguistic features. Gumperz uses the term **co-occurrence rules** for cases in which one linguistic form predicts the existence of another, and in the case of dialects like Ranamål and Bokmål, we get both **horizontal** and **vertical co-occurrence**. This notion is schematized in Figure 3.7. Thus Ranamål, as an entity, is identifiable because, when speakers articulate sounds at the Ranamål end of variables, they also produce Ranamål grammar and lexis. This is vertical co-occurrence across the linguistic levels. But also, in a given utterance, if a speaker is speaking at the Ranamål end of various continua, this selects Ranamål for the next and successive linguistic items produced. This is horizontal co-occurrence as it proceeds sequentially in a text.

What, then, from the linguistic point of view, is code-switching between dialects? Labov (1972: 188) writes, ' . . . to demonstrate that we have a true case of code-switching, it is necessary to show that the speaker moves from one consistent

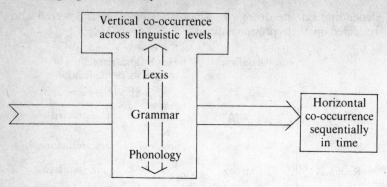

Figure 3.7 Defining a variety by co-occurrence rules

set of co-occurring rules to another.' But in many instances this sort of clarity will not exist. As Blom and Gumperz point out, we get degrees of shifting, sometimes a breakdown in co-occurrence rules. It is this which provides linguistic problems for the analyst who is using the conceptual framework of codes and code-switching to relate social explanations to the details of linguistic variation. It is only justified to talk of distinct codes if, in fact, co-occurrence rules define such distinct entities which also are conventionally used by speakers to implicate social meanings, relative to social norms in a speech community. But it is also the case that *single variable features* can correlate independently with social factors and also independently can encode social meanings. This is typically what happens when social boundaries are not sharp. It is to the study of such continuously varying features, and the sociolinguistic structures of which they are part, that we shall now turn.

Before doing that, though, glance back to the stanza from A. M. Klein's poem with which this chapter began. Its macro-structure is clearly English. But consider the allusive fluctuations of code within it. There are French or French-like words – '*parle*', '*vocabulaire*', '*Ecosse*' – and syntactic forms in the text. Since the two languages are distinct codes, defined by co-occurrence, and not related on a continuum, these intrusions might best be interpreted as metaphorical code-switches of some kind. Notice then how we could say that there has been a weakening of the horizontal and vertical co-occurrence rules, and hence the boundaries between the varieties. This is a witty, light poem, a mock epic.

Note that this is achieved by allusion to yet another variety, to the latinate syntax and vocabulary of the English epic, itself a translation-equivalent of Latin forms. The poet is intentionally creating a linguistic mix, including a pastiche of 'franglais', to actualize his meanings. This illustrates how the social meanings of whole varieties can be used and large-scale patterning related to individual acts of speech.

4. Discovering the Structure in Variation

'Free variation' is of course a label, not an explanation. It does not tell us where the variants came from nor why the speakers use them in differing proportions, but is rather a way of excluding such questions from the scope of immediate inquiry.

Fischer (1958)

Variability

In the last chapter, we looked at code-switching and saw that sometimes it was not plausible to account for variation as an alternation between two distinct codes. Sometimes we find instead a rapid and seemingly random fluctuation between linguistic forms. Let us make this problem concrete, so we can visualize what such variation is like. Consider words ending in the suffix '-ing', such as 'hunting' or 'working'. Very widely within the English-speaking world, people pronounce such items as either *working* or *workin'*. Sometimes the suffix is pronounced as '-*ing*'; sometimes as '-*in*'. Although from the point of view of the written word, this looks like 'dropping the g', that is not what happens. Phonetically neither form of the suffix contains [g]; the contrast is between whether the final nasal is pronounced at the back, [ɪŋ], or the front, [ɪn], of the mouth.

To imagine the variability here, let the /ɪn/ form be represented by 1 and the /ɪŋ/ form by 0. Now imagine utterances by three speakers on a given occasion where there are ten opportunities of pronouncing words which have the '-ing' suffix. The production of the two variant forms might be as follows:

Occasion 1
Speaker A 1 1 0 0 1 0 1 1 0 0 (5 /ɪn/)
Speaker B 0 1 0 0 1 1 0 1 0 0 (4 /ɪn/)   out of 10
Speaker C 1 0 1 0 0 0 0 0 0 0 (2 /ɪn/)

On another occasion, however, we might find something like this:

Occasion 2
Speaker A 1 1 1 0 1 0 1 1 1 1 (8 /ɪn/)
Speaker B 1 1 0 0 1 0 1 1 0 0 (5 /ɪn/)   out of 10
Speaker C 1 1 0 0 1 0 1 0 0 0 (4 /ɪn/)

This is indeed a rapid fluctuation between forms. And such variation is pervasive throughout language. We will be seeing many examples in the course of the following chapters. The problem for the linguist faced with such inconsistency is to find a structure which can explain it. To do this, both a theoretical outlook and a methodology is required, and these were first provided by William Labov who revolutionized dialect studies with the publication in 1966 of *The Social Stratification of English in New York City*. Labov's research provided a paradigm for research into variation. This chapter will be devoted to an exploration of this new methodology and its consequences.

But first, what sort of explanations of variation are superseded by this new paradigm? Earlier explanations of variation fell into two categories: namely that it is the result of **dialect mixture**, or that it is a case of **free variation**.

These explanations are implicit in two traditional approaches to language. The concept of a 'dialect' as a variety of language is, of course, a 'given' in tradition dialectology, which has as its aim the empirical study of such entities. A variety, or code, or dialect, as we saw earlier, is a 'clustering together' in terms of co-occurrence rules of linguistic features into a single coherent linguistic object. It can be given a name like 'Bokmål'. Such entities are the things that switch in code-switching. It could follow that our rapid fluctuation is simply the result of a mixing of dialects in communities and individuals. The trouble is that variability of the '-ing' kind simply does not find its origin in two distinguishable dialects that then mix. We would be postulating two distinct codes on the basis of observed fluctuation simply to explain that fluctuation as a mixture of them. But such variables fluctuate more or less independently of each other in any case. In other words, both in individuals and communities, certain features vary continuously within a single language system. We saw this with the degrees of palatalization and the height and retraction of vowels in Hemnesberget. A language seems to be a 'loose' system.

Nor can this variability be dealt with by the mainstream tradition of linguistic theorizing. We saw in Chapter 1 how abstract a language is from the point of view of Chomsky's linguistic theory. Properties of language viewed as sets of sentences are explained by invariant rules which ultimately reflect universal features of human linguistic abilities. Variation is abstracted out in getting at the essential properties of the system. A language is viewed as an idealized 'frozen' system outside time and social space. And, as Fischer points out in the quotation that begins this chapter, 'free' variation is simply a way of excluding variability from the object of inquiry.

Labov's aim, however, is to confront the 'looseness' of the system as the data of linguistics itself, and thus to lower the degree of idealization of the object of inquiry – to study the language in use in the speech community. His initial intuition was that large-scale variation was not without pattern, but that it was socially determined. It could only be explained by social and historical factors interacting with factors within the linguistic system. One had to look for the wood in which the variation was the trees. With a sophisticated method for investigating speech within the community, consistency in the use of one variant over another in individuals, groups and contexts would be found. This is true of many 'aggregate' human phenomena, for example, in economics. Without a description in institutional or group terms, the phenomenon is invisible or incoherent viewed as individual behaviour. (Whether the group solely explains or determines the individual behaviour is another matter!)

Sociolinguistic variables

The hypothesis is that variation is socially conditioned. Although it may appear incoherent in the speech of an individual, a structure will emerge if the variation is studied socially. But in order to do this, a quantitative method is necessary. One has to be able to count the frequencies of the variants in order to compare them between individuals, groups and contexts. Therefore Labov introduced the notion of the **linguistic variable**. (If a variable can be correlated with a non-linguistic variable of social context, such as class, style, sex, or age, then it can be called a **sociolinguistic variable**.) The variable itself is written in brackets: (ing). This symbol is an abstract construct representing any given linguistic feature which can be freely realized by two or more variants, which are the **values** of the variable. Each variant has a number and these can be written inside the brackets. For example, (ing) represents the variable, and (ing - 1), (ing - 0) the two values of the variable. (ing - 1) represents the /ɪn/ form, as in 'workin'', and (ing - 0) the /ɪŋ/ as in 'working'.

$$(ing) \begin{cases} (ing - 1) = in' \text{ (nasal in front of mouth)} \\ (ing - 0) = ing \text{ (nasal at back of mouth)} \end{cases}$$

The next step is to count the instances of each of the values of the variable feature in the utterances in question and calculate an index. This allows the analyst to work out the quantity, for example, of the '-in'' form used, as opposed to the '-ing' form, for individuals and for groups. In the case of the variable (ing) the calculation of the index is very straightforward. It is a straight percentage of the number of '-in'' ('workin'') forms used in the total number of cases where either (ing) form is possible, thus:

$$(ing) \text{ index} = \frac{\text{number of '-in'' forms}}{\text{total number of occurrences of (ing)}} \times 100$$

We are now in a position to calculate (ing) index scores for the utterances of a given individual. This will give us a quantitative representation of variation, first for individuals and then for social groups of which they are members. Consider our hypothetical occasions of (ing) above. On occasion 1, Speaker A produced '-in'' (pronouncing the nasal with closure at the front of his mouth), five times out of ten. This gives him an index score of fifty. On occasion 2, however, the same speaker pronounced '-in'' eight times out of ten possible occurrences of the (ing) variable. And his score was therefore eighty on this occasion. We can now precisely compare individuals and individuals as between different occasions with respect to this particular variable feature of their speech.

Sociolinguistic structures

The sociolinguistic variable is a tool which allows us next to establish average index scores for any group or sub-group within a larger population. People can be grouped with respect to any social attribute which the analyst suspects is relevant, for example, age, sex, ethnic group, education, place of residence, socio-economic class and so on, and the average score calculated. Similarly, if a method can be found to control features of situation, features such as whether the utterance is relatively casual or formal, average scores for **styles** can also be arrived at. In other words, the analyst can *correlate index scores with non-linguistic variables* for large and complex populations and reveal the 'aggregate' structure of variation.

When this is done, the degree of structure revealed is extraordinary. Figure 4.1 shows the average (ing) index scores of Labov's informants in his survey of the Lower East Side of New York City according to their socio-economic class and

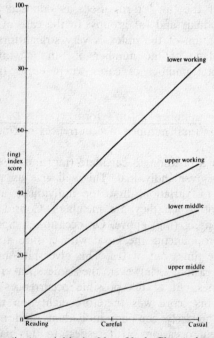

Figure 4.1 The (ing) variable in New York City (*adapted from Labov, 1972*)

simultaneously correlated with the degree of formality in the style of their speech. I shall return in a moment to the notions of 'class' and 'style' used in this type of research. For the moment, note that the diagram reveals a clear structure for the (ing) variable, a stratification in the use of '-in'' versus '-ing' according to class and style, which is not apparent in the seemingly random fluctuations in the pronunciation of any one individual in isolation. Clearly, the variation is not 'free'. The use of the linguistic variants are socially conditioned. As we shall see, such **sociolinguistic structures**, determined on the dimensions of class and style, are just one significant correlation made possible by the use of quantitative methodology.

Note some of the important features of Figure 4.1. The variable (ing) is stratified by class. In each style, the average index scores of the informants grouped by class form a hierarchy according to the class stratification of the society.

Simultaneously, the variable is differentiated by style. The behaviour of each class varies systematically according to whether their speech is casual, careful or reading style. Although each class has different average scores in each style, all groups **style-shift**. And each does so in the same direction. They produce higher (ing) scores in the more casual styles; the lines of the graph all rise as the degree of formality becomes less and less. And yet, as they rise, they each remain regularly stratified by class.

This kind of variable, called a **marker** by Labov, is structured two ways at once, both by a hierarchy of social status and a hierarchy of formality, or care in speech. There is clearly a connection between these two social factors. It would seem that the form produced with the highest frequency by the upper middle class in all contexts, including the most casual (the '-ing' variant), is also the form aimed at by all social classes, the more attention they pay to their speech. As Labov says (1972: 240), it would be "difficult to interpret any signal by itself – to distinguish, for example, a casual salesman from a careful pipefitter." This style-shifting suggests that relatively lower (ing) scores (a higher percentage of the '-ing' variant) not only characterizes the speech of the highest class, but marks the standard of prestige for the community as a whole – presumably because of the social meaning of that variant. The '-ing' variant is the prestige form, at least overtly, and the '-in'' variant is stigmatized, and this seems intuitively correct.

The (ing) variable, like all the variables we will look at, also reflects a particular point in the dynamics of language change. Variability, which we see now as systematic differential frequencies in the use of the variants of a single variable, is central to the process of change. Both (ing) variants go back as far as early Middle English (Wells, 1982: 262). The literature suggests that in early modern English the presently stigmatized '-in'' variant was, in fact, the most frequent form for all social groups. Wells remarks that '-in'' was the fashionable pronunciation in eighteenth-century England, and that a folk memory of this exists in the phrase 'huntin', shootin' and fishin'', used to refer to such prestige pastimes. It was only in the late eighteenth and early nineteenth centuries that a 'spelling' pronunciation gained prestige (written '-ing' being associated with closure in the back of the mouth) and there was a prescriptive condemnation of the '-in'' form by teachers and grammarians (Labov, 1966: 395). We see here a connection between attitudes, prestige, language change and sociolinguistic structure. The (ing) variable is now stable, however, and there has been virtually no change involving this feature for nearly a hundred years. The kind of sociolinguistic structure in Figure 4.1 therefore represents the typical pattern for a *stable* variable. Thus, individual variables have histories. Other recurring types of sociolinguistic structures are diagnostic of changes taking place within the linguistic system as it interacts with social structure in complex ways. We will be interpreting some other types of sociolinguistic structures later. And we will need to do so in socio-historical terms.

Perhaps the most important point to make about Figure 4.1 is that the difference between the pronunciation of social groups is a question of *relative frequencies*, not of absolutes; similarly with the stylistic variation. Thus, both in the community as a whole and for an individual, it is *not* possible to say categorically that their speech has *only* '-in'' forms or *only* '-ing' forms. Rather, they have varying frequencies in the production of the variants which correlate with their position in society. The discovery that accent is a question of frequency of occurrence is one of the most important features of Labov's type of dialectology.

The (ing) variable occurs in almost every English-speaking community. (The exception is among English-speaking South Africans where the '-ing' form is categorical and, of course, where the social stratification is unique; Wells, 1982: 263.) That the differences are statistical can be further illustrated by looking at the variable for other groups. Thus, Labov only included adult white informants in Figure 4.1. Black informants displayed a much higher use of the '-in'' variant than did white speakers. In careful style, the average score for all white adult New York City informants was thirty-one, for all black New York City informants, sixty-two. For black informants from outside the city the average score was even higher, seventy-seven. Thus, ethnicity is also reflected in (ing) scores. And this is related to geographical differences. Northern black communities have origins in the southern states, and both whites and blacks in the South in general have higher (ing) scores, higher even than speakers of non-standard northern varieties. Thus, in the Appalachian region, Wolfram and Christian (1976: 62) found scores ranging from eighty to one hundred in casual speech. Here are the figures for six individual white informants in West Virgina:

Speaker	Age	Sex	(ing) score
1.	67	M	94.4
2.	13	M	99.1
3.	15	F	84.9
4.	42	F	96.6
5.	12	M	100.0
6.	57	M	84.4

We now have a picture of language as being variable, both individually and collectively. This variability can only be systematically investigated using quantitative methods. When this is done, we find that the variation is not 'free', but that there are patterns of distribution in the frequencies of variants conditioned by social, including stylistic, factors.

Linguistic constraints on variables

But the situation is more complex than this. Variables are usually also conditioned by internal linguistic factors. The linguistic environments of the variable, for example the set of items which precede or follow it, can affect the frequency with which one or the other variant appears. These sets of environments inside the language combine with social factors to yield the scores we observe. Such variation is termed **inherent variability**.

External ———→		←——— Internal
social ———→	VARIABLE	←——— linguistic
factors ———→		←——— environments

This can be illustrated by another variable which occurs in the speech of virtually all English speakers. This is final consonant cluster simplification or **/t,d/ deletion**.

When words end with two consonants and the second of these is /t/ or /d/, then it is possible that the final sound may be deleted. This is a phonological simplification which turns words like 'act', 'hand' or 'fist' into 'ac' ', 'han' ', or 'fis' ':

hand → han'

But how likely is this rule to apply? How many times will it apply out of the number of times it could apply? This is conditioned both by internal linguistic and by external social factors. The rule may be said to be more or less favoured in the frequency of its application by given environments. Thus, the environments provide variable constraints on the rule. Of course, the limiting cases in such favouring or inhibiting of the application of a rule are when it always applies or never applies in a given environment. If it always applies, it is **categorical** in that environment. Environments can be ranked in the order in which they favour the rule applying.

In the case of /t,d/ deletion, the two most important linguistic constraints on the rule are listed on the right of the circle below, and some of the external social factors on the left. There are more factors (Guy, 1980), but we will limit the discussion to these.

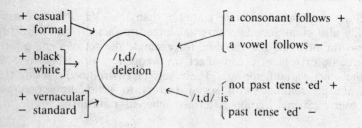

First, the internal constraints. The rule is favoured if the sound which immediately follows the /t/ or /d/ is a consonant, rather than a vowel. Thus, we are more likely to find post card → pos'card

than we are to hear

last October → las' October

Secondly, the rule is favoured if the /t/ or /d/ is part of the structure of the word itself, as in 'hand', then if it has been suffixed to a verb as the past tense marker, '-ed'; for example in 'pass' becoming 'passed'. Thus, we are more likely to find

hand grip → han' grip

than we are to hear

passed Mary → pass' Mary

The least favoured environment is that in which we have a past tense '-ed' preceding a vowel. We are least likely to find

rolled over → roll' over
ripped off → rip' off

It is most important to note that all of these forms occur in the speech of *some* speakers; what we are talking about is the relative likelihood of their occurrence. These internal factors interact with external factors, which further influence whether or not the rule applies. For white standard varieties the rule is tightly constrained. It applies virtually only in the environment of a following consonant, and then usually only in casual speech. For some white vernaculars, although the environmental constraint remains the same, the frequency of application differs. Thus, Chambers and Trudgill (1980: 148) note that among speakers of a rural vernacular in northern England the rule applies about 80 per cent of the time, a frequency higher than in standard white accents. In some white non-standards, and very markedly in the black English vernacular of New York and Detroit, a following vowel also favours the rule, but less so than a following consonant. In these accents the rule may also some- times apply when the /t/ or /d/ is the '-ed' past tense form, but is favoured when the sound is part of the structure of the word and not the suffix, 'not -ed'. Frequency also varies by social class.

So, in conditioning frequency, there are four interacting environments. In the order of how strongly they favour application of the rule, these are consonant or vowel, and 'not -ed' or 'ed'. Figure 4.2 shows the effects of this interaction for a number of American varieties (Wolfram and Christian, 1976: 56). Observe that in column four, '-ed' followed by a vowel, the two weakest constraints, produce the lowest scores, but with a significant difference between white and black speakers. By contrast, the percentage of simplification is highest in column one, where the two strongest constraints favour the application of the rule. The relative difference between black and white speakers remains roughly the same, however.

Issues of method

Labov has provided us with a **quantitative paradigm** for the study of variation. But that is only the first step in the story. In the remainder of this chapter we will be examining, in turn, the following issues which arise out of this method of inquiry: *investigation*, *representation* and *interpretation*.

First, how are we to *investigate* the practices of social groups and the ways individuals speak? What are the assumptions and consequences of different ways of approaching the community? This is both a practical and a theoretical matter. Second, how are we to *represent* the results of such investigations? It stands to reason that the kind of representation will influence and be influenced by the kinds of interpretations we make of what we have found. How we represent something implicitly tells us how we view it.

Third, how are we to *interpret* what we have found? Tabulations like 4.1 tell us that there is a systematic correlation between linguistic variables and social factors such as class and style. What is the significance of such findings for our understanding of the place of variation in language? How can we explain what we have found?

These three issues are deeply interrelated.

Language variety:	1 'Not -ed', followed by consonant % simplification	2 '-ed', followed by consonant % simplification	3 'Not -ed', followed by vowel % simplification	4 '-ed', followed by vowel % simplification
Middle-class white Detroit speech	66	36	12	3
Working-class black Detroit speech	97	76	72	34
Working-class white New York City adolescent speech	67	23	19	3
Working-class white adolescent, rural Georgia-Florida speech	56	16	25	10
Working-class black adolescent rural Georgia-Florida speech	88	50	72	36
Southeastern West Virginia speech	74	67	17	5

Figure 4.2 Consonant cluster simplification in some American varieties (*from Wolfram and Christian 1976: 56*)

Approaching the community: assumptions

A linguist investigating actual speech is interested ultimately in individual speakers. But he is studying them also, inevitably, as members of groups. At every stage he is confronted with the classical difficulty of the individual and the group. There are individual actions and behaviour and there are practices which typify groups of individuals. It is the latter which the linguist wants to discover. Groups may exhibit 'emergent' properties, patterns not visible when one regards only the individual. Conversely, any given individual's behaviour may not conform to the pattern of the group.

In the course of the book we will have to refer to many different kinds of human groups – classes, ethnic groups, geographically defined communities, neighbourboods, peer groups, age groups, social networks, families, kin groups, and the largest group, a society as a whole. These categories, of course, differ a lot among themselves. But they have some features in common which allow us to talk about them as groups in our ordinary usage. The most important point to make is that they are all human institutions, they are 'collectivities', not just 'collections' of individuals. Macdonald and Pettit (1981: 107f.) write,

> The set or collection is conceptualized in such a way that A and B are the same set if and only if they have the same members. This means then that a set changes identity if it loses or gains a single member. Such a principle however does not go through with groups, for a family does not become a different entity through the birth or death of a child, a company does not mutate in the turnover of its directors, a nation does not lose its identity as one generation replaces another. The failure of the principle to apply indicates that groups are assigned by us to a different ontological category from that of the collection, an assignment that warrants describing them as collectives.

Groups have some very peculiar properties. One such is that just mentioned, which they share with physical objects: they remain the *same* entity through time even when their parts are replaced. Another is that we treat them as autonomous agents. An individual may do something, acting for a group as its agent, irrespective of his personal feelings – corporate agency means that the individual acts 'not in his own name'. We talk of

'Britain' and 'America' as autonomous agents represented by individuals' actions. Such is the power of conceptualization.

There is a large sociological literature on human groups which we cannot deal with here. However, in Figure 4.3 I have listed some of those features of human groups which will be of significance for language as we proceed. Only point 11, Groups and practices, needs explanation at this stage. A **practice** is an implicit regularity of behaviour that characterizes a group (Macdonald and Pettit, 1981, 110f), such things, for example, as 'accepting the authority of Parliament' or 'using banking facilities properly'. A general regularity of this sort can underlie a whole range of actions. We will return to such phenomena later on. For now, consider a practice as rather like a norm or a convention such that *there is a general expectation within a group that everyone will conform with the practice.* As such, practices form a stable social background for making sense of what people do. We need to know the relevant practices of a group in order that any individual's behaviour be intelligible. This leads to point 12. The central importance for our understanding of each other, of mutual expectation, combined with the significance of group identity for individual identities (points 8 and 9), exerts **normative pressure** on individuals to do what they are expected to do.

A scientist normally generates his data with hypotheses already in mind. We shall see that linguists approach the community with differing assumptions about relevant groups. Different groups reveal different correlations between language and society.

But there are also three further important assumptions about practices which are made in sociolinguistic research. The first is that individuals have a **vernacular**. Labov writes (1972: 208),

> Not every style or point on the stylistic continuum is of equal interest to linguists. Some styles show irregular ... patterns ... In other styles, we find more systematic speech, where the fundamental relations which determine the course of linguistic evolution can be seen most clearly. This is the 'vernacular' – the style in which the minimum attention is given to the monitoring of speech. Observation of the vernacular gives us the most systematic data for our analysis of linguistic structure.

The second assumption is that individuals style-shift away from their vernaculars in situations where they are paying more

1. *Changing membership.* A group remains the *same* group although the individuals who constitute it may change.
2. *Continuity in time.* A group remains the *same* group as it continues in time, and in spite of changes in membership.
3. *Individuals shared by different groups.* The individuals who constitute a group may *at the same time* be members of other groups.
4. *Physical discontinuity of membership.* The individuals who constitute a group need not be in physical proximity.
5. *Primary and secondary groups.* In primary groups the members are directly related in face-to-face interaction. In secondary groups the members are indirectly related, according to some wider criterion.
6. *Enduring or evanescent.* A group may endure for generations, or may be evanescent, forming for a particular purpose or circumstance and dissolving afterwards.
7. *Stratification.* Groups may be stratified relative to other groups in a hierarchy from higher to lower according to some evaluative criteria.
8. *Self-conscious significance.* Individuals can be grouped together on any criteria. Not all criteria are equally salient. The most important criteria is the self-conscious significance of the group – how it views itself as significantly different from other groups, and how solidary its members feel.
9. *Identity.* An individual's multiple group memberships make up his social identity.
10. *Reference groups.* An individual may find his identity or values in those of some group of which he is not a member.
11. *Groups and practices.* Practices are regularities of behaviour which characterize groups.
12. *Normative pressures.* Pressures are exerted on a group's members to make them conform to the practices of the group.
13. *Centrality and peripherality.* Individuals may be central or peripheral members of the group.
14. *Internal structure.* Groups have different kinds of internal structure. Some are integrated, some diffuse. Some are informally organized while others are institutions, with formally specified roles and statuses.

Figure 4.3 Some features of groups

attention to speech. There is a dimension of casual to formal, in which the vernacular is the most casual style.

The third assumption is what makes observation of the vernacular a problem. The very presence of the linguist, observing speech, affects the style of the speech observed. In particular, the presence of the linguist makes the speech more formal than it might otherwise be. Labov calls this **the observer's paradox**. As he puts it, how does one know whether or not the light is off inside the fridge when the door is shut?

Approaching the community: techniques

As a practical matter, the linguist must come up with solutions to these problems in order to investigate speech. There are three basic classes of techniques which have been used:

Anonymous observation;
The sociolinguistic interview;
Participant observation of (a) natural groups, and
(b) social networks.

These methods of investigation all have strengths and weaknesses. Anonymous observation side-steps the observer's paradox, since the speakers do not know they are being observed. But the linguist cannot easily identify or control either the social groups or the stylistic variation. The classic form of investigation is the interview as developed by Labov (1966). The data for sociolinguistic structures such as Figure 4.1 was obtained this way. Let us see how this was done. The hypothesis was that linguistic variables were conditioned by class and style.

Social class

Socio-economic class is one example of **stratification** within a society. To say that any group of people is stratified is to say that they can be ranked in a hierarchy, from highest to lowest, on some scale. Consider the examination results of a group of students. The students can be ranked on the scale of examination grades and thus stratified with respect to that property. Note that there has to be an evaluative dimension to this in order to establish the hierarchical ranking and thus stratify, rather than merely differentiate, the population. There has to be tacit agreement that peoples' relative positions can be arranged from higher to lower. The stratification of a society is constituted subjectively by its members' attitudes to themselves and to each other concerning their relative positions within a hierarchy. So stratification will be deeply tied up with **evaluation**, with prestige and stigmatization.

Within sociology there is a large literature on social class. In our ordinary use of the term 'class', we probably use it to refer to our various perceptions of people's differential access to resources and power, as well as the differing cultural practices and beliefs which represent, reflect and justify that differential access. For sociolinguistic research work, however, some way is needed to establish objectively the social class of the informants. Very often, as in Labov's work, pre-existing sociological data for the population is used. The objective measures used to establish social class were the scales of income, education and occupation. An individual's socio-economic class was established by his combined rank on these three scales. Using these combined criteria, a single continuum of class stratification can be established on which one can differentiate individuals as finely as the measure allows. The actual socio-economic classes used are cuts along this continuum. Labov initially divided it into ten social classes. It is important to realize, then, that social class is an abstract construct. Because of the scales chosen, it should reflect the objective stratification of society and people's subjective perceptions, whatever the deeper causes of such phenomenon.

The next step for the researcher is to correlate the index scores for the linguistic variables with the social class continuum. Logically, there are a number of possible ways to do this. One possibility is to treat a set number of social classes as given, and simply work out the average score for the individuals in each of the classes. Another possibility, used in recent research by Pellowe and Jones (1978) on Tyneside, is to process the linguistic data first and then see how its intrinsic internal structure corresponds with combinations of social factors. A third possibility, the one used by Labov and most other researchers, is to cut the social-class continuum into social classes in such a way that it best reflects the regularities in the linguistic data.

In many cases the correlation between average index scores and social class is such that the variable exhibits **fine stratification**. This means that the average scores for each successive group, as one ascends or descends the continuum of stratification, grades into that of the group above or below it with no sharp discontinuities. Thus, no matter how finely one cuts the continuum in establishing average scores for social strata, the scores will be stratified (arranged in a hierarchy) for all styles. The usages of the classes, although different, blend into one another. The kind of stratification seems to be typical of phonological variables. It is exhibited by the (ing) variable in New York.

Other variables, by contrast, exhibit **sharp stratification**. In these cases, often syntactic variables, the average index scores seem to divide the social continuum into two, with a major discontinuity in the scores of upper and lower strata. An example of this feature is the (ing) variable in Norwich investigated by Peter Trudgill in *The Social Differentiation of English in Norwich* (1974). The Norwich (ing) scores are given in Figure 4.4. Note that, as in New York, there is a completely consistent correspondence between the stratification of linguistic scores and that of the social classes in every style. I have put boxes around those pairs of figures that exhibit sharp stratification.

We noted before that the frequencies observed were *simultaneously* a reflection of the informant's style and his social class. This means that an individual with a score of, say, forty-three, could be either a middle-working-class informant in reading style, or a lower-middle-class speaker in casual style. The class stratification is obscured unless some way is found to hold style constant, or for the linguist to know what style of speech he is observing. The difficulty was the observer's paradox.

Speech style

The technique which Labov used in the sociolinguistic interview is the paradigm solution to this problem. He utilized the observer's paradox itself to define a speech style, which he called **Careful Speech**. This is the speech elicited by the very presence of the interviewer, used as a point of reference. Any utterance in reply to the interviewer's formal questions during the interview is labelled as 'careful'. The assumption is that there are styles both more casual and more formal than this. Figure 4.5 schematizes how these styles are elicited. Careful speech is the starting point. The principle is to control the amount of attention which the informant pays to the way he speaks. More formal styles, those above 'careful speech' in the figure, are those which successively

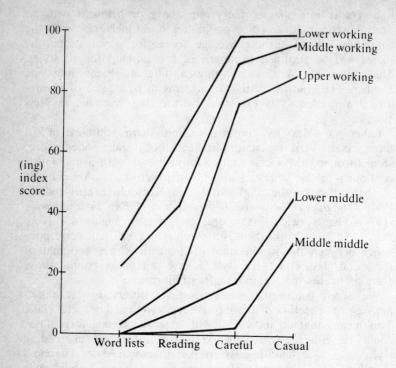

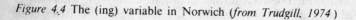

	Class	Word list	Reading	Careful	Casual
I	Middle middle	000	000	003	028
II	Lower middle	000	010	015	042
III	Upper working	005	015	074	087
IV	Middle working	023	044	088	095
V	Lower working	029	066	098	100

Figure 4.4 The (ing) variable in Norwich (*from Trudgill, 1974*)

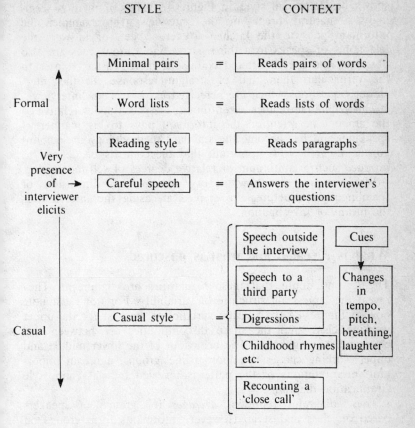

STYLE   CONTEXT

Formal

Very
presence
of   →
interviewer
elicits

Casual

Minimal pairs	=	Reads pairs of words
Word lists	=	Reads lists of words
Reading style	=	Reads paragraphs
Careful speech	=	Answers the interviewer's questions

Casual style = {
Speech outside the interview
Speech to a third party
Digressions
Childhood rhymes etc.
Recounting a 'close call'
}

Cues

Changes in tempo, pitch, breathing, laughter

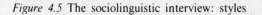

Figure 4.5 The sociolinguistic interview: styles

produce more conscious care in the informant. Thus, the context of 'reading paragraphs' of connected prose produces a **Reading Style**, which is itself more self-conscious than the already relatively careful speech of the responses to questions. Reading **Word Lists**, because it draws further attention to linguistic items and their pronunciation, is more formal again. Even more attention is paid to the act of speaking itself. **Casual Style**, by contrast, is defined as those utterances made in contexts which *decrease* the amount of attention paid to the manner of speech, relative to the central reference point. The contexts are those shown beside 'casual style' in Figure 4.5. Thus, if there is seemingly a natural break in the interview (for example, the informant goes to the kitchen to get a beer, or answers the telephone, or speaks to a third party) and various **cues** are also observed, the speech uttered counts as more 'casual', closer to the vernacular, than that of straight responses to the interviewer's questions which are perceived as part of an 'interview'.

This technique defines a continuum of speech styles relative to the amount of attention the informant pays to his manner of speaking, and has become the standard methodology in sociolinguistic research. It is important that the contexts be defined to produce such a continuum of relative degrees of self-monitoring.

We have now seen how the two non-linguistic dimensions of sociolinguistic structures are arrived at, using the interview as the means of investigation.

What is revealed and what is obscured

There is no doubt that these regularities are significant. They reveal the large-scale structure of variability. For now, just note how in Figure 4.4 the stylistic variation is steepest for the upper working class, and the sharp discontinuities are between this class and its neighbours. The behaviour of the lower middle and upper working classes, the 'border-line' groups, figure in important interpretations of the patterns revealed by class and style stratification diagrams.

These diagrams represent *averages* for groups of speakers based on class and style. However, informants form groups on other criteria as well. Data obtained from interviews allows the linguist to get average scores for other obvious secondary group characteristics; for example, sex, age, ethnicity, locale etc. Thus, Trudgill (1974) found that women consistently had lower (ing) index scores than men. Women produced relatively more of the prestige '-ing' variants than men. The other side of this coin was that both men's speech and working-class speech were typified by relatively higher (ing) scores, more of the '-in'' variant.

A social identity is partially made up of the various large secondary groups of which the individual is a member. I am a member of a class in a stratified overall society; I am in a certain age group, of a certain sex, and so on. The averages for individuals grouped by any one of these social factors does not reveal correlations for the others. The data needs analysis. The linguist has to look to the *interaction of social variables* and evaluate their relative weight in determining scores. Other factors are also buried within the correlations. The relative effects of the purely linguistic environments, such as those mentioned in our discussion of /t,d/ deletion, need to be separated out. Finally, what about the individual within the averages? An average score of forty for some group does not tell us exactly what individuals are doing. The explanation of individuals with deviant scores may tell us a great deal about the significance of the group scores. Indeed, the correlations themselves need to be interpreted. Where does the variability itself originate? If it is part of the process of language change (the assumption we made in Chapter 2), then how do these large-scale correlations help us to explain how language changes? We will be looking at these issues in Chapters 6 and 7.

Sources of normative pressure

The sociolinguistic interview is not a particularly good way to observe the vernacular. (Its strength is the breadth of information it yields.) Its point of reference is the speech elicited by the presence of the interviewer himself, and the interview situation. But the interviewer, as an 'outsider', invokes the norms of the 'outside', those normative pressures coming from the society as a whole. Note that in Figure 4.4 three of the four styles involve formality. Where reading is involved we gain access to how the individual self-consciously thinks the language ought to be pronounced. This is by definition, as it were, since those styles were set up to increase his awareness of speech. The identification of informants by social class also produces structures which give us access to the normative pressures of the society as a whole. Class involves the stratification of this largest of all groups. In Figures 4.1 (from America) and 4.4 (from England) speakers of all classes style-shift towards the forms used most frequently by the highest social class in casual speech. The upper middle classes are, it would seem, the custodians of the standard of good pronunciation. We are therefore gaining access to 'pressures from above the level of conscious awareness'. The interview reveals the normative pressure exerted by a stratified structure.

However, we will see later that there are many variables in the process of change *towards* non-standard forms and *away* from the prestige forms; for example, the Norwich (e) and the New York (oh). Paradoxically, the observed style-shifting in these cases is away from the direction of change and still towards the standard forms used by the middle classes.

It follows that there are normative pressures from other sources. Of course, any social group exercises such normative influence. One is, for example, under pressure to speak in a way appropriate to whether one is a man or a woman. But the places to look are those primary groups in which the vernacular is based; those groups based on intimate face-to-face association. The solidarity of the group exerts a normative pressure away from the values of the larger society, and towards its own vernacular culture. The identity of the individual, both given and chosen, is at the complex intersection of differing groups and their normative pressures. The intensity of these pressures will vary according to how integrated or diffuse are the structures of the groups. In large, mobile populations the pressure will be less than in those groups which are 'local' and 'vernacular'. (Milroy, 1980, 178f).

Primary groups

Access to the vernacular will clearly be gained through the study of individuals within primary groups. A number of studies, including that of Hemnesberget by Blom and Gumperz (1972), used techniques developed to do just this. What is needed is a way of obtaining large quantities of spontaneous speech in as natural a situation as possible, and still to overcome the observer's paradox. This can be done by long-term participation in and observation of 'natural' groups. Labov, Cohen, Robins and Lewis (1968) developed such a method in their study of the vernacular of black adolescent peer groups in Harlem: the Thunderbirds, the Jets and the Cobras.

After contact was established with the groups, multiple techniques were used to investigate speech. The main techniques were formal sociolinguistic interviews and the recording of group outings and group sessions. Investigation began with the Thunderbirds, and spread to the Jets and Cobras. In these last two groups participant observation was done by John Lewis, one of those interviewed in early exploratory work. The presence of an 'insider', who controlled the vernacular, helps to override the observer's paradox. Lewis rented a clubhouse and had daily contact with the Jets through 1966. Labov found that the group sessions yielded very natural vernacular speech. He writes, "the setting was essentially that of a party rather than an interview, with card games, eating and drinking, singing and sounding. The effect of observation and recording was, of course, present, but the natural interaction of the group overrode all other effects" (Labov, 1972a, xviii–xix). The observer's paradox can thus be overcome by the pressures of face-to-face interaction in primary groups in natural situations.

Blom and Gumperz (1972) found the same effects. They write, "Methodologically, self-recruitment of groups is important for two reasons. It ensures that groups are defined by locally recognized relationships and enables the investigator to predict the norms relevant to their interaction. Furthermore, the fact that participants have pre-existing obligations towards each other means that, given the situation, they are likely to respond to such obligations in spite of the presence of strangers. Our tape recording and our visual observations give clear evidence that this in fact was what occurred" (Blom and Gumperz, 1972: 426–7).

In both of these studies, the speech was not viewed out of context. In Chapter 3, we discussed the social analysis made by Gumperz and Blom. Labov *et al.* (1968) used multiple methods of observation and testing. The vernacular black culture and its values and speech event types were studied. (For example, the word 'sounding' was used a moment ago; this is the New York term for exchanging ritual insults: Labov, 1972a; Mitchell-Kernan, 1972.) Systematic studies of adult black speakers and white adolescent speakers were done. And a social analysis of the gangs were carried out. Members were categorized according to their degree of integration into the vernacular sub-culture, and index scores calculated on this basis.

Social networks

Such studies, however, are constrained in that they can only be carried out in naturally occurring groups. They are group based. An alternative approach has recently been developed by the Milroys and used to study the working-class vernacular in Belfast, Northern Ireland (Milroy and Milroy, 1978; Milroy, 1980).

They found it possible to begin at the other end, as it were, and base their investigation of the vernacular on the speech of individuals. The familiar quantitative method of scoring variables could be applied to an individual's **social network**, his face-to-face associations. Average scores for other social variables – neighbourhood, style, sex, age and so on – could be studied in relation to both individual and group network scores. This method of investigation makes assumptions: it postulates that the kinds and density of relationship which an individual has within primary groups is significant for linguistic variability; just as the interview methodology presupposes that the stratification of the society as a whole is significant.

A social network is a way of representing the individual's pattern of social transactions within a community. Figure 4.6 portrays an idealized social network graph. Starting at EGO, where

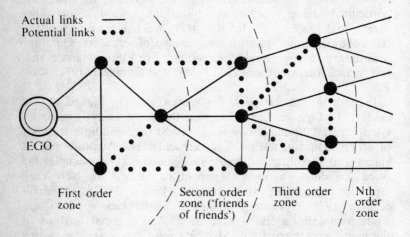

Figure 4.6 Social networks (*after Boissevain, 1974*)

the network is anchored, an individual's social relations with other persons are represented by lines. Some of these persons also interact with each other. All the persons who directly interact with EGO form his **first order zone**. But each of these persons interacts with further individuals who are not in touch with EGO, but who could be. These form his **second order zone**. Such people are 'friends of friends', and, in community life, serve many useful functions for EGO: the 'I can get it for you wholesale' functions. Social networks involve more than simply communication. They form the web of transactions which make up the intimate texture of daily life, and as such involve individuals in rights and obligations towards each other.

There are a number of important features which allow comparisons between networks of different types. Networks may be more or less **dense**. If the members of an individual's network are also in touch with each other independently, that network has a high **density**. In other words, a network's density is a measure of how many potential links are in fact actual links. A **cluster** is a part of a network with a high density. Networks may also be **multiplex** or **uniplex**. Multiplexity means that there is more than one transactional basis for the social relationships in the network. Figure 4.7 shows the diversity of linkages that could exist in multiplex network. The same individuals can be

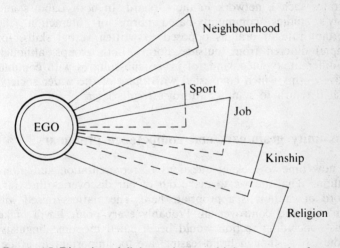

Figure 4.7 Diversity of linkages in a multiplex network (*from Boissevain, 1974*)

simultaneously linked by kinship, employment and neighbourhood. It was the relativity, density, and multiplexity of their networks that formed the basis of individual's network scores.

Intuitively, the more dense and multiplex a network is, the more social cohesion one would expect. Each individual has transactions with each of the other individuals independently and in a multiplicity of ways. They are kin, who live and work together. Such networks exert a strong normative pressure on their members based on a sense of solidarity – the pressure comes from 'inside' the network. In general, high density and multiplexity, which typified the working-class communities studied in Milroy (1980), sustained non-standard norms.

The sociolinguistic research was carried on in three deprived inner city areas of Belfast; Ballymacarrett, a Protestant area of East Belfast, the Hammer, in West Belfast, also Protestant, and the Clonard, a Catholic area of West Belfast. The aim was the study of the working-class vernaculars of these territorially based communities in as natural a way as possible.

Milroy gained access to the community as a participant-observer by using the natural status of 'a friend of a friend'. She introduced herself into the community through mutually known individuals and entered networks 'of kith and kin'. Figure 4.8 illustrates such a network in the Clonard. In both Labov's and Milroy's studies, community-based norms of interaction (the important role of oral as opposed to written verbal skills, for example) differed from 'outside' norms. Both groups, although very different, typified kinds of urban sub-cultures with communicative norms which contrasted with those of the wider society. We shall return to some of Milroy's results later.

Community grammars and competence grammars

It is now time to look at questions of representation and interpretation. What are we to make out of our discoveries thus far? A word of caution is appropriate here. The matters raised will be difficult and controversial. Probably every point I will make in this concluding section would be disputed by some linguists. But the issues, though brain-teasing, are too important to evade.

Variability, Labov argues, is not explicable if we look only to the speech of the individual. He writes (Labov, 1972a: 124),

> ...we now know enough about language in its social context to realise that the grammar of the speech community is more regular and systematic than the behaviour of one individual. Unless the speech pattern is studied within the overall system of the community, it will appear as a mosaic of unaccountable and sporadic variation.

The occasions of Speakers A, B and C at the beginning of this chapter allowed us to visualize how this would look. And Figure 4.1 and 4.4 showed us the regular patterns observable

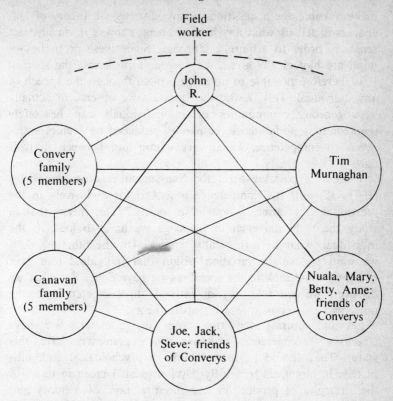

Figure 4.8 A portion of the Clonard network, showing density of 100 (*from Milroy, 1980:58*)

through the social investigation of speech. Labov is arguing for community grammars, which will represent such sociolinguistic structures. But what would be the status of such grammars?

Modern linguistics has not had to face this problem before. Since de Saussure's *Course in General Linguistics* laid the foundations of the subject early this century, it has been possible to ignore variation in speech. As we saw in Chapter 1, the aim of the linguist is to characterize 'competence'. In Saussure's terms this was **langue**, or language, viewed as a system of relations between categories, abstracted from the variation implicit in individual utterances, historical evolution of the system, or dialects. In Chomsky's terms, in order to find out 'what language is', we have to discover the universal properties of mind that make possible the acquisition of any language. A theory of language will tell us what any human being 'knows', in an abstract sense, in order to acquire a language. Since these properties of mind are biologically given, they are uniform across the species. It is therefore possible to investigate them through the speech of any individual. This is why the variation we observe in actually heterogeneous communities or in individuals can be safely ignored. It is **performance**, or **parole**, produced by factors extraneous to competence, which vary within and between individuals.

There is a paradox here: **the Saussurean paradox**. As Bailey (1973: 35) puts it, "competence is looked for exclusively in the individual, but variety is sought in society." This means that to study the truly universal in language we have to look to the individual, what he intrinsically 'knows'. On the other hand, if we want to explain variation within that individual (our task here), we must look to the social, as we have done. But what we discover, we are told, is not intrinsic to competence, to the universals that constitute a linguistic theory.

Let us contrast the two types of grammar. We have Chomsky's competence grammar. Such grammars have this status. They should be interpretable in psychological and, ultimately, in biological terms. By psychological, I mean in terms of the strategies of production and interpretation, of memory and so on; the sort of thing for which we can get behavioural evidence. By biological, I mean the actual neurological structures in which the knowledge is realized. For Chomsky, knowledge of language is ultimately a matter of biology. We are genetically preprogrammed to learn language: that is ultimately the locus of grammar. He argues that it is the present impossibility of directly investigating this, together with ethical considerations, that make us proceed abstractly. We investigate what any individual 'knows' via his judgements of grammaticality, paraphrase relations, and so on.

Now contrast this with Labov's community grammar. This formalizes the quantitative patterns which are only visible when speech is investigated socially. It is a collective grammar, but not a universal one. The question then arises as to the status of the quantitative rules of which such grammars consist.

Interpreting community grammars

This is problematic. Some people working on variation believe that **variable rules**, rules that formalize in probabalistic terms frequencies such as those we observed, are psychologically real. That is to say, such rules are part of competence. They are not only the rules of a community grammar, but are part of the intrinsic knowledge of language which any individual has.

The theory of variable rules, as a model of the quantitative patterns such as Labov and others have revealed, are an exceedingly technical matter.

We can sketch out the basic principle. Variable rules are constructed on the basis of the 'aggregate' data of average scores, and observed frequencies, such as those discussed above. Then probabilities are assigned to the various internal linguistic environments predicting, in order, the way they constrain the probability of the rule applying in that environment. There is a prior input probability of the rule applying, determined by the extralinguistic factors such as class, style, ethnic group etc.

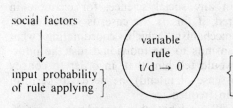

Such a device accurately predicts the observed frequencies. It is derived from an analysis of the whole community. It therefore states a quantitative relationship between any two informants, such that what one speaker does is mathematically tied to what another speaker does.

Now the problem is that it is hard to make sense of any psychological interpretation of these rules (Bickerton, 1971; Bailey, 1973; for a discussion, see Romaine, 1982: 247f). Bickerton argues that speakers could not conceivably keep track of the frequencies of variables in their speech relative to thousands of other members of the community with whom they have never had contact. Indeed, how could such 'community grammars' be acquired by an individual? The problem is not that individuals apply the rule with the probabilities stated in the rule. This, in fact, happens. There is no disputing that the rules *do* predict the occurrences of variants. They predict them for groups and for individuals. The problem is that in the representation the individual probabilities are mathematically tied, the one to the other. How could individuals 'know' this, as psychological reality would demand? In brief, how could an individual 'know' a community grammar?

Any model needs to be interpreted. The variable-rule model can be understood as a community grammar, and as an individual grammar. As a model of the individual it may represent what he knows. The individual *can* know, indeed, he *must* know, the probability with which to apply the rule, because, if it is correct, he does as the model predicts. But as a community grammar, its claims to psychological reality are doubtful without some concept of a 'group' mind. It formalizes mathematically the quantitative relations the linguist has discovered in aggregate data. An individual, whatever he does, simply *cannot know this* in the way the linguist does. In any case, the model simply represents the facts: it does not tell us what the connections are such that variables are mathematically related in this way in the speech of the community. There is a similar problem with mathematical modelling in any social science, for example in economics. What is required, if this is the case, is some sort of collective 'coordinative' mechanism which, coordinating what whole communities do, transmits to the individual just the information that he needs. It would tell him that, in order to convey what he intends (in some sense of intend), he needs to perform certain variants with certain frequencies.

Variable rules do not tell us what this 'coordinative mechanism' is; nor why the probabilities of individuals are tied together in the way the model says. As community grammars, however, let us agree that they are not psychologically real, that there is no group competence. Competence must be universal and individual.

Autonomous social facts

Let us try again. There is another possible interpretation of community grammars. They arguably could be **autonomous social objects**. This is very much the sense in which Durkheim (1938) used the term 'social fact'. In this case, community grammars would exist in some sense independently, 'over and above' the individuals who constitute the community. No individual 'knows' such emergent properties of the group. They are ontologically independent of individual knowledge. It seems to me that some such conception of language itself was involved in the notion of langue, before it was reinterpreted by Chomsky. (The locus of Chomsky's grammar is the human brain, remember.)

Clearly, social facts do exist, since we are able to talk about them. They have, at least, 'expressive autonomy' (Macdonald and Pettit, 1981: 115f). But what kind of relationship can we say might exist between such entities as community grammars and individuals who constitute the community?

Generalizations expressing social facts are often considered the social equivalent of scientific laws in the physical sciences. We have two variables; for example, a dependent linguistic variable like (ing) and an independent social variable such as socio-economic class. The two co-vary. The investigator claims to have discovered a *casual* connection between the two. If this interpretation is made, then the individual's behaviour is casually determined in conformity with the generalization. We could interpret sociolinguistic structures like Figure 4.1 in this way.

Much depends on what one means by the word 'cause' here. In ordinary speech we use 'because' to cover many different kinds of connection between X and Y.

$$X \quad \text{cause} \quad Y$$
$$\uparrow$$
$$\text{connection}$$

The crucial factor is the kind of connection we posit between X and Y. The strongest connection we can make is, 'caused by a physical law of nature'. Let us call these *strong* causal explanations. A weaker sense of 'cause' is possible, in which a correlation is observed between X and Y. If X occurs, Y occurs. We know that there is a connection, and it is an empirical connection; that is, it could be otherwise. We don't know what this connection actually is, but we have rejected a physical law of nature as a candidate. Let us call this a *weak* causal explanation. The co-variance betwen (ing) scores and class is of this type.

It seems to me that only the stronger, physically interpretable, sense of causation is properly explanatory. It says that something is the way it is because that is how *nature* works, although it could be otherwise. Now this is the sort of explanation Chomsky is seeking for his linguistics, grounding competence in biology as he does. If we have a 'Chomsky' universal, telling us the form of a linguistic rule, then it would be absurd to doubt that the individual is not determined by it in the strongest sense.

But the weaker sense of 'cause' arguably explains much less. It makes social facts 'visible', but it doesn't tell us why they exist – social facts such as suicide rates, the relation between money supply and inflation, or the correlation between (ing) scores, class and style. In this weak sense, individual behaviour is not determined in any absolute sense by the general law in question. Individuals may behave in conformity with the generalization, if it is correct, but we still do not know why they do so. This is relevant to the study of variation because there has been some tendency to interpret sociolinguistic structures in causal terms. We shall return to these issues in Chapter 11.

We have, then, in the patterns of a community grammar, a precise presentation of social facts. These are the quantitative relationships between social and linguistic facts 'made visible'. The model is weakly causally explanatory; as Romaine (1982: 187) puts it, "a valuable analytic device". The only way in which a law of nature could strongly cause a collective regularity in human beings would be if we were biologically (hence physiologically and psychologically) so constructed. It seems to me that, in general, the connection between social variables is not of a physical or psychological kind. We have rejected psychological reality for community grammars, let alone a biological explanation of variability. So we must reject strongly causal explanations of variability in language. This is not to say that we haven't an intrinsic ability to do things with a certain frequency, merely that the community grammar does not tell us why we do so – does not tell us the connection between social variables and index scores. It simply displays social facts. This is a very important activity, however. Without it, we wouldn't know that such regularities existed.

It would seem, then, that we must return to the idea that there is a coordinating mechanism which will explain why groups do, in fact, behave with such astonishing regularity.

Figure 4.9 presents the alternative ways of interpreting the correlations we have discovered between linguistic and social factors. We have rejected A, strongly causal explanations, for dealing with variation in language. However, A legitimately provides such explanations for Chomsky's universal grammar. We have denied social facts, such as community grammars, strong causal efficacy. We opt, then, for B. In this case, what individuals do is 'coordinated' in such a way that regularities emerge.

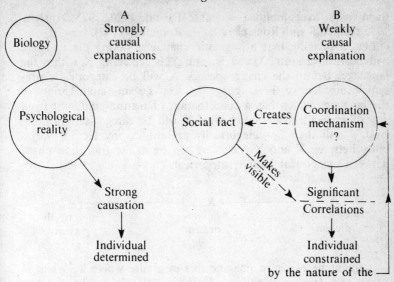

Figure 4.9 Ways of interpreting correlations between linguistic and social factors

We will look next at a candidate for such a 'coordinative' mechanism.

Waves of change revisited

In Chapter 2, we talked of the diffusion of linguistic changes as waves moving through both social and linguistic environments. This was illustrated in Figure 2.2. So far we have investigated variation in terms of the correlations between the frequency of variants and social groups and styles and linguistic environments. This has been represented by variable rules, rules which represent what a community does. The behaviour of all individuals in all contexts is quantitatively related. We noted above the difficulty involved in saying that an individual 'knows' such a grammar. There is an alternative approach to the significance of variation. This represents and interprets inherent variation in terms of the wave-like movement of change through language.

This **dynamic paradigm** has largely been due to the work of Bailey (1973) and Bickerton (1971, 1973). The issues raised are complicated and controversial, and I must necessarily present them in an oversimplified way (see Fasold, 1970, 1975; Anshen, 1975; Sankoff and Rousseau, 1979; Romaine, 1982).

Let us imagine that a linguistic change is taking place. There will be two variants, X and Y, and Y is replacing X within the language. Before the change occurs, X will be categorically present in any **lect** of the language. (A lect is a minimum variety of the language which has a combination of features different from any other lect.) After the change, X will be categorically absent. And Y will then be categorically present in any lect. If variability between X and Y occurs, it will be in the transition phase between categorical X and categorical Y.

$$X \longrightarrow X, Y \longrightarrow Y$$

X	X, Y	Y
categorically present	variably present	categorically present

It might be easier to imagine this in a case where a variant is being lost from a language. First, it will always be present. Then, it will sometimes be present and sometimes absent; it will be variable. Finally, it will always be absent. And the reverse happens if a feature is being gained. A change from X to Y involves the loss of X, the gaining of Y, and a phase where both occur and are variable. The notion of a wave itself implies that change is not instantaneous.

The wave model traces this process. Look at Figure 4.10. In

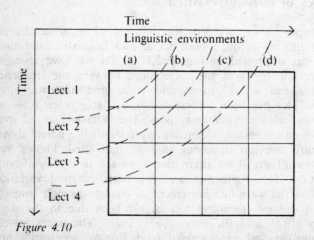

Figure 4.10

this example we can trace a change as it moves, in time, through four linguistic environments, (a), (b), (c) and (d), and through four lects. (These can be represented as four minimally different grammars.) The wave hypothesis is that the change proceeds systematically through the environments in the order represented in the diagram. Simultaneously, it moves through the lects, first lect 1, then 2, then 3, then 4. The order depends on the point of origin of the change.

Let us look at the wave front as it moves through the environments and the grammars. The change begins at the top left-hand corner of the diagram. It originates in a specific linguistic context, and among a small group of speakers: lect 1, environment (a). The change has a definite directionality inside the grammar of lect 1. The linguistic environments can be arranged in a ranking according to the degree to which they favour the change or not. Thus, it spreads from 1 (a), to (b), (c) and (d) in this lect. In our diagram, the wave front is just reaching environment (d) in lect 1. It is virtually complete in environment (c) for this first lect.

But, simultaneously, the change is moving into the other lects. In Figure 4.10 the wave front has just reached lect 4. How far the change has gone in the environments of a lect is related to how close that lect is to lect 1, where the change originated. Thus, in lect 2, it is midway through environment (c); in lect 3, it has not yet reached environment (c); in lect 4, it is just beginning in the first environment. In each lect, in turn, it goes through the environments in the same order, but does so *later*.

We said a moment ago that variability will occur in the process of transition. This means that at the time when the wave front is moving through the cells in our diagram, the two forms will be variable and will occur with a given frequency. When the change is complete the new variant will appear 100 per cent of the time. Before it has reached a given environment or a given lect, it will appear '0' times or be categorically absent. In between, *where* and *when* it is variable, it will appear a certain percentage of the time. One would expect, then, that the frequencies will be ordered in exactly the order of environment and lect, decreasing from 100 per cent, in terms of how far they are from the point of origin. Scores of 0 will occur in environments and lects which the wave front has not reached. This would be the case at any chosen time, if the 'clock is stopped'. As time goes on, the scores for each cell will rise, preserving their relations determined by their relative distances from the origin of the wave, with new cells rising above 0 as the wave front spreads to new environments and lects, which then become variable. Cells closest to the origin will start reaching 100 per cent at these later times.

How exactly the frequencies will look depends on how, in fact, wave fronts move from cell to cell. Different views of this give different distributions of the frequencies, although we get the same direction in the rise of frequencies. If one claimed that the rate of change increased as it neared completion, then frequencies will rise more *quickly* closer to the point of origin. If one claimed that a change had to be relatively complete in one cell, before it spread to the next cells, then we would observe quite large jumps in frequencies between cells where the innovation was first appearing, and adjacent cells where it was relatively complete – rather than a gradual, smooth increase. Bickerton (1971, 1973) makes the very strong claim that, for any lect, only *one* cell may contain *both* forms (be variable) at any time. This means that the whole top left part of Figure 4.10 would be categorically 100 per cent, and the whole bottom right, categorically 0. We would observe frequencies only in a line of cells running from the top right corner to the bottom left corner of the diagram, a line at the outer edge of the wave front. On this view the group frequencies which Labov's correlational studies obtain are a 'statistical illusion', caused by working from averaged group scores. In fact, many speakers have lects which are either categorical, or only variable in one environment.

It would seem that this claim is too strong. We will take Bailey's view of the matter. Figure 4.11 shows the sort of frequencies we might expect to obtain at three relative times in Bailey's theory (Bailey, 1973: 79). Observe the regular increases in the percentages of the new variant as it approaches the point of origin, lect 1, environment (a). Observe also how the percentages of the new form increase, preserving their relations with each other, at the two later times as the change continues to work its way through the language.

Consequences of the dynamic paradigm

The Bailey wave model represents inherent variation in terms of the dynamics of the way changes move through language. This has consequences for investigation, and for the way in which variability can be interpreted.

Linguistic environments

		(a)	(b)	(c)	(d)
	Lect 1	100	90	80	20
Relative	Lect 2	90	80	20	10
time 1	Lect 3	80	20	10	
	Lect 4	20	10		

		(a)	(b)	(c)	(d)
	Lect 1	100	100	90	80
Relative	Lect 2	100	90	80	20
time 2	Lect 3	90	80	20	10
	Lect 4	80	20	10	

		(a)	(b)	(c)	(d)
	Lect 1	100	100	100	90
Relative	Lect 2	100	100	90	80
time 3	Lect 3	100	90	80	20
	Lect 4	90	80	20	10

Figure 4.11 (adapted from Bailey, 1973:79)

Methodologically, it is possible to work with data from individuals. Once collected, the problem is to determine the correct order of the linguistic environments and the correct order of the grammars so that the data exhibits more or less the relations displayed in our diagrams. The data is arranged implicationally on **implicational scales**. Put simply, this means that if a feature appears with a certain value in one cell, that **implies** that it occurs with a predictably lower value in the next cell below or to the right, and so on, as a result of the wave of change. We can assign the patterns so generated to the grammars of individual informants. The method is, at heart, linguistic, in that its concern is with the linguistic patterning of change. The order of grammars ought, however, to group individual speakers together in terms of those social and geographical spaces through which the change is working. But social factors are 'outside' the analysis of change, in that the social groupings and styles are not used to explain the wave front's progress; to explicate the dynamism. One advantage of working with individuals, however, is that when we observe deviant cells that break the implicational pattern (as we will), we can account for this through the idiosyncratic, personal biographies of those informants (Bickerton, 1971).

The picture of language which emerges is that of a system of related grammars, each minimally different from the next with respect to waves of change. The overall representation of language can be conceived of as a **panlectal grid**: an arrangement of possible grammars, implicationally related, for some given space and time. The variation between and within lects is thus an intrinsic part of language. Contrast this with the categorical grammars of Chomsky's view of language, in which variation is a matter of performance.

We can also contrast this panlectal, or 'polylectal' view with Labov's conception of a community grammar. In the polylectal view, the frequency with which an individual produces a given variant is understood in terms of the position of his particular lect on a wave of change. He needn't 'know' the grammars of other people's lects. This dissolves the problem of how an individual speaker may be said to 'know', in Chomsky's sense of competence, a community grammar. He need not know it. The grammars of the community and of the individual are not the same. He is able to deduce the frequencies we observe without having internalized the probabilities derived from the distribution of frequency in the whole community (Bailey, 1971: 82). For any variable feature, the quantities are greater later, and lesser earlier. His frequency of one variant over another, by environment or lect, simply depend on *when* he acquired the feature.

Does this suggest that it is the waves of change that provide the 'coordinative' mechanism which relates what an individual does to the pattern observed in the whole community? In one sense, the answer must be "yes". It accounts for what an individual does, relative to other remote individuals, to produce the overall pattern, without the individuals 'knowing' that overall pattern.

In another sense, the answer must still be "no". Too much is still left unexplained. Precisely what is left unexplained are the social correlations made visible by the Labov paradigm. Let us look at this from the point of view of the kinds of explanation we discussed earlier.

Assume that we could develop a theory of language change that depended *only* on psychological and physiological factors. Language changes solely because of the way in which we physically produce it, or psychologically produce and perceive it, or the way in which children acquire it in each succeeding generation. Such factors are, in fact, central to any theory of language change (see, for example, Lightfoot, 1979). Our theory of change would then account for the facts in a 'strong' causal way. Language changes because of universal characteristics of the human organism. We are simply built that way. But such explanations are only part of the story.

The evidence derived from Labov's quantitative paradigm overwhelmingly suggests that social factors interpenetrate with psychological and physical ones in producing that variability which is the result of language change (some variability has other sources). We are thus pushed back again to the explanatory status of correlations between social and linguistic variables. We saw that they were 'weakly' causal. They made the pattern visible, but did not tell us the underlying connection.

The problem remains. What makes it the case that individual's utterances, remote in time and space, are 'coordinated' in such a way as to produce the large-scale pattern that quantitative studies make visible? The waves of change, generating implicational patterns, are clearly the mode of transmission of the information required to produce the pattern of frequencies. But what is the 'coordination' between individuals' utterances, in the first place, such that they are generating and diffusing waves of change? And this apart from psychological or internal linguistic factors.

In the course of the rest of the book, aspects of some answers to this question will be explored. In the next chapter, however, we will look at a single variable in some detail. We will do this with an eye open for social factors at work in language change.

5. Rhoticity

The generally more distinct utterance of Americans preserves a number of consonants that have begun to decay in
Standard English....In 1913 the late Robert Bridges
belaboured the English clergy for saying 'the *sawed* of the
Laud' instead of 'the *sword* of the *Lord*'.... The violent
Anglophile, Henry James, revisiting the United States after
many years in England, was so distressed by this clear
sounding of *r*, that he denounced it as a 'morose grinding
of the back teeth'....

Mencken (1919)

The feature in question is **postvocalic** *r*. This is the *r* in words
like 'guard', 'art', 'lord' and 'fourth', and at the end of words
like 'floor', 'far' and 'rider'.

In line with our popular beliefs about accents, a basic
dichotomy can be set up about how people pronounce words
like these in English. It is often said that English speakers of
English drop their *r*s, and, in contrast to this, Americans pronounce all the *r*s that appear in the written language. The
accents are *r*-less and *r*-full, respectively.

Even folk perceptions are more fine-grained than this, however, and within Britain there is an awareness that Scottish, Irish
and West Country accents are *r*-full. As mentioned in Chapter 1,
for English English speakers *r*-fullness has a social meaning, not
only of transatlantic English, but, at home, of both rusticity and
bucolic genuineness. Accordingly, it is sometimes used to adver-
tise such wholesome products as 'butte*r*' and 'cide*r*'. In the
United States, on the other hand, over and against a norm of
r-full pronunciation, people think of *r*-less English principally as
a feature of Southern accents, 'confederate' English as it is
sometimes called, and also of what is loosely called an 'Oxford'
accent – the prestige pronunciation of southern England. As we
shall see in Chapter 7, stereotypes associated with people's *atti-*

tudes towards differing forms of speech are themselves significant facts, and an important part of the study of variability.

After the methodological emphasis of the last chapter, this chapter will look at some descriptive studies, and will concentrate on a single feature, postvocalic *r*. There are reasons why this is appropriate. This sound-feature has been extensively studied in a number of different communities on both sides of the Atlantic. The pattern that emerges is very interesting, partly because of its scale in space and time. The sound has been involved in a long-term pattern of changes in many accents of English. It is currently in the process of change in New York City and was one of the features studied by Labov (1966). Because of the change in progress, we will find an interestingly different sociolinguistic structure for the variable (r), as compared to that of (ing). We will also begin to see how social factors are inextricably involved, not only in language variation at a given time and place, but in the diffusion of linguistic change.

Before beginning, however, a note on jargon. Wells (1982) comments on the use of 'rhotic', 'rhoticity' etc. in place of the more straightforward '*r*-full', '*r*-fullness' etc. It seems that for some people with *r*-less accents, the term '*r*-full' may easily be mistaken for 'awful'. We would then be describing awful accents! Shades of Henry James – see the quote at the beginning of the chapter!

Rhotic and non-rhotic

The situation is, of course, much more subtle and complex than any simple dichotomy. Let us consider exactly what is meant by saying an accent is rhotic or non-rhotic. The first point is that *r* occurs in a number of different linguistic environments. In some of these, it is never or very rarely dropped. Places where either all or almost all speakers never drop *r*, are:

1. Word initial; reed, raw etc.
2. Between two vowels: arrow, borrow etc.
3. In consonant clusters before a vowel: bread, bring etc.

Because of its appearance in these positions, the sound *r* is part of the sound system of English in general. It serves to tell words apart, for example, 'raw' v. 'law', 'rum' v. 'bum', and 'drank' v. 'dank'.

When we talk of *r*-dropping in *r*-less accents, we are actually talking about its loss in *two* specific environments. What these have in common is that the *r* follows a vowel, hence the term 'postvocalic *r*'. These two environments are:

4. After a vowel: guard, board etc.
5. Word final: floor, rider etc.

The environments of *r*-dropping can be made more delicate: in terms of the class of the preceding vowel, whether the syllable is stressed or not, whether the next word begins with a vowel or a consonant, and so on.

Now there are three possibilities for an accent in relation to *r* in these latter environments. It may:

(Historical	Categorically retain *r*	(Rhotic	= *r*-full)
direction	Variably retain and drop *r*	(Variable	= has *variable* (r))
of change)	Categorically drop *r*	(Non-rhotic	= *r*-less)

These are the three phases, noted above, that occur in the process of a language change. Historically, if we look at the English language overall, the dropping of *r* is an innovation. In earlier periods, English would have been rhotic throughout. That this is the case can be readily seen if we think of the system of spelling that we have been handed down, and that was regularized in the eighteenth century. In general, though not always, the presence of *r* in the spelling tells us the positions of the historic *r*.

If we look at English today, all three of the possibilities relevant to *r* can be found. Later on, we will be concentrating on speech communities where there is a **variable (r)**. Figure 5.1 surveys the overall distribution of rhoticity, variable rhoticity and non-rhoticity among English accents (Wells, 1982). In dealing with this feature, we are talking about accents, not dialect differences. You will recall that accents differed only on the level of sound, and not necessarily on any other level. Remember also that the terms in Figure 5.1 are misleading in the way that they label accents as things, as discrete objects. In fact, we are dealing with continua, as we shall see. So Figure 5.1 is just a general guide. One point is quite clear from it, however.

Rhotic	Variably rhotic	Non-rhotic
General American class of accents: midland, north central, middle Atlantic etc.	Local accents in the west of England	RP (Received Pronunciation) in England and Wales
Southern mountain accents in US, 'hill type' of speech	A few local accents in the north of England. New York City	Local accents of the east and north of England
General Canadian	'Borderline' rhotic/non-rhotic areas in US, e.g. South, eastern New England, black English vernacular	Most accents of Wales and New Zealand
Scottish accents		Australia
Irish accents		South Africa
Some West Indian, e.g. Barbados		Black English vernacular in US
		Some parts of eastern New England
		Southern speech area in US. 'plantation' type
		Some West Indian, e.g. Trinidad

Figure 5.1 Rhoticity in the accents of English

Although prestige accents in Britain and North America – RP and General American respectively – provide 'polar norms' of non-rhotic and rhotic speech, there is not any simple dichotomy between the two sides of the Atlantic. Variability and the opposite categorical pronunciations are common in both societies, in particular speech communities.

How *r* is made

Consider, for a moment, how different to the ear an *r* sound appears in American, West Country, or Scottish speech – in these three rhotic varieties. Whether we classify an accent as rhotic or not depends solely on the presence or absence of postvocalic *r*. As we saw before, this is a part of the systematic arrangement of sounds as they function in the language, permitting speakers to tell words apart; for example, 'guard' from 'god', or 'board' from 'bawd'. However, there are also considerable variations 'beneath' this, so to speak, on the purely phonetic level. There are a number of different ways in which the sound *r* can be made with the organs of speech. The *r* sounds different depending on how it is made, and this is irrespective of whether the speaker's accent is rhotic or not. We all have *r*s in some environments.

In word-initial position, most accents make *r* in roughly the same way. In this position, it is a consonant sound, shaping the beginning of an initial syllable. Usually, the tip of the tongue is held near to, but not touching, the ridge just behind the upper teeth. The tongue tip is usually turned slightly backwards. This is called **retroflexion**. The sides of the tongue are touching the molars and there is a lateral bunching of the tongue. The air stream escapes continuously and freely out of the mouth, without friction, and the vocal chords are vibrating, giving the sound 'voice'. Bronstein (1960) points out, in connection with a common American pronunciation of this initial sound, that it can be alternatively made with the tongue-tip held low, and the central part of the tongue bunched and raised upwards and rearwards. One major difference between accents has to do with the **degree of retroflexion** in articulating the sound. Thus, RP has slight or no retroflexion, while American and West Country accents have more. Such movements produce the *r* impressions that we perceive.

There are other ways in which *r* can be pronounced. It is one of the most various of English consonants. It was originally a **trill**, a series of rapid taps by the tongue against the teeth ridge. This still occurs in some accents and some individuals in certain styles. It later became a **fricative** sound, in which audible friction can be heard in the narrowed gap between the tongue and the teeth ridge. This still occurs when *r* follows *d*, as in 'drink' in RP and other accents. Also, in RP, in the position between two vowels, for example in 'very' or 'marry', *r* is often realized as a **flap**, a single tap of the tongue-tip on the teeth ridge. We will be mentioning these various pronunciations of the same abstract *r* sound later, as they are relevant.

The English pyramid

Figure 5.1 tells us that RP is non-rhotic. This accent is the national prestige norm of England and Wales. Before looking specifically at *r*-lessness in England and Wales, we must look at how various accents are related to each other within the overall society.

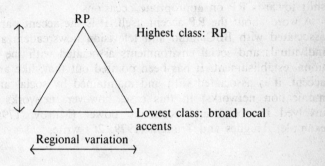

It is generally agreed that the relationship of accents to each other in England takes the form of a pyramid (Wells, 1982: 14; Hughes and Trudgill, 1979: 6). The pyramid represents two continua of variation. The base represents geographical variations, local accents. The vertical dimension represents social stratification. At the apex is RP.

It can't be emphasized enough that RP, at the top of the pyramid, is a national norm. *It is not localized.* It is distributed in the highest social classes up and down the country. At the opposite end of the social scale, at the base of the pyramid, we find the speech of the lowest classes – which is also the most highly localized pronunciation. It is the broad local accent of that area. Working-class accents vary markedly from region to region; Cockney, Scouse, Tyneside, West Midlands and so on. These can be broadly classified, of course, in larger regional terms, as southern or northern, for example. But the most localized accents are also those at the bottom end of the social scale.

The middle social strata are distributed between these two norms. In each geographical area, therefore, as we move up the social scale, speech becomes more RP-like. Conversely, as we move down the social scale pronunciation becomes less RP-like, and, at the same time more local. We saw this situation in the

Norwich (ing). In the case of this feature, consistent use of the 'ing' variant, scored as 000, represented consistent RP pronunciation. This was achieved by the middle class in two reading contexts. At the other end of the scale, the lower working class scored 100, or complete use of the 'in'' form in casual speech. Middle-class accents, therefore, can be 'mildly regional', in different parts of the country, in their approximation to the national RP norm. Style-shifting tells us also that individuals can shift towards RP on appropriate occasions.

A word about the RP accent itself. It is the accent particularly associated with BBC radio and television newsreaders and with individuals and social environments associated with the conventional establishment. It has been pointed out that, like any other accent, it is associated with and maintained by social and communication networks; in this case, however, networks directly involved in social and economic power (Milroy, 179f , for example). Hughes and Trudgill (1979: 2f) write,

> RP has ... remained the accent of those in the upper reaches of the social scale, as measured by education, income and profession, or title. It is essentially the accent of those educated at public schools (which are, of course, private, and beyond the means of most parents). It is largely through these schools that the accent is perpetuated. For RP, unlike prestige accents in other countries, is not the accent of any region (except historically: its origins were in the speech of London and the surrounding area). It is quite impossible to say from his pronunciation where an RP speaker comes from.

Although RP has been extensively described in phonetic and phonological terms, there is an urgent need for empirical studies of how such overtly prestigious standards are created, maintained, and convey normative pressure. There is also internal variation and change within RP, though not on a geographical basis. Note also that the use of RP as a prestige accent must be interpreted as relative to the meaning which its use conveys in a given context. There are occasions when it would be seen as 'affected'.

The diffusion of r-lessness

It was in the eighteenth century in the south-east of England that English began to lose postvocalic *r*. Let us look at the situation geographically. If today we plot on a map of England those areas where any rhoticity still survives, as in Figure 5.2, what are we looking at? If we put ourselves at the point of origin of the change, the south and east, we are looking *outwards* to the limits of where the loss of *r* has diffused as a categorical property of all accents. This is the white area of Figure 5.2. In this area, pronunciation is *r*-less, from RP down. We are looking at the past diffusion of the change through geographical space.

But we are also, simultaneously, looking *downwards* towards the lower end of the social scale, towards the base of the pyramid. We can assume that the loss of *r* was a prestige innovation, and therefore related to the norm of higher status groups. The fact that RP is categorically non-rhotic tells us this. Therefore, those areas where rhoticity survives, since they are plotted in geographical and therefore 'local' terms, also represent the situation looking down towards the bottom of the pyramid, down the scale of social variation. We know that RP speakers are *r*-less. How far downwards through social space has the loss of *r* progressed? Figure 5.2 tells us something about this. The shaded *r*-pronouncing areas represent the accents of the informants of the *Survey of English Dialects*. These are the most conservative speakers of all – older, working-class and *rural* speakers.

The categorical area of *r*-lessness, the white area, is larger if one plots regions where *r* is observed in *urban* speech, as in Figure 5.3. We can immediately see by comparing the two maps that the extension of rhoticity is much shrunken. The change has diffused all the way down the social scale more widely in urban areas than in rural ones, so that urban areas shaded in Figure 5.2 – for example, Merseyside or Tyneside – are not shaded in Figure 5.3. The working-class (most local) speech of these conurbations is non-rhotic. This suggests, as we shall see in Chapter 6, that urban areas act as foci in the diffusion of change. Its progress does not proceed smoothly from the point of origin.

It is possible to infer from Figures 5.2 and 5.3 that a complex wave of change has passed through geographical and social space, leading to a loss of rhoticity in most English accents. The process has gone further in the north than in the west. In the north, urban rhoticity has practically disappeared. Wells (1982:

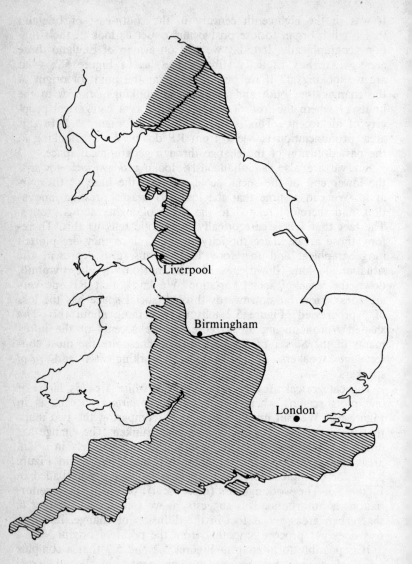

Figure 5.2 Areas (*shaded*) of England where /r/ may still occur in the speech of older, rural, working-class speakers (*from Chambers and Trudgill, 1980:110*)

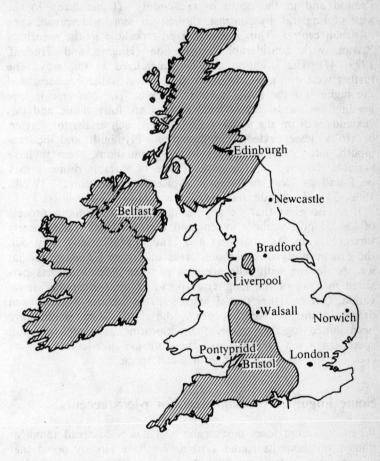

Figure 5.3 Areas (*shaded*) of Great Britain where /r/ still occurs in *urban* accents (*from Hughes and Trudgill, 1979:33*)

368) says, "The patch of residual urban rhoticity, ever shrinking under the pressure of the non-rhotic majority, now seems to be located to the north of Manchester, in places such as Rochdale and Accrington. It remains also in the country areas around Preston and in the north of the county" (Lancashire). In the west of England, by contrast, rhoticity is more widespread, even in urban centres. Thus, there is a postvocalic *r* in the speech of Bristol, with considerable retroflexion (Hughes and Trudgill, 1979: 47). The situation can be generalized in this way. The further west one goes, the more widespread is the *r*-fullness and the higher up the social scale it extends. The converse is true heading eastwards. Broad local accents are fully rhotic and this "extends well up the social scale in cities such as Bristol, Exeter, or (to a lesser extent) Southampton. Plymouth and Bourne-mouth, large cities with very mixed populations, seem to have variable rhoticity or even none. Traces of variable rhoticity may be found as close to London as Reading (Berkshire)" (Wells, 1982: 341). In 'borderline' areas, *r* is clearly a variable (r).

It is also clear that we are dealing with a continuous process of loss of postvocalic *r* in England that may have lasted nearly three centuries. As Chambers and Trudgill (1980: 109) point out, the discontinuity of the rhotic areas in Figure 5.2 show us that we are dealing with **relic areas**, where the older form has per-sisted in spite of the long-term spread of the '*r*-dropping' inno-vation. One imagines that if maps such as 5.2 and 5.3 had been drawn in the nineteenth century, the rhotic areas would have been joined together, rather than appearing as islands of *r*-full speech in a sea of *r*-lessness. The diffusion of *r*-lessness makes concrete the waves of change in social space.

Some linguistic consequences for r-less accents

When an accent loses postvocalic *r*, it has widespread ramifica-tions throughout its sound system. We have already noted that in non-rhotic accents we get homonyms which we do not find in rhotic ones, for example 'bawd' and 'board' in RP, or 'guard' and 'god' in New York City. What happens is in fact very com-plex and beyond the scope of this book. So, I will briefly sketch some basic consequences, to give an idea of what happens when *r* is lost, and to show that changes in one sound affect other sounds.

The consequences we are going to consider apply in varying

ways to all non-rhotic accents, although RP will be the main example. One major consequence takes place in the vowels. There is a wider range of contrastive vowel sounds in non-rhotic than in rhotic accents. To explain why this should be so, we need to be able to describe differing vowel sounds and how they are made. We will have to describe vowels in dealing with variables in later chapters in any case. Imagine the trapezium shape below as representing a cross-section of the oral cavity (i.e., the inside of the mouth) as viewed from the side. The diagram is, of course, highly idealized. A vowel sound is produced by the completely unobstructed outward movement of the air-stream through this chamber, with the vocal chords vibrating. The sound quality of each particular vowel sound is determined by the shape given to the chamber by the position of the tongue.

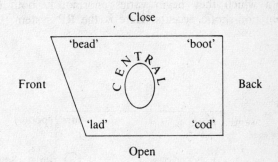

Using **vowel diagrams** like this, the vowels of a language can be charted according to where in the mouth the highest part of the tongue is put as the sound is made. Vowels can be front or back and close or open. Try to observe the four peripheral vowel sounds, indicated by the four key words in the diagram, by noting the position of your own tongue as you make the sound. The oval at the centre of the diagram represents the central area of the mouth where central vowels are made. These are sounds such as the last sound in 'the', in rapid connected speech, or the vowel in RP 'bird' or 'fur'.

To appreciate what happens in non-rhotic accents, we should first look at how postvocalic *r* is made in accents that have it. (Above, we looked at how *r* was made in initial position.) I will follow Bronstein's (1960) analysis of General American. In general, the tongue is held in the position of a central vowel. This sound is then *r*-coloured. Either the tongue-tip is turned back towards the hard palate in retroflexion (the amount of retroflexion varies from accent to accent), or the tongue is bunched and retracted upwards, or both. This is a very vowel-like sound. Conceive of it as a constriction of a central vowel that produces an audible *r*-colour to the sound.

When *r* is dropped from an accent, the constriction disappears. The process could be thought of as the absorption of the r-coloured central sound into the preceding vowel. In cases other than word-final 'er', where we gain a syllable consisting of *only* a central vowel, the outcome for non-rhotic accents is a system of centring glides or **diphthongs**. These are vowel sounds in the course of which the tongue changes position. In centring glides the tongue ends up in the central area of the mouth. The number of distinct, centring diphthongs, and the range of positions from which they begin varies enormously both between and within non-rhotic accents. Here is the RP system (Gimson, 1962):

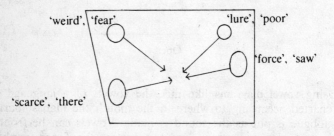

Other things also follow, with much possibility for variability. Thus, these diphthongs can become simple vowels, so that words like 'fear', 'poor', 'scarce' and 'force', especially the last two, have variants which are *not* diphthongs, but a single lengthened vowel. For most RP speakers, in fact, the 'force' sound is always a long vowel. In varieties where rhoticity *also* exists, variably, such as that of New York City, the situation can become very complex indeed.

Linking r

Another consequence of the loss of *r* is its reappearance under certain conditions. Thus, it is a common characteristic of non-rhotic accents that *r* appears in word-final position to serve as a link with a following word – but *only* when the following word begins with a vowel. Thus,

with linking r	without linking r
far away	fa...country
answer it	answe...badly
car engine	ca...port

Intrusive r

But the reappearance can go further than this. The *r* can appear before vowels *where there never was an historic r* and where, accordingly, there is no written *r*. This **intrusive r** is common in non-rhotic accents. Thus,

intrusive r
idea-r-of
area-r-of agreement
Shah-r-of Iran
draw-r-ing

This is a very interesting feature because of what it tells us about the rules of non-rhotic accents. It suggests that *r*-less speakers, in fact, don't 'know' which words historically end in *r*, and that therefore they do not represent final *r* in the way they 'store' these words. Therefore, for such words, the rule is not to *drop r* before a consonant, but rather to *insert r* whenever there is a following vowel. This rule applies to words where historic *r* occurred, and we observe linking *r*. But it *also* applies to similar words where there was no historic r, and we observe the so-called 'intrusive' sound. Since this tells us that the accent is fundamentally *r*-less and cannot have a 'dropping' rule in final position, it is an excellent diagnostic of *r*-lessness. In fact, intrusive *r* never occurs in rhotic accents. But it is a perfectly natural phonological process for non-rhotic accents. It follows from their rules.

In spite of this, intrusive *r* is stigmatized in Britain. Speakers of non-rhotic accents accordingly attempt to suppress it, especially inside words (as in 'drawring'). But think about how difficult this will be! In the absence of *r* in one's knowledge of the word, one has to be guided solely by the preceding vowel's class, and the *spelling*. The spelling tells us which words had *r* historically. In fact, the stigmatization is related to the existence of these final *r* s in the written language, and shows us the power of literacy in relation to notions of correctness. A standard written form in this case is a vehicle of normative pressure in terms of the prestige norm. This will ensure that intrusive *r* will tend towards lower frequencies in more careful styles. In fact, suppression usually involves suppression of linking *r* as well, or its realization by an alternative sound. This set of rules, consequences of loss of *r*, thus opens up new possibilities for variation.

Scotland: rhotic accents

A look at the map in Figure 5.3 shows that Scottish accents exhibit full-blown rhoticity; a striking contrast to English norms.

We can see in Scottish accents how vowels combine with *r* and contrast this with the centring diphthongs of *r*-less speech. The diagram below illustrates how *r* functions in rhotic accents (adapted from Wells, 1982: 408). Ideally, each set of words is

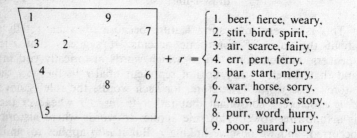

$$+ \, r = \begin{cases} 1. \ \text{beer, fierce, weary,} \\ 2. \ \text{stir, bird, spirit,} \\ 3. \ \text{air, scarce, fairy,} \\ 4. \ \text{err, pert, ferry,} \\ 5. \ \text{bar, start, merry,} \\ 6. \ \text{war, horse, sorry,} \\ 7. \ \text{ware, hoarse, story,} \\ 8. \ \text{purr, word, hurry,} \\ 9. \ \text{poor, guard, jury} \end{cases}$$

distinguished by a simple vowel sound, numbered 1–9 in our diagram, plus an *r*-sound. Of course, there is much variation between Scottish varieties. Thus, in general, Scottish vowels 2, 4 and 8 are kept distinct; the pronunciation of 'bird', 'pert' and 'word' are different. In popular Glasgow speech, however, 2 merges with 8, and 'bird' and 'word' rhyme, although remaining distinct from 'pert'. By contrast, in middle-class Edinburgh pronunciation all three categories are merged into a constricted central vowel, and all the words of 2, 4 and 8 rhyme. We find similar processes in General American.

Let us look now at how this systematic *r* is actually articulated in Scottish English. Nearly the full range of variants occurs. We discussed how each of these was made above. They are:

    (a) trilled *r* (popularly, rolling your *r*s)
    (b) flapped *r* (a single tap on the teeth ridge)
    (c) the frictionless continuant (described above)
    (d) *r*-lessness (newly observed by Romaine, 1978)

I noted earlier that the trill was the original form of English *r*. The literature and popular opinion suggest that this persisted in Scotland until this century as a major pronunciation (Wells, 1982; Romaine, 1978). Today, however, this sound has been largely replaced by the two middle variants, the flap and the continuant. The rolled *r* is mainly confined to special formal contexts. The latter two forms are variable, and conditioned by both linguistic and social factors. We thus have an **(r) variable**, with the flap and the continuant as its values (although the trill could be included as a third value).

Romaine (1978: 145) reports that in Edinburgh it is the continuant form which is the prestige variant. It is more frequently found in Scottish standard English, is a marker of 'polite' Edinburgh speech, and is endorsed for teaching. But both Romaine and Abercrombie had also informally observed some cases of apparently *r*-less speech in the city. This, in the context of complete Scottish rhoticity, was remarkable.

Romaine (1978) investigated this *r*-variability by studying the speech of twenty-four working-class Edinburgh schoolchildren aged from six to ten years old. Her (r) variable had the three values below. The (r) scores were the percentage of each variant observed. The study was restricted (unfortunately) to *r* in word-final position.

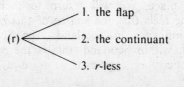

                          1. the flap

(r)   2. the continuant

                          3. *r*-less

The overall index scores for all speakers show that the flap was the most commonly used form, the continuant next, and *r*-lessness last. Although *r*-lessness did occur among Scottish schoolchildren, it did so relatively little. Remember also that it was restricted to word-final position and was most favoured by utterance-final position. The figures are

Total index scores (r) <
1. the flap   47
2. the continuant   38
3. *r*-less   15

The correlations that proved really suggestive, however, only emerge when sex and style are looked at. The boys produced more of the flap, and of the *r*-less variants. In contrast, the girls produced more of the continuant than the other sounds, and had very little *r*-lessness. So, the continuant seemed to mark female speech, and the flap and non-rhoticity, male speech. The style-shifting was even more interesting. Among the ten-year-olds, when reading passages the boys shifted from the flap to *r*-lessness and the continuant, in that order. But the girls also shifted to *r*-lessness in reading style!

Romaine (1978) interprets her results in this way. There seem to be two norms at work. The Edinburgh prestige norm is the continuant. This accounts for the sex differentiation of the scores. Girls are responding more positively than boys to the prestige norm. The girls are closer to the middle-class variant. But, at the same time, there is a vernacular norm – the *r*-less innovation. The 'innovation' seems to be located among the boys. Both boys and girls also recognize the prestige of this form (a covert prestige perhaps) because they both shift towards it in reading style, although boys also shift towards the overtly prestigious continuant as well. Such patterns suggest that a change is taking place. We will return to such matters later. However, Romaine feels that the source of this *r*-lessness is separate from RP influence in Scotland. The Scottish norm is clearly *r*-full, and, within Scotland, this is the prestige form. If the local non-rhoticity is significant, it is as a vernacular and male innovation.

Transatlantic

The rhoticity plot really thickens when we look to the other side of the water.

The map in Figure 5.4 sets out the main dialect areas of the eastern United States. The particular speech communities which we shall look at in the course of this chapter are labelled. The shaded areas show us that rhoticity is a feature of the accents in the centre of America; more specifically of the north central, central midland, middle Atlantic and mountain speech areas. Sometimes all these rhotic accents are grouped together under the label, 'General American'. They have in common the fact that they exclude those Eastern and Southern accents which are *r*-less. It is important to realize, therefore, that General American is not the same sort of thing as RP. Rather, it is a class of accents which are *geographically* defined.

So let's be geographical. It is usually said that *r*-less speech occurs in eastern New England, New York City, and in the coastal plain of the South. We can think of American *r*-lessness as radiating outwards from the major ports of the eastern seaboard. (There is a gap in the middle Atlantic region at Philadelphia.) Such a pattern is suggestive of diffusion. Thus we find the eminent American dialectologist Hans Kurath writing, "the socalled 'r-less' type is spreading as a prestige pronunciation from the old cultural centres within these areas, a process that in all probability has been in progress for generations" (Kurath, 1965,

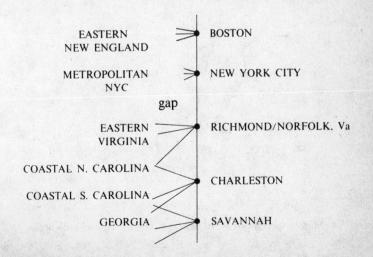

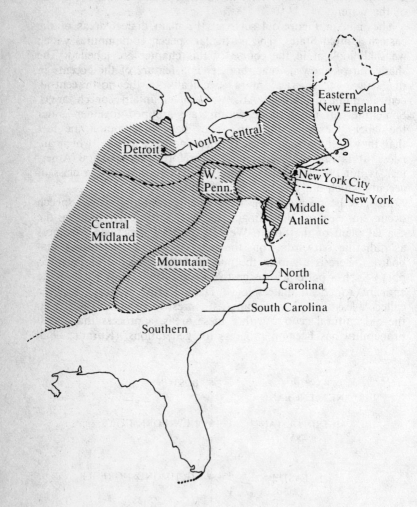

Figure 5.4 Major speech areas of eastern USA, with rhotic areas shaded

in Williamson and Burke, 1971: 105).

Maps like Figure 5.4 are very frustrating because they are highly idealized. This is because, as the results of research conducted for linguistic atlases, they are largely based on the geographical distribution of variants. It ought to be obvious by now that space is only one dimension against which variants can be plotted. Internal linguistic, and a multiplicity of external social dimensions condition variation – so the resulting structures are multi-dimensional. Without quantitative methods and social correlations we cannot observe these patterns. So the maps represent a static yes/no situation which hides social variation, and the processes that have happened and are happening in time.

We find another important dialectologist, Raven McDavid, who worked on the *Linguistic Atlas of the South Atlantic States* (1947), commenting,

> The conventional statement about the Southern postvocalic *r* is that it does not occur as constriction . . . . The fact that in every Southern state one may find locally rooted native speakers with constriction in at least some of the words has been either overlooked or deliberately ignored.

It seems that, in fact, the feature was *variable* for at least some speakers in the *r*-less areas.

The sources of r-lessness in America

The shaded areas in Figure 5.5 and 5.6 show the distribution of rhoticity in the 1930s and 1940s in New England and South Carolina respectively. These two areas have in common the fact that *r*-lessness seems to radiate outwards from the cultural centres of Boston and Charleston.

Bernard Bloch, writing in 1939, and drawing on the records of the *Linguistic Atlas of New England*, reported the highest frequencies of *r*-pronunciation in the western part of New England. In the east, focusing on the Boston area, loss of *r* predominated. This had spread to New Hampshire and Maine. One sure sign that one is dealing with the diffusion of an innovation is the existence of discontinuous relic areas, as we noted above. Figure 5.5 shows a number of fairly self-contained communities bypassed by the spread of non-rhoticity. These included the islands off the coast. (We shall have occasion to look at one of

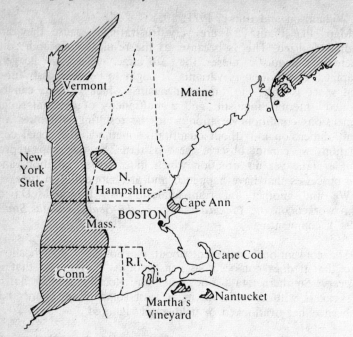

Figure 5.5 Main *r*-pronouncing areas (*shaded*) of eastern New England, circa 1930s (*after Bloch, 1939*)

these, Martha's Vineyard, later on.) There were signs in these relic areas and in certain parts of the boundary between the two types that younger speakers preferred the Boston pronunciation. This would indicate that loss of *r* was still spreading.

Writing in 1947, Raven McDavid argues, in a classic article, that a purely geographical account of *r*-pronunciation in South Carolina could not account for the facts of its distribution at that date. Traditional explanations of geographical data tend to be in terms of the historical pattern of settlement. Note, for example, the 'mountain' speech area in Figure 5.4. The accents of the Appalachian mountains differ markedly from those of the coastal south. This can be explained in terms of the speech of the original settlers. It was Scotch-Irish (Ulster) people who first settled the mountains, and they migrated to that area from Pennsylvania. Their presence therefore explains this southward prong of rhotic midland type speech. We have a reason to divide southern speech into 'hill type' (rhotic) and 'plantation type' (non-rhotic) (Stephenson, 1977: 75).

McDavid argued that complexity of distribution in the 1940s could not be explained so simply. The coastal areas settled by speakers from England, who therefore might be expected to be both rhotic and non-rhotic, was very small compared to the extent of contemporary *r*-lessness. It was, indeed, the case that Scotch-Irish had settled the two areas where rhoticity was densest (see Figure 5.6), but both rhoticity and non-rhoticity occurred in areas where the other was expected.

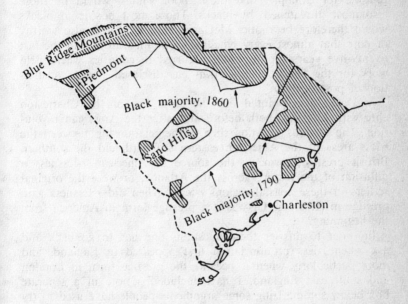

Figure 5.6 South Carolina: the spread of the plantation system. Shaded areas are those where *r* was found in 'worm', 'father', 'barn', and 'bread', circa 1940s (*after McDavid, 1947*)

This required a *social* explanation. McDavid noted that rhoticity was associated with lower levels of education, older speakers, and rural, as opposed to urban, speech. His conclusion was that, in South Carolina, *r*-pronunciation was a mark of cultural isolation. Various communities were outside the historically dominant social pattern of the state. Conversely, *r*-less speech was associated with the dominant pattern, which was the plantation system of agriculture, and the planter caste, focused on the culturally and commercially dominant city of Charleston. His argument was that *r*-lessness had diffused outwards from

Charleston along with the plantation system, and had, as its social meaning, the prestige of that city and the social system of which it was the focus. Constriction had survived among 'poor white' speakers outside the system. These were people living in areas unsuitable for plantation agriculture.

Figure 5.6 shows this quite clearly, by illustrating that *r*-less areas largely coincide with those into which plantations had spread, as evidenced by black majorities in 1790 and 1860. It follows, for example, that those 'poor whites' would be those also most 'threatened' by blacks. Those most hostile to blacks would therefore be rhotic. McDavid remarks, "It is also worthy of note that almost every lynching in South Carolina in the last twenty-five years [up to 1947] occurred in counties where field work for the *South Atlantic Atlas* has disclosed strong constriction of postvocalic *r*."

McDavid also pointed out the close ties of the Charleston elite with England, both before and after the American revolution. The obvious question then is the relationship between the *r*-less areas of the American eastern seaboard and the southern British prestige norm. Is the source of American *r*-lessness a diffusion of the feature across the Atlantic, or were the original settlers in these coastal regions *r*-less? When did *r*-lessness gain prestige in America? Or was it a prestige form in America from the beginning?

In order to answer these questions one has to go back and ask when *r*-less pronunciation first appeared in England, and more particularly when it became the prestige form in London and south-east England. I have included a note in a separate box below summarizing some arguments people have used to try to establish these dates, because I think the methods and evidence used are intrinsically fascinating. (If we are going to look at *r*, we might as well go 'whole hog', right back to the beginnings of the variants.) For those that want to skip this, however, we can conclude that both forms very probably crossed the Atlantic as 'folk' pronunciations. But we can also say that the period at which loss of postvocalic *r* became a feature of the English prestige norm is quite late. This suggests that loss of *r* as a prestige form was, in all probability, diffused from British English to American English via the coastal centres, and from there to the hinterland; as Kurath suggested.

The Kurath-McDavid theory tells the following story. Postvocalic *r* would have come to America, at least latterly, as a variable feature. The original settlement patterns would include both

The original loss of postvocalic r: a note

Early loss of r. There seems to be agreement that r-less speech became the standard of London speech in the late eighteenth century. But some writers have suggested earlier dates. Archibald Hill (1940) describes a loss of *r* as early as the fourteenth century. But this is in a single restricted environment: in stressed syllables before just those consonants which are made by the tongue-tip and the teeth. It looks as if *r* was assimilated to the dental sound which followed it in words like 'barn' and 'bird' at a very early period.

A second view of early loss of *r* is that of Wyld (1920) and Jesperson (1954). They argue that there was a very general 'weakening' in the pronunciation of *r* from the fifteenth century. Jesperson notes a very general movement from a trilled to a continuant *r* over a number of centuries. In the seventeenth century we find Ben Jonson writing that *r* was 'sounded firm in the beginning of the words, and more liquid in middle and ends' (1639). Wyld cites written forms like *Woseter* – Worcester, and *Dasset* – Dorset, from a sixteenth-century diarist of humble origins, Henry Machyn. Similarly, Kurath (1965) points to spellings like *libity* – liberty, and *patchis* – purchase, as evidence that some American colonists were *r*-less, even by 1700.

Wyld paints the following picture. The loss of *r* began in the east of England by the middle of the fifteenth century, especially before *s*. By the middle of the sixteenth century it had extended both to other consonants, and to the London vernacular. (The forms used by Henry Machyn are an example.) By 1650 it had diffused upwards to London society. In this case, both pronunciations would go to America, but *r*-less speech would go as a prestige form.

Eighteenth-century origins. There are reasons for thinking these dates are too early. Stephenson (1977) points out that there are three places where *r* fluctuates in rhotic accents *without indicating a general loss of the sound.* These are

1. in unstressed syllables: 'adve(r)tise', 'su(r)prise' etc.
2. before a following dental: 'ho(r)se', 'nu(r)se', me(r)cy' etc.
3. when two *r*'s appear in the same word: 'co(r)poration', 'fa(r)ther' etc.

These are all reported in rhotic speech. And most of the evidence for early loss is based on cases like these; for example Machyn's spellings above.

Actual comments on *r* are more valuable, and these *do not* start appearing until the eighteenth century. We find Walker referring to London speech in 1775 and 1791. He says that in England and particularly in London words like 'bard', 'card', and 'regard', are pronounced as 'baad', 'caad', and 'regaad'. Even more revealing is Hill (1821), who writes that *r*

> ought more carefully to be preserved for posterity, than can be hoped, if the provincialists of the Metropolis and their tasteless imitators are to be tolerated in such rhymes as *fawn* and *morn*, *straw* and *for*, *grass* and *farce*, etc. etc. to the end of the reader's patience.

For Hill in 1821 this is clearly a new innovation as a prestige pronunciation. *r*-lessness is thus not probably part of a prestige norm till at least late in the eighteenth century. It clearly would have been variable at this time and earlier. In this case, *r*-less speech would *not* have originally gone to America as a prestige form.

rhotic and non-rhotic speakers from England, reflecting the state of the loss of *r* in the part of England from which they came. (Of course, all Scottish and Irish settlers, like those of the mountain region, would be rhotic.) On our dating, the weight of accents would be towards *r*-full speech the further back one went in time. The relic areas tell us this.

The *r*-less form acquired prestige in America, when it was adopted from Britain by the elite classes of New England and the Southern aristocracy. Kurath points out the transmission mechanism: the very close ties between these groups and southern England. The planters and merchants of the South, especially, had their children educated at the English universities or by imported English tutors, and were accepted as equals in London society. In other words, there was a single culture and a dense network of communication between the elites of New England, the South, and southern England. The change then diffused downwards and outwards from the coastal centres as a new 'prestige' form. We saw how this process had worked itself out in South Carolina. But on the borderlines, the feature remained variable.

There is one last piece of evidence that something like the above account is plausible. Very often, when a group adopts the form of another more prestigious group, the practice of the borrower goes beyond that of those from whom they did the borrowing. In the Southern states one sometimes finds a sort of hyper-*r*-lessness which drops *r* in environments where it is not normally dropped in Britain. Some Southern accents, for example, have not only no intrusive *r*, but no linking *r*. In some non-standard varieties, *r* between two vowels, as in 'hurry', is dropped, and 'Paris' can be identical to 'pass' (Wells, 1982; 544). Such features suggest attempts by successive groups to approximate to a prestige innovation, pushing the change further and further along.

A reversal of the pattern

Much evidence has been accumulated recently that a major change is taking place with regard to rhoticity in the *r*-less speech communities we have been discussing in the eastern United States. We have been looking at the spread of *r*-less speech focused on the coastal centres. There is evidence also of the spread of rhoticity back into these enclaves, as if two contrasting waves of preference were meeting each other.

Thus, Bloch (1939) noted that on the boundary between the two forms in western New England and in the Connecticut River valley *r*-pronunciation was becoming more general. It was spreading through western Connecticut from the rhotic areas in the north central USA. In other words, the two types were 'spreading vigorously from opposite centres': the *r*-less variant from the Boston focus, the *r*-full variant from the interior. As far as *r* was concerned, New England was not a single dialect area and the speech of many individuals was variable. When Boston was re-examined by Parslow in 1967, he found that *r* was being *widely re-introduced* even into the speech of the city. Comparison of his study with that of the Atlas survey of 1939–43, on which Bloch's analysis was based, 'demonstrates a steady progression to *r*-timbre for all regions and social levels' (Parslow, 1971: 622).

In 1947, McDavid had noted that there were some slight hints of a reversal of the trend in prestige values in South Carolina; that rhoticity, formerly associated with social peripherality, might possibly become respectable. He remarked that, even in the low country, some girls in their late teens and early twenties were sporting newly acquired *r*s. By the time of O'Cain's study of Charleston in 1972, however, *r* had *reappeared* in the city itself. McDavid and O'Cain (1977) write, "Postvocalic *r* has advanced at a rate that surpasses almost every innovation in Charleston speech. Only aristocrats and older whites of other classes consistently approach fully *r*-less speech." In other words, it is variable for all other groups. McDavid (1975) notes that this feature, formerly associated with Southern poor white speech, seems to have become part of the regional standard, although it is not yet used by all standard speakers.

In 1966, Levine and Crockett, in a classic piece of research, studied *r*-pronunciation in Hillsboro, North Carolina. This is a piedmont community at the western edge of the coastal plain, not far from the Virginia border. The community is at the confluence of several dialect areas and near the boundary of midland and Southern speech types. They wondered if "inhabitants spoke some 'transitional' dialect, or, instead, one or more of the nearby dialects in relatively unmixed form" (Levine and Crockett, 1966: 77).

They found *two r-pronouncing norms* within the community. But the community was not regularly stratified, from higher to lower, according to frequency of *r*-pronunciation. High-status speakers were associated *either* with the *r*-full norm, *or* the *r*-less norm. Low-status speakers fell *between* the two norms. Levine and Crockett concluded that is was the 'clarity' or 'strength' of the norm that was associated with social position. So both norms could be models of prestige speech in Hillsboro.

The interesting point here was the direction of change observed! In more formal styles of pronunciation, *r* was more frequent, and it was also more frequent among the young. There was evidence that older people, men, blue-collar workers, and those who had resided in the community longer favoured *r*-lessness. Younger speakers, women, short-term residents, and those near the top of the 'white-collar' class (but not at the top of this class) favoured rhoticity in that they conceived it to be 'correct'. All this led to the conclusion that the community was transitional, and moving towards rhoticity under the pressure of outside norms. If this is right, then rhotic General American would become the prestige norm for this community.

The evidence emerges that rhotic speech is spreading as the prestige form into formerly *r*-less areas.

New York City

Labov comments that a New Yorker's overt attitudes to its own vernacular speech patterns are extremely negative; that it is a 'sink of negative prestige'. Vernacular New York City features have been stigmatized. Consider the 'Brooklynese' stereotype of working-class New York speech. This can be the subject of humour.

Toity doity boids sittin' on de koib, choipin' and boipin' an eatin' doity woims.

Thirty dirty birds sitting on the curb, chirping and burping and eating dirty worms.

In fact this '*toity-toid* street' diphthong has attracted such stigma that it is rapidly disappearing from the speech of the city, and now survives only among lower-class speakers. If the British reader wants to get some general idea of how the New York City vernacular sounds, he can think of Archie Bunker in *All in the Family* or the Telly Savalas New York cop in *Kojak*.

Perhaps connected with this general stigmatization is the self-contained nature of the New York City speech community. Metropolitan speech patterns do not extend further than the outer suburbs. In pure geographical terms, it is by far the smallest of the speech areas on the map in Figure 5.4. In terms of *r*-lessness, it became a non-rhotic island surrounded by rhoticity. Contrast this with the extent of the spread of 'plantation' type speech in the South. Stephenson (1977) reports *r*-less speech as characteristic of the 'cultivated' classes in much of the South. Reporting on San Antonio, Texas, Sawyer (1959) notes the variability of retroflexion. R-less speech characterized older informants. Even here, however, *r*-less speech showed signs of decline. Middle-aged informants pronounced *r* half the time or more, and the young educated informants were fully rhotic.

Historically, New York City has followed the same pattern as the other coastal centres. An *r*-full area in the eighteenth century, it had become *r*-less by the end of the nineteenth century, under the influence of eastern New England and southern British norms. Berger (1980) also points out a strong maritime connection with the South.

Labov (1972) writes thus about the adoption of *r*-less speech:

It seems to be one of our best examples of a 'change from above' – originating in the highest social group – which eventually spread to the entire speech community and became the vernacular form. Our first documented evidence for r-less pronunciation in New York City dates to the middle of the nineteenth century; Richard Norman has observed that the New York poet Frederick Cozzens rhymed 'shore' and 'pshaw' in 1856. Babbitt's study of 1896 was the first linguistic report, and it showed that the r-less speech was the regular vernacular pattern of the city. Babbitt's report as well as Linguistic Atlas interviews of the 1930s show a completely r-less dialect.

By the time of Hubbell's study in 1950 and Labov's own study in 1966, the situation had changed substantially. In the speech of any given New Yorker in the area which Labov studied, the lower east side of Manhattan, there was a great deal of apparently random fluctuation between the production of constriction and its absence. The two forms appeared to be variable. They were freely substitutable for each other in the same environments. This was true for the various instances where *r* would be possible during a single utterance, as well as between different utterances by the same speaker and, of course, between speakers. The speech both of individuals and of the community was inconsistent. Hubbell (1950) had assessed New Yorker's usage as follows (quoted by Labov, 1966; 36):

> The pronunciation of a very large number of New Yorkers exhibits a pattern ... that might most accurately be described as the complete absence of any pattern. Such speakers sometimes pronounce /r/ before a consonant or in final position and sometimes omit it, in a thoroughly haphazard fashion.

The department stores

Labov's work in New York City includes one of the best examples of anonymous observation which we have. You will recall that this was one of the techniques of investigation mentioned in Chapter 4. One of the ways of overcoming the observer's paradox was to engineer a situation in which people's speech could be observed without their knowing it. Labov (1966) was able to do this in three New York City department stores. The suspicion he was working on was that rhoticity was being reintroduced into the city as a prestige feature. Labov (1966: 64) predicted: "If any two subgroups of New York City speakers are ranked in a scale of social stratification, they will be ranked in the same order by their differential use of (r)."

The groups of speakers in question were the salespeople of three large department stores in Manhattan. Labov, using a series of quite objective criteria, ranked the stores in the following order: (1) Saks Fifth Avenue; (2) Macy's; (3) S. Klein. He argued that jobs in the three stores would be socially evaluated in the same order, if only in terms of the working conditions and relative prestige of the stores.

Now, how was he to observe the salespeople pronouncing or dropping their *r*s? The technique was both ingenious and amusing. He chose a department which was located on the fourth floor of each store, and asked salespeople, "Excuse me, where are the−?", which would, of course, elicit, "Fou*r*th Floo*r*," as a reply. The investigator would then lean forward and say, "Excuse me?" This would normally cause the unwitting informant to repeat, in a more careful and emphatic way, "Fou*r*th floo*r*." In this way, Labov was able to get four instances of postvocalic *r*, in two contrasting styles and two linguistic environments, for each informant.

The results are below. And they are as predicted. The sales personnel, ranked according to the three stores, could also be ranked by their differential use of *r*. The overall stratification of (r) by store is Saks 62 per cent, Macy's 51 per cent, and Klein's 21 per cent of *r*s pronounced.

Saks	Macy's	S. Klein

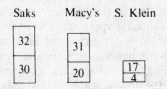

The bottom figure in each column is the percentage of *all* *r*-pronunciation; the top figure is the percentage of *some* *r*-pronunciation (Labov, 1966: 73).

But the results were even more fine-grained than this. There was style-shifting. In each store, the amount of rhoticity was greater in the more emphatic style. And, amazingly, there was a difference in (r) scores inside the Saks store itself. On the quieter and more expensive upper floors of Saks, the percentage of all or some (r) was 74 per cent. In the hustle and bustle of the ground floor the figure was 46 per cent.

Sociolinguistic structure of (r)

Figure 5.7 displays the stratification of (r) by class and style as revealed by further sociolinguistic interviews in Labov's study of the lower east side. The (r) index score is the percentage of postvocalic *r*s used out of number of times *r could* have been used. The general shape of the diagram is familiar to us from our study of the (ing) variable in Chapter 4.

But the structure of the (r) variable is different. On the dimension of social class, each class is differentiated from the other. On the dimension of style, there is a clear style-shift towards more rhoticity for all social classes. This confirms that *r*-full speech is now the prestige form in New York City. The difference is that there is a **cross-over** pattern in the more formal styles. In casual speech only the upper middle class really has any significant rhoticity. However, in the more formal styles, the *r*-score for the lower middle class (classes 6–8) rapidly increases and, crossing over, is higher than that of the upper middle class (class 9) in the most formal styles.

Labov calls this phenomenon **hypercorrection**. In this case, we observe hypercorrect behaviour by the lower middle class. Earlier on, when we were discussing the 'sharp stratification' of the Norwich (ing), in Figure 4.4, these 'borderline' classes also came to our attention. In the case of (ing), however, we had a stable and regular structure, without hypercorrection. We will be making generalizations about irregular structures later on. Suffice to say at this point that both hypercorrection and irregular structures are diagnostic of linguistic change in progress. In particular, hypercorrection by the lower middle class tells us in this case that a new prestige norm is entering the community.

Let us see exactly what we find out about informants in the most formal styles. Remember how these styles were defined in Chapter 4. They were designed to produce relatively more self-conscious attention to speech. They therefore measure, not what people's vernacular is like when they are being casual and not paying attention to how they speak, but rather what Labov (1966: 241) calls their **phonic intention**. They tell us the norms of the speaker, rather than his everyday performance. The dotted lines in Figure 5.7 represent these norms.

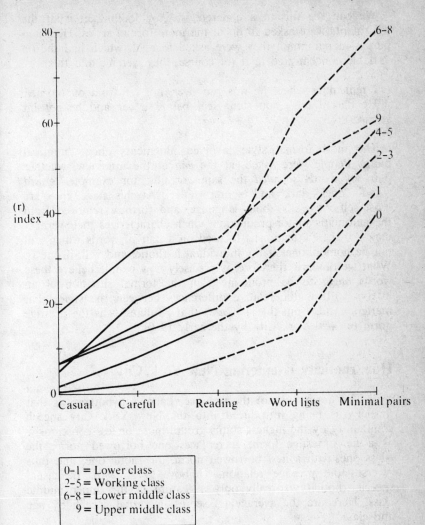

Figure 5.7 (r) in New York City (*from Labov, 1966*)

We can see this in a concrete way by looking at what the informants were asked to do in the more formal styles. Here is a part of a paragraph they were asked to read, which had the (r) variable concentrated in it (of course, they weren't told this).

I remember where he was run over, not far from our corner. He darted out about four feet before a car and he got hit hard etc.

The most formal style involved judgments about 'minimal pairs'. People were asked, at the *end* of the interview, whether pairs of words *sounded* the same or not; for example, 'guard —god', 'dock—dark' and 'source—sauce'. At this stage, they are most self-conscious about language, and furthest removed from the automatic motor-production which characterizes their vernacular. All their attention is focused on a pair of words which will not be homophones if the individual is rhotic, and will, if one is. What we observe, therefore, is precisely how people believe these words *ought* to be pronounced in the formal situation of an interview. It is the relative differences between the styles that matters. And, from this, it seems that *r*-fullness was the prestige norm in New York City by the early 1960s.

How rhoticity is entering New York City

Yes! The norm but not the practice. Labov's hypothesis is that rhoticity is being introduced into the New York City speech community by the highest status group, more or less consciously, as a new prestige form. It replaces one borrowed norm, the *r*-less one, with a new borrowed norm, the rhotic one; and thus reverses the prestige relations (Labov, 1972: 290). In casual speech, rhoticity is really only a feature of the upper middle class. Here are the average (r) scores in casual speech by age and class:

Age	Lower	Working	Lower Middle	Upper Middle
8-19	00	01	00	48
20-29	00	00	00	35
30-39	00	00	00	32
40-49	00	06	10	18
50+	00	08	00	05

Since 00 means a complete absence of rhoticity, these figures tell us that New York City, in its everyday styles, is very largely an *r*-less community. It is only the upper middle class, who are introducing the change, who have respectable amounts of constriction.

But note how, in the upper middle class, there is a steady decrease in *r*-scores as the informants get older. We said earlier that *average* scores for classes and styles conceal significant patterns in variation on other dimensions. This is the case with *age* in New York City. Speakers over forty have much lower amounts of constriction than do their younger counterparts. Speakers over fifty have virtually none. This suggests that the change entered the city, in the upper middle classes, in the 1940s.

But notice there is no age-grading in the other classes. Rhoticity, as a practice, has not reached them. But it *has* as a norm. We can see this from hypercorrection and style-shifting. The younger upper middle class is the 'reference group' for this new norm. In fact, it is the older lower middle class speakers who hypercorrect; those over forty. And so, for this class, average scores rise by age because they are using the younger speakers of the class above them as their model of correct speech.

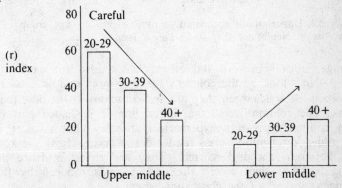

This pattern only really becomes clear if you look at the two diagrams in Figure 5.8. The dotted line in each diagram is the upper-middle-class score for each age group. In both styles, this line steps down to the left. It is clear that rhoticity is a property of younger upper-middle-class speakers. They are introducing the new form.

The columns in the two diagrams in Figure 5.8 represent the

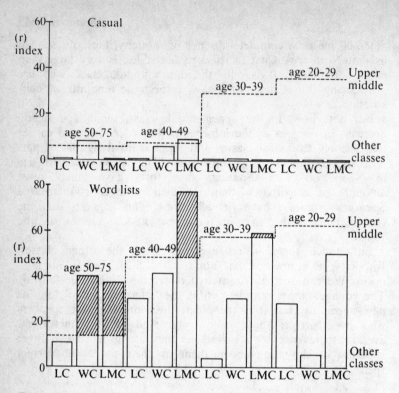

Figure 5.8 Upper middle compared to other classes by age group in two styles, New York City (*from Labov, 1966*)

average index scores of the other classes, also for each age group. Now look at the columns for the lower middle class in the word-list style, when they are self-conscious about how they speak. The columns cross the dotted line. The shaded part of each column represents hypercorrect speech. What is clear is that older lower-middle-class (and oldest working-class) speakers are the ones who hypercorrect. They are giving evidence, in doing so, that they accept the new norm introduced by the younger speakers of the class above them.

Labov (1972: 136f) has tentatively suggested that this pattern serves to accelerate the process of change. By hypercorrecting, lower-middle-class speakers provide a model of the new norm for their own children. This leads to its more rapid diffusion downwards through successive classes, in successive generations.

We now have a precise picture of how an innovation may be introduced by higher-status groups into a stratified society, and a possible role for hypercorrection in its diffusion. We will be returning to these matters later. But note how, in New York City, Labov's quantitative methodology has made visible the way in which rhoticity is being reintroduced into that community. Contrast this with the frustrating and very partial accounts which we have had in the earlier part of our study of *r*; those done before or outside of the new quantitative paradigm.

Black Detroit

To conclude, we will look at one more speech community – in order to make some very important final points about our discussion in this chapter.

The speech of black people has been the subject of research and controversy in America since the 1960s. Here we will examine just one feature in one community: the (r) variable as described in Wolfram's 1969 study of Detroit Negro speech. In contrast with New York City, *r* is not a variable feature in the pronunciation of the white community in Detroit, a city which is in the north central speech area of the US, and, as Figure 5.4 shows, is categorically rhotic. However, the feature is variable for the black community in Detroit.

The top diagram in Figure 5.9 shows the percentage of times postvocalic *r* is absent in the speech of Black Detroit for four social classes. For comparison, the average score is also given for a group of upper-middle-class white speakers. Variability of *r* only really characterizes the black ethnic group. The two main groups in American society whose speech is *r*-less are whites of the coastal enclaves and speakers of the black English vernacular. These two groups are not unconnected.

In the 1960s, the majority of black Michigan residents were not born in the state. Older persons were internal migrants from *r*-less areas of the American South, and younger persons were overwhelmingly the children of recent arrivals. The parents of 53 per cent of Wolfram's informants were born in the three deep Southern states of Mississippi, Alabama and Georgia. Another 21 per cent were born in other Southern states. Thus a linguistic boundary coincident with an ethnic boundary exists in Detroit. But is is not a full explanation to say that *r*-lessness among Detroit blacks was caused by the movement of people who speak a non-rhotic vernacular into a northern city in which the basic pattern is rhotic. As Wolfram (1969: 25) points out, "One

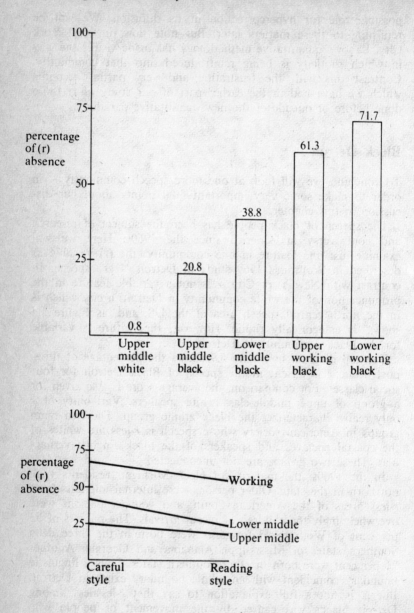

Figure 5.9 (r) absence in Detroit Negro speech, by social class (*from Wolfram, 1969*)

of the most important factors accounting for speech behaviour in the Detroit Negro population is racial isolation. Patterns of Northern segregation are a main source for transforming many Southern speech characteristics into ethnic and class patterns of speech in Northern cities." In fact, class, sex, age and racial isolation interact in complex ways. The migration of black people into inner cities in the north – the inner city of Detroit has very high densities of black people as a percentage of the population –. has led to the emergence of a "uniform caste dialect – the black English vernacular of Harlem and other inner cities" (Labov, 1972: 299). Labov sees this as part of a general tendency connected with worldwide urbanizaton in the past several centuries: the transformation of local dialects into language varieties defined in terms of stratification. Innovations emerge that reflect the processes of urbanization.

Wolfram's study showed that within the black community (r) reflects social class differences among Blacks. Figure 5.9 shows the fine stratification of (r) absence by social class. Each class increases its amount of rhoticity as one moves up the social scale. The bottom diagram in Figure 5.9 shows the style-shift between careful and reading styles. We see that this is also in the direction of rhoticity, but no hypercorrection is visible. Wolfram's data on age, which shows no age-grading for (r), suggests that working-class adults are persistently retaining a nonrhotic Southern norm (Wolfram, 1969: 118). However, the picture that emerges for *r* in terms of class and style is one in which, for the black middle class at any rate, there has been an acceptance of the norm of General American. Clearly what has happened is that the pronunciation of the host community has become the form with *overt* prestige within the black ethnic group's upper strata.

But the upper strata in the black ethnic group is a much smaller percentage of the total black population than for a comparable white community. Less than 15 per cent of blacks are middle class, while over 40 per cent of whites are in this group. This means that the sociolinguistic process will be different. The black vernacular has proved highly resistant to institutional pressures from higher up the social scale. Labov (1972: 299f) says, "in the larger ghetto areas, we find black speakers participating in a very different set of changes bearing no direct relation to the characteristic pattern of the white community ... " He continues, "similar processes appear to be operating ... wherever large capital cities are developing at the expense of the hinterland. In the traditional literature... the social setting of language change is discussed in terms of the spread of the prestige patterns of urban capitals such as London and Paris. The creation of low prestige working class dialects is a pattern of equal linguistic interest... "

Specificity of explanations

Our sketch of rhoticity has been on a very wide canvas. We have looked at the diffusion of the loss of postvocalic *r*, and the gain of postvocalic *r*, in many speech communities: from Charleston, to Edinburgh, to eighteenth-century London, to postwar New York. The inescapable effects of social factors in the diffusion of linguistic change was clearly visible.

One reason why it is possible to study *r* so widely is that the innovations we have looked at have characteristically been introduced by the highest status groups in the community. This was the first sort of normative pressure we discussed in the last chapter, and is a reflex of stratification as characteristic social structure. The processes involved are analagous, on the level of the single variable feature, to those involved in standardization, as discussed in Chapter 2. In the next chapter, we shall see that social stratification and its concomitant stratification of styles is just one social dimension relevant to linguistic variation.

Even more important is the way in which *r* must be explained differently in different communities. In England, *r*-lessness is the prestige norm. In New York City, *r*-fullness is being introduced by the highest ranked social group from outside the community. In Edinburgh, *r*-less speech has appeared in one sex, in one social and age group. That looks like a vernacular innovation, which probably will not spread because of the prestige rhotic norm of Edinburgh English. There seems to have been a reversal in the fortunes of *r* as a variable in the speech of coastal South Carolina. How could this be explained? If a new prestige norm has replaced an older one, we could look for the way institutions create and sustain prestige norms. For example, in England, how is RP maintained as the prestige norm? The system of stratification is probably central to this; and the control of large-scale institutions by the upper strata of society, including education, public culture, state institutions, and the media. But could *that* apply to *r*-less speech in Charleston? McDavid (1975) argues instead that the profound postwar changes in Southern society, including a great increase in educational and economic opportunity for the formerly disadvantaged, has led to upward mobility by rhotic whites. Such people have modified the Charleston standard. If this is true, it would be an example of a change introduced by a lower strata of society.

Whatever the case, this explanation will clearly not do for either New York City or Detroit. The point, then, is that postvocalic *r* is a *different* sociolinguistic variable in each of these communities. The rhoticity or otherwise of speech means something different in different speech communities.

6. *At the Intersection of Social Factors*

Thereupon those who had been presented with the head answered, 'Your majesty, an elephant is just like a pot,' and those who had only observed the ear replied, 'An elephant is just like a winnowing basket.' Those who had been presented with the tusk said that it was a plough share. Those who knew only the trunk said it was a plough. 'The body', said they, 'is a granary: the foot, a pillar: the back, a mortar: its tail, a pestle . . . '

Some Sayings of the Buddha
(tr. F.L. Woodward, 1973)

When we introduced sociolinguistic variables it was mainly in relation to the two interconnected social factors of class and style. This is important but somewhat misleading, since it highlights only one particular sociolinguistic structure. It quickly became obvious that other social variables also reveal patterns in linguistic variability which are significant. An index score, whether individual or averaged for primary or secondary groups, is at the intersection of social factors.

In this chapter, we will look at some of these factors in turn and try to see how they intersect in particular cases. The main factors are: (1) geographical space; (2) stratification; (3) social networks; (4) sex; (5) ethnicity; (6) age. These are woven together in a very subtle and complex way in a speech community. They interact differently for different variables. Using quantitative methods to study correlations with one social factor makes the pattern partially visible. Like the blind men in the quotation above, we see only a bit of the elephant and can easily misinterpret that bit. The aim, of course, is to view each sociolinguistic structure as evidence for a theory of how language structure and change must, in part, be explained in terms of social structure and change. We will look at that issue in Chapter 7.

Spatial diffusion

I remarked earlier that 'where one lived' was a social characteristic of people which affected their use of language. The study of the way in which linguistic variants were geographically distributed was very much the province of traditional dialect geography. That this is important can be seen from the very clear evidence of spatial diffusion which we observed in connection with r; for example, in Figures 5.2, 5.3, 5.5 and 5.6. The use of quantitative methodology can make the study of spatial distribution of variants more exact and rigorous.

We can illustrate some of the possibilities by looking at a proposal by Trudgill (1974a) for the application of some of the techniques of modern geography to the study of the diffusion of linguistic variants. Trudgill adapted the methodology of the Swedish geographer Hägerstrand to the examination of the spatial diffusion of a linguistic innovation in the Brunlanes peninsula, Norway. The study was meant to be mainly illustrative of what might be possible if the notion of a linguistic variable is joined with sophistication in geographical method.

In the Brunlanes area, the variable studied was the vowel (ae). This has to do with the relative height of the vowel. Evidence suggested that the pronunciation of the sound was in the process of being 'lowered', or pronounced more openly, so that it was variable within and between the communities of the peninsula.

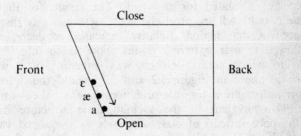

The score of 000 marked a consistently high pronunciation and a score of 400 indicated a consistently low pronunciation. The higher an informant's score, the further the change towards 'lowering' had gone in his speech.

The relative height of the vowel is a gradient, or 'more or less' phenomenon. The individual score for each informant is a measure of where, more close or more open, he pronounces (ae). We have seen how average scores were determined for categories such as class and style. But how can this be done for space?

The method is to find out the quantitative relationship between two spaces of equal magnitude. One divides into a series of equally sized cells the geographical space through which one is trying to observe some innovation moving. For each cell, the percentage of times the new innovation appears, out of the total number of times the variable occurs overall, is calculated, giving the ratio of new to old for each cell. Then, by comparing any two cells, it is possible to measure precisely the increase or decrease of new cases as opposed to old for the two spaces. At a point in time, a relatively higher score for a cell suggests that the innovation is further advanced in that space. At the same point in time, a relatively lower score for a cell suggests that the innovation is less advanced in that space.

One could imagine how this method might, for example, be used to measure the spread of non-rhotic pronunciation through geographical space. If (r) index scores were the percentage of *r*s used out of the total number of possible postvocalic *r*s, then a lower score would represent an increase in *r*-less speech. To apply the method, the space in question (say the West Country of England) would have to be divided into cells of equal magnitude. Using Labov's techniques, an average index score would then be calculated for each cell. The result, for that point in time, would tell us precisely how *r*-lessness was distributed in space for that region. Relative increases or decreases, if they followed regular patterns, would allow us to infer from which and to which areas *r*-lessness was spreading, if it was. Maps, such as those in Figure 5.2 and 5.3, would thus present much more information for interpretation. In fact, they would be the spatial equivalent of the sociolinguistic structure diagrams – with space instead of class and style as the social variable. As Trudgill (1974a: 223) points out, spatial cells are the equivalent of Labov's social class cells.

The immediate interest is spatial diffusion of change. Hägerstrand suggested that this ultimately depends on the 'sender's network of interpersonal contacts and that the configuration of this network is primarily dependent on various barriers' (Trudgill, 1974a: 223). Social barriers have the same effect as physical barriers. We mentioned this notion when discussing the differentiation of varieties in Chapter 2: that the boundaries between dialects will be along lines of weakness in communication networks (Bloomfield, 1933: 328). It is also possible that social networks may be useful here. Changes will spread from individual to individual along networks. Clustering, density and multiplexity will facilitate diffusion within a group. But weak network links between groups will slow down the process.

The sheer geographical distance between people will itself have an effect on diffusion. If everything else is equal, people who live close together are likely to be similar in their adoption of the innovation, as opposed to those who live further apart. In the theory, this is called the **neighbourhood effect**.

But patterns of communication are clearly not dependent only upon spatial proximity. Changes diffuse more rapidly between urban areas which are in close contact than they do between those centres and their respective closer rural areas. Changes can 'jump' between these **central places**. And then they will spread out from such foci to the intervening hinterlands later. Both these effects were observed in Brunlanes.

Trudgill's first step was to impose a grid of cells on a map of the Brunlanes peninsula to divide it into spaces of equal magnitude. Figure 6.1 shows how this looks. Average (ae) index scores were then calculated for cells in a profile from east to west. This is represented by the dotted lines between the centres of Larvik and Hamna. Figure 6.2 represents the average index scores for the cells through which the dotted line passes as it crosses the peninsula.

Remember that higher scores represent relatively low vowel height, and that this 'lowering' is the direction of the change we are studying. The lowest vowels are to be found in the urban communities. The highest variants are in the rural area most remote from these centres, gradually increasing the further one gets from the centres of influence. Trudgill suggests that the linguistic change is radiating from Larvik, spreading by the 'neighbourhood effect' to the surrounding area. It has 'jumped' to Hamna, a central place, and is also radiating from that secondary centre. The next step is to represent scores in maps which will graphically display the dynamics of diffusion.

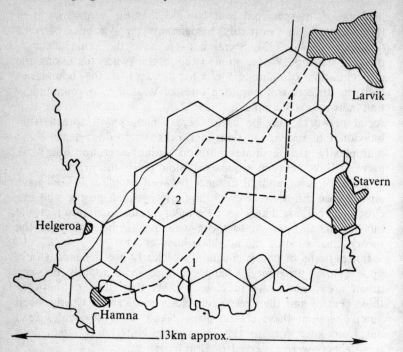

Figure 6.1 Grid imposed on Brunlanes peninsula, Norway (*from Trudgill, 1974a*)

Space and time

The profile in Figure 6.2 gives us the spatial pattern at one time. But an innovation diffuses through space in time. At progressively later times, a change will not only be more widely diffused, but will also be more advanced in its purely linguistic development. In the case of Brunlanes, the scores will be higher later, as the 'lowering' of the vowel develops. As we shall see in more detail in the next chapter, on the assumption that a change is in progress, lower scores ought to characterize *older* speakers, and higher scores ought to characterize *younger* speakers. We saw such age grading in (r) in New York in Chapter 5.

But this will be in systematic relationship with the spaces through which the change is diffusing. Although the young ought to be most advanced in each space, we ought also to preserve both the *relative* differences in age in every space and the *relative*

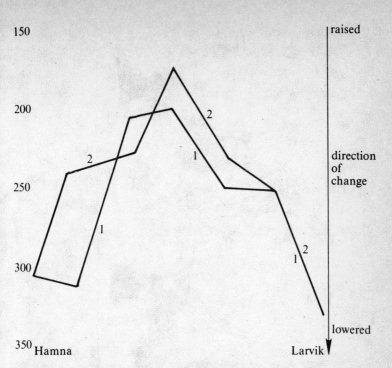

150

200

250

300

350 Hamna

raised

direction
of
change

lowered

Larvik

Figure 6.2 Average (ae) index scores from east to west. The numbers
1 and 2 represent the routes of the profiles marked by the dotted
lines in Figure 6.1 (*from Trudgill, 1974a*)

differences between the spaces, depending on how far the change
has gone in each one.

Figure 6.3 shows that this is the case on the Brunlanes peninsula. Average (ae) index scores for each cell by age group have
been worked out, and isoglosses drawn which reflect these
average scores. The top map shows the scores for those aged
seventy and over, the middle map for those aged twenty-five to
sixty-nine, and the bottom map for those aged twenty-four and
younger. The scores clearly increase by age group for all spaces,
with younger speakers having higher scores, and therefore 'lowered' (ae) variants. For Larvik's neighbourhood the scores are
240+ at seventy and over, 280+ at twenty-five to sixty-nine,
and 320+ for twenty-four and younger. But spatial differentials
are preserved. Thus Larvik is always ahead of Helgeroa in the
innovation for each age group. Increasing scores also spread out
further from the 'central places' into their 'neighbourhoods' for
each successively younger age group.

The nature of change tells us that the highest scores (the most

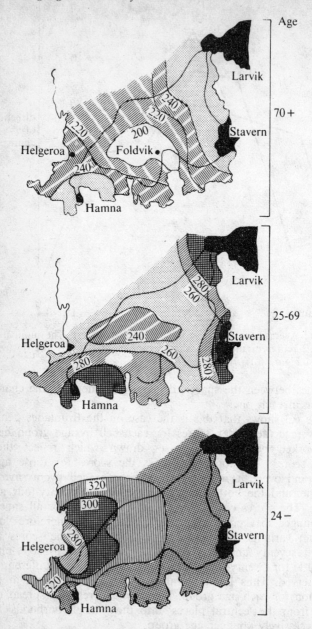

Figure 6.3 Brunlanes (ae) by age *(from Trudgill, 1974a)*

'lowered' vowel heights) will be for the younger speakers in a relatively larger area in the neighbourhood of the place where the change began. As predicted, the highest scores are for the under twenty-fives in a large neighbourhood around Larvik. The lowest scores ought to be for the oldest speakers at the place which the change reached last – a place at the outer limits of the neighbourhoods of the central places. The top map, in fact, does show the lowest average scores for the oldest speakers, those aged seventy and over, in the intermediate area north of Foldvik. The origin of the 'lowering' at Larvik, its spread to its neighbourhood, its 'jump' to Hamna and its diffusion from there are all made clear by the application of quantitative methods to the study of the diffusion of this change.

Trudgill's research is illustrative of the possibilities. Processes such as these were clearly taking place during the spread of *r*-lessness and *r*-fullness in the speech communities we looked at in Chapter 5.

There have also been attempts to determine whether spatial weaknesses in networks of communication do correlate with isogloss bundles. Labov (1974) was concerned to see if this traditional hypothesis, that language differentiation was caused by relatively less communication between rather than within groups, could be empirically corroborated.

There is a major isogloss bundle that runs east to west across Pennsylvania, separating its northern tier of counties from the rest of the state. It reflects differences both in vocabulary and pronunciation. The usual assumption is that what most affects people's vernacular speech are face-to-face contacts with other people. (Passive contact through the media etc. probably serves to transmit norms 'from above', and therefore principally affects attitudes rather than practices.) It follows from this assumption that if we could measure the daily density of travel between the residents of different areas, we would also have a rough measure of the amount of communication between the areas. In the USA, up to 90 per cent of inter-city passenger traffic is by road.

Accordingly, Labov calculated the number of primary highways crossing the east-west dialect boundary from north to south. There were 2.2 crossings per hundred miles. But this needs to be compared with the number of north-south crossings of east-west lines up and down the state to see if it is a low or a high figure. Imaginary lines were drawn on the map east to west at thirty-mile intervals, and the number of north-south crossings per hundred miles was calculated. In fact, the dialect boundary *was* in a trough of north-south links. This converged with data about traffic flows. Using traffic-flow maps he was able to show that there was also a trough in average daily traffic flows roughly at the point where the isogloss passes through the state. Similar results were obtained for many, but not all, major dialect boundaries in the eastern states.

The exceptions are crucial. For example, we noted before how small and stable the New York City speech area was in geographical terms, compared to that of other cities. It is almost 'the prototype of a concentrated metropolis', in Labov's words. Yet the average daily traffic flows in and out of New York City are very large indeed, over fifty times greater than the Pennsylvania isogloss. This means that density of communication and weaknesses in lines of communication *alone* cannot account for the diffusion of innovations – although it might have some validity in accounting for broad regional differentiation.

We have seen that the distribution of variants is spatially structured in relation to change through time; that there are 'city effects' and 'neighbourhood effects', and that lines of communication are significant, but not definitively so. Changes diffuse to and from 'places' in a patterned way.

Social stratification

In variables like (ing) and (r) we observed scores stratified by class and style. These two social variables were clearly interdependent. The variable was simultaneously structured on both dimensions. The shifts of style that occurred in the more formal contexts are towards the variant used most frequently by the highest class in casual speech. This is a reflex of social stratification.

When informants are most consciously aware of their speech and 'phonic intention' can be observed, we can talk about variants being produced under **pressure from above**. The word 'above' here is being used in the sense of 'above' the level of conscious awareness. People are aware of the normative pressure being brought to bear on them, for example, in terms of the overt prestige or stigma of a variant, notions of correctness, and so on. As we shall see, however, there is also the opposite case. Normative pressures can affect peoples' speech without them being aware of it. It is below the level of consciousness, and hence termed **pressure from below** – pressure to conform to norms of which people are not self-consciously aware, in response, as Labov puts it (1972: 123), 'to social motivations which are relatively obscure'.

Now notice how we can map these two kinds of normative pressure on to social stratification. Pressure from above, that of which people are aware, has also come from above in the social sense. It has typically been an awareness of what is overtly treated as having prestige or stigma in the society. These 'society-wide' normative pressures have been associated with the higher ranked social strata, although all strata may consciously accept them. We saw how the design of the classic sociolinguistic interview revealed, through style-shifting, the connection between overt prestige, conscious norms and the practice of the upper middle class. Conversely, the non-standard stigmatized variant was characteristically the practice of the lower strata in casual speech. Style and class interact to reveal this conscious, evaluative stratification of the variants.

But there is a possible source of confusion here. The connections just described seem to be a matter of fact, but they are not necessary connections. There is no reason why 'pressures from above', conscious awareness of a norm, could not be exerted on behalf of a non-standard variant. People would attach overt prestige to the vernacular, and judge the use of standard forms negatively. Judgments of 'affectation' are of this type. More characteristically, it is 'pressure from below', without conscious awareness of the norm, that attaches a hidden **covert prestige** to the vernacular. But we must be careful not to assume that all conscious norms and overt prestige are by definition generated from the top down, as it were, and then generalized throughout the overall society. There are both conscious and unconscious pressures acting on all strata. Linguistic innovation can emerge at any point in the social system, and eventually become overtly prestigious.

The distinctions we have just made can be clarified by the diagram below. Solid arrows show the links between strata and normative pressures which seem to reflect the system of stratification. The dotted arrows show the other possibilities. Stratification involves both differentiation and ranking from higher to lower. Talcott Parsons, for example, sees the process of differentiation producing stratification, as different social roles are associated with different statuses within the social system. The ranking is the source of the differing evaluations we find, which presumably serve to *integrate* this kind of social organization.

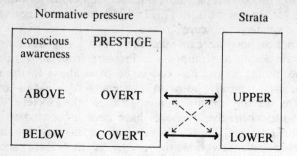

Stratification characterizes complex societies, which are highly differentiated. Urban industrial societies exhibit *class* stratification. One of the trends observable in the modern period has been the relative decline of rural speech varieties. In urban melting-pots these have been transformed and there has emerged variation that reflects the overall system of urban class stratification and the social attitudes that serve to sustain it.

We can make a useful distinction here, borrowed from the sociolinguist Ferdinant Toennies, between *gemeinschaft* and *gesellschaft* types of society. The former type is based on community, and the latter on more impersonal relationships. Community, as a form of social organization, is based on stable personal relationships, for example systems of kinship. In the latter type of society, by contrast, relationships are characteristically mediated through institutions. People relate to each other in a fundamentally different and more impersonal way. When we look at language variation in terms of a *class-style* structure, we are observing the *gesellschaft*-type pattern that reflects the large-scale organization of our society. The *prestige—stigma* axis reflects the evaluative dimension of this structure.

A number of basic kinds of such sociolinguistic structures have been discovered. Four recurring types are illustrated in Figure 6.4.

Sociolinguistic indicators. Sometimes a variable is stratified by class but hardly at all by style. There is no significant shift in average index scores between casual and formal styles. Such variables are called **indicators**. The variable (aː) in Norwich provides us with an example of this type. Its sociolinguistic structure is illustrated in Figure 6.4a (Trudgill, 1974: 98).

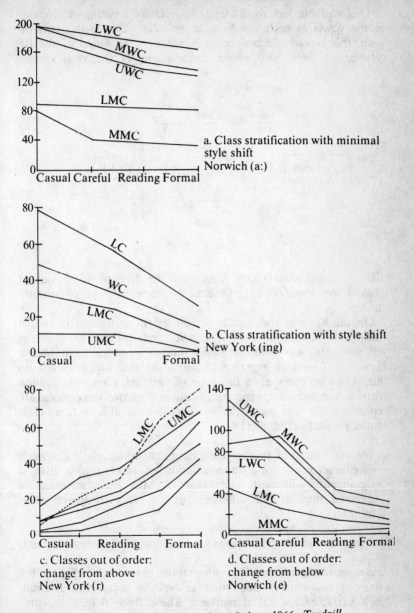

Figure 6.4 Sociolinguistic structures (*from Labov, 1966; Trudgill, 1974*)

This variable has to do with the relative fronting or backing of the vowel in such words as 'after', 'cart' and 'path'. In Norwich, this is variable between a relatively back vowel of the RP type and a very front vowel characteristic of the local vernac-

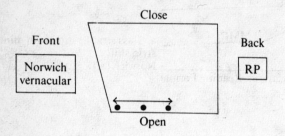

ular. A high score (200) represents the fronted local variant while a low score (000) represents the back RP type of pronunciation.

On the basis of the regular sociolinguistic structures discussed earlier, we should be able to predict style-shifting towards the RP norm in more formal styles due to pressure from above. However, a look at Figure 6.4a will show that (aː) does not do this. Thus we observe, in this type of variable, class stratification with only minimal stylistic stratification. The two dimensions are separable. This is particularly noticeable in the working-class scores for (aː). Trudgill (1974: 98) writes:

> We can interpret this as indicating that although WC speech is characterised by a pronunciation of this variable that is significantly different from that of MC, little attention is directed towards this difference in the Norwich speech community.

We shall return to the whys and wherefores of this in a moment.

Sociolinguistic markers. The other three diagrams in Figure 6.4 all exhibit stylistic stratification as well as social stratification. Such variables are called **markers**. These three diagrams represent recurring types of markers.

Figure 6.4b returns us to the (ing) variable in New York City.

In contrast to Norwich (aɪ) the slope of the lines for all classes shows clear style-shifting. Although the classes remain stratified in the same order for all styles, each one's average index score slopes regularly towards the most formal styles. The question is, why are the structures of this type different from structures of the first 'indicator' type? Why are style and class separated in the first, but not in the second?

Trudgill's analysis of the (aɪ) variable in Norwich gives us an answer. The Norwich (aɪ) does not seem to be subject to any of the normative pressures from above which shape pronunciations towards standard forms. Trudgill (1974: 98f) gives a number of reasons for the lack of style shift in (aɪ).

First, the fronted variant is not stigmatized in Norwich, nor is it overtly stereotyped as an object of humour. It is not corrected in educational institutions. It would seem, then, that although the classes are stratified with respect to (aɪ), there is little correction towards the RP variant. Trudgill notes that overtly stigmatized forms are quite often those that deviate from a spelling pronunciation, as popularly conceived. Thus, people are consciously taught not to 'drop' their 'h's, 't's and 'g's. In this case, the vowel position cannot be conceived of in those terms. So, in contrast to '*in*'', a front (aɪ) does not attract stigma.

Second, the (aɪ) variable is not involved in linguistic change. Trudgill argues that speakers will be more self-consciously aware of variables which are in the process of change, if only because within the group people of different ages will pronounce the form differently. Attention will be drawn to the conflicting forms co-existing within the same social group. From this, we can conclude that *sociolinguistic indicators represent variables which are not in the process of change*. So we can have

$$+ \text{class} \ - \text{style} \ - \text{stigma} \ - \text{change}$$

as represented by Norwich (aɪ) and diagrams like Figure 6.4a.

Does this mean that contrasting diagrams which exhibit style-shifting indicate that the variable is involved in a linguistic change? Not at all. We can get both stigmatization and style-shift (as in New York (ing)) in a variable which is *not* undergoing change. You will recall that we termed (ing) a 'stable sociolinguistic marker'. Chambers and Trudgill (1980: 83ff) point out that, in fact, the following combinations occur for sociolinguistic markers:

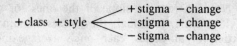

This last category is different from the others, in that style-shift without stigma or change can be accounted for by phonological features of the variable which make speakers aware of the contrast between the variant forms. We can say, in general, that stylistic stratification, and the self-conscious awareness of language it indicates, can be produced by either stigmatization or change or both. It follows that a sociolinguistic marker by itself is not diagnostic of a linguistic change in progress. It is a necessary but not a sufficient condition for change.

Diagrams c and d in Figure 6.4 represent markers that *are* diagnostic of linguistic change. In both cases this can be corroborated by the age-grading of the index scores. These types of structure have in common that social classes are 'out of order' in relation to their index scores.

Prestige innovation. Figure 6.4c represents the by now familiar pattern of the (r) variable in New York City. The contrast with a marker such as Figure 6.4b is very clear. The slope of style-shifting is accentuated for a 'borderline' class. We observe hypercorrection by the lower middle class, represented by the dotted line in the diagram.

This third common pattern is characteristic of a linguistic change taking place within a speech community under pressure from above. (Recall that the new prestige norm of rhoticity was being introduced to New York by younger members of the upper middle class.) By contrast, the first pattern usually represents a stable situation; and the second may or may not involve change.

We saw how hypercorrection from above worked to accelerate the diffusion of an innovation through the class system. Let us now look rather more deeply at this phenomenon. Why should the second highest ranked class behave in this way?

The standard answer to this question is that this group is in the most vulnerable and potentially mobile position in the system of class stratification. Because of this, such people are also the most sensitive to the social significance of prestige and stigmatized variants, and therefore most susceptible to pressure from above in their speech. This becomes obvious when they are consciously exercising control over their speech in the more formal styles.

We saw above that the role of the lower middle class was *not* to originate the innovation, but to be the driving force in its diffusion. Hypercorrection accelerated the spread of a linguistic change. Now we see that hypercorrection is driven by the linguistic insecurity of this, the second highest status group. We should look at this more closely.

Labov (1966) studied his informants' reports of their own usage. On the whole, New Yorkers were very inaccurate in their reports of how they spoke. They consistently over-reported the prestige forms of pronunciation. Labov considered that when a speaker reports his own usage, he is in fact reporting his norms of correctness. This works in the following way (Labov 1966: 455):

> It appears that most New Yorkers have acquired a set of governing norms which they use in the audio-monitoring of their own speech ... the process of stylistic variation ... is governed by the degree of audio-monitoring which is superimposed upon the motor-controlled patterns of native speech. The audio-monitoring norm is the form which is perceived by the speaker himself as he speaks. He does not hear the actual sound he produces, but the norm which he imposes.

Pressure from above produces a cleavage between vernacular pattern and superimposed norm because the norm arises outside the speaker's own group and is transmitted to him through notions of correctness. The degree of over-reporting will measure this cleavage and the strength of the externally imposed norm. And just as the degree of hypercorrection was greatest in the second highest status group, the same tendency appeared in its reports of its own usage. For some variables, the lower middle class over-reported the use of the prestige variant more than the other classes.

There were more overt indications of this linguistic insecurity. A **linguistic insecurity index** was worked out by measuring the difference between how informants reported that they *actually* pronounced certain diagnostic words, and how they said that they believed those same words *should* be pronounced. This, in fact, measures people's willingness to admit to the 'badness' of their own accents – and nothing could measure insecurity more profoundly. On this measure, the lower middle class turned out to be the most linguistically insecure. Some informants roundly condemned their own kind of speech as rendering persons who spoke *that* way unsuitable for prestige occupations.

Social mobility was also related to hypercorrection. Labov (1967) investigated this relationship. Four types of social mobility were distinguished: *upward, steady, downward* and *up and down*. These were based on the present social level of the informant's occupation, compared to the occupational status of his father, and his own first employment. The ranking of occupations into four levels followed the practice of the Census Bureau. Upward mobility was largely a feature of the middle classes, and, to a lesser degree, of the upper section of the working class. Of Labov's informants, the consistently most upwardly mobile group was the lower middle class. (For later, it is important to note that the *steady* type was most marked in the working class.)

It was upwardly mobile groups that showed the pattern of hypercorrection in the use of *r*. Upwardly mobile members of the lower middle class and of the upper stratum of the working class went beyond upper-middle-class scores in formal styles. It was upward mobility, even more than class membership, that characterized the hypercorrecting groups.

This suggests that those who are upwardly mobile are more likely to adopt those exterior norms which are prestigious throughout the community. This is in contrast with stable groups, who are less likely to be subject to normative pressures from outside. For upwardly mobile people, the group just above them in the scale of stratification acts as a 'reference group' for norms of pronunciation. Downwardly mobile people were found not to be influenced by normative pressure from above, and stable groups were governed by their own norms, balanced in behaviour by a recognition of external norms. As we saw, the acceptance of an external norm which differs from one's own vernacular also leads to insecurity. So upward mobility and insecurity converge on those on the 'borderline' between the working and upper middle classes, and generate hypercorrect linguistic patterns.

Labov (1967: 74) sees linguistic behaviour, then, as governed by such normative pressures and the values they encode. These operate irrespective of contact and this shows us again that we cannot account for linguistic boundaries simply in terms of lines of weakness in communication networks. Rather, it is the system of norms that is at work.

Vernacular innovation. Now let us look at a contrasting situation, in which the classes are' again 'out of order', that is, a linguistic change is occurring; but this time the change and its spread is from below in the system of social stratification. This pattern occurs in the Norwich (e) variable studied by Trudgill (1974). It is illustrated in Figure 6.4d.

The Norwich (e) represents the progressive centralizing of the vowel sound in words such as *tell*, *well*, *bell* before an *l*, and in words like *better* and *metal*. The front variant of this variable is the same vowel as in RP. The other variants fall along a con-

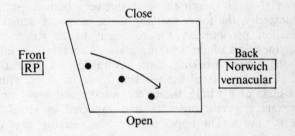

tinuum in which the tongue is retracted and lowered from the RP position. The vernacular vowel is centralized and lowered so that in extreme Norwich pronunciation *hell* is identical with *hull* (Chambers and Trudgill, 1980: 94). Index scores are calculated for (e) along this continuum so that 000 represents a totally RP pronunciation and 200 a totally vernacular pronunciation. The higher the index score, the more non-standard' is the pronunciation.

Now look at the average index scores for Norwich (e) by class and style. Figure 6.4d shows the familiar pattern in some ways. The middle middle class approximates most closely to the prestige RP norm in all styles. With average scores ranging from 000 to 003, this is a virtually consistent RP pronunciation. All other classes style-shift towards this norm in more formal styles. Note the sharp rightward slope of the lines in the diagram. We see, therefore, that the whole community is aware of this larger norm.

But otherwise the pattern is quite different from what we have come to expect. Look at the figures for each class in casual style:

Social Classes	Casual
Middle Middle	002
Lower Middle	042
Upper Working	127
Middle Working	087
Lower Working	077

The classes are strikingly 'out of order' at the working-class end of the social scale. The score for the lower working class is immediately below that of the lower middle class. That means that in any given style of speech those at the very bottom end of the social hierarchy, the lower working class, have less non-standard centralization, pronounce (e) more closely to the RP norm than do other members of the working class. Note also that in casual speech the upper working class centralizes its pronunciation more than the middle of the working class. In short, within the working class as a whole, the upper, middle and lower parts are in the exact opposite order to that expected in terms of the prestige RP norm. The upper parts of the working class diverge most from the standard.

Trudgill interprets this pattern as a linguistic innovation originating in the upper part of the working class in Norwich; an innovation *away from* the RP norm. Norwich (e) is becoming more centralized. In this case, the working-class 'borderline' is leading the process of change. The other 'borderline' class, the lower middle class, is also participating in the change, and so is the lower working class. The upper middle class alone seems insulated from centralization. In fact, a look at Figure 6.4d shows a virtually flat line for this class. It is clear that innovation in the upper working class is also serving as a norm for other parts of the working class. See how the middle working class 'crosses over' the upper working class in more formal styles, and increases its centralization.

In Chapter 4, I mentioned varying sources of normative pressure. In this data we are witnessing covert prestige driving a linguisitc change. Contrasting with what the overall society overtly recognizes as the norm and what is portrayed by the direction of style-shifting (which is consistently towards RP), the actual direction of this change is away from the standard. Clearly, working-class speech also has prestige. But we cannot reach it through the concept of formality, the degree of self-conscious attention to speech. This only gives us access to those forms which people overtly believe are 'correct', those that have the prestige of overt institutional support which we noted in discussing 'standardization' earlier on. They are the forms learned through contact with the larger structures of society – in school, at work, in church or the media – and connected with the written standard. It is these forms of which people approve when overtly asked. *But the positive social significance of vernacular speech resides in the community and culture of its speakers.* This will often diverge from superimposed norms. Although overtly 'stigmatized', its actual 'social meaning' may be positive from the point of view of those to whom it is the vernacular, and deeply tied up with their identity.

Thus, we can see normative pressures affecting people from two directions. Both of these can drive linguistic innovation and its diffusion within the system of stratification. By 'pressure from below' we mean both 'below' in the class hierarchy and 'below' in the sense of not affected by the norms that govern conscious

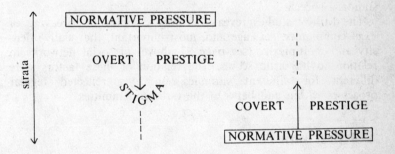

audio-monitoring of basic motor patterns. Far from 'pressure from above' smoothing out language variation, in city after city vernacular innovations originate and spread. The vernacular is extremely alive. It finds its sources in the *gemeinschaft*, or community type of social life.

Social networks

In Chapter 4 we saw that vernacular speech, the speech of working-class communities, could be studied using the notion of the individual's social network. Informally, an individual's social network simply is that network of relationships in which he is embedded and that make up the texture of his daily life. It must be emphasized that this provides us with a radically different perspective from that of an analysis based on secondary group membership. For one thing, the methodology has universal application. As we saw, stratification applies only to one type of society. But everyone lives within a social network irrespective of the type of larger society. By using networks, we can get a picture of the individual within the local community.

We can see how different kinds of networks both make up and are affected by the social conditions in the community. And language variation can be observed in the actual patterns of relationship where the vernacular emerges and is used. In principle, social networks could be studied in any strata. However, our concern here will be the Milroys' study of the working-class vernacular in three Belfast communities (Milroy and Milroy, 1978; Milroy, 1980; Milroy and Margrain, 1980). We are now going 'inside' the large-scale social groups that have preoccupied us thus far. The aim is to gain insight into the dynamics of non-standard speech.

The Milroy studies revealed a very complex interweaving of local community, sex, age and, most important, the relative density and multiplexity (see page 97 above) of social networks in relation to linguistic scores. The relation of these factors were different for different variables, and yet reflected regular processes within and between the three communities.

A Belfast variable

We will look at the interpretation of one variable feature. The communities studied were Ballymacarrett, in East Belfast, and Hammer and Clonard in West Belfast.

One of the most interesting variables was (a), the vowel sound in words such as *man*. The middle-class norm in Belfast for this sound locates it in the lower front area of the mouth. Working-class Belfast speech is currently in the process of *backing* this sound – the tongue moves back and is raised and the lips are rounded. (In other words, the vowel in *man* sounds somewhat like that in the RP pronunciation of the word *father*.) There is a linguistic change in progress in the direction *away* from the middle-class norm. The index scores in Figure 6.5a indicate the

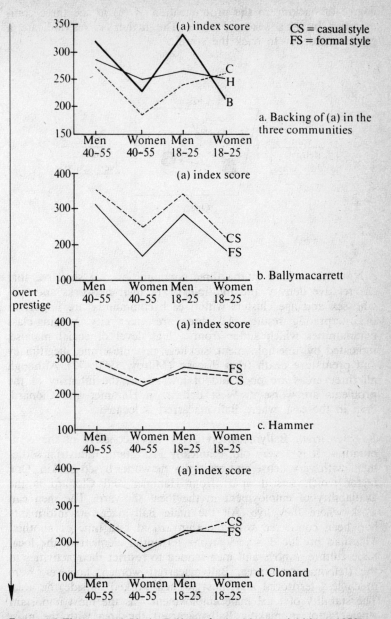

Figure 6.5 The (a) variable in Belfast (*from Milroy and Milroy, 1978*)

degree of backing in the pronunciation of (a) in the three communities by age, sex and style. The higher scores indicate a
greater tendency to back the vowel.

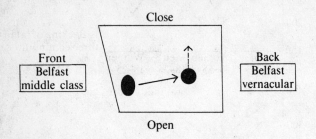

Now let us look at the three communities. We shall see that
the relative density and multiplexity of their networks and specific sex and age clusters within each community are important
in interpreting results. All three are inner city working-class
communities which suffer from a high level of social malaise,
indicated by 'unemployment, sickness, juvenile crime, illegitimacy
and premature death from disease' (Milroy, 1980: 72). Although
all three areas are poor and of low status, the intensity of the
problems are worse in West Belfast, in Hammer and Clonard,
than in the east, where Ballymacarrett is located.

Ballymacarrett. Ballymacarrett is the most cohesive of the communities. It is a very old, ethnically Protestant, industrial settlement with very dense and multiplex networks based on kin. One
factor which sets it apart from Hammer and Clonard is the
availability of employment in the local shipyard. The men can
work where they live. All the male Ballymacarrett informants
had been connected with the shipyard at one time or another.
This had produced a very strong territorial element in the local
male culture – boys and men tended to restrict their activities to
the Ballymacarrett area. Ballymacarrett women, however, were
much less territorial and most women worked outside the area.
The stability of local male employment was the most important
single factor in making Ballymacarrett the area with the most
dense and multiplex networks.

The other two communities, by contrast, suffered from a lack of local male employment.

Hammer. The Hammer, a Protestant area, had been extensively redeveloped and a large part of its population dispersed to other nearby areas. But Hammer people still based their recreational and daily interaction on the old neighbourhood. However, the disruption to social networks caused by the dispersal of the population served to make the social networks of the Hammer less dense and multiplex than those of Ballymacarrett.

Clonard. The Clonard was the only Catholic area studied. In Belfast, ethnicity is cast in terms of Protestant and Catholic, and these labels also serve to rank communities in terms of status. As a Catholic area, the Clonard had the lowest status of the three communities. It also had the worst levels of male unemployment. Only two of the Clonard men whose networks were studied were employed. This lack of local opportunity made the Clonard men less territorial than the men of Ballymacarrett. Consequently, the male social networks were less dense and multiplex. By contrast, the Clonard women were almost all employed.

Against this background, let us now try to interpret the linguistic facts in Figure 6.5. Recall that the (a) variable measures the tendency to 'back' the vowel and that, since the middle-class Belfast norm is a front pronunciation, the more a speaker backs the vowel, the more he deviates from the standard and towards the vernacular. I will treat the diagrams in turn.

6.5a The first diagram shows the backing of (a) in the three communities. *In general, the scores are stratified according to the density and multiplexity of the social networks in the areas.* Ballymacarrett, the most cohesive working-class community, has the most vernacular pronunciations, especially among the men, and the Clonard the least vernacular pronunciation. The degree of backing of the vowel roughly reflects the degree of cohesion in the community, But the situation has many subtleties.

6.5b The second diagram displays the distribution of the scores by age and sex, in casual and formal styles, for the Ballymacarrett area alone. Of particular importance is the sharp sex stratification. The men 'back' the vowels more in both styles, while the women approximate more closely to the middle-class norms. Ballymacarrett has the most dense and multiplex networks found. Milroy (1980: 79f.) argues that density of network goes with polarization of sexual roles. It is the men in Ballymacarrett, with local employment, who form the most dense and multiplex network found. The women's personal networks are 'measurably and significantly less dense than the men's'. The nature of the networks and the linguistic scores by sex correlate in this community. Presumably, the women of Ballymacarrett have *less normative pressure from local patterns of interaction than do the men, and a wider experience of the 'outside', and this is reflected in their scores.*

6.5c, The remaining diagrams give the results for the Hammer
6.5d and the Clonard. The most striking contrast with Ballymacarrett is that there is relatively little sex differentiation of the scores in these two areas. This reflects the fact that only Ballymacarrett has the traditional structure of a working-class community with local employment, dense networks and clearly demarcated sex roles. In the case of the Hammer, the collapse of social networks and the mobility of the inhabitants has levelled out the sex differences in network density and multiplexity. In the Clonard, this effect is due to the extensive male unemployment. There remains one extremely important result. In diagrams a and d, it is clear that the *younger Clonard women* 'cross over' and have unexpectedly high linguistic scores. The women aged from eighteen to twenty-five in the Clonard who were interviewed formed a single localized cluster. As a group, their networks were the most dense and multiplex in west Belfast. That is, the network structure of the young women in Clonard was denser and more multiplex than that of the men, reversing the Ballymacarrett pattern. The high linguistic scores of the young women in the Clonard correlated with their high network density and multiplexity.

The (a) variable in Belfast is a case of linguistic innovation away from middle-class norms. The innovation began within the most socially stable and most highly ranked of the working-class communities, Ballymacarrett, and is most advanced among the men there. They form a very dense and multiplex network, based on local employment and its consequent territoriality. The norms of the other two lower ranked communities are paradoxically closer to that of the middle classes. The 'backing' innovation is spreading to the Hammer and Clonard. In particular it is being introduced into the Clonard by its young women. This is striking because it is a non-standard innovation. What these points of innovation and diffusion have in common is homogeneity and tight social cohesion. The individuals at these points have the highest degree of integration, in terms of their interactions, into close-knit communities which thus exert strong normative pressure. Overt 'society-wide' norms exercise less influence in these circumstances.

These findings are extremely important. What we can say, in general, is that the strength of social networks serves as a norm enforcement mechanism. It stands to reason that in primary groups, where there is dense and varied face-to-face interaction, people will have a powerful normative effect on each other. Normative pressures are focused, rather than diffuse (Milroy, 1980: 178f). A strong sense of group identity and solidarity generates cultural focusing, and this results in both the clarity of the linguistic norms of the group (as opposed to other groups) and a pressure to conform as an expression of individual identity.

In linguistic terms, a high degree of social cohesion sustains and reinforces the vernacular. If that cohesion weakens or breaks down – for example, as a result of urban renewal and dispersion – then norms become more diffuse. Weakening of network strength opens the way for normative pressures from outside the group, normally the society-wide norms of overt prestige, to have a greater effect. This is exactly what we observed when we looked at Labov's research into social mobility. Recall that it was the upwardly mobile strata who hypercorrected – who seemingly were most subject to pressure from above. Mobility thus relates to diffuseness of norms. Individuals fall in varying ways between normative pressures, and where and how they fall depends on their social networks.

We should not assume, however, that strength of social networks, and focused norms, are features only of working-class community and vernacular. We saw in Chapter 3 the importance of residential segregation and clearly defined domains in the maintenance of separate languages. Milroy (1980: 180) argues that close-knit networks and consequent focusing can occur in any strata. In British society focusing in fact characterizes the highest and lowest classes. The argument here is that it is from dense and multiplex social networks at the upper edge of society that the highly focused RP norm emerges and is sustained. To this degree, it is like any vernacular. But, unlike the others, it is also legitimated by the overall ideology of the society – by, for example, its notions of status and mobility. It is institutionalized and thus becomes a society-wide force.

Sex

The concepts of social network and normative pressure can help us understand the way in which sex correlates with the linguistic scores of an informant. The typical pattern in Western urban society is one in which female speakers use the prestige forms more frequently than do male speakers. The two top diagrams in Figure 6.6 reveal this patterning for two widely separated examples: (r) absence in Detroit, and the (ing) contrast in Norwich. You will remember that sexual differentiation occurred even in the speech of schoolchildren in Romaine's Edinburgh study. And it was the boys who deviated most widely from the prestige forms with regard to the Scottish (r). Labov notes that it is the women among the lower middle classes of New York who are most linguistically insecure, and style-shift towards the prestige norms most sharply.

There are exceptions and complexities which will emerge in a moment. But the data from many studies suggests that, in general, women are more sensitive to the social significance of speech than men. By every measure, women consistently achieve scores closer to the overt prestige norm of the standard in the community, and seem therefore to be more susceptible to 'pressure from above' with respect to the variants they prefer. Why this should be so is usually explained in terms of the subordinate status and role of women in the society. Linguistic 'status-consciousness' is seen as a reflex of subordination in social life.

Social status in stratified societies is ascribed or achieved in relation to the social role a person has in its public institutions: to a person's job or wealth. Everything else, like costume, residence, lifestyle, follows from that and signals the social status of the individual. Adult men usually have direct access to these sources of social identity. They have occupational status and its

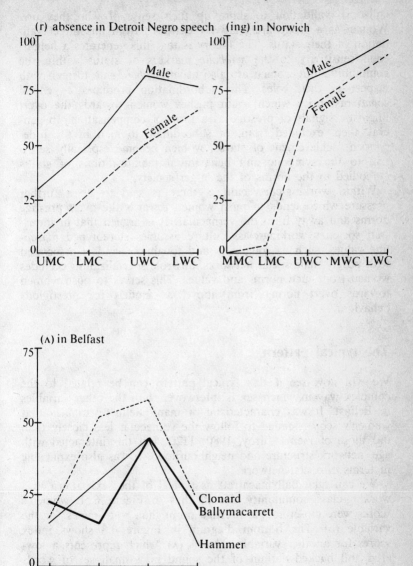

Figure 6.6 Sex differences in speech (*from Wolfram, 1969; Trudgill, 1974; and Milroy and Milroy, 1978*)

collective validation to shore up their sense of who they are. Women as a group are relatively excluded from this direct validation of their status. The theory is that this generates a heightened sensitivity to the *symbolic* markers of status within the community. But women are also usually *subordinate* to men with respect to their roles. This subordination produces a general social insecurity which again pushes women towards the overt linguistic signals of prestige as a form of compensation. In general, then, excluded from, or subordinate to men in the independent achievement of status, women become especially sensitive to the symbolic and behavioural manifestations of status embodied in the norms of the larger society.

Within working-class culture, there is said to be a further pressure which tends to push women towards the overt prestige norms and away from the vernacular. It is argued that in industrial societies working-class culture assumes stereotyped masculine values, such as roughness and toughness, and is associated with purely male social networks. Sex-role specialization excludes women from such norms and values. This serves to push women towards overt norms 'from above' as models for prestigious behaviour.

The typical pattern

We will now see if this typical pattern can be related to the complex way in which sex is interwoven with the other variables in Belfast. It was characteristic of many Belfast variables that women's scores tended to follow the vernacular less closely than did those of men (Milroy, 1980: 112f). But this interacted with age, network structure and neighbourhood. It was also explicable in terms of social network.

We can take Ballymacarrett as typical of the sex pattern in a working-class community. Recall that in Figure 6.5b women's scores were closer to the prestige norm than were men's for the variable (a). The bottom diagram in Figure 6.6 shows index scores for another variable. This is (ʌ), which represents a lowered and backed variant of the sound in a small set of words like *'pull'*, *'took'*, *'shook'* and *'foot'*. (In other words, in this community, the vowel is pronounced somewhat like the RP vowel in the words *hut* and *shut*.) The index score is the percentage of this lower variant in such words, as opposed to a raised and centralized alternant. The lower form is stigmatized in Belfast, so lower scores signify the prestige variant. As we would expect, Ballymacarrett women in both age groups have lower scores in Figure 6.6 than do their men. For both (a) and (ʌ) the typical sex pattern can be observed in this community.

But Ballymacarrett is also typical of the way sex roles are handled in working-class communities in general. Milroy points out, as we said above, that dense and multiplex networks foster sex-role differentiation. Quoting Bott (1971), Milroy (1980: 135) points out that the kinds of social networks which people have determines the way that they divide up responsibility for tasks within marriage and, in general, how independent they are of each other. The idea is that dense and multiplex social networks contracted before marriage enforce group norms even after marriage, and so there is marital segregation – sharp differences between men and women – in communities with such networks. We saw that Ballymacarrett was the most dense and multiplex of the communities studied.

This separation of the sexes is sustained by the *local* male employment in the shipyards and the territoriality of Ballymacarrett. Male social networks were more dense and multiplex than women's in this community. There was enhanced male solidarity. The women, on the other hand, had lower network scores and worked *outside* the local community. In this way, we can account for the typical pattern of sex differentiation in terms of social networks.

Female innovations

The other communities give us another perspective on this issue because, for some variables, they deviate so markedly from the typical pattern. In the Hammer there was virtually no sex difference at all for (a). This is very clear in the flat lines of Figure 6.5c. Milroy argues that high male unemployment and redevelopment, with its consequent dispersal of the traditional community, has lessened the network strength of Hammer. This has led to a less regular and symmetrical distribution of linguistic scores than elsewhere (Milroy and Milroy, 1978: 23).

The sex differentiation in the Clonard is the most interesting of all. In a community with the lowest network density and multiplexity of the three due to high male unemployment, it was younger women who had introduced the backing of (a) into the community. The young Clonard women formed a very dense and multiplex cluster – they worked together and spent their leisure time together. In fact, the shape of their social life was of a kind that would, in a more typical community, characterize younger male groups. They had the highest network scores of any sub-group. (By contrast, young Ballymacarrett women had the lowest network scores of any sub-group.) Milroy (1980: 144) writes:

> ... very dense, multiplex networks are associated particularly with men living in working class communities of a traditional kind, with a locally-based homogeneous form of employment. More specifically, network structures in the three areas ... seem likely to co-vary to some extent with factors like the stability of the area and availability of male employment locally. The men in Ballymacarrett lived in conditions particularly likely to favour the formation of dense, multiplex networks and polarization of the sexes. Conversely, the young women in the Clonard contrast with the men in being fully employed, and have developed the solidary relationships of the kind usually associated with *men* of the same age.

So this group of women has introduced a vernacular innovation, the backing of (a), originally associated with men in Ballymacarrett, into the Clonard.

Now let us look at the variable (ʌ) in Figure 6.6. We saw how in Belfast as a whole it is the higher, central variant which has overt prestige, and the lower, backed variant which carries overt stigma. But this is not so in terms of *vernacular* prestige. The lower, backed (ʌ) has conscious vernacular prestige – 'it is almost *prescribed* amongst adolescent and other close-knit male peer groups' (Milroy and Milroy, 1978: 26). This would seem to be an example of pressure from above being overtly exerted in favour of a non-standard within a specific sub-group. A variant which is overtly stigmatized in the wider society nevertheless has overt prestige in the sub-group.

These norms are reflected in the bottom diagram in Figure 6.6. Older men seem to favour the standard variant in all the communities. Women in Hammer and Ballymacarrett and the younger women in the Clonard also favour the form with society-wide prestige. But younger men and *older women* in the Clonard have high percentages of the vernacular form. The conclusion is that just as today's young women have introduced the backing of (a) into the Clonard from a higher-status community outside, so when today's older women were younger they had done the same thing with (ʌ).

For these variables, Clonard women do not follow the typical pattern. Other studies, by Trudgill (1972) and Chambers and Trudgill (1980: 99), also suggest that younger women are sensitive to covert prestige and non-standard forms. We saw in Edinburgh that there was some shifting to the boys' vernacular among girls in reading style. Our conclusion is that the relation of sex to linguistic variables involves other social variables, for example age and network structure. The typical pattern is an indirect reflection of the typical position of women in the kinds of society which have been studied. Where the pattern differs, for example within social networks, the linguistic structure also differs.

Ethnicity

Ethnic group is another place where community exists within the overall structure of society – where we find *gemeinschaft* inside *gesellschaft* (these terms were defined on page 162). In ethnic groups one would expect to find tight-knit social networks and cohesive community. This would be especially so when ethnic groups were also associated with neighbourhoods. Indeed, the Belfast communities are ethnic neighbourhoods, although this is expressed in terms of religion. In a study of ethnicity and linguistic variation in Boston, Massachusetts, Martha Laferriere (1979) puts it very well:

Ethnic and religious groups tend to form subcultures within larger cultures. Part of the 'institutional completeness' of subcultures is their distinguishing and highly valued occupational, educational and linguistic traits. Furthermore, the occupational and linguistic values which are held in esteem by a subculture may or may not correspond to the values of the larger mainstream culture . . . . An ethnic group is a family par excellence. It comprises an extended circle of relatives and acquaintances of all ages who are often bound together by an ancestral language, country, food and folklore. These elements may be reinforced by socio-religious organisation – including youth groups which provide the *cultural force* to transmit the particular groups esteemed, educational, occupational and linguistic values.

Laferriere studied the (or) variable in Boston. This has to do with the relative height of the vowel in words like '*form*', '*short*' and '*horse*'. The lower variant characterized the Boston vernacular while the more close variant characterized a standard pronunciation. For vernacular speakers, using the lower variant, the word '*short*' would rhyme with '*shot*'.

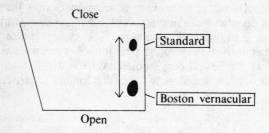

In the Boston study, ethnic group was found to correlate with the percentage of the lower variant found. (The significance of ethnic group was not surprising since this was also a major factor for the variables in Labov's New York research.) In Boston, speakers aged over sixty, in all three of the ethnic groups studied, almost exclusively used the vernacular form. It seemed that the standard variant had entered ethnic speech as an alternative way of pronouncing words of this type. A variable feature had been created for speakers under sixty. Clearly a linguistic change was occurring. The ethnic groups differed in their treatment of this new prestige variant. Figure 6.7 displays the percentages of the lower vernacular variant for the three ethnic groups.

Laferriere advanced the hypothesis that the change was proceeding through the ethnic groups in the following way. In the first stage, some members of an ethnic group acquire, mainly as a by-product of education, a positive knowledge of the norms of the wider community. They know that the vernacular is stigmatized but it remains their active, automatic form of. speech. People in this position ought to be very sensitive to the stylistic significance of the variants, and style-shift in an extreme way. In stage two, this knowledge is transmitted to some younger speakers in their ethnic group. These make the prestige variant their 'active' automatic form. In the final stage, acceptance of the new standard becomes generalized among the younger

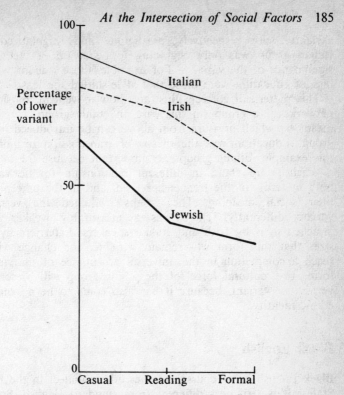

Figure 6.7 Variation by ethnic group in Boston (*from Laferriere, 1979*)

speakers of the ethnic group. At this stage, for speakers in this ethnic group the older vernacular form is both stimatized and perceived as representing those other ethnic groups who have not yet begun to participate in the change.

A study of educational levels and age, and the utilization of the stylistic significance of the variants, led to the conclusion that the Jewish ethnic group had completed all three stages of the change. By contrast, the Irish group was at the second stage, and for the Italians stage one was just beginning. The fact that only *older* Jewish speakers utilized the stylistic distinctiveness of the variants, although the Jewish group had the most standard scores overall, suggested that the change was most advanced in this group. The Irish were the only group where there was a systematic relationship between the years of education a speaker had and his proclivity to use the variants stylistically. For these speakers, education had brought with it an awareness that the variants were respectively prestigious and stigmatized. The Italian group was only beginning to be aware of the stylistic significance of the variants. For example, those Italians with the highest education were those that style-shifted the least.

This pattern, if correct, illustrates how movement 'outside' the networks of a group (in this case an ethnic group) can be the means by which pressure from above can be introduced into the group. Education was the means of transmission of norms in this example. Ethnic groups are important because the members of each group stand in different relationship to the variants, both in terms of the frequencies used, and in the perception of their social meaning. The groups evaluated the vernacular variant differently. There was a measurably weaker stigma attached to it by Irish and Italian speakers. Laferriere hypothesizes that this form will remain variable; the change will not reach a completion in the universal acceptance of the standard form. The 'cultural force' of the ethnic group will preserve the vernacular variant, because it has also come to be a symbol of ethnic identity.

Black English

Black English is, of course, another ethnic dialect in the United States. It is strikingly different from standard English. Some of the reasons for this are historical. I have outlined some views about the origins of black English in the box on page · 187. Another reason for its divergence may be found in the more recent emergence of **black English vernacular** in the northern cities. This is the ethnic dialect of the inner city studied in detail in Labov's investigation into pre-adolescent and adolescent peer groups in Harlem (Labov, 1972a, and Labov *et al.*, 1968). It is a vital and innovative urban vernacular highly resistant to pressure from above. In Laferriere's terms, it is the product of a powerful 'cultural force'.

There is one well-known feature of all varieties of black English in the United States which we will look at. It is the deletion of the **copula** '*be*' in many environments. The aim is to see exactly how this feature relates to standard English. It appears to be very different, but in fact, as we shall see, it is in a systematic relation to the rules for other varieties of the language.

There are three possibilities with regard to the copula in Eng-

The Origins of Black English: a Note

Why should there be such a degree of divergence between black and white ethnic dialects in the United States? Presumably this will be rooted in the historical circumstances in which black English originated and has developed.

The creole hypothesis. One widely accepted view is that black English began as a contact language of the sort described in Chapter 2. Under the historical conditions of slavery, people of diverse West African mother tongues would have been thrown together under a single superordinate variety, English. These are precisely the conditions under which first pidgins, then creoles emerge. It has been argued that contemporary black English began life as a creole. Subsequently, it has been and still is in the process of decreolization, a general evolution towards the standard (Bailey, 1965; Stewart, 1967; Labov, 1972a). Stewart writes:

> the Negro slaves who constituted the field labour force on North American plantations ... spoke a variety of English which was in fact a true creole language – differing markedly in grammatical structure from those English dialects which were brought directly from Great Britain ... and, although this creole English subsequently underwent modification in the direction of the more prestigious British-derived dialects, the merging process was neither instantaneous nor uniform. Indeed, the non-standard speech of present day American Negros still seems to exhibit structural traces of a creole predecessor, and this is probably a reason why it is in some ways more deviant from standard English than is non-standard speech of even the most uneducated American whites.

Pidgins and Creoles are *types of language* with the same properties whatever the superordinate variety. Syntactic features, such as the overt absence of the copula, are a common feature. The striking resemblance between Negro non-standard English in the USA and other Caribbean creoles strongly supports the creole hypothesis. Like these other creoles (in Jamaica or Guyana, for example) black English will *vary along a creole continuum* between standard English on the one hand, and most creole-like variants on the other. Some varieties, like Gullah (spoken in the coastal regions of Georgia and South Carolina) are quite deeply creole and replete with Africanisms (Turner, 1945; 1948).

White non-standards. Some dialectologists claim, however, that Negro non-standard shares most, if not all, of its features with various white non-standards – that it has its origins in the white dialects with which blacks came into contact. Its greater divergence is the result of cultural isolation. For example, Shuy, Fasold and Wolfram (1971) investigated variable features in the speech of lower class black and white children in a rural area of Mississippi. Both black *and* white children were found to delete the copula, but differentially. For the white group, deletion was largely restricted to the plural form *are*. These white Southern children would say, '*They ugly.*'

However, similarities between white and black non-standards in the South could be the result of influences in either direction.

lish: the full form, the contracted form (captured by the apostrophe in the written language) and the deleted form:

Full variant	Contracted variant	Deleted variant
She is real nice	*She's real nice*	*She real nice*
She is a nurse	*She's a nurse*	*She a nurse*
Some say you are going to die	*Some say you're gonna die*	*Some say you gonna die*

This variable is one in which superficially there is a real discontinuity between white and black communities. Only black English permits deletion. But the situation is more subtle than that. Figure 6.8 displays Wolfram's analysis of the percentage of contracted and deleted forms for the black social classes in Detroit and the white upper-middle-class group. Out of the total number of possibilities for 'doing something' to *be*, whether contraction or deletion, all the groups are roughly the same: That is, they all have roughly the same percentages of full forms. And this includes the white group.

The crucial factor for the black groups is the ratio of deleted to contracted forms. The white group uses no deleted forms at all, as expected. But the relative percentage of deletions for the black groups increases as one moves downward through the social classes, relative to the number of contractions, until it reaches 56.9 per cent deletion and 25.0 per cent contraction in members of the black lower working class. As was the case with (r), the black middle classes, under pressure from above, have adopted the white norm of contraction and delete very little. Style-shifting is in the direction of contraction, testifying to its

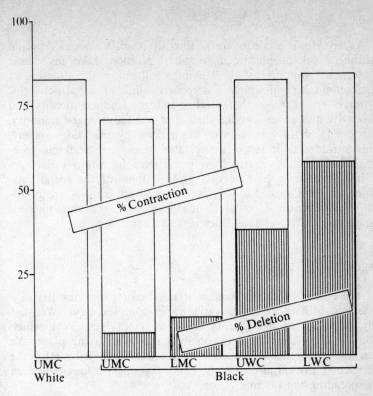

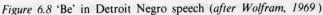

Figure 6.8 'Be' in Detroit Negro speech (*after Wolfram, 1969*)

overt prestige. Conversely, the black working-class vernacular is characterized by deletion.

But to return to the question of the apparently sharp linguistic discontinuity between the ethnic groups: it is true that the white groups in Detroit never delete, but the varieties are in a systematic, structured relation to one another. Black and white treatments can be covered under a single rule. Both groups can optionally reduce the full form of the copula in certain specific environments – these are practically the same for either variety. In the standard, the form can only be contracted. *And wherever it can be contracted in the standard it can be either contracted or deleted in the vernacular.* The reduction process is carried one step further – but it is still part of the same process.

There is a good deal more that could be said about the copula and other features of black English. I have only scratched the surface; the reader is referred to the literature, especially Dillard (1975), Labov (1972a), Baugh (1980), Fasold (1969, 1972) and Wolfram (1971, 1974).

As an ethnic dialect, black English is in a special position because black people are in a special position. Like any ethnic dialect, the structure of the language will reflect the structure of the communities in which it is spoken: kinds of social networks, attitudes to language, the social meanings of ethnic identity and solidarity and so on. As the dialect of a disadvantaged minority, black English is very heavily stigmatized by the wider society, and attitudes to it reflect many false stereotypes and misapprehensions. These are part of the racial tensions within society.

It is interesting to note that at least three of the social variables we have looked at – class, sex and ethnicity – are politically problematic. It is as if, in these cases, the variability of language runs along fault-lines in social structure.

Age

In the course of these chapters it has become obvious that age interacts with other social variables in complex ways. We saw, for example, the age-grading effect in (r) in New York which allowed us to say that a linguistic change was taking place. We saw the preference of younger male speakers in Belfast for the vernacular (ʌ) variant, and the role of younger Clonard women in spreading the (a) innovation.

There is a recurring pattern in which scores of younger speakers are closer to the vernacular, and away from overt prestige norms. If one wants to observe the most extreme forms of vernacular speech, the place to look is among male adolescent 'peer groups'. For example, Labov's (1972a) study of the peer groups in Harlem found higher percentages of copula-deletion than among adult blacks. The peer groups, close-knit clusters in social network terms, differed also between each other. Peer groups of young people exert great normative pressure on each other, and are correspondingly less susceptible to society-wide norms conveyed to them by the institutions of the adult and outside world, for example, in schools. When this is reinforced by ethnicity, one gets a strikingly different dialect such as the black English vernacular.

The normal patterns of age differentiation, when a variable is not in the process of change, has roughly the shape illustrated opposite. We can explain this diagram in terms of the pressures of different sorts of norms for different age groups. It is those in the middle age groups, those who are working and who are con-

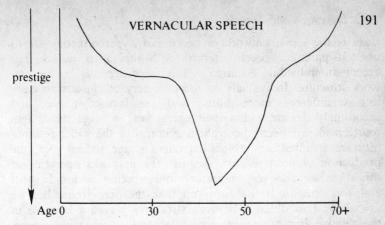

Figure 6.9

tacting other groups and other society-wide values, whose social identity must deal with pressure from 'outside'. Lives become more 'public' at the middle period.

The relationship between age and variation also depends on the way in which accent is acquired and made part of 'automatic' motor production. It is this automatic speech that is an individual's vernacular. It contrasts with the speech that occurs when people exercise conscious control of their pronunciation in formal styles. At different ages individuals are subject to different normative pressures. It is the normative pressures that effect them when their vernacular is being acquired that are crucial. Of course, later circumstances can lead people to adapt their accents. We will be discussing linguistic accommodation in the next chapter. But from the point of view of the linguistic system itself, and from the point of view of that system changing, it is the continuum of vernaculars in time and social space that is significant. Self-conscious speech reflects the conflict and interaction of norms. We saw how hypercorrection transmits pressures from above to a younger generation, providing a model which is more 'standard' than parents' vernacular, and thus accelerating linguistic change.

One basic fact is that, as far as accent is concerned, children speak more like their peers than like their parents. There is controversy about the mechanism by which the vernacular accent is acquired. Labov (1972) distinguishes three stages. In stage one, ages two to three, the child has his first experience of language. At this stage the relevant social network is the child's immediate family. In stage two, ages four to thirteen, the basic vernacular accent is created. The most important normative pressure at this stage is the social network of peers. But hypercorrection shows us that parental speech interacts with this as a model. The accent an individual acquires at this stage depends on his network structure. Individuals on the periphery of clusters are subject to different, more diffuse and less focused norms, and accordingly deviate within their age group. In stage three, ages fourteen to seventeen, the evaluative norms of the wider community are acquired, and somewhat later, at age sixteen plus, the production of prestige forms begins. The networks operating at this stage are also very important for enforcing norms. In general, the structure is less tight-knit than the peer group. But we saw above how different network structures played a key role in the relative importance of vernacular and society-wide norms. These latter norms exert their greatest pressure during the working ages, and taper off again in favour of the vernacular over the age of fifty.

We have seen that if a linguistic change is taking place in the pronunciation of a variable, this is reflected in the average score by age. As each generation acquires its vernacular, the average score of that age group is further along the direction of the change than that of the immediately preceding generation. Each successive generation, having acquired the form later, will have gone further than the last; so, in general, younger speakers will be more advanced, and older speakers less advanced with respect to the change. This is observable as age-grading when age is plotted against average index scores. Normally, youngest speakers are most advanced in the change, although this is not always so.

Figure 6.10 shows such a pattern for Norwich (e). You will recall that this involved a vernacular innovation of centralizing the vowel sound in words like 'bell' and 'tell'. Higher scores signified a greater degree of centralization. Note the significant increases in the degree of centralization for speakers under thirty, but especially in the unconscious casual style, which most closely reveals the basic form of the vernacular. We will be looking at this kind of pattern in the next chapter when we study the problem of language change.

In this chapter we have seen how the frequency of a variant reflects the intersection of various social variables and the normative pressures associated with them. It was the norms, rather than density of communication by itself, that accounted for differentiation. An individual's speech was the outcome of these intersecting pressures which reflect the overall complexity of our social structure.

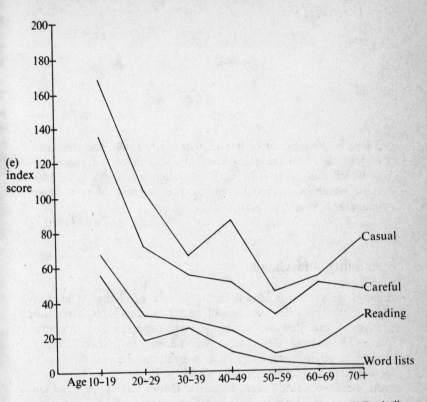

Figure 6.10 Norwich (e) by age and style (*from Chambers and Trudgill, 1980*)

7. Change, Meaning and Acts of Identity

> There is the element of habit, custom, tradition, the element of the past, and the element of innovation, of the moment, in which the future is being born. When you speak you fuse these elements in verbal creation, the outcome of your language and your personality.
>
> Firth (1950)

Variability and change

A language system is always in the process of change. The study of such change is the province of **Historical linguistics**, a separate branch of the study of language (see, for example, Aitchison, 1981). The role of this chapter will be, not to discuss language change in all its complexity, but to examine the role that social factors play in the process of change.

As we have already seen, linguistic theory has approached language in an idealized way. It has been characterized as governed by a homogeneous system of rules. The historical and social dimensions of language, including its use to make utterances in context, is not in general admitted as primary data for a linguistic theory, because the aim of that theory (as we saw with Chomsky) is to specify just those universal psychological principles that define what *any* natural language is. The regularities looked for are very abstract, and sets of sentences, with variability omitted, will do as the data for such an enterprise.

The idealization is a 'convenient fiction' of the sort used in any science. The fiction is that it is possible to make statements about 'a state of the language', as if time were frozen, and with all the heterogeneity and inherent variability smoothed out. But we have seen in the last few chapters the actual extent of the

variability within a language. Each linguistic variable is a statement that for some linguistic category, for example the front
vowel found in some class of words, there is a continuum of
alternative forms which appear. Individuals and groups have different frequencies, starting with categorical presence or absence,
of one alternative as opposed to the other.

As we saw in Chapter 4, a stage of variability is a necessary
condition for a linguistic change. In some cases, therefore, we
observe systematic heterogeneity because a change is taking
place. Recall the Bailey wave model. The distribution of the variants was systematic in terms of the purely linguistic environments through which a change was moving. Linguistic environments could be ranked according to how they favoured one form
over the other. The distribution of the variants was also systematic in terms of lects. In different peoples' grammars the change
had reached different stages depending on their remoteness from
its point of origin. So the systematic nature of linguistic heterogeneity reflects different points in the direction of linguistic
change.

Linguistic change can be viewed as change in the rule system
of a language. For example, rules can be added to or lost from
a language. They can be reordered or simplified. An innovation,
a new specific change, may appear and then propagate until it
entirely replaces the earlier rule. While this process is occurring,
the rule is likely to be variable because, within both the individual and the group, older and newer forms co-exist. In order
to fully explain why such dynamic processes take place within a
language, one must consider both *internal* and *external* factors.
Internally, the rules of language are interdependent. A change in
one rule will always have complicated effects upon other rules.
Innovations may appear and be driven, not by pressures from
outside language, but by interaction with another change in
some related rule, rather like a chain reaction. Such processes
are psychological. Psychological pressure, whether it be pressure
towards simplifying the overall system, or producing symmetry
or equilibrium within it, or in order to facilitate production and
comprehension, can cause change. The process by which language is acquired by each generation in turn also causes change
to occur in a systematic way. So explanations of some language
change can be found internally to language itself.

It is such internal factors that account for why linguistic environments can be ranked in the order in which they favour one
variant over another in the wave model. For example, an item is

always produced or perceived in the context of neighbouring items. Some neighbouring items favour one variant more than another for purely psychological or physiological reasons. One variant may make some distinction easier or harder to perceive, for example, or may collapse one set of words into another. It is ramifications of this sort that cause one change in the language system to produce other changes. For example, a later change may restore a distinction that was lost; and in this sense be caused by another earlier change.

But these internal factors only offer a partial explanation of the systematic fluctuation between forms. (There is always some 'noise' or non-systematic random fluctuation as well.) Internal factors always interact with external causes of change. These are social and situational factors. Variation is only fully systematic when viewed in relation to social context. We have seen the correlations between sociolinguistic variables and a number of intersecting social factors: class, age, sex, social network characteristics, ethnicity and spatial distribution. One reason why groups which are established on these bases may differ in their index scores for a variable is that they may each stand in a different relationship to the linguistic change that the variable is undergoing. Our aim now is to try to make more explicit how the mechanism of change works, and how social groups and their values figure in it.

With the advent of quantitative techniques it became feasible to study linguistic change in the context of the community, as it was happening (Labov, 1963; Weinreich, Labov and Herzog, 1968; Labov 1972: ch. 7 and 9). The classic study of linguistic change in progress is Labov's research on the island of Martha's Vineyard, Massachusetts, three miles off the southern coast of Cape Cod. We came across this area earlier, as a 'relic area' or 'speech island' which still preserved constriction over and against the *r*-lessness of eastern New England (see Figure 5.5). Martha's Vineyard will provide our main example of the mechanism of change, because of its clarity and relative simplicity.

The task of studying linguistic change in progress may be broken down into three separate problems:

The transition problem. What is the route by which a linguistic state of affairs has evolved from an earlier state of affairs? Can this route be traced?

The embedding problem. Can the social and linguistic conditions in which this change has been embedded be found? The variable which is changing is correlated with dimensions of social context. It is also correlated with factors internal to the linguistic system – the linguistic setting in which it is embedded.

The evaluation problem. What subjective factors in the population correlate with the observed change in the variable? What do the forms involved 'mean' to the speakers and how does this relate to the process of change?

Answers to these specific questions in any one community will point the way to more general answers to the question of how changes originate and spread, and the specific role of social factors, including subjective attitudes, to this process.

Real and apparent time

The distinction between **real** and **apparent time** provides a solution to the temporal transition problem. Any change entails at

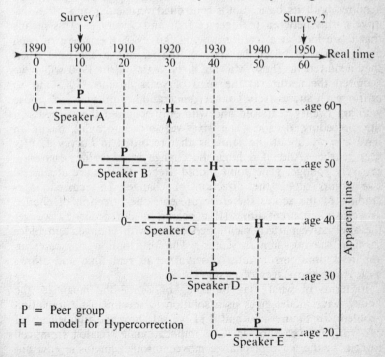

Figure 7.1 Real and apparent time in language change

least one difference in what is the same thing (a linguistic variable) at, at least, two successive points in real time. Real time is calendar time. Imagine that a linguistic change has been occurring in the period between 1890 and 1950. The solid arrow in Figure 7.1 represents the sixty years in real time between the two dates. If we are examining some feature which we think has changed in this time, one avenue open to us is to consult a study conducted earlier in real time, say 1900, if one exists. If the feature differs between the two surveys, then we can conclude that a change has occurred in the interim.

But we can also observe the change in another way. Earlier on, I remarked that a linguistic change in progress would be reflected in the age-grading of index scores. (Although the normal pattern for the age-grading of a linguistic change in progress is a correlation between chronological age and index score, with the youngest speakers being most advanced as regards the change, there are exceptions to this pattern.) How this happens is made explicit in Figure 7.1. Each generation acquires both its basic motor-controlled vernacular and its evaluative norms between the ages of four and seventeen. This means that if we look at a feature now, at Survey 2, the accent of each age group will reflect the state of the feature at the time when they acquired it. Those who are sixty years old in 1950 will have acquired the feature in the span of years around 1900, and so on for each successively younger generation, until we reach those who are twenty years old and who only acquired their accents in the preceding decade. The sixty-year-old informant ought to have a score about the same as that recorded in Survey 1, fifty years earlier. And, if a linguistic change is occurring, each successively younger generation should 'freeze' the feature at successive points along the direction of change. The current age-grading of the scores therefore presents the direction of change 'frozen' in apparent time. (If a change is not occurring we get the alternative pattern mentioned earlier with younger and older speakers having similar scores.) The distribution of scores in apparent time corroborates observation in real time and allows us to trace the stages of change.

In terms of what may be going on *inside* the language, the Bailey wave model gives us a solution to the linguistic transition problem. In Figure 4.10 and 4.11 we saw how the frequencies of one variant over another were implicationally related from cell to cell, as the wave of change moved through linguistic environments and lects. So our progressively younger speakers in Figure

7.1 will, in each generation, have more cells in which the change has gone to completion, or has high frequency. This will produce higher scores in younger speakers.

To say that a linguistic change is taking place is to say that the movement to categoricality is increasing as time goes on. Why should frequencies increase as the speakers in Figure 7.1 get younger? After all, are not the older speakers nearer to the beginning of change; thus, according to Figures 4.10 and 4.11, should they not have gone further towards its completion and have higher scores?

The answer to this question has to be in terms of the *relative* stability of the motor-controlled vernacular of most individuals throughout their lifetime. The speech of an individual can change stylistically, but that is when the underlying vernacular is consciously overridden. There are regular age-effects, which we have seen before, caused by the varying normative pressures of different ages. There also can be a certain amount of adaptive change to new norms in the course of a lifetime. But these patterns are not sufficient to speed up the change in an individual's vernacular to the extent that it becomes anything like the change that occurs between generations. So for long-term changes in the vernacular, the change is visible in apparent time, as age-grading.

The question then is, why should younger speakers acquire a variable feature with a higher frequency, and in more linguistic environments, than the variable has in the speech of those older speakers from whom they acquired it? We can refer back for two possible answers. The first is hypercorrection. The **H**s in Figure 7.1 show us the locus of hypercorrect models in the older generation's more formal styles. These can be internalized as casual norms by younger speakers. The second is the normative pressure of the peer group; the principal factor in the acquisition of accent. The peer group (**P** in Figure 7.1) enforces the innovative form with frequencies higher than that of the older speakers who provide the model, as a distinguishing feature of its own identity.

Speakers A to E in Figure 7.1 are the *same group* of people persisting in time. The change is moving through this group. Other groups will participate in the change, beginning at later times.

Centralization on Martha's Vineyard

Labov studied the centralization of (aw) in Martha's Vineyard.
This sound is a diphthong. That is, it involves a gliding change
from one vowel position to another.

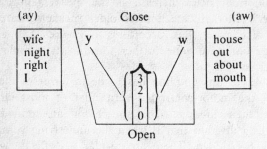

In the case of (aw), the glide is towards the upper back part of
the mouth, in words like '*house*', '*out*' and '*mouth*'. However, the
first part of the diphthong was variable. It could be very 'open',
represented as 0 in the diagram, or very centralized, represented
as 3 in the diagram. (Centralization means that the first part of
the diphthong, the a, becomes somewhat like the schwa at the
end of *sofa*.) The variable (aw) represented the degree of centralization in the first part of the diphthong, with 3.00 marking
completely centralized, and 0.00 marking a completely open pronunciation. There was another parallel variable (ay) in which the
first part of the diphthong in words like '*wife*' and '*night*' also
varied between centralized and open. In this case the glide was
towards the upper front of the mouth. So we find (aw)
embedded in a system of upgliding diphthongs. The long-term
process within the English language since the sixteenth and seventeenth centuries has been towards the lowering of both of
these sounds. In the mainland USA, both sounds are in general
pronounced in the lowered form. However, on Martha's Vineyard it appears that this historic pattern has been reversed.
Labov found increasing centralization of both sounds.

Figure 7.2 presents the index scores by age group in both real
and apparent time. The top row shows the results of the 1933
Linguistic Atlas of New England survey. At this date the (aw)
variable showed virtually no centralization. The (ay) variable
showed moderate centralization. Historically, this might be

expected. The 'lowering' process had already occurred. In the case of (aw) it was complete. With regard to (ay) Martha's Vineyard was a relic area, preserving the older form, just as with rhoticity.

Now look at the 1961 distribution of index scores in apparent

Real time 1933–61

		(aw)	(ay)
1933	Linguistic Atlas of New England	0.06	moderate
1961	Average scores for age levels		
	75+	0.22	0.25
	61-75	0.37	0.35
	46-60	0.44	0.62
	31-45	0.88	0.81

Apparent time 1961

1961	Speakers in a critical subgroup		(aw)
	Mr H.H., Sr	aged 92	0.10
	Mrs S.H.	aged 87	0.20
	Mr E.M.	aged 83	0.52
	Mr H.H., Jr	aged 60	1.18
	Mr D.P.	aged 57	1.11
	Mr P.N.	aged 52	1.31
	Mr E.P.	aged 31	2.11

Figure 7.2 Increase of centralization of (aw) in real and apparent time, Martha's Vineyard (*after Labov, 1963, 1972*)

time. It is most striking how the average scores for both (aw) and (ay) increase regularly at each successive age level. This regular increase in centralization is even more striking when the individual scores of a critical subgroup, a social network of descendents of original settlers is examined. This provides clear evidence of transition in the direction of increasing centralization. Note also that although (ay) begins with more centralization, and although this process continues, (aw) passes (ay) in degree of centralization for younger speakers. Transition from 'lowered' to 'centralized' can thus be clearly traced.

Embedding and evaluation

How is this process of centralization embedded in both the linguistic and social structure of the community? I have attempted to schematize the main points of Labov's solutions to the embedding and evaluation problems in Figure 7.3. The island's permanent population consists of three main ethnic groups: the Yankees, descendents of the original settlers; the Indians, the remnant of the island's aboriginal inhabitants who are few in number and concentrated on Gay Head, a remote headland; and the Portuguese who are the most recent incomers, having only been established on the island for a few generations. Geographically, Martha's Vineyard can be divided into Up-Island, which is rural and of which Gay Head forms the tip, and Down-Island, where the main towns are located.

The general embedding pattern for the change can be seen in Figure 7.3. The innovation began Up-Island among the Chilmark fishermen, rural Yankee descendents of the original settlers. This group had the highest centralization scores. The initial change began in (ay) which had retained some centralization over and against the historic lowering of the sound on the mainland. From the Chilmark fishermen centralization of (ay) spread to the rest of the Yankee community.

This change in (ay) affected the symmetrical upgliding (aw). Here the purely internal linguistic embedding had an effect. The (aw) variable also began to increase in centralization, following along slighly behind the (ay).

From the Yankee community, the change spread to the adjacent Indian group. After the lapse of a generation, diffusion continued to the Portuguese. These latter two ethnic groups hypercorrect in the case of (aw), and the centralization of that variable is greater than that of (ay). Portuguese and Indian informants had higher index scores for (aw) than for (ay), although this was not true of the Yankee group.

The task now is to elucidate this pattern in terms of the social and evaluative context. Because of economic change, the traditional way of life and social fabric of Martha's Vineyard was under considerable strain. The original economy of the island, based on whaling, commercial fishing and agriculture, had

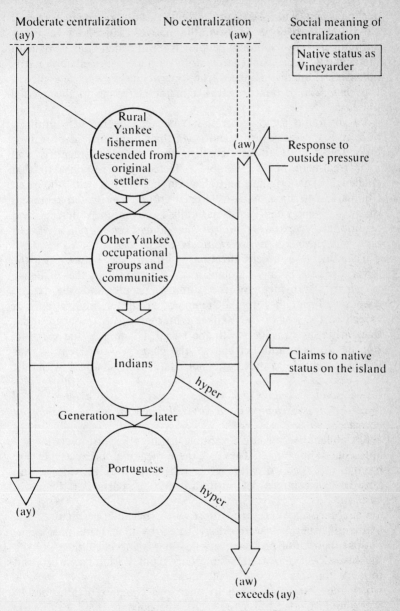

Figure 7.3 Interaction of social and linguistic factors in centralization of (aw) and (ay), Martha's Vineyard

declined and had been largely replaced by a service economy based on tourism. In season, the native islanders were vastly outnumbered by 'summer people' from the mainland. Much of the island was being alienated from its permanent inhabitants by outsiders. For the Yankee group particularly, who felt that it was *their* island, this provided a major challenge to their social identity.

Labov found a close correlation between degree of centralization and a positive attitude to Martha's Vineyard. Each ethnic group on the island was challenged in terms of identity, and their treatment of the variable reflected their response to that challenge. The original centralization had begun with the rural Chilmark fishermen. As a 'reference group' they would represent island **indigenousness** most naturally – given their descent and traditional occupation. *Through their usage, centralization encodes the social meaning, 'native status as an islander'.*

Their increase in centralization, contrasting as it does with the lower variants of the mainland, was a response to the challenge to identity provided by the summer people and the tourist economy. From the original 'reference group', centralization had spread to the rest of the Yankee ethnic group to the degree that their attitudes coincided with the social meaning of the variable. For the Indians and Portuguese, the claim was different; it was to be accepted as having equal status as islanders with the Yankees.

The point of central importance here is that the external social force driving the change is mediated through the social meaning of centralization.

Social factors can effect variable features because certain variants encode meanings. They get these meanings because they are originally associated with some subgroup who provide a link between a complex of attitudes and a particular linguistic variant.

On Martha's Vineyard, those who began the change, the Chilmark fishermen, were differentiated by their traditional occupation, their rural provenance, and their Yankee ethnicity. Given the historical context, this subgroup typifies island identity and thus, within the context of language heterogeneity, variants which they use can potentially encode a complex of attitudes to the island. Under pressure, such subgroups respond below the level of conscious awareness by developing such a variant more fully in the direction which encodes the social meaning. The form spreads to the rest of the group, and successive generations further the change.

It is the social meaning of the form, its encoding of attitudes, that diffuses the change to other groups within the community. The form is employed symbolically by other groups, each in response to its own social circumstances. It is at this point that variants spread or not, depending on whether the social meaning invokes a positive or negative response in other groups.

The role of internal factors must also be taken into account. Given structural pressures inside the language, some changes take place solely due to the effect of other prior changes. In other words, not all variation in itself is socially significant. On Martha's Vineyard, the centralization of (aw) was, in the first place, a response to the centralization of (ay).

Other groups who adopt the change later can respond *both* to the original change and to other variables which have begun changing due to structural pressure. The social meaning is now encoded by these latter variables as well as by the original change. In Martha's Vineyard, the concomitant variable (aw) has been driven even further along in the direction of the change than (ay). Labov calls this process the **recycling** of the change by successive groups. It is this which accounts for very high scores for (aw) among the Indians and Portuguese on Martha's Vineyard.

Subjective evaluation of the variables

The complex of attitudes which links society and linguistic forms can be explored independently. On Martha's Vineyard, Labov found a high correlation between centralization and attitudes towards the island. Islanders were divided into those who expressed positive, negative or neutral feelings about Martha's Vineyard (Labov, 1963: 306).

Persons		(ay)	(aw)
40	Positive	63	62
19	Neutral	32	42
6	Negative	09	08

Correlation between such attitudes and index scores is sharper than for any more objective social category. Labov found this very fine-grained indeed. Scores even correlated with the specific intentions and life histories of individuals.

One of those with the highest degree of centralization, for example, was the son of a Chilmark lobsterman. He was a university graduate who had returned to the island after having tried and rejected mainland life. Among high school students, too, Labov found a significant relationship between index scores and whether or not individuals intended to leave the island and seek educational and career opportunities elsewhere. The very significant and detailed relationship between centralization and orientation to Martha's Vineyard suggests that it is the social symbolism of this linguistic feature which best explains its change.

We shall return to the question of attitudes in a moment.

The stages of a sound change

Let us now step back and take a broader view of the stages of a linguistic change. Figure 7.4 represents some of the basic stages proposed by Labov (1972) and which we have observed on Martha's Vineyard. Some points about how changes begin need further clarification.

Basic heterogeneity

Heterogeneity is the normal state of a language. At any given point in time many features are variable. As we saw, a change from one form to another necessarily involves a phase in which there is a fluctuation between the two forms. But although variation is a necessary condition for change, it is not a sufficient condition. Much of the pervasive fluctuation in language is not diagnostic of a change in progress.

But the various types of 'inherent variability' in the language system are usually the result of earlier change, concomitant pressure as the result of a change elsewhere in the system, factors of production and perception, contact between languages or varieties, or the requirements of communication in context. What *may* change is selected from this pervasive fluctuation. Thus, in Martha's Vineyard the centralization of the diphthongs emerged

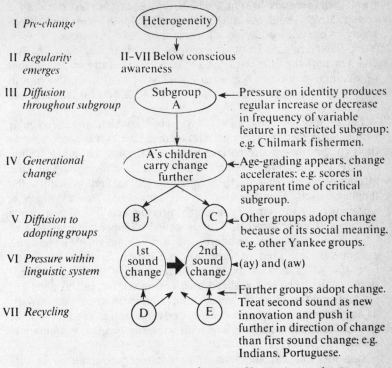

I   *Pre-change*

II *Regularity emerges*

III *Diffusion throughout subgroup*

IV *Generational change*

V   *Diffusion to adopting groups*

VI *Pressure within linguistic system*

VII *Recycling*

Heterogeneity

II–VII Below conscious awareness

Subgroup A ← Pressure on identity produces regular increase or decrease in frequency of variable feature in restricted subgroup: e.g. Chilmark fishermen.

A's children carry change further ← Age-grading appears, change accelerates: e.g. scores in apparent time of critical subgroup.

B   C ← Other groups adopt change because of its social meaning. e.g. other Yankee groups.

1st sound change → 2nd sound change ◄ (ay) and (aw)

D   E ← Further groups adopt change. Treat second sound as new innovation and push it further in direction of change than first sound change: e.g. Indians, Portuguese.

VIII *Pressure from above = Conscious evaluation v. Unconscious evaluation*

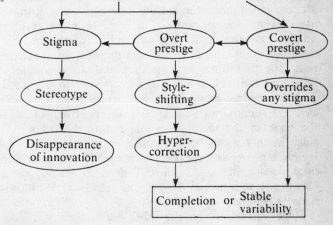

Stigma ← Overt prestige ↔ Covert prestige

Stereotype   Style-shifting   Overrides any stigma

Disappearance of innovation   Hyper-correction

Completion or Stable variability

Figure 7.4 The stages of a sound change

from their *previous* lowering which created a contrast between a conservative island variant, (ay), and a lower mainland diphthong. The reintroduction of *r* as a linguistic change in New York City emerged from its *previous* loss. In some cases, earlier changes and the effects they have on other sounds in the system of distinctive sounds seems to *rotate* vowels around the mouth over a long period of time (Labov, 1974: 225ff, for an example of this).

Let us look at some cases of variability which are the regular result of linguistic processes. Remember that a variable consists of two or more alternative ways of doing the *same* thing. 'Inherent' variability occurs when the conditioning of the alternants is at least partially attributable to factors within the language itself. For example, in any language a sound which is systematically the same is regularly pronounced in different ways in different environments. This is called **allophonic variation** and is a basic structural property of any language. We had an example of this kind of variation in Chapter 5, when we noted how the /r/ sound is made in different ways in different positions. In RP, /r/ was **realized** as a continuant in initial position, a fricative after *d* as in '*drink*', and a flap between two vowels, at least for some speakers. One finds the same kind of conditioned variation when dealing with meaning-bearing grammatical items.

Consider the category **plural**. This category is realized in different ways in different kinds of word. The following words have plurals which are pronounced differently: *dog-z*, *cat-s*, *horse-iz*, *men*, *sheep*, *children* and so on. Yet the same grammatical distinction is being made. This variability is 'inherent' because it is conditioned by the linguistic environment of the item in question. The first three variants of plural, for example, are conditioned by the way in which the last sound in the word to which it is attached is pronounced. Sounds are regularly **assimilated** to adjacent sounds in casual speech. Hence, the *n* of *in* is made on the back of the teeth in *in the*, but further back on the teeth ridge in *in heaven*; or *n* becomes *m* in *ten men* to give us *tem men* when we are speaking quickly. The simplification of the final consonant cluster in t/d deletion which we studied in Chapter 4 was favoured, you will recall, by a following consonant as opposed to a vowel.

Some variability, on the other hand, appears random. It has been argued that **phonetic drift** can account for sound change (Hockett, 1958). Drift is the product of scatter in the pronuncia-

A note on pervasive variability

Lexical

Most of the variation we have considered is at the phonological level of language. However, variation is also pervasive at other higher levels of language structure, for example, **lexically** and **syntactically**. On the lexical level, **synonyms** – words that mean the same thing – are variables. Often, such synonyms differ in formality, for example, *eat-dine* (see Geertz, 1960). Some are dialectical variants, for example, *lift-elevator*, *hood-bonnet*, and so on. Others stand in more complex relations to context, for example, technical terms (*urinate-pee-piss*) and *terms of address*. Consider the implications of addressing someone by either their title alone, title and last name, first name alone, last name alone, or multiple names (Brown and Ford, 1964; Brown and Gilman, 1960). The partial nature of synonymy is a function of the differing social meanings within a set of terms which are otherwise 'cognitively' synonymous.

Syntactic

Syntax is the level of language in which words are put together to make sentences. Variability is also pervasive at this level. Inherent variability is the case where the linguistic environment affects which of the alternative forms will appear, or appear with a certain frequency. We find inherent variability in the case of **contraction and deletion of the copula** and in the **rules of negation**, discussed earlier. Thus, contraction and deletion of the copula is most favoured when a noun phrase follows *be*, and least favoured when a verb in the '*-ing*' form or the 'future' verb *gonna* ('going to'), follows *be*. Both of these constructions also vary in terms of social group, and are therefore dialectical variants (see Labov, 1972a: ch. 3 and 4; Baugh, 1980).

Sentence relatedness

Perhaps the most pervasive and most significant variability in the linguistic system is termed **sentence relatedness**, or sometimes **stylistic variation**. This occurs when two or more stable grammatical structures can be used to 'say the same thing' – i.e., be true or false under the same conditions. Sentences and phrases which are related in this way are **conventional paraphrases** of each other. This phenomenon is a central property of syntactic structure and involves most constructions in standard English. Here are nine examples:

1 (Dative)	The vicar gave a book to the saint → The vicar gave the saint a book.
2 (Passive)	The vicar killed the shark → The shark was killed by the vicar.
3 (Extraposition)	That he killed the shark surprised us → It surprised us that he killed the shark.
4 (Dislocation) left	My mother was a saint → My mother, she was a saint.
right	My mother was a saint → She was a saint, my mother.
5 (Topicalization)	I like that sort of music → That sort of music I like.
6 (Adverb preposing)	The car started yesterday → Yesterday the car started.
7 (Though movement)	Though it's big, it's not dangerous → Big though it is, it's not dangerous.
8 (Cleft)	The vicar is clever → It's the vicar who is clever.
9 (Pseudo-cleft)	The vicar loves good food → What the vicar loves is good food.

Variables of this kind are difficult to study using quantitative methodology, primarily due to low frequencies of occurrence (Labov, 1972: 247; Romaine, 1982: 29f.; Sankoff, 1974). However, explanation of such variants' potential for use in contexts of speech is an important part of the study of the pervasive variability of language. Some syntactic structures also form implicational scales of the sort we saw in Chapter 4. This suggests that variation on this level also plays a part in linguistic change. We shall return to these matters in Chapter 11.

tion of a sound around a 'target' at which people are aiming. The 'targets' at which speakers aim in making a sound are internal models of the distribution of the sound. These are based on what they hear in the speech of others and their monitoring of their own speech. Such 'targets' drift because of the only approximate nature of the hits. These produce changes in a speaker's 'expectation distribution' through time. The drifting may not be in a determinate direction. Nevertheless, according to Hockett, it constitutes sound change.

Orderly differentiation

However, the type of pervasive fluctuation which we have looked at does *not* in itself constitute a change in the language. Rather, it provides the 'material' out of which a change can be unconsciously established, or **actuated**, by some *group* of speakers. For a change to have happened, it is not enough for an individual's speech to vary in a new way. Other speakers must interactively share the change in the variable in a consistent way. In other words, it must take on a regular change of frequency in a determinate direction within a group before we can actually speak of a 'change' occurring. The point is made in a classic article by Weinreich, Labov and Herzog (1968: 187):

> Linguistic change is not to be identified with random drift proceeding from inherent variation in speech. Linguistic change begins when the generalisation of a particular alternation in a given subgroup of the speech community assumes direction and takes on the character of orderly differentiation.

On this view, a change cannot really be usefully distinguished from its diffusion. It has diffused, has become a joint feature of those in some subgroup, by the time we can use the word 'change' to describe it at all – a process which, if not checked, would lead to the replacement of one variant by another in a variety of language. (Say we observed a change like this in the speech of only one individual: that would not be language change.)

To illustrate the relationship between fluctuations of the sort just described and change, reflect on the original loss of *r* as discussed in the note in Chapter 5. We saw reports of very early but environmentally restricted loss of *r*, before dental consonants, and particularly before *s* (e.g. '*horse*'). This looks like a case of assimilation. There were other specific environments in which *r* is or has been lost within otherwise fully rhotic accents. One was in unstressed syllables; another was a kind of **dissimilation** that occurred when there was more than one *r* in a word. Each of these are cases of regular phonological processes – they can be given a recognizable physical or psychological account.

We argued then that the observation of such variation in rhotic accents is not in itself evidence for a general loss of *r*. It could be that this variability might become the beginnings of a linguistic change. It has the 'potential' of a change because (in restricted circumstances) there is more than one way of doing the same thing. But if it *is* a pre-change state of the language, we could only know that retrospectively. It is a case of inherent variation which is not necessarily involved in change.

Similarly, the earlier change in English allophones of *r* in postvocalic position, which might have been from trill, to fricative, to continuant (the 'weakening' of r) would 'set the stage' for loss of *r*, but doesn't necessarily mean that *r*-dropping will follow.

A personal anecdote might be instructive here. Over the years it has been pointed out to me that I consistently spell the word '*surprise*' incorrectly, writing '*suprise*' instead. This mistake is so entrenched that I have had to look up the word more than once in the course of writing this book. Now, I speak with a fully rhotic accent, and don't misspell similar words like '*surmount*' or '*surpass*'. This misspelling reflects the fact that, although my speech is *r*-full, I variably drop the historic *r* in this class of words in rapid speech. If my attention was drawn to the word, however, I would 'correct' my pronunciation by inserting an *r*. This is a nice example of variable *r* in an unstressed syllable in otherwise *r*-full speech.

A contemporary example of *r*-loss in this one environment is also provided in Wolfram and Christian's (1976) study of Appalachian or 'mountain' speech in West Virginia. Unstressed syllables were the only environment in which significant *r*-loss was observed. The point here is that this kind of fluctuation is not a language change. It only becomes a language change when it becomes generalized to a group and direction emerges. When this has happened we observe a uniform statistical structure for the variable in that group, and a systematic change in the frequency of one variant over another in apparent time.

Why and where?

But why should change begin? Why should variability take on the character of an orderly differentiation in a group? The answer for Martha's Vineyard is quite clear: it is because of the social significance of the two ends of the articulatory scale. The relatively centralized end of the scale stands for 'native status as a Vineyarder'; the relatively open end of the scale, its opposite. As Labov (1980: 262) writes: "The functions of language reflected in these sound changes cannot be limited to the communication of referential information. We are clearly dealing with the emblematic function of phonetic differentiation: the identification of a particular way of speaking with the norms of a local community." The argument, then, is that the origin/ spread of change is due to the 'social meaning' attached to a variant within a subgroup – and the emergence of a new 'norm' of pronunciation, as part of the system of norms which constitute and identify that group, and govern its practices.

There is another 'why' question that follows! That is, why should a subgroup generate a new norm of pronunciation? (Presumably, at any given stage its current norms, the result of earlier changes, already have social significance for the group.) Martha's Vineyard again suggests where to look. Labov sugests (1972: 178) that the separate identity of the group is subject to internal or external pressure. More generally, we can say that social changes affecting a group lead it to change its norms and practices as a response to the pressures brought to bear on it. It is also likely that linguistic changes in *other* groups, or in other parts of the linguistic system, may change the 'value' of a feature governed by an older norm, and hence exert pressure for a normative change in order to preserve the possibility of conveying the same social meaning in a different way.

Before going into this any further, we should see if we can locate where in the social system language change is likely to originate: in which groups, for example. Which groups characteristically tend to lead in linguistic change?

In terms of the system of social stratification, the most recent evidence suggests that in systematic linguistic changes the highest and lowest social classes lag behind. The groups who innovate are those 'borderline' classes centrally placed in the hierarchy, the upper-working and lower-middle classes (Labov, 1980: 253f.). The reasons for this may differ for these two strata, as we saw before, but they are in a position in the hierarchy to be particularly susceptible to either focused internal normative pressure or pressure from above. Changes introduced by the highest classes always seem to be borrowed from outside the community, like *r* in New York (Labov, 1972). Labov tentatively goes on to identify more precisely those who lead in linguistic change. He writes (Labov, 1980: 261):

It appears that the speakers who are most advanced in the sound changes are those with the highest status in their local community.... But the communication networks provide additional information, discriminating among those with comparable status. The most advanced speakers are the persons with the largest number of local contacts within the neighbourhood, yet who have at the same time the highest proportion of their acquaintances outside the neighbourhood. Thus we have a portrait of individuals with the highest local prestige who are responsive to a somewhat broader form of prestige at the next larger level of social communication.

It is such individuals who lead in local, i.e. vernacular, change as opposed to changes in the direction of the standard originating in the upper-middle class.

It is striking that Labov's account at least partially converges with that of the Milroys. The individuals mentioned are clearly those with the most dense and multiplex social networks, who at the same time have contact with networks outside their own. This, for example, is suggestively similar to the pattern of the young Clonard women described in Chapter 6, who had introduced the (a) innovation into their community from the higher ranked Ballymaccarrett neighbourhood. It was argued there that highly focused norms are produced by close-knit social networks. Such focusing serves to maintain vernacular norms, over and against the standard. Social mobility, the break-up of such tightly knit networks, is likely to lead to linguistic change in the direction of the standard. It is members of the 'borderline' classes who are 'between norms' to the greatest extent – they experience the social meanings of competing norms.

Norms and change in norms

A language change involves a change in norms. We have used the words 'norm', 'normative pressure' etc. freely so far, but without trying to be precise about what we mean. We have said that the norms we are referring to are norms of pronunciation at which speakers aim in producing the variants of a variable feature; and an interpretation of the variants in terms of their social meaning. The norm is also what makes it possible to say that centralization encodes local identity. So, a norm has two sides.

We should explore this more fully. Within sociology, 'norm' is a crucial idea. In general, a norm is said to be a **rule**, or a **standard**, for an action. (The term comes from the Latin, *norma*, 'a carpenter's square', according to the Oxford Dictionary.) Williams (1968) writes, 'A norm ... is not a statistical average of actual behaviour but rather a cultural (shared) definition of desirable behaviour.' So when we are talking about a norm in relation to a sociolinguistic variable, we are not talking about the actual frequencies speakers produce, but rather the intersubjective group standard, or the rule, that guides or motivates the act of its production. Note that this rule, being intersubjective, coordinates the individuals who constitute the group. It may do so, definitively, if the rule in question guides a practice that defines the group. If the norm is effective, we will 'observe a marked regularity of social acts in recurrent situations of a particular kind' (Williams, 1968). The regularity of the frequencies we have observed in sociolinguistic variables are not now the object of our study, but rather the norms, rules or standard that led speakers to use such frequencies.

Why should an action need a standard to which people are expected to conform? In terms of 'desirability', it is usually said that norms are legitimated by *values* and *beliefs*. Behind every norm is a value. We have already seen one such value in Martha's Vineyard: that of local identity, and the beliefs intertwined with considering that of value.

But there is another reason why actions are governed by norms or standards. The norm in fact makes it possible to understand what act it is – to interpret the act as of a certain kind, and not of another kind. So, for example, centralization as opposed to non-centralization can be reliably interpreted as conveying that the speaker is positively oriented to Martha's Vineyard (everything else being equal). The norm, or rule, is what makes it possible to interpret the action as conveying what it does. It says, do *this* in this context, and anyone who knows the rule will find what you are doing intelligible; in this case, 'speaking with a certain accent' and therefore 'claiming a certain identity' in relation to the hearer. Without this norm, the frequencies would be uninterpretable in this way. Within the community where the rule is known, it creates intelligible action, and governs mutual expectation in interaction. Such norms or rules make *possible* a social life which is constituted by actions, because they *constitute* the very actions themselves (Parsons, 1951: 11; Searle, 1969; Winch, 1958).

We have now detached the observed frequencies with which a variant occurs from the norm which governs that pattern by making it convey something about the values of the community.

But there is no reason why the norm should specify actual frequency level as the action to be interpreted. The rule itself can be put in invariant terms (LePage, 1980). All that is required is that, in any given context, the speaker produce a high or low enough relative frequency so that his action can be interpreted one way or the other. The norm can simply be put thus: centralization will convey local identity, openness will not. That is, the norm may be categorical although the actual performance it governs is not. In a context, the frequencies required to convey the distinction will only approach the norm in a rough way, sufficient in that instance to convey the social meaning. This accounts for why accents or dialects are perceived or, at least, talked about categorically, although their linguistic nature is statistical. Conversely, of course, the 'more or less' nature of the variable means that frequencies can be adjusted to convey very 'fine-tuned' degrees of identity.

Given what we have said about norms, we can reconsider the notions of normative pressure, focusing, diffuseness etc. In LePage's view, we are motivated in our linguistic behaviour such that "we create our 'rules' so as to resemble as closely as possible those of the group or groups with which from time to time we wish to identify" (LePage, 1980: 15). LePage uses a cinematic metaphor. We *project* the model norms onto the social screen and bring these into *focus* with those of others.

Focusing will be easier in groups which have a strong sense of their own identity, a consensus in values and beliefs, and also in relation to the norms or rules which govern their practices. Conformity to these norms will be mutually expected within the group as definitive of membership. In each face-to-face interaction the same members will 'take for granted' in each other a knowledge of the norms which make what they say intelligible. Not to conform to the expectations would, in fact, convey to the others that one is, to that degree, not identifying with the group. So tight-knit territorial social networks enforce norms. Nonconformity matters because it is incorrigibly communicative.

In alternative types of group, it may be harder to identify models, or one may be faced with conflicting models. The rule itself may not be clear, in that there may be uncertainty as to what is being conveyed in a situation of use. If a group has a weak, or externally imposed, sense of identity, and less consensus in values and beliefs, it is more open to outside models as norms. Normative pressures would be more likely to derive from authority and status in institutional structures instead of arising out of interaction itself. Focusing in these cases is less easy. The models are the written language (spelling pronunciation), public speech (the media etc.), and notions of correctness explicitly articulated by high-status figures of authority, for example, by teachers. The norms enforced in these situations are also different; what I convey by 'taking them for granted' is authority and/or deference and other values of the wider society.

It follows from what we have said *that language change must necessarily involve normative change.* Milroy (1980: 187) notes that 'focusing – the formation of a recognizable set of linguistic norms – is in itself an aspect of linguistic change.' Consider now three sets of circumstances in which Williams (1968) suggests normative change is likely to occur:

A demand for norms is likely to arise from persons who find their interactions confusing or vaguely defined; for this reason, unstructured situations often create a pressure for the development of new norms. Enduring social conflicts, when not of too great an intensity, also generate new norms, developed out of negotiation, compromise, mediation . . . . Another major source of new norms lies in collective reaction to shared 'strain' experienced in relation to old norms.

We have seen language change emerging also under such conditions. Milroy (1980) postulates the break-up of social networks as a situation of change, and we have seen that social mobility is associated with hypercorrection. In Canada, we saw social conflict leading to new norms in the allocation of English and French; and, conversely, the importance of clarity of norms in terms of 'domain' for language maintenance. Finally, we saw the reaction to 'strain' in Martha's Vineyard. Labov (1980: 263) suggests that the entrance of new ethnic groups into a community also motivates diversification in language. This would be a situation of 'strain' to older norms, as each group, including the new entrants, redefines its identity and relative position within the larger society.

Attitudes to language: matched guises

In connection with Martha's Vineyard, we saw that it was possible to explore informants' attitudes to linguistic variables. In doing this we are trying to discover the content of the 'social meaning' of the contrasting variants. This is the same thing as finding out what their use conveys in context. Remember that it is by following the norm or rule in the use of the variant that the speaker conveys this meaning. So, in exploring the complex of attitudes to a variant, we are also exploring the norms which govern its use.

The most important research into the evaluation of speech has been done by social psychologists. Pioneering studies were conducted into language and inter-ethnic attitudes in Canada by Wallace Lambert and his associates at McGill University in Montreal. The methodology developed by Lambert (1967) has been applied to the study of attitudes to language in the USA, Britain and elsewhere. For surveys of social psychological research into language, see Ryan and Giles (1982), Giles (1977), and Fraser and Scherer (1982).

The central research method evolved by Lambert is the **matched-guise** technique. The problem is to elicit from informants only their reactions to the form of speech, for example to a particular accent, not to the content or to any of the expressive features of speech that mark individuals or vary with situations. What we are after is not 'what people say', but merely reactions to 'how they say it' with regard to certain features of the language they use.

The matched-guise technique employs a single speaker but in two or more 'guises'. This speaker produces the same utterances, first in the 'guise' of one language or accent, and then in the 'guise' of another. The subjects, who are unaware that the different forms are produced by a single speaker, respond not to any individual feature of the speaker's voice, or the text, which remain constant, but only to the language or accent he is employing. Using this technique, responses solely to code can be studied.

Empirical studies have produced three kinds of findings. First, it has been found that accents vary in terms of perceived status. Secondly, and even more interestingly, the accent or language used signals a **stereotype** of a certain kind of personality. And thirdly, *speakers' attitudes to language are more regular and uniform than the actual usage within the community.*

We can illustrate the first point by some British findings. When we investigated the pattern of variation for British variables earlier, it was clear that style-shifting, when it occurred, was always in the direction of the prestige norm of Received Pronunciation, or RP. In the more formal styles, when speakers came under greater 'pressure from above', because they were more self-conscious about their speech, the frequencies moved towards the RP norm. This was true even when the direction of change was towards the non-standard. Clearly, this pressure reflects a speaker's perception of the relative status of accents, and this can provide pressures which affect change.

Howard Giles (1970, 1971) found that accents in Britain could be arranged in a continuum of relative prestige. For example, thirteen accents were presented to 177 South Welsh and Somerset schoolchildren using the matched-guise technique. The informants rated the thirteen 'guises' both in terms of the prestige of the speaker and aesthetically, in terms of the pleasantness of the voice. The children were of two age groups: twelve and seventeen years old. They were unaware that they were listening to a single speaker.

The prestige of RP was confirmed. The rating of accents, in general, placed RP first on the continuum of prestige. Birmingham, Cockney and Indian accented English came at the bottom of the scale, with the first having least prestige. In the middle were foreign-accented English (North American, French and German) then the various 'national' accents within the British Isles (South Welsh, Irish) and last, various English regional accents (Northern, Somerset). The least prestige attached to the speech of the industrial towns.

There were important age differences. The younger informants, at twelve years of age, did not on the whole conform as closely to the above pattern as did the seventeen-year-olds. The younger speakers exhibited more **accent loyalty** to their own South Welsh and Somerset varieties. Unlike the seventeen-year-olds, the younger speakers 'unrealistically' attributed high prestige and pleasantness to 'accent identical to their own'. Both age groups in both areas exhibited some loyalty to speech 'like their own' but they still ranked the named local accent inferior to RP. There was evidence too that male and working-class informants had more accent loyalty than female and middle-class ones. This latter result is presumably the attitudinal correlate of the linguistic patterns with regard to class and sex which we discussed earlier.

Subjective evaluation in New York

Labov (1966) adopted similar techniques in order to study attitudes, not to whole accents or languages, but to individual variables in New York City. The voices of speakers were arranged on a tape recording so that they would be heard reading sentences of a text in three ways: one in which there was no occurrence of the (r) variable at all; one in which *r* was used consistently; and one in which *r* was used inconsistently. This provided both *r*-less and *r*-full 'guises' for the same speaker.

A scale of occupations was presented to informants. The occupations were ranked in order of prestige: television personality, executive secretary, receptionist, switchboard operator, salesgirl, factory worker, and 'none of these'. They were asked to imagine themselves a personnel manager and to rate voices on the tape according to suitability for jobs on the scale.

Using the differences between the judgements the informants made about the job suitability of the *same* speaker in the three 'guises', Labov calculated the percentages of (r)-positive and (r)-negative responses. Positive responses were those in which rhoticity signalled suitability for a higher ranking job. When (r)-positive responses were plotted against age, as in Figure 7.5, the results showed the remarkable uniformity mentioned earlier. For speakers aged between eighteen and thirty-nine (r)-positive

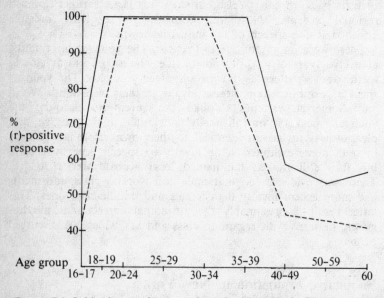

Figure 7.5 Subjective evaluation of (r) in New York City by age group

responses equalled 100 per cent for all social classes. This is more uniform than the actual index scores. That is, there is far more social agreement in evaluation of the variable within the community than there is in members' actual performance. Recall that in casual style, no class achieved an average *r*-score of more than 20 per cent. This uniformity is in all likelihood because by studying the evaluation of speech, rather than its production, we have gained access to the norms which govern the social meanings of the variants. The norm appears to be uniform in the community.

Note also the age distribution of a positive orientation to *r*. Sensitivity to the feature begins at the period when the wider norms of the society are internalized and corroborates Giles's findings. It then drops off abruptly at around age forty, which is evidence that this (r)-positive norm is a fairly recent introduction. As we saw in Chapter 5, there is a similar age stratification in actual index scores.

The uniformity of attitudes to (r) reflects the pressure exerted overtly by its social meaning: the fact that it encodes high status within the community. Such norms, because they reflect the uniform knowledge of what it 'means' to speak in a certain way, reflect the **communicative competence** a member must have in order to interpret the social significance of speech. An outsider, faced with the variation in *r* in New York City, would not know what it means. For this reason, and because of their uniformity, norms provide a better definition of a 'speech community' than does actual performance.

The above investigation revealed the subjective dimension of the overt prestige of a variant. We saw earlier, however, evidence for the existence of 'covert' prestige, the sort of social meanings attached to non-standard or overtly stigmatized forms. This is harder to study directly than overt prestige, since by definition people do not usually reveal positive orientations towards non-standard forms when questioned about their attitudes. The evidence for its existence tends to be indirect. However, Labov (1972) also sought to explore covert prestige in his subjective evaluation test. The 'job suitability' question clearly gives access to overt norms. But Labov also asked: "If the speaker was in a street fight, how likely would he be to come out on top?" and "If you knew the speaker for a long time, how likely would he be to become a good friend of yours?" The 'fight' question produced the opposite response to the 'job' question. Speakers of non-standard and stigmatized variants are 'tougher' than speakers of prestige variants. Answers to the 'friend' question were extremely interesting, and provide some direct evidence of the solidarity function of the vernacular. Informants of the lower working class produced the same scores for 'friendship' as for 'toughness'. Those who would be most likely to win in a street fight would also be most likely to become friends with informants from the lowest strata. Conversely, for the upper-working and middle-class informants, the parellelism was between 'friendship' and 'job suitability'. The confirmation of both covert and overt attitudes to variables reflects the two types of social structure we discussed in Chapter 6: overt prestige being a function of the impersonal, stratified dimension, and covert prestige that of the network or community structure. It is significant that the same linguistic form can convey meanings which refer to *both* kinds of structure. Thus, in one context, a use of non-standard forms could convey group identification. In another context, the same forms might convey low status in terms of social stratification.

Social stereotypes

These results also suggest that attitudes to language involve more than merely the attribution of relative perceived status. Listeners also typically make judgements about the speaker's personality from the way he speaks. The research by social psychologists has shown that linguistic forms, whether accents or whole languages, seem systematically to elicit perceptions of the personality of the speaker as a representative of his type. These take the form of stereotypes of a 'typical' member of a group. Investigations of such group evaluations coded in speech usually employ the matched-guise technique. Listeners are asked to evaluate a speaker in various 'guises' using adjectives which express personality judgements. For example, Lambert's (1967) judges were asked to evaluate 'guises' with respect to the following traits:

Competence	*Personal integrity*	*Social attractiveness*
intelligence	dependability	sociability
ambition	sincerity	likeability
self-confidence	character	entertainingness
leadership	conscientiousness	sense of humour
courage	kindness	affectionateness

(Other categories used are religiousness, good looks and height.)

Simplifying the often subtle results of this research, it seems to be the case in general that guises involving prestige forms, such as RP, elicit high ratings in terms of competence. Vernacular forms, by contrast, are more favourably regarded in terms of personal integrity and social attractiveness. These contrasting evaluations, the features of personality emphasized in the stereotype, seem to reflect the two social relationships of **power** and **solidarity**, just as did the 'job-friend-fight' continuum in Labov's investigation. Informants seem willing to grant status-related attributes, such as leadership, intelligence and ambition, to stereotypes of personality elicited by superordinate linguistic guises. This leads to unfavourable attitudes with respect to 'own group'. But solidarity-related attributes – kindness, sincerity, and so on – are part of the perceived personality encoded in vernacular speech. What is important for our purposes, however, is that 'social meanings' related to variability in a speech community are complex, involving stereotypes and a number of alternative norms of interpretation, each of which puts pressure of a different kind upon a speaker in terms of the meaning of 'what he does'.

Power and solidarity

We have said that the subjective evaluation of variants is patterned in terms of two dimensions. We will explore this further.

Giles and Ryan (1982) argue that informants' evaluation of speech varies according to the **situation** in which it is used. And it varies in a principled way. In Figure 7.6 situation types are classified according to two dimensions: first, the degree to which they are status-stressing or solidarity-stressing; and secondly, the degree to which they are group-centred or person-centred. Prototype situations for the combinations of types from each axis are given. Linguistic variations tend to elicit the evaluations listed under 'Rating dimensions' if the situation is of the type defined by the two dimensions which form the sides of that quarter of the diagram. For example, in a situation which is both status-stressing and person-centred, the relevant evaluations would be in terms of the competence, expertise etc. conveyed by the speaker's accent, or variety. On the other hand, in a situation which is solidarity-stressing and group-centred, the evaluations of

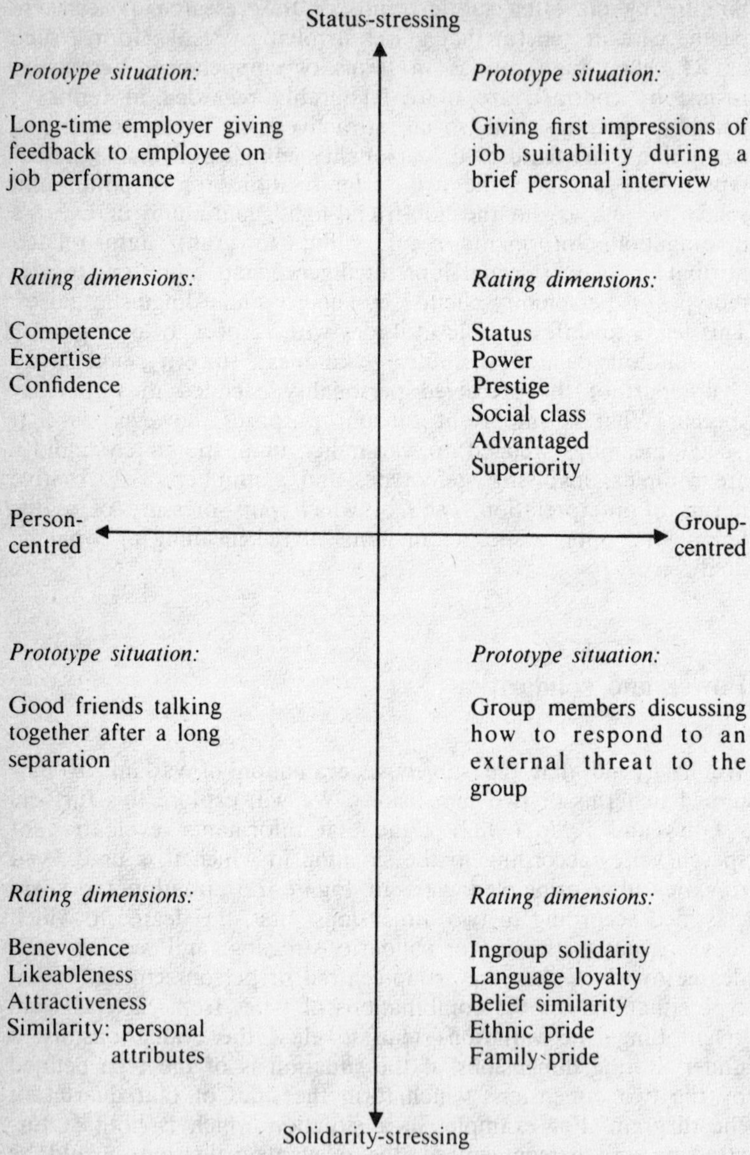

Status-stressing

Prototype situation:

Long-time employer giving
feedback to employee on
job performance

Prototype situation:

Giving first impressions of
job suitability during a
brief personal interview

Rating dimensions:

Competence
Expertise
Confidence

Rating dimensions:

Status
Power
Prestige
Social class
Advantaged
Superiority

Person-   Group-
centred ←————————————————————————————————————→ centred

Prototype situation:

Good friends talking
together after a long
separation

Prototype situation:

Group members discussing
how to respond to an
external threat to the
group

Rating dimensions:

Benevolence
Likeableness
Attractiveness
Similarity: personal
           attributes

Rating dimensions:

Ingroup solidarity
Language loyalty
Belief similarity
Ethnic pride
Family pride

Solidarity-stressing

Figure 7.6 Perceived language attitude situations and evaluative ratings vary along two dimensions (*from Giles and Ryan, 1982*)

the speaker would be in terms of their perceived ingroup solidarity, belief similarity (to the hearer) and group pride etc. These evaluations are everyday inferences, in terms of stereotypes, which we make from the 'social meanings' conveyed by how people speak.

We can exemplify how these dimensions might work. Say that we have a sociolinguistic variable (a), with two variants. One variant is in the direction of the standard, S, and the other in the direction of the vernacular, V. S has overt prestige, and V has covert prestige.

We would predict that in a status-stressing and group-centred situation – for example, in giving a first impression of job suitability during a brief personal interview – the use of S would elicit positive responses on evaluative dimensions such as prestige, social superiority, status etc., and the use of V would elicit negative responses on these dimensions. This is the sort of thing Labov (1966) found in measuring subjective reactions to *r* in terms of 'job suitability'. By contrast, if the situation were solidarity-stressing and group-centred, the *use of the same forms* would produce positive ratings for V in terms of solidarity, loyalty, pride etc., and negative ratings for S on these evaluative dimensions.

There are some very important points to consider here. The obvious one is the way in which people respond to a variant. *What it conveys depends on the situation of use.* It conveys a part of the stereotypical picture of a social group. The second point is that these responses follow from the social meaning of the variants of the variable. The argument goes like this. Because of the norm in the community, the variant at one end of the scale conveys *identity with* one social group and the set of social values that are believed to typify that group. Conversely, because of the norm in the community, the variant at the other end of the scale conveys *identity with* another social group and the set of social values that it typifies. The norm or rule is the shared knowledge that these connections obtain in the community and that therefore the use of one form or the other in varying degrees will convey these identifications. We have a complex of attitudes to these different *groups* within the society, and the values they represent. If linguistic forms convey *identity with* such groups, it follows that they will also elicit, depending on the situation, aspects of our stereotypical attitudes to these groups. For example, to hear someone use a form like our own in a solidarity-stressing and person-centred situation will make us perceive him as positively benevolent, likeable and attractive, and similar to us in personal attributes. The stereotypes reveal attitudes to groups, which become attitudes to language, because of the normative connection between variants and group identity. The norm says that the variant 'stands for' the group.

The third point is that in the types of society we have been discussing, these identifications tend to be interpreted in terms of the two basic dimensions of power and solidarity. Presumably this is because the relationship we enact normally place participants in two ways: whether they are members of the same group or not, and all that that entails for their relationship; and whether they are of equal status or not and all that that entails. Much politeness phenomenon is involved in negotiating these relationships using language (Brown and Levinson, 1978; Lakoff, 1972; Brown and Ford, 1961; Brown and Gilman, 1960). But why should relationships be placed on *these* two dimensions? An answer could be that these are the fundamental dimensions in which our society is structured and which we have seen all along: institutionalized and therefore impersonal hierarchy, and social network or community. In relational terms, power and solidarity. Other types of society could be organized in different ways.

The fourth point is that, to the degree that he can adjust the frequency of one form over the other, the individual can place himself in relation to these meanings, according to the situation. We saw this in the phenomenon of style-shifting. The sociolinguistic interview, and especially when informants were asked to read within it, is probably best viewed as a status-stressing and person-centred situation. In such cases, increases in the frequency of the prestige variant regularly occur. In terms of Figure 7.6, these will convey the degree of the speaker's identification with superordinate groups in the society and their values, and lead to a positive evaluation of the speaker's social competence, expertise and confidence. That is what the speaker is attempting to convey.

The individual and variation

The individual speaker lives in a multi-dimensional set of relationships to the various groups within his society, including his own group, his own social network. From this, it is clear that the individual speaks subject to a multiplicity of conflicting pressures derived from the social symbolism of the variants. His **idiolect** not only reflects his unique position in relation to the purely structural heterogeneity of a language system which is changing, but also his particular relationship to the normative pressure exerted by the various groups in the society. The speaker is 'between norms'. From his social network comes pressure deriving from solidarity. His actions will be interpretable in the light of this norm, as expressive of his solidarity with his own group. From other groups come other norms, including those made legitimate by the institutions of the society at large and deriving from status. His actions will also be interpretable in the light of these norms – for example, the social status he claims according to his use of a variable.

Lames

There is strong evidence that an individual's unique index score reflects his own particular personal relationship to these norms. We saw on Martha's Vineyard how fine-tuned were index scores to personal attitude and biography. Milroy (1980: 131f) found also that individual linguistic variability strongly correlated with degree of integration into local social networks. For example, of two individuals, Hannah McK. and Paula C., the latter approximated more closely to the vernacular. This was not explicable in terms of any objective social attribute, but in terms of Hannah's isolation, relative to Paula, within the community. Similarly, Labov (1972: 255f) noted that individuals on the periphery of the adolescent peer groups in Harlem, called **lames** in the vernacular, differed significantly in speech from core members of the gang. In the case of lames, weakened pressure from the peer group could in fact open the way to a more positive orientation towards the institutional norms of the wider society. This is similar to the relationship established by Milroy between group cohesion, measured by network density and multiplexity, and adhesion to the vernacular norm and its symbolism of solidarity. Disruption of networks, or the less dense and more uniplex networks characteristic of middle class life, could lead to the opposite effect.

Accommodation theory

Social psychologists have recently been developing a paradigm of research based on the notion that speakers modify their speech in interactions with respect to listeners, by becoming more like the listener or less like the listener. In other words, people's speech can come together, or **converge** in interactions, or alternatively, their speech may **diverge**. The aim of **accommodation theory** is to understand the processes underlying these phenomenon.

We have not time here to survey the literature in this field (Giles, 1980; Thakerar, Giles and Cheshire, 1982). In general, linguistic convergence is normally taken to reflect a group's perhaps unconscious wish for mutual identification. That is, it is expressive of a wish for approval and solidarity. On the other hand, linguistic divergence (or the maintenance of a speaker's own speech pattern) will occur when speakers, "either (a) define the encounter in intergroup terms and desire positive ingroup identity, or (b) wish to dissociate personally from another interindividual encounter (both identity-maintenance functions)" (Thakerar, Giles and Cheshire, 1982: 248).

In other words, two of the principal factors behind accommodation involve identity – either its maintenance as *distinct* from that of the recipient, or a wish to be seen as *similar* to the recipient and hence win social approval. It has been shown, for example, that convergence produces positive reactions in hearers. The situation is made very complex, however, because psychological convergence and divergence (what people subjectively believe they are doing) is not in a simple relationship to objective linguistic convergence and divergence. People may converge towards what they 'believe' to be the norms of another's speech, without this being objectively the case (Thakerar, Giles and Cheshire, 1982).

Nevertheless, in accommodation theory we see individual speech shifting in relation to perceived norms, and to enact social relationships. This area of research may be extremely important in connection with the mechanisms of diffusion of change and maintenance of differences, because it views them on the level of interaction.

Acts of identity

The individual is 'between norms'. How he says what he says conveys social meanings about him and his relationship to the hearer and to the larger social structure. The fact that speech is systematically meaningful even on the phonological level is shown by the social psychological research. I am using 'meaningful' here to signify that something is being regularly conveyed in context by the relative use of one variant as opposed to another. It is the norm, or rule that makes this possible. It does this by establishing a connection between variants of a variable and identity in terms of groups. This link appears to be originally non-arbitrary in that a group is 'naturally' relatively connected to a variant in its vernacular. But it becomes arbitrary and conventional in the norm. One sense in which it becomes conventional is that each speaker can be assured that other speakers know that to use more or less of a variant conveys more or less identification with different groups, and they also know he knows this. The speech community can be viewed as a system of such norms reflecting its various social identities, on to which variables can be mapped.

Now an utterance is also an action. Given the framework of norms, each utterance is also incorrigibly what LePage (1980) has called an **act of identity**. We saw earlier how LePage argues that people create their linguistic rules to resemble those of the groups with which they wish to identify. He writes (1980: 14):

> Each speech act is an announcement: "to this extent I wish to be thought of as my own man, to this extent like A, to this extent like B, to this extent like C . . . " and so on, where A, B, and C – and myself, and their properties, are the speakers own constructs . . .

That is, A, B and C can be viewed as idealized models constructed by projection and focusing from the speech of relevant groups. From the variability he observes, the individual constructs invariant models. His speech will be '*a variable mix of idealized invariable norms'*. There are constraints on constructing models: difficulty in identifying model groups, difficulty of access to model groups, strength of motivation with regard to various groups, and ability to modify speech patterns.

Within this last constraint, this approach also admits the possibility of intentional action, in negotiating identity, into issues of variability. Variability can thus be integrated, using the notion of norms, into the analysis of language as social action. The system of norms provides the mechanism by which an individual's actions are intelligible to others. Leaving aside the question of how conscious people are of their intentions, the question of choice in formulating identity has also been introduced into the picture. We will turn to questions of speech as action in the next part of the book.

To conclude, let us return to the question of the 'coordinative mechanism' that puzzled us in Chapter 4. How was it that speakers who had never contacted each other could produce frequencies that were related in such a precise and regular way over a whole community? We rejected as incoherent the notion of a community grammar in the Chomskyan 'competence' sense, and such notions as a 'group mind'. We also rejected, later on, the internal implicational relations of lects vis-á-vis a language change as the sole mechanism.

However, we can now propose that the 'coordinative mechanism', that which makes countless 'acts of identity' exhibit statistical structure, are the norms which make such actions intelligible. Since norms are conventions which govern action, they behave like the other conventions that constitute and regulate human groups, and are learned and maintained in the same way. Each individual cooperates in the system of mutual taken-for-granted rules because to do so makes social life possible; the rules both constitute his actions and make them intelligible. He takes them for granted because he knows that to do so is a *sine qua non* for everyone else taking them for granted too.

8. *Discourse Games*

> Here the term 'language-*game*' is meant to bring into promi-
> nence the fact that the *speaking* of language is part of an
> activity, or of a form of life.
>
> Wittgenstein (1953)

In the last chapter, we concluded with a change of perspective.
We looked at features of the speech of an individual. More particularly, we brought in the notion of an 'act of identity' when
we looked at language from the point of view of the utterances
which speakers perform when they are using language. We also
saw that to understand the meaning of the utterances, we had to
know the norms or rules which governed their use. Now we will
put aside the study of aggregate behaviour – large-scale sociolinguistic patterns – and turn to the study of individual utterances.
Social regularities will figure in the discussion but in a different
way; principally in terms of the rules that constitute the way
language is used.

When a person speaks, they perform an **utterance**. Utterances
have certain general properties which make them quite different
from other categories such as sentences or propositions.

An utterance is always the utterance *of* a speaker, and uttered
to a hearer or hearers. It is part of an event. It is something
speakers *do* within the event. Therefore, it is an activity. Because
it is part of an event, its performance will always be located in a
particular setting and take place at a particular time. The participants are engaged in **discourse**. And their discourse is
embedded in a **context**. The context of an utterance is quite a
complicated idea, as we shall see. It includes not only participants, time and setting, but also the previous utterances of the
discourse and the background knowledge required for the talk to
be understood.

I said that an utterance is a constituent of an event. When we
use the word 'discourse', we are referring to an aspect of the

class of social events in which utterances occur. Of course, virtually all social events have both verbal and nonverbal constituents woven inextricably together in various ways. Discourse, as we are using the term, is the verbal aspect of such events. This verbal aspect has certain basic properties which mirror the structure of social events in general. Consider a largely nonverbal example such as a tennis match. This has participants who have roles and associated activities specified by the fact that they are playing tennis. The participants take turns. Their actions are coordinated. We have names for the things they do when they hit or miss the ball. Similarly, utterances are activities in discourse. People bat the conversation backwards and forwards like the participants in a game of tennis.

Activities and rules

Once we have said that utterances are activities, we must immediately return to the question of norms or rules. We saw above that actions were essentially rule-following behaviour. When people *do* something, *what* they are doing is only intelligible if we know the rules they are following: intelligible both to themselves and to others. Following the rule makes the activity *count as* an activity of a certain kind. The use of the words 'intelligible' and 'count as' here means that action is not mere behaviour, but that it is meaningful and therefore incorrigibly interpretable. Something is being conveyed to an observer, namely, that the actor did such and such an act. But both actors and observers (or, in the case of discourse, speakers and hearers) can only recognize what was done if they both share a knowledge of the criteria for the act, the rule that is being followed. It follows that such rules are social. I would not be able to convey anything if only *I* knew the rule – I can make up rules for myself and play games with myself, but in principle my action would be unintelligible to others unless they can infer the rule I am following. Because rules are social, they work by convention; that is, they are solutions to coordination problems between participants. Each participant tries normally to follow some rule so that other participants can rely on him doing so, and because he therefore can rely on them also to follow the rule. The regularity mutually achieved can be taken for granted as a solution to a coordination problem. It is in everyone's interest that what each one does is interpretable, and communicates in a predictable way. Our main point, then, is, in the words of Gumperz (1975: xiii), 'that human activity, to the extent that it communicates, is always constrained by shared norms.'

We can think of a culture as being a system of such rules governing activity and making it intelligible for participants. The view of social action as 'meaningful' because 'rule-following' which I have presented here is roughly that of Peter Winch (1958) which itself grew out of the later philosophy of Wittgenstein. But it has also been a central strand in both sociological and anthropological thought (for a discussion, see Ryan, 1970: ch.6; Giddens, 1976; and Wilson, 1970). From this perspective, the task of the social scientist is the explication of the rules or norms which constitute social activities.

Language is the paradigm case of meaningful human action; and it is the language-like nature of activity in general that is the starting point for Winch's arguments. Indeed, in most events both utterance acts and nonverbal, but still communicative, acts are interwoven together and are mutually dependent for their interpretation. One feature of discourse is that there must be at least two participants. Now let us see some of the rules they follow.

A cooperative activity

To converse is a good cooperative activity. Just as it takes two to tango or play tennis it takes (at least) two people to have a conversation. And, as if they were dancing together, people engaged in conversation are successfully doing something together; mutually accomplishing the creation of a social event, 'the conversation' itself. Think of the simple matter of taking turns. How is it that the participants speak one at a time for the most part, with very little overlap? How does one know when it is one's turn, or go about getting a chance to speak? How does one know 'what one is supposed to say'?

The fundamental aim of this conversational cooperation is for each participant to achieve the understanding of what the other intends to convey. In other words, to communicate. But for people jointly to perform this activity, they have to be able to assume also about each other that they know the rules of the game. These are the conventions which make cooperation possible. Such conventions in conversation are of two kinds. They govern both practical machinery of conversation itself, such as

turn-taking, and they tell us how utterances should normally be interpreted in the specific kinds of contexts in which we find ourselves and which the utterances themselves at least partially constitute. They are essential tacit assumptions about conversation and context which we can assume our interlocutors share (at least in our own speech community) and which are necessary to **gloss** what the other chap is doing. They enable one to say to oneself, 'It's my turn to speak' or 'He's ready to close the conversation' or 'In this situation, that can't be a real question'.

The social organization of conversation has been studied extensively in an approach to sociology which is termed **ethnomethodology**. I will explain the term later, but first we will look at some of its relevant results.

Openings

Emanuel Schegloff in his important article, 'Sequencing in conversational openings' (1968), studied the problem of how participants achieve coordinated entry into a conversational exchange. Conversation has a basic structure *ab*, *ab*, *ab*, in which participants a and b speak successively in turns. The question is how they begin to 'lock' themselves into such a structure. How do you begin to engage someone in talk and guarantee yourself a further turn later? How does one begin to create this conversational social relationship?

Schegloff studied this in the **openings** of telephone conversations. His research was carried out by analysing the tape-recorded telephone calls to and from the complaints desk of the police department in an American city. Although the data was very specific, Schegloff's aim was to find the deeper structural generalizations underlying the openings of conversations. I have summarized his conclusions in Figure 8.1.

Schegloff found that the basic structure of such openings could be generalized into what he called **summons-answer sequences**, which were 'a general way that participants initiate a conversation, provide a coordinated entry to interaction and establish that they are available to interact.'

To account for his data, Schegloff had to view the ringing of the telephone as an integral part of the exchange, a **summons**. Note that in this case, an act which conveys a participant's intentions, the summons, is realized by a bell ringing. Although in other situations we often summon someone verbally, this

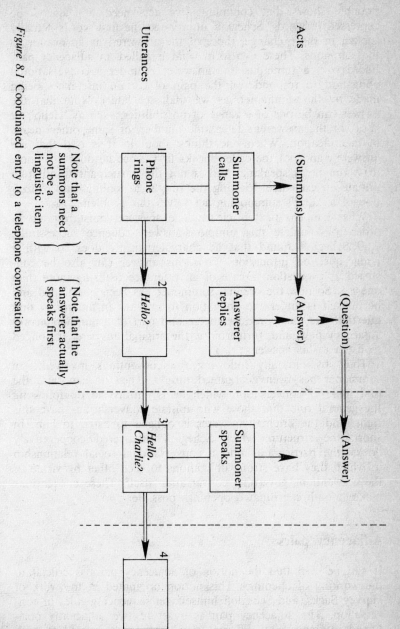

Figure 8.1 Coordinated entry to a telephone conversation

example shows that communicative acts need not always be expressed in words. Schegloff interpreted the first words actually spoken in the exchange, those of the answerer, as an **answer** to the summons. These two form what is called an **adjacency pair**. Faced with a summons, the answerer is under a conversational obligation to respond (on the pain of certain inferences being made by the summoner, as we shall see later). Note that the answer can be one of a range of possibilities, such as 'Hello', or 'Yes', or the answerer's telephone number, or some other means of identification. When one thinks about it, it is odd that the answerer, and not the caller speaks first, since he does not know to whom he is speaking, and is not the participant wanting to initiate an exchange. Viewing the ring as a nonlinguistic realization of a caller's summoning act solves this problem.

What happens next is clever. The answerer must respond in order to complete this summons-answer sequence successfully. And Schegloff found that he characteristically does so with a rising question intonation. Thus, his answer can also be construed as a **question**, a case of an utterance realizing more than one act. So now the original summoner has been questioned and he himself is under the obligation to provide an answer to that question. He must produce the second part of a **question-answer** adjacency pair, and, furthermore, the original answerer is obliged to listen to his answer.

Thus, by mutually following the conventions involved, the summoner has been guaranteed turn 3. Then he can raise the first **topic** of conversation which he is entitled to do following the general rule that those who initiate conversations have this right, and the original answerer is obliged to listen to him. In short, the structure which Schegloff discovered cooperatively 'locks' the participants into a conversational social relationship in which they have strong obligations to each other by virtue of the conventions governing conversation itself. These conventions make smooth coordinated openings possible.

Adjacency pairs

It can be seen that the notion of adjacency pairs is crucial to the working of openings. This notion originated in the work of Harvey Sacks, and Schegloff himself, on sequencing rules in conversation. The adjacency pair is a set of two adjacently positioned utterances, by different speakers, closely related to each other in a specific way. We have already seen two examples – the summons-answer and the question-answer sequences. Other examples in the literature are, a **greeting** and its **return of greeting**; an **offer** and its **acceptance** or **refusal**; a **thanks** and its **acknowledgement**; an **apology** and its **acceptance**; a **complaint** and its two sorts of replies, a **diminisher** or a **sympathizer**; a **challenge** and its **rejection**; and a **compliment** and its **acceptance** or **rejection**. It is clear that these types are little institutions; coordinated pairs of communicative acts. Many acts, then, conventionally require replies of specific kinds and put the hearer under a conversational obligation to provide them.

Adjacency pairs have the following properties. Their crucial feature is what Sacks calls 'the conditional relevance' of the second part on the first, and the 'sequential implicitiveness' of the first on the second. Basically this means that when the first part is produced, the next turn has an expected interpretation projected on it. Therefore, whatever is produced second will be specifically interpreted as an act of the kind required by the first part. Questions demand answers, for example, or greetings require greetings in return.

We assume that an interpretation of the second utterance as a relevant reply to the first must be calculable from the two utterances, and we will ransack the background information in order to be able to construe the second utterance in the appropriate relation to the first. We are now talking about very powerful conversational constraints on how we are to construe utterances which come immediately after, for example, a summons, a question, or a greeting. This power can be seen from the notion of **official absence**. Say, for example, I am ringing you on the telephone and there is no answer. In fact, nothing has happened at all between the successive rings of the telephone, the series of summonses which I have uttered. But this nothing is not nothing. The silence *will* be interpreted. I conclude that either you are out, or otherwise unavailable to interact. Sacks writes, 'If there is no answer, then inferences are warranted in the culture.' Think of how we interpret the official absence of a reply to a greeting we have just issued. The kindest inference which is warranted is that our acquaintance did not see or hear our greeting. Similarly, consider the case of the officially absent answer to a question. The convention of adjacency pairs generates these inferences.

Why should pairs of acts of this type characterize the close-ordering of conversation? What sort of 'work' has to be done by participants that is reflected in adjacency pairs? Remember that we are studying *'inter-action'*. As the form of the word itself suggests, we are dealing with the normal coordination of actions as a mutual accomplishment of participants. The rules are conventions which *enable* this accomplishment. One thing that adjacency pairs provide for is that, when the first pair part has been uttered, a future event – the next pair part – is guaranteed to occur (or to be officially absent) as a reply. A future turn by the current hearer is therefore to this degree controlled by the speaker; a 'projection' of a future event is made by his utterances of the first pair part. The current hearer's next turn will be expected to be relevant, so the utterance of the speaker at this turn 'projects' just what the *other* participant's utterance is required to be relevant to. Against this expectation, deviations can be interpreted, and thus can convey specific meanings. The absence of a reply, or the particular form a reply takes, is communicative over and against the norm established by the adjacency pair structure. Any act that flouts normative expectations is 'meaningful', as we shall see later.

Another accomplishment enabled by this close-ordering is described by Schegloff and Sacks (1973; in Turner, 1974: 240):

> What two utterances, produced by different speakers, can do that one utterance cannot do is: by an adjacently positioned second, a speaker can show that he understood what a prior aimed at, and that he is willing to go along with that. Also, by virtue of the occurrence of an adjacently produced second, the doer of a first can see that what he intended was indeed understood, and that it was or was not accepted. Also, of course, a second can assert his failure to understand, or disagreement, and inspection of a second by a first can allow the first speaker to see that while the second thought he understood, indeed he misunderstood. It is then through the use of adjacent positioning that appreciations, failures, correctings, etc., can be themselves understandably attempted.

There are other important features of adjacency structure. Once the successful accomplishment of a pair is 'brought off' by the participants, some pairs are then **repeatable** and some are **non-repeatable**. Of course, if a speaker judges that a second pair part has not been achieved at all according to rule – if the current hearer's next turn is *not* construable in such a way as it can be said that it occurred at all – then the first act can be **reinstated**.

For example, if someone clearly did not hear my greeting, or did not understand that I was making a request, then I can reinstate my greeting or request. But once an exchange of greetings has been accomplished to the mutual satisfaction of the participants, it cannot be repeated in the same interaction. This 'mutual satisfaction' rider which I have included on the rule can, of course, cause 'trouble' in those cases where participants differ in their view of what counts as successful accomplishment of the pair. Other kinds of pairs can be repeated as a matter of course. Thus, the successful bringing off of a question-answer sequence allows the questioner to pose further questions. So we sometimes observe a conversational organization composed of a chaining together of question-answer adjacency pairs:

Q-A, Q-A, Q-A, etc.

The use of such repeatable rules is one way of structuring an overall conversation. We shall see later, however, that what superficially appears to be a question and its answer is not always or even usually a question. It may look like a question, for example, if it is an interrogative form, but at the same time it may be realizing other acts. In such cases, conversational reasons for the use of a repeatable adjacency structure may be to provide a superficial way of organizing speaker control over successive turns, or to introduce new topics, or simultaneously to do other kinds of 'work' in the discourse.

Also, in those cases of adjacency pairs where there are alternatives for a pair part, one of these may be **preferred** to the other in most circumstances. Alternatives are normally available in second pair parts, as replies to first pair parts. For example, in the class of acts which attempt to get the hearer to do something, there are two types of reply, compliance or refusal. Similarly, in supportive actions, such as invitations, compliments and so on, the first pair part may be either accepted or rejected. In general, it it the compliance and the acceptance which are preferred outcomes, and the refusals and rejections which are less preferred, by *both* participants. In the figures which follow, I have marked preferred alternatives with an asterisk.

Schegloff (1979: 49) points out that this preference can project the influence of an intended, but not yet performed, adjacency pair 'backwards' to a turn, before the first pair part is actually uttered. A speaker may attempt to pre-emp a dispreferred outcome (or guarantee a preferred one) by use of a **pre-sequence**, which is mutually understood to preface a later turn. A clear example of such a construal is the **pre-invitation**, as in the following:

(pre-invitation)	1. Are you doing anything tonight?
	2. Not really – no.
(invitation)	3. How about we go to the show?
(acceptance)	4. OK.

The first pair part, 3, will be placed or not in the speaker's next turn, depending on the reply, 2, to the pre-invitation, 1. From another point of view, what we are observing here is also the 'forwards' projection of the pre-sequence. The form of the later adjacency pair is conditional on the outcome of the earlier one. We will see such 'projection' later on when we look at closing sequences.

Adjacency pairs: compliment responses

Adjacency pairs are on the whole not as simple as the notion first appears. Let us look at one sequence in more detail. This is the pair compliment and compliment response (Pomerantz, 1978). Three main points will emerge. First, that the relation between the first and second acts is *dynamic*; it is not merely a question of recognizing a compliment, and responding with a fixed type of reply. The second pair part is, in fact, an 'outcome point' where what is uttered becomes *intelligible as a reply* because both participants know the rules involved. The adjacency pair is more a norm of interpretation than it is a list of appropriate utterances. Although certain words do recur in adjacency pairs of the more institutional types and certain words are conventional, in fact it is how the words are interpreted that is important. Secondly, many pairs enable solutions to conversational *problems*. Thirdly, the pair parts may be doing more than one thing at the same time. In Pomerantz's terms, compliment replies are subject to multiple constraints.

This last point first. Pomerantz argues that there are three systems of constraints which govern the action of replying to a compliment. Two of these exist because the utterance of a compliment can be viewed as simultaneously two different types of action. Characteristically, these require different kinds of replies.

The action types and their appropriate replies are illustrated in Figure 8.2.

A compliment is a **supportive action**, akin to 'offers', 'gifts' and 'congratulations', which sequentially imply an acceptance or rejection as second pair part. At the same time, a compliment is also what Pomerantz terms an **assessment action**, which sequentially implies agreement or disagreement as a second pair part. This latter type of act presumably includes all those acts, like 'stating' discussed above, in which the speaker in uttering a proposition also intends the utterance to count as an undertaking that the utterance is true. It is this truth claim that makes agreement or disagreement a relevant reply. Other assessment actions would include 'remarks', 'assertions', 'statements' etc. Now think about compliments from this point of view. An utterance which is to count as a compliment must also convey, in some way, that the proposition on which the hearer is being complimented is *true*. In the examples below this undertaking is explicit. Characteristically, therefore, such utterances perform the two types of acts simultaneously. *An utterance is a complex · of related actions.* This property will concern us again in Chapters 10 and 11.

As we said, each type sequentially implies different classes of reply. As a supportive act, the rule is that hearers either accept or reject the compliment. But the rule goes further than this. There is a 'preferred' response, namely acceptance, particularly by means of an appreciation token, such as 'thank you'. There is an affiliation between acceptance (supportive actions) and agreement (assessment actions). This means that a compliment can also be accepted through the expression of agreement with its content. This is a secondary way of accepting compliments. Sequentially, if both positive replies occur they do so in the order, accept and agree. Pomerantz (1978: 84ff) gives the following examples:

1. Why, it's the loveliest record I ever heard. And the organ –
2. Well, thank you.

1. Oh, it was just beautiful.
2. Well, thank you + Uh, I thought it was quite nice . . . .

Because of the affiliation of accept/agree and reject/disagree, just as one can accept through agreement, one can reject a com-

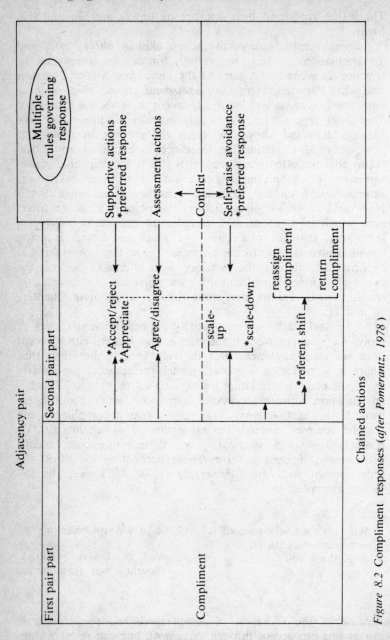

Figure 8.2 Compliment responses (*after Pomerantz, 1978*)

pliment through disagreement with the truth of its content, (Pomerantz, 1978:87):

1. (You) did a great job cleaning up the house.
2. Well, I guess you haven't seen the kids' room.

Interestingly, this is the preferred method of rejecting a compliment. This is because it avoids *explicit* rejection, which is the dispreferred response to supportive actions. The preference for explicitness in acceptance leads to the preference for inexplicitness in rejection.

Politeness

But a third norm complicates the picture. Although acceptance is the preferred outcome of the adjacency pair, the prevalent empirical response to compliments is disagreement and rejection. How could this be? Pomerantz invokes a third rule to account for this: **self-praise avoidance**. Participants should, at least conventionally, avoid assenting to enhancements of their own status/prestige. Therefore, one who has received a compliment has a problem of conflicting norms. Stated categorically, he should accept the supportive action and the truth of the speaker's assessment with a token of appreciation. On the other hand, he should avoid agreement with a proposition to which his assent will count as self-praise. To disagree, however, threatens both parties. It repudiates both the complimenter's supportive act and his competence in uttering the truth, and, for the hearer, it involves him in self-deprecation. Compliment response, therefore, is problematic.

This is reflected in the solutions which exhibit an 'in-betweenness' in attempting to resolve the conflict. Remember, earlier we saw a similar 'in-between-ness' in that, for a given phonological variable, an individual was *between* norms. The outcome was the statistical positioning of the 'act of identity' in relation to the various norms. Note, however, that identity claims always imply relationship claims relative to some hearer, on the dimensions of status and solidarity. Presumably to receive a compliment is status-enhancing and simultaneously an expression of solidarity. Self-deprecation in a response is status-reducing, and therefore expresses solidarity in return. A speaker may 'scale down' an agreement following an acceptance. To do so exhibits features of *both* agreement and disagreement (Pomerantz, 1978: .95):

| Compliment | 1. She's a fox (of the hearer's new bride). |
| Agree 'scaled down' | 2. Yeh, she's a pretty girl. |

But, given the problematic nature of responses, why should one compliment anyone at all? Clearly, in the terms we have been discussing, the speaker is following *another* politeness rule such that he should express his solidarity with and enhance the status of the interlocutor where possible. To compliment (congratulate, offer, praise etc.) him does this.

However, there are two dangers in complimenting. One we have already seen. By enhancing his status, it puts the hearer on the spot. If he agrees, he both commits self-praise and weakens solidarity by virtue of accepting this enhanced prestige. The other danger involves the complimenter. Although complimenting someone *does* express solidarity towards them, it often does so at the price of obtruding rather badly into that area of the personal that is the possession of every 'other'. To compliment necessarily involves making public an assessment, albeit a favourable one, of the 'other'. This is presumptious and can be potentially an enactment of a power asymmetry in favour of the complimenter. Imagine a compliment issued by an employer, for example, to an employee. This danger is inherent in enacting the norm of expressing solidarity through the means of compliments (praise, offers etc.). The complimenter must obtrude to do so.

Conventionally, the 'scaled-down' agreement as a response is beautifully 'poised' between the potential inferences generated by the conflicting rules. The receiver of the compliment accepts it, with reservations, by agreeing with the assessment, also with reservations. He thus accepts, and does not repudiate the other's supportive expression of solidarity and *returns* it by partially rejecting any enhanced prestige/status that might accrue to him by virtue of being praised. At the same time, he restores the privacy of his 'area of the personal' by partially disagreeing with the assessment. This reduces the status of the complimenter and restores symmetry of power. Any 'presumptiveness' is repaired. Ironing out any possible asymmetry of power itself enacts solidarity and lets the complimenter know that the compliment was taken and accepted according to that norm. The problem is resolved and the adjacency pair 'brought off'.

Once symmetry is assured and intent cleared up, the complimenter sometimes reasserts his position; 2 above is followed by
3: 'Oh, she's gorgeous.'

Agreement which is 'scaled down' typically follows compliments which do not directly refer to the hearer. In the example
above, the referent was the hearer's new bride. Usually, a more
overt disagreement follows a compliment that directly refers to
its recipient. For example, (Pomerantz, 1978: 98):

1. Well, we'll haftuh *frame* that.
2. Yee -*Uh*ghh, it's not worth fra(hh)mi(h)ing.
3. W'*sure* it is.

Sometimes disagreements do not completely counter-assert the
proposition but rather qualify the compliment:

1. You brought - like a *ton* of things.
2. *Just* a few little things.

Presumably, when compliments directly refer to their recipients,
the danger to both participants' status is more overt, as opposed
to less direct compliments. Overt disagreement, correspondingly,
is both more self-deprecatory and has a greater effect on the
possible 'presumptive' status on the complimenter. When the
status problem is thus resolved, the mutual accomplishment of a
compliment-response pair can be interpreted as the expression,
acceptance and return of solidarity.

Another solution to the problem is to reassign the compliment
elsewhere, or return a compliment to the original speaker.

So far, then, we have demonstrated that much more is
involved in adjacency pairs than the simple occurrence of two
acts in sequence. In general, it seems that close ordering is a
framework of expectations which can be used for the solution of
problems in the enacting of relationships. The adjacency structure in this sense enables, and is a resource for, coordination of
actions. In the above examples, *the participants are negotiating
their relationship*. Now just what is the best outcome for them?
What, in general, are people trying to 'bring off' together in a
compliment-response pair?

We expect that the speaker ought to be intending to reinforce
or establish solidarity by 'building up' the socially accredited
identity of the hearer, doing something good to him. Given this,
the hearer ought to accept the offer and in so doing make the

solidarity mutual. In this light of this norm, the prevalence of rejection in compliments is only *ritual* rejection. The response is not really rejecting the compliment. The conflict of norms produces indirect rejections as responses (disagreements, reference shifts etc.) but in fact the preferred response of acceptance is being accomplished on another level. The preference for acceptance is what generates this interpretation.

Of course, when we use the word 'preference' here we are talking about a social rule. At this point, we ought to distinguish between two uses of the word rule, which up to now we have conflated. Most of the rules we have talked about so far have been rules which one must follow in order that what one is doing can count as *that* kind of action at all. They make what one is doing intelligible as an action of a certain kind. If one does not know, or follow, the rule, the action will not count as doing *that*. The adjacency-pair rules are of this type. The rule is simply that the second pair part, produced on the completion of the first pair part, will count as a reply to it. The necessary condition of a reply is that it be a reply to something. On the assumption that this rule holds, not following it will be communicative, witness the notion of 'official absence' of a reply. The rule is both **constitutive** of the act and our means of interpreting what people do. The second sense of rule, by contrast, is its **regulative** aspect. Such a rule stipulates that an act 'ought' to be performed or avoided. Constitutive rules are logically prior to regulative ones; for example, one has to know what counts as murder in order to be able to obey the rule which says not to murder. Many constitutive rules are also regulatively interpreted. So participants 'ought' to cooperate in adjacency pairs by producing the second pair part. But within this conversational obligation are more specific regulative constraints. Participants 'ought' to produce preferred alternatives and hence work towards preferred outcomes in 'bringing off' the pair. Failure to accomplish the pair in this *way* will also warrant inferences and be communicative. Preferences, therefore, are regulative aspects of language use – the 'ought' aspect.

This helps us to understand something more of the possible force of normative pressures. The largest part of this pressure has to do with the requirement that one follows the rule or norm simply in order to convey the meanings one intends and be understood. This is the enabling aspect of rules. A participant follows rules under this aspect because it is *rational* to do so. When the rule is also interpreted regulatively by the community, then a moral, legal, aesthetic etc. pressure is also exerted by the group and its judgements. The two aspects are not only connected by the priority of the enabling aspect, but by the incorrigible communicativeness of real or apparent violations under both aspects. The interpretations differ as between aspects, however. Under the constitutive aspect we ask what the participant intended to convey in acting that way. Note how this assumes both rationality and the 'taken-for-granted' nature of the rule. Under the 'regulative' aspect, besides the first kind of interpretative activity, there is also a judgement of the act in moral, legal, aesthetic etc. terms. The normative pressure exerted through language usually has this regulative aspect. In extreme cases it can take the form of language legislation. More often it has the form of prescription regarding correctness or aesthetics. But it pervades the interpretation of every speech act under the heading of **politeness**. We have already seen that the use of variants is expressive of power (relative status) and solidarity (degree of social distance).

Let us see what kinds of generalizations can be made about politeness phenomenon. Arguably, it can be derived from the notion of **face** as this is used in the analysis of 'face-to-face' interaction by Erving Goffman (1955, 1967). For Goffman, a participant's face is his image of himself in terms of approved social attributes. In an encounter, a participant claims a face for himself which is 'lodged in mutual appraisal' between himself and the other participants. All the participants are responsible for maintaining their own and each other's faces cooperatively in the course of the interaction. This responsibility leads to a pair of related rules: the **rule of self-respect**, wherein a participant must stand guard over his own face, and the **rule of considerateness**, wherein he must go to certain lengths to respect the face of others. Participants cooperate to try to make sure that neither themselves nor others are defaced, out of face, or in the wrong face.

This is evident in **repairs**. Repairs occur when there is some source of 'trouble' in a conversation. The trouble need not be a mistake. It can be any of a range of difficulties. For example, a hearer may not have heard or understood some remark, or a speaker may not be able to remember a name, or find the right word for what he wants to say. Schegloff, Jefferson and Sacks (1977) show that conversation is so organized that there is a preference for **self-repair** over **other-repair** in dealing with such troubles.

In a major study of politeness, Brown and Levinson (1978: 66ff) distinguish between negative and positive face. The former is, 'the basic claim to territories, personal preserves, rights to non-distraction – i.e., to freedom of action and freedom from imposition'. The latter is, 'the positive consistent self-image or "personality" (crucially including the desire that this self image be appreciated and approved of) claimed by interactants'. These two aspects of face can be framed in terms of participant's wants, to be unimpeded in action, and to be desirable at least to some others. Many activities are intrinsically face-threatening. Earlier we saw the face-threatening aspects of compliments to their recipients. Although compliments enhance positive face, they threaten the hearer's negative face because they predicate some desire towards the hearer and/or his goods. This limits his actions because, in response to this imposition, he feels impelled to self-effacement (Brown and Levinson, 1978: 71-3).

Participants adopt **strategies of politeness** in order to avoid or minimize face-threatening activities. There are positive strategies, such as claiming common ground or fulfilling the hearer's wants. (Issuing compliments to someone might be an example of this latter aim.) There are negative strategies, aimed at the hearer's negative face, such as avoiding overt coercion, not making assumptions, being direct about one's intentions and so on. A particular linguistic form in itself is not usually polite or impolite, rather its politness has to do with how it is interpreted relative to the available strategies and the context. For example, what is' polite or impolite to a particular participant is relative to the dimensions of power (relative status) and solidarity (social distance) claimed and granted in the faces which have been accredited in the encounter. What actually threatens face, and therefore motivates choice of strategy, for example, depends on relative status and intimacy. To receive a compliment from a superior differs from receiving one from an intimate. In general, in modern Western societies, the preference seems to be to mask status differences (which threatens hearer's negative face) and reinforce solidarity (which enhances hearer's positive face). The particular preferences we have noted – acceptance, agreement, self-correction etc. – would seem to reflect this. Keep in mind as well the ritual nature of these meanings. Politeness interpretations decode just one dimension of the complex of activities done in the performance of an utterance.

Identification

So far we have seen that interaction between participants is dynamic (involving the continuing negotiation and mutual definition of their relationship), coordinative, oriented to problem-solving, and enabled by conventions. Another problem for participants is that of the achievement of mutual recognition, that is, to identify to whom you are talking from the resources available. Schegloff (1979) analyses this aspect of the organization of conversation.

Usually, identification is accomplished in what Schegloff terms the **pre-opening** sequence, and among acquaintances this is achieved through 'inspectables' – very simply, by what people look and sound like. The preferred method of identification involves the minimum use of recognitional resources. The basic resource is self-reference by the use of one's name, but the resources a speaker provides are **recipient-designed**; that is, they give just the amount of information the speaker believes the hearer requires to identify him, and in the appropriate form. The preference is to achieve mutual recognition with less than the basic resource, by appearance and/or a minimal sample of voice, and to do so immediately and without problems.

Schegloff (1979: 50) writes, 'This is a specification, in the domain of reference to persons, of the general recipient design preference: don't tell the recipient what you ought to suppose he already knows; use it. This principle builds in a preference for "oversuppose and undertell".' Again, a preference reflects a general politeness strategy – in this case, one oriented to the hearer's positive face. To set things up so that a hearer will identify you with minimal resources also conveys, and can allow the hearer to infer, that you suppose that he and you are solidary. Conversely, there are dangers in this assumption of 'common ground' or 'intimacy', since it obtrudes on the speaker's negative face. His freedom is limited by the assumption that he can identify the speaker from minimal resources. Consequently, if there is doubt, the speaker can 'undersuppose and overtell'. This switches strategy to one of negative politeness. By 'being direct', any threat is removed to the hearer's negative face.

Identification becomes particularly problematic when visual cues are unavailable and there is no pre-opening sequence. So let us confine ourselves to such a case: the opening of telephone conversations. Schegloff's analysis is very complex and subtle. Here I can only summarize a few of its main points.

There are *two* identification problems, that of the caller in identifying the answerer, and that of the answerer in identifying the caller. Figure 8.3 shows the locus of each problem. 'Identity?' marks the point where the resource is provided. 'Solution'

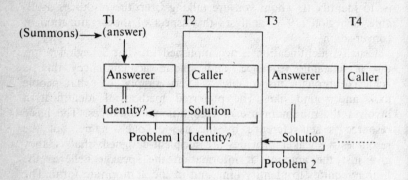

Figure 8.3 The problem of identification (*after Schegloff, 1979*)

marks the turn where, as preferred, the earliest resolution of the problem can be accomplished. Turn 2 is the most problematic. At this point the caller (who knows whom he intended to call) ought to achieve recognition of the answerer and, at the same time, provide just the right resource for the answerer successfully to recognize him. This is accomplished at the same time as other adjacency pairs, which appear to be the main business of the conversation. Earlier, we saw that the answerer's first turn, T, was an answer to a summons. Next we commonly observe an exchange of greetings.

Answerer	1. H'llo?	(answer to summons)
Caller	2. hHi	(greeting)
Answerer	3. Hi:?	(greeting)

Schegloff points out that these utterances are at the same time acts which invite and give recognition. Again we see that the same utterance is used to perform a complex of acts. Schegloff (1979: 35) describes this:

The doing of an initial greeting in second turn has two aspects at least. First, it is the first part of a basic sequential unit we call an adjacency pair... its recipient properly responds with a second greeting, or greeting return. Second, it is a claim to have recognised the answerer and a claim to have the answerer recognise the caller. These two aspects of the caller's initial 'Hi' are intertwined. A first greeting having been done, a second greeting is what should relevantly occupy the next turn. But as the first greeting displays recognition, so will a second greeting; it will thus do more than complete the greeting exchange, it will stand as a claim that the answerer has reciprocally recognized the caller.

There is strong evidence that this is what is going on. The second greeting may be withheld, if recognition has not been achieved:

Answerer	1. Hello?	(answer to summons)
Caller	2. Hello, Charles.	(greeting)
pause	(0.2)	
Caller	This is Yolk.	
Answerer	3. Oh, *hello*, Yolk.	(greeting)

The second part is officially absent (note the pause). The silence conveys that the caller has not been recognized. He, therefore, provides a further resource over and above the minimum voice sample. Since this is dispreferred, the recognition, when it comes, is in the form of 'the big hello' and is accompanied by an 'Oh' which signifies 'success now'.

Schegloff has isolated a number of solutions to the identification problem. Let us just look at one more very interesting type. In some cases, the caller's first turn consists of the answerer's (presumed) name pronounced with an interrogative or quasi-interrogative intonation. For example:

Answerer	1. Hello.
Caller	2. Connie?
Answerer	3. Yeah. Joanie.

Schegloff (1979: 50ff) argues that the use of this intonation conveys that the caller doubts that merely a minimal sample of his voice will be sufficient for the answerer successfully to identify him. It is a form of presequence designed to pre-empt the dis-preferred result of not being identifiable from such a sample. It conveys that the speaker, recognizes the danger, to himself, of oversupposition. His display of doubt in fact provides a turn for the answerer to confirm that he *does* recognize the caller. This happens in the example above. The answerer, as requested, does confirm that mutual recognition has ben achieved. Another common reply is for the answerer to utter the first pair part of a new adjacency pair in turn 3, for example; 'Oh, hi. How are you?' This signals that the problem of identification has been solved, and that the conversation may proceed.

Turn-taking

Another problem for conversation organization is that of the orderly allocation of turns to speak among the participants. The rules for coordinating turns in casual conversation were explored by Sacks, Schegloff and Jefferson (1974). In Figure 8.4 I have designed a machine which displays the main points of their analysis.

The machine starts at those points in the current speaker's turn where it is relevant for the floor to be taken by someone else. These **transition relevance points** are the boundaries of lin-guistic items such as sentences, clauses, phrases and even, in some cases, words. The participants, knowing the structure of such items, can collectively project each construction to its formal conclusion and therefore foresee those points at which a change of speaker is possible. If I am uttering a sentence, say a grammatical interrogative, all the participants will know the places where that construction could be considered completed.

At each transition relevance point, a number of things can happen. The current speaker can select the next speaker. If this happens, the party selected has the right and the obligation to speak. There are a number of ways in which the current speaker can select his successor. Remember that the adjacency pair cre-ates an *interpersonal* conversational obligation. Thus, by issuing a particular first pair part, for example a question, I can oblige the participant to whom the question is addressed to reply (on pain of warranted inferences caused by its official absence) and thus select him as the next speaker. This is a common mode of cur-rent speaker selection. Recent research has also shown that paralinguistic factors, such as the use of the eyes and features of

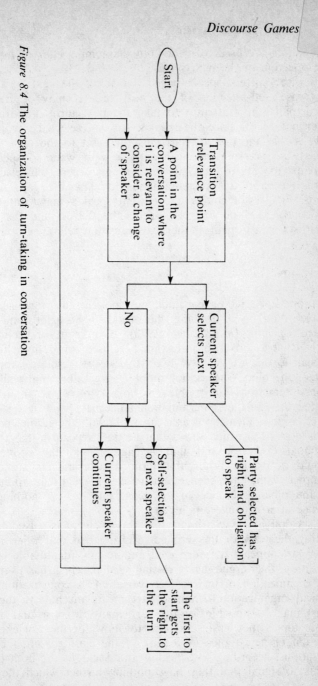

Figure 8.4 The organization of turn-taking in conversation

intonation, are used to mark both the coming ends of turns and the selection of the next speaker.

But the current speaker need not select the next speaker. In this case, self-selection of the next speaker may occur. Other participants may attempt to take the next turn at a transition relevance point, since the speaker has not selected anyone. The rule is that the first to start gets the right to the turn. This is called the **pressure rule**, since those who want to speak will attempt to 'get in first' at those points where self-selection is permitted, and this pressure tends to close the gaps between turns. Finally, of course, the current speaker may continue (he may have to if no one else selects themselves) and the system returns to start again at the next transition relevance point.

Closings

Appropriately, let us conclude our look at the organization of conversation by examining the work of Schegloff and Sacks called *Opening Up Closings* (1973). A moment's reflection will reveal that a conversation cannot be closed simply by a **terminal exchange** such as, A: 'Bye bye'; B: 'See you around', appearing out of the blue. One cannot simply say goodbye and walk away from interaction. The problem is how to recognize an utterance as the first part of a termination adjacency pair. If it is recognized as this, then the hearer can reply with the second part (his own 'goodbye') which shows that he does recognize that this is a terminal exchange and that he agrees that the conversation should now end. When this terminal exchange is successfully completed, then the silence which follows will be interpreted not as the official absence of anything, but just as nothing. The silence after a conversation.

Schegloff and Sacks argue that this problem is solved by preparing the way for the terminal exchange, so that when its first pair part appears it is expected and readily identifiable. A conversation, they argue, has a **closing section**, which has to do with the organization of **topics** of conversation. A conversation has a topical organization. Another part of its machinery, therefore, must make it possible for the participants to raise and develop those topics they wish, and also to allow for the efficient introduction of new topics. A feature of the closing section of conversations, according to Schegloff and Sacks, is for both participants to signal that they have nothing further which they wish to raise. They do this by, in effect, 'passing' a turn. Thus exchanges like the following occur:

A: Well....
B: OK, then....

A conveys that he has nothing further to mention and simultaneously gives B a change to introduce a further 'mentionable'. B, in reply, conveys that he also has nothing further to mention. Since this is now agreed, the stage is set for the terminal exchange and it will be possible to recognize the first part of it when it appears. Conversational acts like the above are termed by Schegloff and Sacks as **pre-closings**.

It is clear from the above that ethnomethodology is concerned with the explanation of the methods (hence its name) that we employ in constituting our everyday social life. Talk, conversation, is a central, commonplace, cooperative activity. It is clearly *ordered by convention*. But exactly how do people 'gloss', that is, understand, the meaning of the activities of everyday life? What is the structure of their practical reasoning? This will reveal the very fabric of assumptions that underly social life and make it possible. For discussions of ethnomethodology see Garfinkel (1967), Turner (1974), and Wallace and Wolf (1980: ch.6).

For us, ethnomethodological research, based on rich data, has demonstrated that *the organization of talk itself is a social institution*. We have seen 'metaconversational' speech acts proposed such as 'replies', 'repairs', 'bringing up a topic' and 'pre-closing', and the phenomenon of the sequencing of successive pairs of acts by different participants. It is clear, then, that part of what participants intend to convey in their utterances will be about the conversation itself. And, therefore, the rules organizing conversation itself will figure crucially in the understanding of what an utterance means.

Situations and speech events

This chapter has shown us so far that utterances are activities and that activities are constituted by participants following rules. More specifically, we have seen that conversation itself has a rich organization and is 'enabled' by specific rules. Participants communicate with each other about their communication.

Every utterance is also made in some social context – inescapably. This is true of any kind of action. Therefore, equally inescapably, we must ask how the nonverbal aspects of social context figure in relation to the activity of speaking. The actual way in which context figures in the production and interpretation of utterances will be discussed in later chapters. Now we want to consider two things. First, what particular features of social context in general figure in the performance of any utterance? Second, since any human action is rule-governed, do the rules for certain kinds of social situations specify the performance of certain speech acts as 'constitutive' of those situations? That is, unless people speak in a certain way, a certain specific social event or situation simply cannot happen; for example, a 'trial' or a 'wedding'. If this is true, as it obviously is, then the rules governing the use of language in these contexts will figure crucially in the production and understanding of utterances.

The anthropologist Dell Hymes (1962, 1964, 1972) has discussed various components which must be included in a complete ethnographic description of the act of speaking. In Figure 8.5 I have summarized sixteen factors. Note how a framework of relevant situational categories, a **context of situation**, constrains the more general features of interaction we have looked at. Thus, particular contexts of situation will specify certain speech acts and adjacency sequences, and not others. Particular outcomes – for example, a 'verdict', a 'sale', or a 'diagnosis' – will be normatively expected to be mutually accomplished. Turn-taking may be specified in relation to particular roles – for example, a teacher and a pupil, or a doctor and a patient. Context of situation provides a grid which can be placed on speech so that its contextually relevant features can be interpreted in relation to recurring features of situations (Halliday *et al.*, 1964; Gregory, 1967; Firth, 1957).

The social actions of a culture enact recurring **situations**. We need to distinguish between situations and settings. Settings are what the word implies: the actual physical setting of the act, a classroom or a pub or a church hall or Leicester Square. But a situation as defined is more abstract. It is a recurring institution in a society, a 'form of life', in which actions are intelligible and meaningful. Situations have differing degrees of formal organization of diffuseness. Consider the differences between a 'religious service', 'the floor of the Stock Exchange', 'Saturday night disco', 'a date', 'a reception', 'a party', or 'a seminar'. Consider the distinction between the setting of a particular church and the values, roles and expectations related to how to act in 'going to

S	situation	1. Setting or locale 2. Scene or situation	The *setting or locale* is local and concrete; the place and time. The *scene or situation* is abstract, a recurring institution, a type of social occasion like 'a committee meeting'.
P	participants	3. Speaker 4. Addressor 5. Hearer, or audience 6. Addressee	Whom the act is addressed to, and who it is uttered by, are significant. In various situations, participants are allocated *communication roles* by the culture, for example, 'a chairman', 'a therapist', 'a patient', 'a client', 'a teacher', 'a pupil', 'an interviewee'.
E	ends	7. Purposes – Outcomes 8. Purposes – Goals	Some speech events have conventional outcomes, for example, 'a diagnosis', 'a sale', or 'a verdict'. These, as well as individual goals, are significant.
A	act sequences	9. Message form 10. Message content	Topics of conversation and particular 'ways of speaking'. In a culture, certain linguistic forms are conventional for certain types of talk. Certain adjacency pairs typical for certain speech events, e.g., a political interview.
K	key	11. Key	Tone, manner or spirit of the act, mock or serious.
I	instrumentalities	12. Channel or mode of discourse	Spoken, written, written but read aloud, recited etc.
		13. Forms of speech	The dialect, accent or other variety of language in which the act is uttered.
N	norms	14. Norms of interpretation	Interpretation that would be normally expected for the speech event in question.
		15. Norms of interaction	Interpretation in relation to the conventions of conversation itself, turn-taking etc.
G	genres	16. Genres	Categories such as poem, myth, tale, riddle, lecture, commercial, editorial etc.

Figure 8.5 Components of speaking (*after Hymes, 1972*)

church'. It is obvious that we only have words for some situations and often tend to use the concrete noun for something much more abstract. For example, we use 'school' for both the building and the 'form of life'. A situation may typically include speech as part of itself. All my examples include talk. But they include a great deal more besides.

By contrast a **speech event** is a social institution which specifically and only constrains the interpretation of talk itself (and therefore also the production of talk if a speaker wants his intents correctly interpreted). Hymes (1972: 56) writes that a speech event is 'restricted to activities, or aspects of activities, that are directly governed by rules or norms for the use of speech'. We have names for such events: 'interview', 'lecture', 'argument', 'quiz', 'casual conversation', 'trial', 'press conference' etc. There are many which we can only refer to by circumlocution or metaphor, like 'chewing the fat' or 'whispering sweet nothings', or 'chatting him up' or 'dressing him down'. Again, speech events have various degrees of organization or diffuseness, but they are real social categories. A mutual recognition of the speech event type, which participants assume they are sharing, is crucial to the reasoning involved in construing utterances. It is part of the background knowledge required if what one utters is to be relevant to the preceding utterance, and to the continuing purposes of the conversation.

Return now to Figure 8.5. Look at the sixteen components. A given speech event's internal structure will include each of these. It will constrain us to certain interpretations of actions in certain sequences of adjacency pairs. It will characteristically assign us to certain communication roles as speakers and hearers. It may require certain specific forms of words or messages and may require them to be delivered in a certain key. As a thought experiment, imagine some speech event, for example a trial. Go through the sixteen features and see how the speech event constrains them.

How to enter a Yakan house

Some illustrations are perhaps in order. There are excellent anthropological descriptions of speech events. See, for example, Bauman and Sherzer (1974), Sanches and Blount (1975), or Frake (1980). We will look at a study by Frake (1975) – *How to*

Enter a Yakan House – which analyses the rules for entering houses among the Yakan, a Moslem people of the Philippines.

The typical layout of a Yakan house, with each part labelled with its Yakan word, is displayed in Figure 8.6. The house is a setting with a limited number of conceptually distinct locales, for example, the 'porch' and the 'head zone'. (The wall opposite the

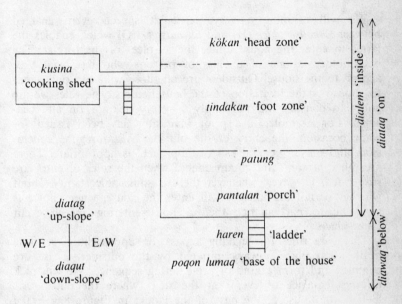

Figure 8.6 Yakan house settings (*from Frake, 1975*)

doorway is the sleeping area of the residents.) Various parts of the house can be the settings for a wide variety of different social situations. For example, the 'porch' is where 'conferences', 'negotiations' and 'litigations' are held. (For these speech events, see Frake, 1969.) The 'head zone' is where rituals are held. Thus, a setting within the house does not uniquely determine one situation, but various situations are appropriate to particular settings.

The organization of the house, and the language used to describe it, is such that if defines a definite sequence of settings which must be followed in gaining entry. Frake (1975: 30) arranges these in order of a progressively deeper penetration into the resident's private space. We can follow this progression in Figure 8.6.

1. From 'vicinity' to 'at'.
2. From 'below' to 'on'.
3. From 'on' to 'inside'.
4. From 'foot zone' to 'head zone'.

We will examine a very particulat speech event enacted between *a householder* (H) and *an outsider* (O) which enables the latter to enter the house under the auspices of the former. The householder is one of a class of persons who has legal 'free access' to the house. Outsiders are all those who can only enter the house at the invitation of the householders. The rules we are going to consider do not apply to everyone, nor on all occasions. For example, if a prior invitation has been issued for some occasion, the entry of the outsider is a foregone conclusion, and only a general call of 'approach' is appropriate. There are other persons and circumstances when the rules of entry are suspended. However, whenever there is some 'uncertainty' about whether or not an outsider will enter the house, when choice is available to participants, then a house-entering speech event takes place.

There are rules for 'making a pass' or 'approaching' a house in the first place, always initiated by the outsider. These are complex and form a kind of pre-entering sequence. We will pick up the sequence of events at the stage where the outsider is 'below' the house at the base of the ladder in Figure 8.6. Frake points out that moving to this position is the functional equivalent of a knock on the door in our society. Like the telephone ringing, it is a summons, and puts the hearer under the obligation to respond. The Yakan sequence at this point is Schegloff's 'summons-answer' adjacency pair (Frake, 1975: 32). The answer takes the form of a 'customary question' or *addat magtilewin*. (Recall the question intonation in the telephone answer pair part.) This utterance could be an answer to the summons, a greeting, and/or a question. In other contexts, which Frake describes, the 'customary question' is taken as a greeting and, if returned, the sequence of exchange of greetings is accomplished. In this context, however, the utterance is not to be interpreted as a greeting, but rather as an answer to the nonverbal summons. Since it is a question, an answer is expected. This enables householder and outsider to 'lock in' and begin the speech event proper. Note how the specific context of situation was crucial for the interpretation of the 'customary question'.

The main body of the speech event has the following form. The householder is only permitted to issue or not issue invitations to the outsider to progress to the next setting. Invitations for each setting have a different form. The outsider, on the other hand, is only permitted *to ask for permission to leave or not*. He can never go deeper into the house without an invitation, and he can never withdraw from a setting without asking permission and receiving it. The householder, on the other hand, cannot end the event but has control over who can enter each of the settings.

Frake (1975: 31) notes the 'game-like' nature of the event. At each setting, each participant has two choices of action. The outcomes are the joint result of what each participant does. The way the rules work is illustrated in Figure 8.7. Possible outcomes are *advance* to the next setting (for example, from 'below' to

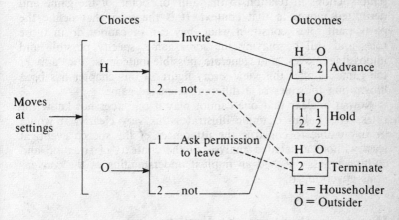

Figure 8.7 Invitation-permission language game (*after Frake, 1975*)

'on'), *terminate* the interaction, or *hold*. The condition for 'advance' is met when the householder invites and the outsider does not ask for permission to leave. The condition for 'terminate' is met when the outsider asks for permission to leave and the householder does not invite. The 'hold' conditions obtain when both participants do the same thing: either both perform 1, or both perform 2, in which case play remains at the same setting. The regulative aspect of these normative rules is the social obligation for the householder to 'render attention' to the outsider and for the outsider to 'display respect' in return. The simple system of rules in Figure 8.7 underlies what is superficially a rich variety of different routines.

A notion which has been implicit throughout this chapter can now usefully be made explicit since it is so clearly illustrated by this example. This is Wittgenstein's concept of a **language game** (Wittgenstein, 1953; Kenny, 1973). This notion captures, by analogy, the game-like character of what people *do* when they say something. (The analogy does not refer to the 'non-serious' nature of games, but rather the game-like properties of the calculus involved in producing and interpreting utterances.) Acts of speaking function only in the context of other linguistic and nonlinguistic activities. Both kinds of activities are constituted and made intelligible to oneself and others by following 'the rules of the game'. These make what people do count as particular kinds of acts, but only in the context of the game. Participants' actions must be construed in relation to other participants' actions in relation to the 'aim' or 'point' of the game and permitted moves in that context. It is the rules that define the participant roles, constrain what they can or cannot do in those roles and still be playing the *same* game, specify possible and impossible moves, and generate possible outcomes, the 'aim of the game'. Under this view, every figure in this chapter has been illustrating the rules of a different language game.

Now it is clear that one cannot play if one does not know the rules. The Yakan example illustrates this very clearly. It would be impossible to construe the utterances of the speech event, at least without a detailed analysis of the contexts of situation and culture, unless one had an implicit understanding of the conventions governing it.

How to teach among the English

Such speech events also characterize our own culture. Imagine yourself for a moment in a typical classroom somewhere in the English-speaking world. Or recall your own schooldays. The teacher has just 'asked a question'. But was it *really* a question? Did the teacher really request information which she believed the pupils knew and she didn't? Well, if it is not a real question, then what is the teacher intending to convey? (Likewise, Searle points out that an examination question is not a real question.) We have to ask ourselves, then, what is the structure of the classroom speech event and what sort of acts conventionally constitute it? There may not be specific names for these. Thus, one possibility is a sort of Socratic pseudoquestion, the intention of which is to lead the pupils step by step through an argument. Another is, by pseudoquestioning, to assess what information the pupils already have. Another may be simply to 'raise a topic' for discussion, or even simply to request that the pupils 'say something' in certain instances.

The language of the classroom has been extensively studied. Sinclair and Coulthard (1975), reporting the results of a research project into classroom discourse, described a typical threefold structure in **teaching-exchanges**. Figure 8.8 illustrates how such an exchange might be analysed by their system.

I cannot examine the complexities of Sinclair and Coulthard's work here, but it is clear that they found characteristic sequences of adjacency pairs, and norms of interaction and interpretation, which correspond to the roles of teacher and pupil in classroom speech events. Thus, a pupil will interpret 'They needed very rich and powerful patrons, didn't they?' not only as a request for confirmation, but as a **starter** in the **initiation** of a teaching exchange. The function of this act, according to Sinclair and Coulthard (1975: 40), is 'to provide information about or direct attention to or thought toward an area in order to make a correct response to the initiation more likely'. And its identification depends on the sequence of acts realizing the sequence of moves which make up the structure of this kind of exchange. The **opening-answer-follow-up** structure is a characteristic of teaching exchanges. The follow-up perhaps also suggests that the elicitations are not real questions.

So, like the Yakan, we also have complex speech events with their norms for the use of speech. In summary: these are conventions of production and interpretation which enable us, in following them, mutually to constitute the event in question and realize its purposes. We are free to perform any utterance with any intent, of course, but its interpretation and its relevance to other utterances is in terms of the speech event which the hearer believes (and believes the speaker believes) has been mutually agreed upon as background knowledge. The language used, together with the social assumptions, creates the event. The constraint on the individual is that the intent behind what he says be **calculable**, makes sense in terms of this assumed background and the meaning of the linguistic forms he utters. Of course, sometimes the speech event which we believe we are in can be

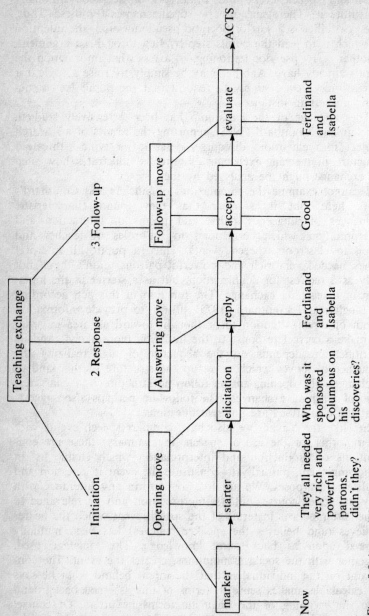

Figure 8.8 A possible teaching exchange

redefined to 'save the sense' of the individual. This also points to the way in which such conventions can themselves evolve and change.

In this chapter, I have looked at some of the things which we tacitly know about the structure of conversation itself, and about its situations and settings insofar as they concern the interpretation of utterances. In the next chapter, I will look at another kind of 'background knowledge'; that which is not specifically concerned with the structure of speaking itself, but is nevertheless crucial to its production and comprehension, namely the frameworks of everyday belief through which we interpret and structure our world.

9. Knowledge of Words and Knowledge of the World

> The uniformity that unites us in communication and belief is a uniformity of resultant patterns overlying a chaotic subjective diversity of connections between words and experience. Uniformity comes in where it matters socially; hence rather in point of intersubjectively conspicuous circumstances of utterance than in point of privately conspicuous ones.
>
> Quine (1960)

A boundary

Consider the following text:

1 Brenda: I'm pregnant... and it's your fault.
2 Brenda: I told you to be careful...
3 Arthur: How do you know?
4 Brenda: I'm twelve days late.
5 Arthur: How do you know it's mine?
6 Brenda: I ain't done owt like that with Jack for a couple of months or more.
7 Arthur: Well, have yer tried owt? Took owt I mean?
6 Brenda: Yes, took pills but they didn't work.

If we consider just the semantics – that is, the meanings of the words and sentences by themselves – it is clear that we would not be able to comprehend in full the connections between the various utterances. A sentence or word meaning by itself, the semantics of the linguistic items, is that which is conveyed by those items universally in any context of use. Consider the meaning of sentence 1, 'I'm pregnant'. What are the states of affairs which it is conventionally agreed are 'picked out' by the combination of 'I', 'am', 'pregnant'? What is contributed by the adjective 'pregnant'? This means, roughly, that the subject of whom it is said 'has a foetus in her/its womb'. (One could argue that it also entails 'is going to have young, give birth', but this is not necessarily, but only probably, the case.) The fact that the subject of whom it is said is female, mammalian and animate, is also part of the meaning of the word. Now consider the relation of 'I'm pregnant' to the successive sentences above. 'It's your fault' means roughly that some state of affairs which the speaker believes is bad or wrong is the responsibility of the hearer. Therefore, a hearer could tell from the meaning of the linguistic items alone only that an adult female speaker 'has a foetus in her womb' and that 'Arthur' is 'responsible for this bad state of affairs'. The connection between these two is taken for granted.

Similarly, in 2, the linguistic meaning of the sentence, which again accuses Arthur by reminding him of Brenda's earlier request that he be careful, does not actually contain the information about how his carefulness can be related to her pregnancy. Again in 4, both the fact that it is her period, not herself, which is late, and the reason why this utterance can count as an answer to 3, 'How do you know? (you are pregnant), are part of the background knowledge invoked in the interpretation of the utterances. Similar relationships hold between the other propositions in the text. It is clear, therefore, that the sequential cohesion of utterances depends not only on the meanings of the linguistic forms, but also on additional information which we infer from them.

In other words, what is taken for granted is information such as: pregnancy is the result of intercourse; pregnancy stops menstruation and therefore an absent period after intercourse is a sign of pregnancy; the father of the putative child also has the responsibility to solve the problem of the pregnancy; pregnancy is a 'bad' thing for Arthur and Brenda because she is married to someone else, and so on and so forth. Such information is not an unstructured set of propositions but is all interconnected in a large-scale structure of knowledge. Certain propositions from this larger structure, which are not part of the linguistic meanings of the text itself but which are needed to make the text cohere, are somehow implied by the text in context. Figure 9.1 is suggestive of the conceptual areas that, interconnected together, make up some sort of large-scale structure of our 'everyday' knowledge in this area of experience. The lines under each word represent

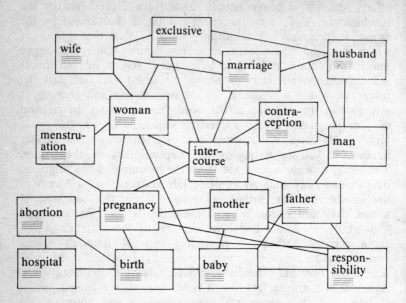

Figure 9.1 The interrelatedness of background knowledge

propositions the content of which is what we know about each area, and the lines between bubbles represent the inferential connections between each set of propositions.

Kinds of contextual information

When discussing background knowledge in the production and interpretation of utterances we must proceed with care. Many of the issues have been discussed by philosophers and many of the points I will make have a philosophical flavour. The first thing to do is to try to sort out the various kinds of contextual information that is, in principle, available to participants. Whether participants *do* use all the contextual resources available for comprehending utterances is another matter. We are interested in finding out what they must use, what they can use, and what they do use. Information that they can and *do* use is a matter of **heuristics**, that is, of strategies adopted to facilitate the discovery of something. The role of contextual resources also depends on what they are resouces for – what we are discovering. The words we have used for this are 'comprehension' or 'interpretation' of utterances. But there are problems in what we mean by these terms. We shall see that to 'comprehend' an utterance is to draw new inferences from its proposition(s) conjoined with the proposition(s) of other utterances in a context. However, there are degrees of comprehension – we can comprehend more from an utterance (draw more inferences) by doing more work and widening the context. But 'comprehending' the utterance in this sense is not exactly the same thing as 'understanding' which of the inferences which could be drawn were those that the speaker intended to be drawn. Figure 9.2 makes some important distinc-

1.	**Background knowledge**	(a) Knowledge of the language.
		(b) Metaconversational rules, norms, conventions (Chapter 8).
		(c) Participants' biographies.
		(d) Metasocial rules, norms, conventions. (situation types).
		(e) The encyclopedia.
2.	**Mutual knowledge**	Each participant's knowledge that the other knows *that p*, inferred on some *basis*
3.	**Context of utterance**	
	(i) Previous utterances in same conversation.	
	(ii) Immediate setting of speech.	
	(iii) Previous conversations of participants.	
	(iv) Background knowledge, *accessed* by (i)–(iii).	

Figure 9.2 Kinds of contextual information

tions about different kinds of **contextual information** available to participants. I will discuss each kind in turn.

First, there is **background knowledge** of the most general sort. As we saw, people know and believe a very great deal about the world and how to live in it. It is probably most useful to think of this information as sets of propositions which participants know or believe to be true.

Knowledge and belief are not the same thing (Hintikka, 1962).

The two have different properties. For example, if I know something, I also believe that it is the case. However, if I believe something is the case, I do not necessarily know for certain it is the case. My belief could be wrong and have to be revised. I can believe something that is actually false. By contrast, I cannot know something that is false. Belief is a wider term than knowledge.

One special kind of knowledge is my knowledge of the language. I know quite a bit because I speak English. For example, if I know that Brenda is pregnant, I also know that in the normal course of events she is going to have a baby, that she is female and so on. Our knowledge and belief are interwoven with the meanings of words and sentences in our language.

It is a characteristic of propositions that they can be either true or false. Another characteristic is our ability to draw **inferences** from them. So if I know or believe that one proposition is true, I also know or believe that the other propositions are true. I can do this without looking at the world. If B follows from A, and I know A is true, then I don't have to check the facts to know with equal certainty that B is true. And so on for B and C etc. This serves to tie together what we believe into a network of inferentially related sets of propositions of potentially unlimited size. A more of less internally consistent chunk of such a network could be legitimately termed a **belief system** for a given area of experience.

These inferential networks are 'anchored' in what a person takes to be undoubtedly true in a multiplicity of ways. Some certainties seem to be anchored in language itself, some rest on observation, some are stipulations, most are warranted socially. Other beliefs, within the network of beliefs, are held because they follow from these.

The sheer size of what an individual knows, believes or assumes is quite marvellous. Consider what one has to know in order to do everyday things, like driving a car, going shopping, or eating in a restaurant. The same knowledge is invoked in understanding utterances about such areas of experience (Schank and Abelson, 1977; Garfinkel, 1967). Some kinds of knowledge and belief seem very basic and general – things we believe about how the physical world is put together. There is knowledge, for example, about what we would admit to the actual world as an object, and, once admitted, how it can be spatially related to other objects: 'above', 'below', 'on', 'beside' etc. This is related to more specific knowledge about how spaces are organized in everyday life; for example, how houses can be laid out, and how individuals move around in them. There is knowledge about when it is appropriate, or not, to attribute causation (of various kinds) in describing the relationship between two events. These sorts of things are assumed in talking about something as everyday as 'a child threw a ball up the flight of stairs and broke the vase on the table on the landing', where assumptions about space and causation are implicitly involved in understanding that the first event is related to the second.

We also know a lot about people. We know about the practices of our community – how to buy and sell, work and play and so forth – in the most minute detail. We know, believe and assume a great deal about what others presumably think, feel or are trying to do. For example, if someone has an anguished look on their face, is hopping about vigorously and clasping their left thumb with their right hand, we would probably say they were 'in pain'. If there was a hammer at their feet etc. we might also be willing to tell a causal story about what happened. If someone treats us badly, we impute certain psychological states to them as possible explanations: that they were 'tired' or 'jealous' or 'spiteful'. Think of what is involved, as background knowledge, in understanding what it means to describe someone's action as 'trying to get even out of spite'. So knowledge of the world involves not only propositions about the world 'out there' which people know or believe, but beliefs about how to understand 'people' and 'practices'. Everyday reasoning involves not only a 'taken for granted' physics, geography etc., but a 'taken for granted' psychology, sociology, politics and so on.

All these aspects of background knowledge can appropriately be referred to as the **encyclopedia**; everything participants know, believe or assume about everything. In Figure 9.2 I mentioned three areas of the encyclopedia which might be accessed in a verbal encounter. These are, first, rules for conversational activity itself, of the sort discussed in Chapter 8; second, general rules for interpreting social actions whether involving language or not; and third, participants' biographies and social characteristics. Within a community we can assume participants to have differing but overlapping encyclopedias reflecting their different experiences.

The second kind of contextual information is **mutual knowledge**. This is the subset of background knowledge which is shared, and known to be shared, between any two participants.

This notion, how speaker and hearer know that each other knows that something is so, is problematic. It is problematic in two ways. First, in how mutual knowledge can be reliably established, and secondly, in terms of the role it plays in comprehension (Clark and Marshall, 1981; Smith, 1982).

Mutual knowledge involves coordination between participants in terms of what they know each other knows. The notion was introduced by David Lewis (1969) in his analysis of conventions, viewed as solutions to 'coordination problems'. (For other treatments and uses of 'mutual knowledge', 'shared knowledge', 'common ground' etc., see Schiffer, 1972; Stalnaker, 1978; Karttunen and Peters, 1979.) Lewis (1969) proposes a number of examples of such problems:

> Suppose you and I both want to meet each other. We will meet if and only if we go to the same place. It matters little to either of us where (within limits) he goes if he meets the other there; and it matters little to either of us where he goes if he fails to meet the other there. We must each choose where to go. The best place for me to go is the place where you will go, so I try to figure out where you will go and to go there myself. You do the same. Each chooses according to his expectation of the other's choice. If either succeeds, so does the other; the outcome is one we both desired.

Such problems occur in everyday life. For example, say one is supposed to meet a relative who is arriving on a known flight at London Airport and the relative knows they are going to be met. Both parties want to meet the other. But no specific meeting place at the airport has been prearranged and communication between the participants is impossible. Each participant will go to the place where he expects the other participant to go. If these mutual expectations are correct, the participants will meet.

Lewis's ultimate point is that if this situation recurs between the same two participants (the relative comes again in succeeding years), their expectations of each other will become regularized and a guide to action. Each will know that the other expects that he will go to a particular point, X, in the terminal. A convention, which solves the coordination problem, will have been established. Mutual knowledge is thus a prerequisite to a convention. And, as we have seen, convention is central to the use of language in context. In Chapter 8, for example, we showed that speech events and sequencing rules (language games, in Wittgenstein's terminology) involved conventional rules. And earlier on, we concluded that it was convention (a norm of interpretation) that was the 'coordinative mechanism' which accounted for how speakers, who had never been in contact with one another, produced variants of a variable feature in community wide patterns. From Lewis's arguments, we can conclude that it is mutual knowledge, as a subset of background knowledge, that is significant for the analysis of discourse.

But how can participants reliably establish that they mutually know something? (Note that I don't have to believe what you know is true. I just have to know that you know it, and you have to know that I know you know it.) There are arguments here about resolving an infinite regression which we cannot go into (Lewis, 1969; 52ff; Clark and Marshall, 1981). However, participants are said to have a **basis** or **grounds** for mutually knowing something, or, in philosophical terminology, for mutually knowing '*that p*'. In Lewis's words, they need a mutual 'ascription of some common inductive standards and background information, rationality, mutual ascription of rationality, and so on'. We have pushed communality one stage further back here. To establish a basis for mutual knowledge *that p*, we assume of each other that we are rational, and reason according to certain everyday standards etc. Another basis for establishing mutual knowledge might be the mutual assumption by participants that they speak the same language – the point being that certain kinds of inference are drawn from sentences as a matter of 'knowing' a language, and that for any one utterance, the rest of the language serves as background knowledge that can be taken to be mutual.

Clark and Marshall (1981: 26ff) carefully sort out and classify the way people ground the assumption of mutual knowledge in their experience. One way is in terms of community membership. If someone is a member of a given social group, then it follows that, in all likelihood, they know what other members of that group know. (We saw earlier that a group's 'knowledge' of rules, norms or conventions was more regular than its actual practice, and, in fact, could be used to define a speech community.) The second major type of tactic is the direct evidence we have of what others know, believe or assume through our own experience of them.

In Figure 9.2 I called this last type of information **context of utterance**. Imagine a discourse as it unfolds and utterances are exchanged. For any given utterance, by either participant, there have been a series of prior utterances. The assertions or presuppositions in these provide a progressively less immediate context for our given utterance. The utterance immediately before a given utterance is its immediately local context: all previous utterances in the conversation are its global context. We can say that each participant has a **commitment slate**: that to which he is committed because of what he has stated in the course of the conversation up to the utterance in question. And each participant's commitment slate includes his assessment, not only of what he himself is committed to because of what he has said, but also of what he believes the other party is committed to. (The term 'commitment slate' originates with Hamblin, 1971; see also Gazdar, 1981.) This is a way of representing that previous utterances in the same conversation provide a good basis for inferring mutual knowledge, and a checkable one. There is always risk in assuming mutual knowledge with another. If I misinterpret or am misinterpreted because I have inferred mutual knowledge wrongly, then this is the case where conversational 'repairs' can be made, following the strategies of faults and repairs mentioned in the last chapter.

The immediate setting of speech is another aspect of context of utterance. The actual physical surroundings which the participants share is a ground for mutual knowledge. So are rather more remotely previous conversations between the same participants and their settings. As a conversation unfolds and its setting changes, we should expect a fairly rapid decay (in short-term memory) of context of utterance as a reliable basis for mutual knowledge of specific propositions. This would vary according to the kind of situation involved in the production of the utterance – prior utterances in written mode can obviously be consulted. It would seem, however, that the most reliable basis for the assumption of mutual knowledge are those elements of context and setting 'closest' to the utterance itself.

I said above that background knowledge took the form of an inferential network of potentially unlimited size. The arrow on the right in Figure 9.2, looping from the context of utterance to background knowledge in general, is meant to suggest how this can be reduced to manageable proportions in any given text. The unfolding commitment slates of participants, and the setting of speech, will have made use of propositions from background knowledge. They will have focused those areas of background knowledge which participants can take as mutual on the basis of 'the conversation thus far'. The propositions in background knowledge which are inferentially related to those in the commitment slates can, of course, also be taken as true, and as mutually known. I can move around the inferential network on this basis with considerable confidence. Thus, once I have added to my commitment slate, on the basis of your utterance, that you know (as I do) that this is 'Yakan house-entering', then I am able to make many more inferences which I can use to interpret what you say next. This tends to preserve a context throughout a discourse, and balance the short-term effect of context decay mentioned above. It is via commitment slates that background knowledge is narrowed down and most reliably established as mutual, immediately prior to the current utterance.

This 'narrowing down' allows us to draw a yet finer distinction within mutual knowledge itself. Clearly, all of the knowledge which participants are able to take as mutual is not required for any one utterance. Therefore, we can distinguish the *actual* mutual knowledge involved in an interpretation as a subset of mutual knowledge.

Role of contextual information

So far, then, we have said that mutual knowledge is of importance in the operation of conventions, and it follows that it is likely to be a necessary condition for those aspects of language which are conventional. Our next question, however, is to ask whether the *prior assumption of mutual knowledge* figures in the comprehension of an utterance, and if so, when and how. What exactly is the role of mutual knowledge in comprehension?

There are two main alternative views. For a debate see the articles in Smith (1982) especially Sperber and Wilson (1982) and replies to them.

View 1: Prior mutual knowledge is a necessary condition for the comprehension of an utterance.

This view claims that the speakers must actually have established to their satisfaction that mutual knowledge between themsel and their hearers exists – that actual mutual knowledge necessary to comprehend the utterance in question.

> *View 2*: Prior mutual knowledge is *not* a necessary condition for the comprehension of utterances; rather the act of interpreting an utterance is in itself context-creating. The hearer draws directly on background knowledge in comprehension and there need be no assumption that this actual knowledge is mutually known beforehand.

This second view is taken by Sperber and Wilson. Let us now look at their theory.

Contextual implications

What do we mean when we say someone comprehends an utterance? As we said before, it is most useful to think of comprehension as *the process of drawing inferences from the linguistic forms of the utterance*. Consider this exchange:

A: She's pregnant.
B: She'll be going into hospital soon.

If we consider A's or B's utterances alone, as if there was no context, we draw these inferences warranted by the meanings of the words in each sentence. Thus from A we can infer roughly that a female adult has a foetus in her womb, and if things proceed normally she will have a baby in due course. From B, we can infer that at some time not too much later than the time when B spoke, a female adult will move towards and enter an institution for the care of the sick or wounded. To make these inferences is to understand the content of the propositions A and B have uttered. This is clearly an important part of comprehension, but it is also clear that there is more to it than that.

Let us look at B's utterance again. We know what inferences an draw when there is no context – we know its propositional content. Now let us put it into context. Start with the A's utterance: its immediately local context. And sudden range of **contextual implications** may be inferred.

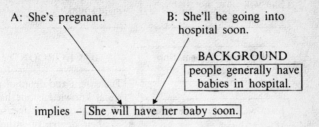

From A and B together, the new information that 'she will have her baby soon' can be inferred. A proposition that could not be inferred from either utterance alone can be inferred from both utterances together. Sperber and Wilson (1982: 73) write: 'A contextual implication of an utterance is a non-trivial logical implication derivable not from the content of the utterance alone, nor from the context alone, but only from context and content combined.'

Now note another factor. In order to comprehend the new information conveyed by B (to draw the contextual implication 'she will have her baby soon') the hearer has to draw on his background knowledge. He has to supply the premiss, 'People generally have babies in hospital', in order to arrive at the contextual implication. So a proposition from background knowledge and the immediately prior utterance, together with the content of B, allow us to comprehend B's utterance as conveying at least that our heroine will have her baby soon. That is one possible interpretation of the point of B's utterance.

More processing, more implications

As an experiment, let us try expanding the context of the exchange between A and B. Imagine, for example, that the exchange immediately preceding our exchange had been about which of A or B was the closer friend of the pregnant lady, call her Brenda. This slight expansion of context, plus further background knowledge, yields further contextual implications from B's utterance:

B: She'll be going into hospital *soon.*

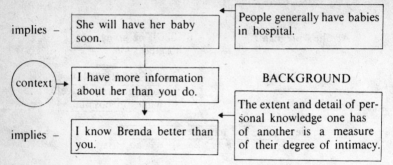

But 'I know Brenda better than you', with the background knowledge on its right as a premiss, is not the only contextual implication that can be inferred due to this extension of context. We could also infer, 'I have gained information re Brenda more recently than you have (if you only know she's pregnant)', as another implication. This could form a link in another inferential chain leading to the conclusion that B knows Brenda better than A does. In other words, this slight expansion of context gives us many more contextual implications.

Let us see what we have established so far:

1. To comprehend an utterance is to draw contextual implications from it.
2. The more the context is extended the more contextual implications can be derived.
3. This increase in the number of implications, involving as it does pushing context back to earlier and earlier utterances, checking setting, and invoking more and more background knowledge, requires more processing. The cost of more contextual implications is more inferential work.

From these three points, it would seem we have a problem in accounting for comprehension. Depending on how the context is expanded, there are very many contextual implications which can be drawn from any one utterance. (By slightly changing the contexts above, or by invoking more or different background knowledge, you can get an indeterminate set of different implications out of our example. Try it!) The problem, then, is to narrow this down to just those interpretations that the speaker intended. Or perhaps a single interpretation.

If we return to our example and take a different tack, another possible contextual implication of B's remark might be:

B: She'll be going into *hospital* soon.

BACKGROUND

```
                              ┌─────────────────────────┐
                              │ People generally are taken │
                              │ into hospital for treatment of │
              │               │ serious medical problems │
              │               │ during pregnancy.        │
              ▼               └─────────────────────────┘
┌─────────────────────────┐
│ There are serious        │
│ medical problems in her  │
│ pregnancy.               │
└─────────────────────────┘
```

Now imagine the context in which A has no particular information about Brenda other than the belief that she is pregnant. A has only recently heard, from a friend of a friend, that Brenda is pregnant. Furthermore, A has no particular reason to believe either that Brenda is near term or that her health has ever been at issue. In such a context as this, what would A do, faced with B's remark?

We can sketch out a strategy, and an assumption, in the following terms. A really has to assume that B's remark is **relevant** to her, as its addressee, in some way or other. Otherwise, the utterance would have no point. A can do two things. She can see what contextual implications are yielded by the minimal context of her own immediately preceding remark, 'She's pregnant', B's remark, and background knowledge. That there are medical problems in Brenda's pregnancy, as diagrammed above, can be inferred immediately. Is that a satisfactory point for B's utterance in this context? Yes, it probably is. But to make sure, A can search the context, back as far as the biographical component of background knowledge if she likes. More probably, she would look out to progressively less local contexts. This takes work, and the work very quickly yields no contextual implications more significant than the one above. A decides that this is the best she can do in comprehending what B said (drawing contextual implications from it). Assuming that B can be assumed to have spoken relevantly, that is probably the correct interpretation.

The reason why that interpretation seems right is, of course, that I imagined a context in which Brenda had not figured until A's remark that she is pregnant. If, however, we stipulate the 'rivalry in friendship' context again, we get the explosion of contextual implications sketched out above. And we get that by expanding the context very little, only one exchange back. The work is worth the gain in comprehension. In this context, A decides that this is, in all likelihood, what B meant to convey.

Context creation

It is a bit puzzling how certain new information is so readily derivable from an utterance, the minimal context of the preceding utterance, and one piece of background knowledge. The fact that this is usually the case guarantees that something will be conveyed in any exchange, even if it is not the point intended by the speaker. (If the hearer feels that this minimal comprehension is not satisfactory, he will search the context to increase the implications.)

Why, then, is something always minimally conveyed? We begin with the fact that participants understand the 'meaning' of the sentences uttered. The contextual implication, 'There are serious medical problems in her pregnancy' (given the background, 'People generally are taken into hospital for treatment etc.), is readily derivable because of the meaning of the word 'hospital' itself, and its contribution to the meaning of the sentence. The Concise Oxford Dictionary's definition of the term is, 'institution for the care of the sick and wounded'. It is a very simple inferential step to arrive at the piece of background knowledge, 'People generally go to the hospital when they are sick or in serious medical difficulty.' In fact, there is no clear-cut boundary in a case like this between the meaning of the proposition and background knowledge inferred from it. Hence the background knowledge required to derive new information is inferable, in the first instance, from the linguistic forms of the utterances themselves.

Now notice that 'hospital' has been italicized in our last version of B's utterance: 'She'll be going into *hospital* soon.' The emphatic way that 'hospital' is pronounced serves to focus our attention on that constituent. We treat it as contributing new information, information that is not retrievable from the context (Halliday, 1967/8). It has been argued, by Smith and Wilson (1979) and Wilson and Sperber (1979), that the effect of such a phonological emphasis is to reorder the inferences warranted by the meaning of the sentence. The inferences thus promoted are those most relevant to the interpretation of the utterance. So with emphasis on 'hospital', inferences dependent on that word are more significant in interpretation than those dependent on other words. And this helped guide us to the correct contextual implication.

By contrast, recall our first interpretation of the utterance. This was, 'She will have her baby soon.' In that example, 'soon' was italicized, and bore emphasis. Accordingly, we took the time of birth, the meaning contributed by that word, as our favoured contextual implication.

Finally, let us return to Sperber and Wilson's (1982) claim that prior assumption of mutual knowledge is not, in principle, required for comprehension. In neither of our interpretations would the speaker have had to determine prior to the utterance that actual mutual knowledge existed between participants. In seeking to construe the utterance in the way most relevant to him, the hearer is led to infer for himself the background knowledge required to do this. In cases like these, the process of comprehension is context-creating. The background knowledge is directly invoked by the process of reasoning, guided by the search for relevance. It need not be assumed to be mutual prior to speaking.

The principle of relevance

The narrowing down of the set of possible implications to that which the speaker intended, and the dispensability of mutual knowledge, is made possible because participants are guided in comprehension by the **principle of relevance**. Sperber and Wilson (1982: 75) state it in this way: 'The speaker tries to express the proposition which is the most relevant one possible to the hearer.' Participants, according to this principle, work on the assumption that each tries, and succeeds, to express propositions which are maximally relevant to the other. Now we need a definition of maximal relevance.

Sperber and Wilson (1982: 74) define degree of relevance as a trade-off between two factors, both quantitative: the number of contextual implications and the amount of processing required to derive them. By amount of processing, they mean the time and attention required to expand the context and infer the implications. They write, 'Degrees of relevance depend on a ratio of input to output, where output is the number of contextual implications, and input is the amount of processing required to derive these contextual implications.' For example, if two utterances are

Input	Output
Amount of processing	Number of contextual implications

equal in the amount of work they require, the one where that work yields more implications is most relevant. On the other hand, if we can derive an equal number of implications from two utterances, then it is the one in which this is done with less work that is most relevant. What a hearer does, according to the theory, is to try to get the best yield of implications for the least processing on the assumption that the speaker was trying and succeeding in conveying just those implications (that he is following the principle of relevance). For criticisms of this view, see Gazdar and Good (1982).

Principle and practices

In general, if we are willing to expand context, including background knowledge, and to keep processing until we find them, we can derive contextual implications which link what has been uttered with the contexts of situation and culture in complex ways – and so elucidate what has been said.

Sperber and Wilson (1982: 76) note that the 'set' of the amount of processing that participants expect to do varies with the type of discourse. Speakers have been able to gauge whether to make utterances which yield their maximum implications in minimal contexts, or to make utterances which do not do so and are relevant only if the hearer searches the context more extensively. In other words, participants have to assess how obscure or indirect to be, and this varies with types of discourse. But doesn't this 'set' to processing effort, and hence to relevance, require prior mutual knowledge? The answer is 'no', not in principle, because presumably the type of discourse that the speaker wants to engage in can itself be contextually implied by the amount of difficulty he builds into his utterances. One would expect that the hearer would interpret this as conveying that the speaker is engaging in discourse of a certain kind. An appropriate reply, showing that he has understood, would establish 'type of discourse' as mutual knowledge at that stage of the encounter. And having this kind of mutual knowledge would have great heuristic value in comprehension. If I am witnessing a trial, or attending a lecture, or entering a Yakan house, or teaching a class, or reading a poem, I do not have to infer this anew in comprehending each utterance. It is mutual knowledge. In practice, context is a great deal more structured and global than it need be in principle.

At this point, we are at a very important crossroads in our argument about the role of mutual and background knowledge in comprehension. In the last chapter we analysed the game-like nature of discourse. We pointed to much evidence that when people speak, they are engaged in rule-governed activities of various kinds. The activities were intelligible only because they were constituted by convention. Now we also saw that conventions presuppose mutual knowledge, if they are solutions to coordination problems. And viewed in social terms, this is what they are.

Once participants have inferred the type of discourse in which they are engaged, the conventions which constitute it come into play. By definition, they have mutual knowledge of those conventions (with a certain amount of 'risk'). In the course of the discourse, therefore, knowledge of conventions involves virtually no processing 'cost'. As we saw, conventions govern relationships between sets of utterances by both participants. Sometimes they are quite local, as in sequencing rules. Sometimes they involve discontinuous utterances.

Remember, for example, how overall 'closing sequences' involved not only terminal exchanges but variably positioned pre-closings. Remember also how the resolution of the identification problem could extend over four turns. Larger-scale constraints, extending over many utterances, governed speech events. Our analysis in Chapter 8 revealed a hierarchy of normative constraints in discourse. Clearly, such conventions serve to preserve an expanded context over many utterances; as a sort of mutually known framework for interpretation. The search for maximally relevant interpretations takes place against this global background of contextual expectations. So I know in advance roughly how much further processing I might have to do in order to get the maximal number of implications. In other words, what is most relevant to me depends on the larger conventional activity which we mutually know we are creating together in our conversation.

We also saw in Chapter 8 that utterances are activities. As such, they are intentional, or performed for a purpose. (We talked above of the 'point' of an utterance.) These issues will come up in following chapters. However, a hearer cannot be said to have understood a speaker's utterance unless he can discern the speaker's intention in uttering it. As Sperber and Wilson (1982: 79) point out, intended inferences require, at least, the prior assumption of mutual knowledge of a specific piece of information without which the hearer cannot comprehend that the speaker intended him to draw the intended inference. We can illustrate both this point, and the point of the previous paragraph, with the following example of a response to a compliment.

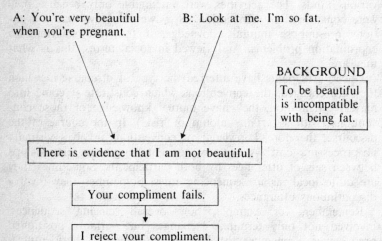

A: You're very beautiful when you're pregnant.

B: Look at me. I'm so fat.

BACKGROUND

To be beautiful is incompatible with being fat.

There is evidence that I am not beautiful.

Your compliment fails.

I reject your compliment.

Given minimal context and background knowledge, it is arguable that the most obvious contextual implication generated by the principle of relevance is the one illustrated, that B disagrees with the assertion, and rejects the compliment. But that may not be the intended inference. I pointed out earlier that the intentionality behind such replies can be quite complex. Rather than rejecting the compliment, the speaker might intend simultaneously to accept it and avoid self-praise. Now to understand that B 'meant' this requires mutual knowledge of a rule of politeness. But, far from involving much processing, this information is instantly available, since it is a convention that is preserved throughout most conversational contexts. Of course, B can say anything in reply to A, but how that will be construed as relevant depends on the constraints of the mutual knowledge of the conventions involved. Say B did seriously intend to reject the compliment, perhaps because she felt the conventional reasons for complimenting were not satisfied (their relationship was such that any possible supportive reason of positive politeness was outweighed by the intrusiveness of the remark). This could be done, assuming the rules of politeness, by remarks such as:

B: Please! Please!
    or
B: Yes, I am very beautiful, aren't I?

Both these replies violate politeness as a norm of interpretation since the preferred reply is acceptance. The first 'defaces' A by conveying that the compliment should never have been attempted, and that the attempt distresses B. The second is ironical, and therefore conveys that B does not consider herself beautiful. Furthermore, it does so in such a way as to call into question both A's judgement and his motives in defining the proposition in the first place. Finally, consider how a 'preserved' context which specified 'non-seriousness' (such as at a cocktail party) could change all these construals, and at the same time, be instantly available mutual knowledge. If those examples are convincing, and utterances enact complexes of intentions of this sort, then it follows that mutual knowledge must figure prominently in the analysis of any exchange. This analysis is possible at minimal processing cost because of the conventional nature of discourse.

Of course, Sperber and Wilson (1982) might well be right when they agree that the principle of relevance generates contexts without prior mutual knowledge. This, in fact, makes orientation and reorientation to different conventions possible in the process of discourse and the learning of new conventions. However, in practice, context is more highly structured, and mutual knowledge of contextual information more pervasively available than their argument might suggest.

One reason for this is that background knowledge is itself highly structured and closely related to, if not inseparable from, knowledge of language. If I can assume that one specific piece of background knowledge is mutually known, I can infer that quite a lot else is mutually known as well. Let us go on to consider this point.

The network of beliefs

Earlier on, we talked of beliefs as part of an inferential network. The philosopher W. Van O. Quine (1953, 1960) draws a picture of beliefs and their relation to language which is of importance here. For Quine, our beliefs about the world do not stand or fall separately. Rather, everything that we believe is a vast single interwoven web of propositions which face experience collectively. Many propositions are assigned the values 'true' or 'false', not entirely because of how they relate to observations of the world, but because of their relations to other propositions. It is only propositions at the boundary of the inferential network which are directly empirical. These boundary propositions can be assigned the values 'true' or 'false' in the light of observations.

On the other hand, propositions at the centre of what we believe, those most deeply integrated into the network, do not relate to observations, except very indirectly. They appear to us to be necessarily true. We are fairly free in how we assign 'true' and 'false', however, to those propositions neither at the boundary not at the centre, in order to maintain equilibrium and stability in the overall system.

Pressures ripple through the system from two directions: at the centre are those propositions which it would be too 'costly' to give up and are more or less immune from revision. At the periphery are those which we are, in principle, willing to revise. So empirical pressure towards revision ripples inwards to meet systematic pressure from the core, which, to varying degrees, resists that pressure or is immune to it. Internally, realignments over what we are willing to call 'true' or 'false' take place. This kind of structure, according to Quine, characterizes the totality of our beliefs – not only our scientific theories, but everyday theories about the world.

We can get at least some hint at how this works by dipping into the totality of our beliefs for an example. The right-hand side of Figure 9.3 shows various kinds of inferential relationships between the proposition 'X is pregnant' and other propositions. Whether the statement 'X is pregnant' is true or false in any given case is clearly an empirical matter. We have criteria for deciding this; for example, we can look at the results of a pregnancy test. Let us say that we agree that the statement is true. The rest of the propositions on the right-hand side of Figure 9.3 then follow from 'X is pregnant' in various ways. For example, we might also believe that X is a woman. This particular belief,

Coordination of Beliefs

1. *X is pregnant* is true.

A believes that B believes *that p*, and, if questioned,

cannot conceive of uncertainty

2. If only females can be pregnant and X is male, then X cannot be pregnant.

3. X is heavy with child.

admits to (more or less) absolute certainty because of words

4. *X has a foetus inside her body*.
5. X is female.

6. X is sexually mature.
7. X ovulates.

because of world

8. Sperm fertilized an ovum of X's.
9. X has not ovulated since fertilization.

believes that a subset of the propositions is true in any case, and all propositions will be true in *normal* cases

10. *X is preparing to have a baby*.
11. X will be a mother.
12. The baby will be X's child.
13. X will become a certain shape etc.
14. X had sexual intercourse with a male of the same species.
15. This male will be the father of X's child.

16. X is married to Y.
17. X has a husband Y.
18. X is Y's wife.
19. Y is the male who is the father of X's child.
20. X had intercourse with Y.

believes that these are empirical questions, salient to p, which may be true or false in context

21. X will have her baby in a hospital.
22. X will have a miscarriage.
23. X will have an abortion.
24. X will be delivered by a midwife.
25. X will have high blood pressure.
26. X will have a short labour.
27. X will have an epidural.

Etc.

Figure 9.3 A network of beliefs

in fact, appears to be pretty well immune from revision (if X is human). Other inferences, for example, that 'X is going to have a baby' or that 'X has a husband Y' and that 'Y will be the father of X's baby' are quite likely to be true, depending on what else we know about the circumstances. We might argue that these will be true in 'normal' cases. However, we would be willing to revise our beliefs and assign them the value 'false' if the facts turn out otherwise. In still other cases, we might want to wait until we have evidence to hand before venturing even an assessment of the likelihood of truth or falsity; for example, about whether X will have a long or short labour. (And notice how many of the inferences would change if X was not human, but a mare – much of the right-hand side of Figure 9.3 would be different.) We are truly dealing with a web of belief. Each of the propositions in Figure 9.3 also has a corresponding set of propositions which it warrants, and those propositions in turn imply another set, and so on.

On the left-hand side of Figure 9.3 I have attempted to show how various kinds of inference vary in the 'tightness' of their relationship to 'X is pregnant'. This 'tightness' is also reflected in the confidence with which participants can assume that other participants will also draw the same inferences. At the top end of the page are those inferences which appear to be indispensable; inferences such as 'X has a foetus inside her body' or 'X is female' or 'X is preparing to have a baby'. It is inferences of this type which tie our beliefs to our language in the deepest way. Our beliefs are 'anchored' to language. According to Quine, inferences of this sort are deeply integrated into the totality of belief. As we move down the page, we come to those beliefs which are clearly contingent on the facts, and context dependent, for example, beliefs about whether X will be delivered by an obstetrician or a midwife, in a hospital or at home, or by a vet in a barn. Notice how the existence of the more apparently indispensable, and therefore intersubjectively reliable, beliefs are essential for the working of language. Without them, we could not reliably infer that our hearer has 'understood' what we had said even in the minimal way. There would be too much indeterminacy in interpretation to guarantee coordination in communication at all.

The inextricability thesis

It is the set of apparently indispensable beliefs which we infer from a sentence irrespective of context which are normally thought of as its 'meaning'. Consider the classic example:

A bachelor is a man who has never been married.

Many linguists and philosophers would say that this sentence is **analytic**. It is necessarily true, not because of the facts, but because of the 'meaning' of the words involved. The sentence has no empirical content. It must be true by definition. The words to the right of 'is' are a paraphrase of the words to the left. Analytic sentences are often viewed as a way of determining the 'meaning' of linguistic expressions.

To claim this, however, leads to a hornet's nest of philosophical and linguistic problems which are beyond the scope of the book (see Quine, 1953; Grice and Strawson, 1956; Putnam, 1962). It is worth noting some of the difficulties in passing. For one thing, the number of 'words' such as 'bachelor', from which one can construct putatively analytic sentences, is quite small. There are many different classes of words and each class behaves somewhat differently. For most classes, constructing analytic sentences is problematic.

Consider two candidates for analytic sentences involving 'pregnant'. The phrases to the right of 'if and only if' purport to be synonymous with, and therefore to represent the 'meaning' of, 'X is pregnant':

4. X is pregnant if and only if X has a foetus inside her body.
10. X is pregnant if and only if X is preparing to have a baby.

Neither of these work as analytic sentences. The trouble with '4' is that it looks to be a sentence which is true as a matter of scientific fact (much as 6 - 9 in Figure 9.3 are matters of scientific fact) rather than true as a matter of meaning. As such, it is one, albeit widely known statement from a physical theory. One could imagine a speaker (for example a child) using the sentence quite correctly and not knowing anything about the technicalities of pregnancy, only that mother is going to have a baby. So what about sentence 10? The trouble with 10 is that it does not seem to be necessarily true at all. X may be known to be arranging things so as *not* to have a baby, and, in the case of 'test tube' fertilization, X may be preparing to have a baby without being pregnant. If we say, however, that we should take 'X is preparing' to mean 'X's body is preparing' to have the baby, then 10, like 4, becomes true as a matter of fact rather than meaning.

Indeed, we can easily imagine a future world in which we might revise our beliefs about both these statements. At the moment, most of us are probably unwilling to say of a woman whose fertilized ovum resides in the laboratory that she is pregnant. Later, after implantation, we would apply the term. However, imagine a world in which extra-uterine fertilization was the normal way in which conception was engineered (as opposed to intercourse). We would have uniform state of affairs in which all mothers-to-be lived for a time. We we have no word for it! In this case, we might be willing to apply the then old-fashioned term 'pregnancy' to this state. We would have revised our beliefs about sentences such as 'X is pregnant'.

According to Quine, even so-called analytic sentences are true because of the way the world is. That is, they are not true because of the meaning of the words, but empirically true. He argues that no statement is immune from revision; even our 'bachelor' example above. But why should such sentences appear to be true because of the language itself? The reason is that statements of this sort express beliefs which are very deeply integrated and interlocked with other things we believe about the world. Although they are, in principle, revisable, to abandon them would be very costly. It would require revision of the rest of our beliefs about the area of experience in question. Figure 9.3 shows how deeply 'pregnant', for example, is embedded into other beliefs about this area of experience.

This leads us to what has been called the **inextricability thesis**. Because it is finally impossible to clearly distinguish between linguistic and factual considerations in assessing the truth of a statement, it is also impossible clearly to distinguish our beliefs about a statement due to its linguistic form, and what Quine calls 'generally shared collateral information' (what we have been calling 'mutual knowledge'). There is no clear boundary between these two classes of inference; between 'meaning' and 'background knowledge'.

This thesis is one with which many linguists would disagree. Indeed, if I want to study semantics, I really do need clearly defined linguistic meanings in order to have something to study. I have to draw a line across Figure 9.3 at some point and say, 'This is the meaning of "pregnant".' The other inferences are background knowledge. Quine denies that drawing this line is possible.

This has a number of important consequences. For one thing, it means that if our hearer 'speaks English', we are warranted in assuming a very wide range of mutual knowledge because of that fact alone. The hearer does not know only the 'meaning' of a statement in isolation from background knowledge. Searle (1980), for example, has pointed out that even within isolated sentences the contribution of a word to truth conditions is only relative to assumed background knowledge. Consider how different are the states of affairs referred to as 'cutting' in the following sentences; and what one would need to assume about the world to determine whether each sentence is true or false:

1. She cut him short when he complained.
2. We can cut our staff and improve services.
3. You must cut the controversial scenes.
4. The criticisms cut him deeply.
5. He cut classes yesterday.
6. He cut the umbilicus.
7. He cut the lawn.
8. We must cut your salary again.
9. I'm going to cut them off at the pass.
10. We can cut across the vacant lot.
11. We got cut off, I'm afraid.

This suggests that, even within a sentence, we draw just that subset of inferences (out of the number of those possible) which allow us to construct a state of affairs that otherwise tallies with our everyday beliefs about how the world works. No English-speaker assumes that lawns are cut with scissors, or that umbilical cords are cut with lawnmowers. A sentence can be viewed, then, as a set of instructions to draw those inferences necessary to construct the state of affairs to which the speaker intends to refer, and to use background knowledge to do so. Similarly, when faced by an utterance in the context of an earlier utterance in conversation, we draw just that joint subset of inferences from the utterances which enable us further to infer the new contextual implications which the speaker intended to convey, according to the principle of relevance. The actual words used are instructions to do this inferencing. They are clues about where to go within the inferential network which we share as members of the speech community. Using old inferences, we can generate new inferences in context.

Another consequence of Quine's position is that there would

be no absolutely clear distinction between changes in our beliefs and changes in our language. Changes in language would occur when systematic changes in our beliefs about an area of experience have affected the network sufficiently that the most deeply integrated beliefs, those that seemed indispensable, also become dispensable and are revised. The periphery of the network will change first, cumulatively over many propositions, and the centre will resist change. In other words, for any given sentence, those inferences most deeply tied to its linguistic form will be relatively more resistant to change, and those which may be either true or false and are only probabilistically tied to other sentences are less resistant to change. Thus, in relation to the truth of 'X is pregnant', those inferences at the bottom of Figure 9.3 are more susceptible to change than those towards the top.

In Quine's analysis, 'observation sentences', those sentences at the periphery of the totality of beliefs, can be revised on empirical grounds. Those at the core appear indispensable. Over many other propositions we are relatively free to assign the values 'true' or 'false' in terms of their inferential relations to these first two classes and in relation to considerations of equilibrium and simplicity.

Now consider, in cases where observation cannot be involved, another possible source for an individual's beliefs. The grounds on which we believe many propositions to be true is social. We believe them to be true because we know other people believe or claim to know they are the case. This is necessary, in fact, because, given the range of propositions to which we are willing to assent, out chances of checking every sentence for ourselves is remote. It is also necessary because our ability to converse with others, and the way we acquire background knowledge, both depend on our building up a knowledge of those inferences that are commonly drawn from sentences by those with whom we interact. Given these origins for, at least some, beliefs, it follows that to believe the same things as our fellows has a useful coordinative function in social life. Given this, we could argue that the assignment of truth values over the totality of beliefs is not so much concerned with the correspondence of propositions with facts, but with whether the beliefs as a whole work as a social form of life. They do not have to be true to work, although we may think they are true if they work.

In earlier chapters, we studied the mechanism of linguistic change paying particular attention to the role of social factors. It is worth suggesting here that similar mechanisms might be at work in the way in which we distribute truth values over propositions within our inferential network. For example, we could propose that redistributions of true and false over propositions will be arranged implicationally in waves. Waves of revision, perhaps ultimately originating in breakdowns in the overall workability of assignments of truth to sentences, would lead to successive reassignments of truth in inferentially related propositions within parts of the network. This would proceed initially through propositions freer to change truth value, and only finally make its way to indispensable beliefs. In other words, the background and contingent beliefs inferable from 'X is pregnant' would have to be revised first, throughout a community, before a revision in the core beliefs can occur. The core beliefs are those that enable us to say that the proposition is true only if a certain state of affairs obtains.

Waves of revision will also be embedded in social structures. Thus, social groups exert normative pressure towards conformity of belief. Convergence of belief within a social group both originates in and facilitates discourse within the group. People find beliefs more credible when they are asserted or assumed by individuals of high status; for example, parents, pundits, teachers, journalists and so on. So we can envisage the two dimensions of social structure – hierarchy and social networks – exerting normative pressures on variations in the structure of belief in a community, just as they do on linguistic structures. It follows that to assign a given truth-value to a proposition can also be a symbol of overt or covert prestige within a community, and thus serve to establish social identity. If the analogy holds, even partially, one would expect to find waves of revision of belief moving through communities, in patterns similar to those observed for linguistic changes.

But, given the inextricability thesis, this process is not clearly separable from linguistic change. The wave of revision will eventually lap against the inferences warranted by linguistic forms. In fact, it is hard to see how these seemingly indispensable beliefs could be maintained or be workable, if large parts of the scaffolding of background beliefs have been revised. At this point, linguistic realignments could occur.

Stereotypes

A lot of our difficulty above arose out of the problem of analytic sentences. Except for sentences containing words like 'bachelor', 'spinster' etc., we found it exceedingly difficult to construct sentences which were necessarily true because of the 'meanings' of the words they contain. In the case of 'X is pregnant' we could not arrive at any single proposition which was necessarily true in this analytic sense.

One way to solve this impasse has been suggested by Hilary Putnam (1970, 1975). Putnam has argued that in dealing with words which refer to **natural kinds**, for example, tigers, or lemons, or tulips, what we need to know in order to use the word correctly is a **stereotype** of the kind in question. Consider 'tiger'. To tell a child how to use this word correctly we tell him that the word means a big, orange and black, striped cat, or, in another example, that 'water' is a clear liquid which is drinkable. To use the word correctly, one needs to know nothing about the objective physical or biological features which distinguish the natural kind: that water is H_2O, for example. Indeed, for most of human history, no one knew the chemical identity of water. This did not prevent them successfully using the word 'water' to refer to water. A stereotype can be wildly wrong as a scientific description. If I came across a tiger which was not striped (an albino tiger, for example) it would still be a tiger. Or if I came across water which was not clear, liquid or drinkable, it would still be water. The stereotype, in Putnam's terms, is a common sense theory about the natural kind which works for normal cases. One can use it to pick out the set referred to for practical purposes. As a common sense theory, it is a sociolinguistic phenomenon – an agreement within a speech community about how to use the words in question.

Now 'pregnant' can be viewed as a natural kind term. Using our example, 'X is pregnant', we can see how Putnam's proposal gives a particular kind of structure to the inferences we draw from the sentence. The word 'normal' lets us off the analytic hook. We no longer have to look for an inference which is necessarily true in every case. Neither do we have to look for empirical facts about pregnancy. What we will infer is a set of propositions, the stereotype, which we believe will be satisfied in normal instances of pregnancy. We would still be willing to assent to the statement that X is pregnant, even if all the propositions were not satisfied in X's case. All we need is a subset of the inferences to be satisfied for us to say, 'Yes, this is a pregnancy, albeit not a normal one.' The common sense theory requires simply that it 'work' for the practical purpose of picking out members of the set in question. Notice how, on this view, we are no longer looking for necessary truths, except perhaps for the small number of single criteria words like 'bachelor'. These are simply a few fixed points in the language (Putnam, 1962). For sentences contining natural kind terms, the set of inferences most closely tied to the language are, as Quine says, matters of fact. Does the stereotype 'work' as a theory about how to refer to the kind? As such, they are clearly revisable if they do not, or if they no longer square with the overall pressures of the totality of belief.

Representation of belief systems: frames

Almost all scholars who have worked on how we comprehend discourse have tried to find some system for representing background knowledge. The extreme difficulty of this task is obvious. For example, there is the problem of infinite regress. As we saw before, each inference leads to further inferences and so on. There is the problem of accessing just those specific pieces of background information required to obtain just the contextual implications that the speaker intended to convey out of a very large number of possible implications, and the difficulty of doing this in a psychologically plausible way. There is the 'inextricability' problem of deciding which part of the representation should be attached to the linguistic items as 'meaning' and which part is truly 'background'. Finally, there is the problem of what form the representation should take. What kind of symbols should the investigator use to represent knowledge?

We have seen that the central processes we have pinpointed involve making inferences. Logic is the discipline which has the nature of inferences and reasoning as its subject matter. On this basis, the proposition has been the most widely used form of representation. However, the proposition itself is an abstract notion (for a survey see Bradley and Swartz, 1979). People do not represent what they know solely in a way which can be adequately replicated in the form of propositions. It has been suggested, for example, that some kinds of knowledge could be internalized in a form akin to a laser hologram. Be that as it may, a theory of discourse need not, in principle, have to be grounded on a psychology of logic, perception, memory and so on. The theory can be more abstract than that, as long as it gives an account of the observations we can make of how utterances join together to form intelligible discourse.

The development of systems for representing knowledge has been of particular concern to scholars working in **artificial intelligence** research, which is a branch of computer science. See, for example, Boden (1977), Bobrow and Collins (1975) or Metzing (1980). This has also been of concern to linguists who are interested in the structure of texts, for example, Van Dijk (1977). For a criticism of the whole enterprise see Dreyfus (1972).

Artificial intelligence, as the name suggests, is the attempt to replicate in computer programs the processes and information required to perform tasks requiring intelligence, those things characteristically done by intelligent creatures such as animals and humans. Such tasks include meaningful interaction with the world in terms of the perception, recognition and manipulation of objects, reasoning, learning and, of course, the use of language. There have been some striking successes in this enterprise, for example, Terry Winograd's (1972) computer system for understanding English. This program can engage in dialogue. It exchanges utterances with the operator about a world consisting of blocks of various shapes and colours. The problem of representing systems of knowledge and belief is a central one in artificial intelligence research. Without some solution, a computer system for discourse production and comprehension would prove impossible.

One of the most influential proposals has been Marvin Minsky's notion of **frames**, which was originally advanced in connection with the computer analysis of visual scenes. Minsky writes (1975: 211):

> ... the ingredients of most theories ... have been on the whole too minute, local, and unstructured to account – either practically or phenomenologically – for the effectiveness of common sense thought. The 'chunks' of reasoning, language, memory and perception ought to be larger and more structured ... in order to explain the apparent power and speed of mental activities .... Here is the essence of the theory: When one encounters a new situation (or makes a substantial change in one's view of the present problem) one selects from memory a substantial structure called a frame. This is a remembered framework to be adapted to fit reality by changing details as necessary. A frame is a data structure for

representing a stereotyped situation, like being in a certain kind of living room, or going to a child's birthday party.

It is most important to note that a frame represents not actual situations, but a stereotype of the situation in question. Minsky suggests that a frame can be thought of as a network made up of nodes or points and the relationships between them. The nodes at the top of the network tell us things which are always true of the situation we are processing. At the bottom of the network are slots or terminals. These terminals, roughly speaking, have conditions on them which must be satisfied by the observations or data of the situation being processed. But terminals can alternatively direct us to other subframes, and also include extra information about typical cases, which may or may not match the observations. Or, we may be told what to do or expect next.

A given situation can also be looked at from different points of view — literally so in the case of visual perception. Minsky allows for this by introducing the notion of a frame-system. This is a set of systematically related frames. In the case of visual analysis, each one of the set of related frames would represent the same scene from a different viewpoint. Move a little to the right, for example, and a given room will look quite different. The two viewpoints will be represented by two different but related frames in the system. Both of these frames, however, have the same terminals. Our conclusion will be that we are viewing the same room, but from a different angle.

There has been a wealth of theories and descriptions along the same line as Minsky's proposals and covering a variety of domains. Systems for the representation of knowledge have been variously termed **schema**, **frames**, **scripts** and **plans**. Employing a range of different formalisms, they have attempted to represent the structure of narrative in stories, the situation of eating in a restaurant, and visual recognition (Schank and Abelson, 1977). It is clear that such formal approaches could be applied to the everyday knowledge of speech events and situations which we discussed earlier. Minsky himself suggests the application of the frame idea to the representation of the structure of, and background knowledge to, discourse and text comprehension.

An example: background

I will conclude this chapter with a brief example of actual discourse. The crucial role of mutual knowledge will, I hope, be clear. The text is a portion of the testimony of the black singer, Paul Robeson, before the House Committee on UnAmerican Activities (HUAC) on 12 June 1956 (from Bentley, 1972). See Figure 9.4.

Unfortunately, we have not space here to do more than merely sketch out informally a portion of the relevant system of beliefs invoked by this text. It invokes what we know and believe about 'the cold war'. (There is a precedent for studying this belief system. One of the most comprehensive representations of belief in artificial intelligence research was developed to generate 'cold war' discourse! See Abelson, 1973.) Presumably, the place to begin would be in a frame-system representing a stereotypical war. So imagine what a war stereotype looks like. It would include such things as: two or more states as belligerents; violent conflict between organized armed forces; battles, with criteria for winners and losers; a 'casus belli' and an 'outbreak' phase; and a final outcome of victory and defeat. Now the phrase 'cold war' is a dead or dying metaphor which would originally have been interpreted in terms of a stereotypical 'hot war'. (In fact, it is an extension of a system of 'fire' metaphors which are part of the idiom of war.) We can understand the phrase 'cold war' as warranting all the inferences that 'war' itself warrants, except that there is little or no physical violence involved. Unless a text itself requires us to add or subtract other inferences, we take a 'cold' war as a normal war without the violence.

Now let us look at some quotations from a major cold warrior, the late Senator Joseph McCarthy. Our aim here is to try to see what alterations are necessary in the notion of a normal war in order to understand 'cold war' beliefs. The following statements are from McCarthy's opening testimony before the Army-McCarthy hearings, March 1954. (The dots represent the normal breaks and hesitations in his speech.)

I The War

... anyone who has followed the ... communist conspiracy ... and can add two and two ... will tell you that ... there is no remote possibility ... of this war which we're in

today and its a war ... war which we have been losing ...
no remote possibility of this ending ... except by victory or
death for this civilisation...

So far, it is a normal war (albeit a verbal one) with its two
possible outcomes. However, the belligerents are unusual. Our
side is obvious, America and the free world. What McCarthy has
to say about the enemy is very interesting. It is 'the communist
conspiracy', a 'brutalitarian force' which 'enslaves' people by
convincing and converting them, rather like a religion. Communists are members of ' ... an organization that wants to destroy
this nation ... that wants to corrupt the mind of youth.'
McCarthy is explicit about the enemy. He says of a communist:

II The Enemy

... he is not a free agent ... he has no freedom of thought
... no freedom of expression ... he must take his orders
from Moscow or he will no longer be a member of the Communist Party.

Let us consider these propositions as part of an inferential network. The last sentence in II looks very much like a stipulation
of the criteria for being a communist, and not an empirical
statement which is subject to revision. If that is so, then we can
consider it an axiom, a proposition treated as self-evidently true
and upon which we can build a deductive system. If we conjoin
this definition with the proposition that we are at war with
Moscow, then other inferences may be drawn. An individual
who, in a war, works under the direction of the enemy is a
traitor. Communists must obey Moscow. Moscow is America's
enemy in a war. Therefore American communists are traitors.
Furthermore, communists are engaged in a conspiracy. By definition, a conspiracy is a secret combination – conspirators necessarily conceal the fact that they conspire. It follows that, if one
confronts a conspirator with his intent, he will deny it. Otherwise the conspiracy will be revealed. We could go on teasing out
the reasoning of this inferential network. But the point is made
that we are dealing, not with specific pieces of information, but
with a web of belief, a theory, which stands or falls as a whole.
This theory finds institutional expression in the activities of
HUAC.

An example: the text

Now look at the Robeson text, Figure 9.4. It is testimony before a committee of Congress. Superficially, the committee appears to be what it constitutionally is: not a court of law, but an investigative subcommittee whose function is to inquire into states of affairs in order to determine the extent of subversive activities in various areas of American life. Ideally, the function of an investigative body is to obtain information and establish the truth regarding its subject matter. Presumably, that is how the public interpret its proceedings. This function is reflected in the superfi-

1.	Mr Arens:	Are you now a member of the Communist Party?
2.	Mr Robeson:	Oh please, please, please.
3.	Mr Scherer:	Please answer, will you, Mr Robeson?
4.	Mr Robeson:	What is the Communist Party? What do you mean by that?
5.	Mr Scherer:	I ask that you direct the witness to answer the question.
6.	Mr Robeson:	What do you mean by the Communist Party? As far as I know it is a legal party like the Republican Party and the Democratic Party. Do you mean a party of people who have sacrificed for my people and for all Americans and workers, that they can live in dignity? Do you mean that party?
7.	Mr Arens:	Are you now a member of the Communist Party?
8.	Mr Robeson:	Would you like to come to the ballot box when I vote and take out the ballot and see?

Figure 9.4 The Robeson Text (*from Bentley, 1972*)

cial form of the discourse. Overtly, it proceeds by means of question-answer sequences, especially at the beginning of the testimony (not included in our text). Robeson is asked questions such as, 'Are you appearing today in response to a subpoena?' But a moment's reflection will reveal that many of the questions in the text are not really questions at all.

Consider utterance 1, 'Are you now a member of the Communist Party?' I would suggest that this utterance is, in fact, an **accusation**. Consider what is involved in asking a question. This act at least involves the speaker requesting some information from the hearer which he does not already know. Is it conceivably the case that the committee believes that Robeson knows the truth of the proposition (that he is now a communist) and that the committee does not? Indeed, the very fact that he is in the stand, as an unfriendly witness, is because the committee has satisfied itself on that account. So it hardly needs to seek this information from him. Perhaps utterance 1 is merely a request for confirmation, for Robeson to confirm their belief that he is a communist. However, given what we have said about the requirement that a conspirator hide his conspiracy, if the committee believes Robeson is a communist and if the committee also shares McCarthy's beliefs about communists, then Robeson could not be expected to reply – if he is a communist. So no reply suggests he is a communist – relative to the belief system. But that is not a genuine request for confirmation by the committee! Let us try again!

To accuse someone of something requires at least two things. The speaker has to assert truly that the accused did the act of which he is being accused, and the speaker has to believe that the act is bad. This is where the 'cold war' beliefs are invoked. Under the assumption that being a communist is 'bad', utterance 1 implies that Arens is accusing Robeson of being a communist. This interpretation, in fact, makes sense of Robeson's reply, 'Oh please, please, please.' More specifically, in terms of the belief system examined above, Robeson is being accused of treason, of conspiring to forward the cause of an enemy with whom his country is at war. Note that the interpretation of utterance 1 as an accusation could not be obtained from the literal meaning of utterance 1 alone. Also note that the interpretation, although it could depend on one specific piece of information, 'that communism is bad', clearly has invoked a more systematic structure of belief. It would be difficult, in fact, for a participant to isolate any one proposition in practice; for example, 'that communists are traitors'. They all depend on one another.

So Robeson is not really in a speech event structured in terms of questions and answers. He is locked into accusation-reply adjacency pairs. Faced with an accusation, there are two possible classes of reply. Either the accused can accept the accusation and apologize, or otherwise repent, or he can reject the accusation on the grounds that it has been infelicitously performed in some way. Robeson initially takes this latter tack. Note that one cannot *not* reply. An 'officially absent' reply, as we saw above, is tantamount to accepting the accusation in this case: the inference of guilt is warranted. Robeson's replies, utterances 4, 6 and 8, show that he is aware of the background knowledge and very specifically realizes that the badness assumption hangs on what his accusers mean by the phrase 'the Communist Party'. The text can thus be viewed as a process of accusation, reply, and successive reinstatements of the accusation, thus:

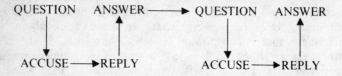

We are witnessing here an institutionalized activity involving language. In this case, the background knowledge is inextricably bound up with the actions constituting the speech event and its norms of interpretation. So we have another instance of a 'language game', as we defined that notion in Chapter 8. This example also demonstrates that utterances can have a real social function. Once a hostile witness has undergone this linguistic process, he publicly 'stands accused' of being a communist, and therefore a traitor. His status in society has been transformed by virtue of the utterances addressed to him. Utterances are real social actions with major effects on individual lives. It is to this question of speech as action that we shall turn next.

10. *A Mode of Action*

> ... the consideration of linguistic uses associated with any practical pursuit, leads us to the conclusion that language ... ought to be regarded and studied against the background of human activities and *as a mode of human behaviour in practical matters* ... language functions as a link in concerted human activity, as a piece of human behaviour. *It is a mode of action and not an instrument of reflection.*
>
> Malinowski (1923)

Action and intention

An underlying theme of the last several chapters has been that to perform an utterance is a mode of human action. When Mr Arens says to Robeson, 'Are you now a member of the Communist Party?' he is doing something. He is performing an action. In the first instance, it is the action of producing this particular English sentence. I suggested in Chapter 9 that it may also be the action of questioning Robeson, and quite possibly also accusing him. It is fundamental to an understanding of discourse to recognize that opening your mouth and uttering is a form of human action. To say something is, in general, like performing many other types of action; for example, opening a window, mailing a letter, hitting a ball with a cricket bat, beckoning to someone, and so on. **Speech acts** have their own particular characteristics but also share certain important properties with other human actions.

Let us examine two such properties. The first was described by the philosopher G.E.M. Anscombe in her book *Intention* (1957). Imagine that we are observing a person, X, standing in front of a window doing something. We ask, 'What is X doing?' How can we describe his action? We can say, 'He's moving his arms' or 'He's moving his arms in that particular way we describe as "lifting"' or 'He's opening the window' or 'He's airing the room' or 'He's causing my papers to blow all over the place' and so on. The point is that we can describe his action in many different ways. In fact, there are as many ways as there are true sentences which describe what he is doing. So the same physical action can be subsumed under any one or more of the descriptions we proposed for it as long as the statements we made are true.

The second property involves an act under one particular class of descriptions. These are intentional descriptions. We know introspectively and by observation that some human actions are intentional and some are not. Thus, most people would agree (to use two of Anscombe's examples) that the peristaltic movement of the gut, or the odd sort of jerk or jump that one's whole body sometimes gives when one is falling asleep, are not intentional. Actions that have the property of **intentionality**, by contrast, are fundamental to understanding human beings and include all speech acts by definition, as we shall soon see. What does it mean to say an action is intentional?

In essence, to say an action is intentional is to describe it in terms of some purpose of the agent to achieve a goal. The act can be truly described or explained in these terms, that he did X (applying a lifting motion to the window) to achieve Y (opening the window). His act is intelligible in those terms.

Anscombe explores this in terms of a particular kind of answer to a 'Why' question. '*Why* is he lifting the window?' 'He *intends* to open the window'. Social life is important to intentionality because in many cases the possibility of describing the act in terms of an intent to pursue a goal is only intelligible in social terms – the relation of an act and its object is part of the form of our collective social life. Asking 'Why' all those students are scribbling in exam books requires a knowledge of the background knowledge that institutionally connects writing exams and, for example, achieving so many A-levels. That is 'Why' they are moving their hands and pens.

Clearly, speech acts share the property of intentionality with other nonlinguistic actions. Think again of Arens's utterance, 'Are you now a member of the Communist Party?' Upon hearing this, we are faced with a problem of interpretation, of how to describe what he is doing with these words in this context. We can consider his action under various descriptions. Here is an easy description. What Arens is doing is uttering a string of English words. Moreover, these words are made up of English speech sounds, they form a certain type of English sentence, and they have a certain meaning. These descriptions are certainly true. But they do not give us an answer to Anscombe's 'Why' question! Let us try again. Let us say that Arens issued the utterance because he was director of the staff of the committee and he was simply doing his job in that role. True again, perhaps, but not really what we are looking for. This description may account for one of his 'motives' in speaking. It may account for his social 'right' and 'obligation' to speak in that role. But it clearly is not the description we want to the 'Why' question.

We want to figure out Arens's specific goal in uttering these words in this way to Robeson. What did he intend to effect in uttering them? In Chapter 9 we tried to reason this out. First we proposed that he intended the utterance to count as an attempt to get the information whether or not Robeson was now a communist. But we abandoned that as a plausible intention in the circumstances. Then we proposed that he intended the utterance as an accusation. These are possible answers to the 'Why' question. The act could be described as a question or an accusation. To perceive Arens's meaning, or 'what he meant', is to perceive the intentionality of his action, an intentionality he assumes the relevant others will be able to perceive.

For a moment, however, let us backtrack into the origins of the insight that utterances are a form of human action. Although this insight might appear to be mere common sense, in fact its first appearance in modern literature was in the later philosophical work of Ludwig Wittgenstein and, independently, and somewhat earlier, in the anthropological studies of Bronislaw Malinowski. Both these thinkers emphasized that utterances were activities within the context of social life.

Malinowski spent much of his professional life studying the culture of the Trobriand Islanders of the South Pacific. His view that utterance was an activity embedded in practical social life and culture arose partly because of the difficulty he found in the translation of texts from their exotic language and cultural setting into ours. Utterances, he argued, could only be comprehended (or translated) relative to the culture and situation in which they were inextricably embedded. Likewise, the 'meanings' of linguistic forms should be thought of not as a relationship between a word or sentence and that to which it refers, but rather as a complex of functional relationships between words, sentences and the contexts in which they are used (Malinowski, 1923; Robins, 1971).

The philosophy of Wittgenstein, however, is the place where the insight that language is an activity occurs most vividly. As we saw in Chapter 8, Wittgenstein (1953) uses the term 'language game' to refer to 'language and the activities into which it is woven', and participant knowledge of 'the technique of using the language.' The term 'language game' is used by Wittgenstein to describe a very wide diversity of kinds of language use. In *Philosophical Investigations* (1. 23), he writes,

> But how many kinds of sentences are there? Say assertion, question, and command?— There are *countless* kinds: countless different kinds of use of what we call 'symbols', 'words', 'sentences'. And this multiplicity is not something fixed, given one for all; but new types of language, new language games, as we may say, come into existence, and others become obsolete and get forgotten.

He lists examples. These include such diverse activities as: 'Giving orders, and obeying them', 'Reporting an event', 'Speculating about an event', 'Guessing riddles', 'Solving a problem in practical arithmetic' and 'Asking, thanking, cursing, greeting, praying'. In Chapter 9, I called Robeson's testimony before HUAC a language game. For Wittgenstein, Arens's utterance, 'Are you now a member of the Communist Party?', would get its particular value in this context because it is a counter in a language game which we might call 'accusation and reply'. (This label refers to a class of actions which could be performed in many contexts. We might want to try to give a more delicate characterization of the activity found in HUAC.) Language, in Arens's utterance, is being used like a tool, in Wittgenstein's metaphor, to achieve his end.

Wittgenstein relates the multiplicity of language games to what he terms 'forms of life'. A language game is only possible within a form of life. This term refers to those patterns of communal activity which make up the shared social life of a group. A form of life is 'a way of living in society' (Kenny, 1973: 163). In our case, the relevant form of life includes the institution of the committee with its function of attaching 'stigma' to individuals to 'purge' them from the body politic and the whole context of belief and action which constitutes 'the cold war'. These are required both for the committee to play the 'public accusation' language game, and for the witnesses and audience to understand their intention. It is in terms of forms of life that the actions which make up the game are possible and meaningful.

The philosophical position of Wittgenstein in his later writings, with all its subtlety and complexity regarding language, is notoriously difficult to interpret. Nevertheless, it has been the basis of one of the major branches of contemporary philosophy of language, called 'ordinary language philosophy'. It is here that we turn to the work of two philosophers in this tradition, J.L. Austin and John Searle.

J.L. Austin was the originator of the term 'speech act', and in his William James Lectures at Harvard University in 1955, subsequently published as *How to Do Things with Words*, he developed the first systematic theory of utterances as human action. We shall be concerned with only three of Austin's terms. The most useful way of thinking about these is to view them as three different descriptions of the same speech act. To illustrate this, consider the text we examined at the beginning of the last chapter. Here it is again in its full form. Arthur is walking with Brenda, who is married and with whom Arthur has been having a surreptitious affair. We will just concentrate on that part of Brenda's utterance which is in the box.

1. Arthur: What's the matter with you tonight?
2. Brenda: I'll tell you what's the matter with me, Arthur.
3. I'm pregnant. Good and proper this time and it's your fault.
4. Arthur: Oh ay, it's bound to be my fault, ain't it?

Brenda has performed at least one speech act. But this act can be described in three different ways. These are illustrated in Figure 10.1.

To begin with the **locutionary act**: this term deals with the act *of* uttering these words. That is, Brenda made noises which happen to have a conventional meaning in English and which realize certain English grammatical forms. We need not discuss this in any more detail now because the more important (for our purposes) descriptions of the speech act are the remaining two.

We'll deal next with the **illocutionary act**. Clearly, Brenda believes she is pregnant. The reason she utters, 'I'm pregnant', is presumably because she intends this utterance to represent an actual situation which she believes is the case. A sentence uttered with this intention is known as a **statement**, when

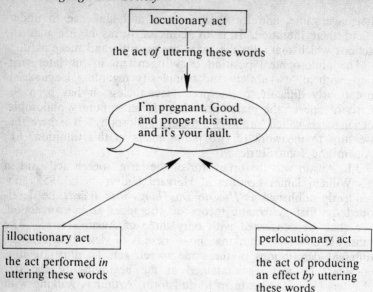

Figure 10.1 Three descriptions of a speech act

someone states that such and such a state of affairs obtains. Consider the next part of what she utters, 'it's your fault'. Given that she has conveyed that she believes she is pregnant, it is further arguable that she also intends to convey that this outcome is because of some bad or reprehensible thing that Arthur has done. An utterance in which the speaker intends to convey that some act or omission of the hearer is reprehensible is an **accusation**. Both stating and accusing are illocutionary acts. In other words, the illocutionary description of a speech act characterizes the speaker's intention, what sort of thing he intended to do *in* making the utterance. (For example, that he intended it to convey that he believed the sentence was true, or that he intended it to convey that the hearer had done something reprehensible.) Austin (1962: 98–100) defines the illocutionary act in the following words:

To perform a locutionary act is in general ... also ... to perform an *illocutionary act* .... Thus in performing a locutionary act we shall also be performing such an act as:
asking or answering a question,
giving some information or an assurance or a warning,
announcing a verdict or an intention,

pronouncing sentence,
making an appointment or an appeal or a criticism,
making an identification or giving a description . . . .
the performance of an 'illocutionary' act, i.e. performance of
an act *in* saying something as opposed to performance of an
act *of* saying something . . .

But such actions also have consequences or effects on the hearer.
It is this that the term **perlocutionary act** describes. Very often
effects are unintentional. Thus, Brenda in performing her accusation probably would not have intended that one of its consequences would be to make Arthur evasive. However, this might
be an effect. Other effects *are* intended. She might have intended
that he accept responsibility for her pregnancy, and certainly
intended that he perceive that in uttering this sentence she conveys that she believes he has done something reprehensible; in
other words, that she accuses him. The effects of saying something, whether intended or not, are the perlocutionary force of
the utterance; in Austin's words, 'what we bring about *by* saying
something, such as convincing, deterring, and even, say, surprising or misleading'. A good example of an intentional effect,
the perlocutionary **uptake** of an illocutionary act, is the answer
which may occur in response to the illocutionary act of asking a
question. The essence of questioning is to try to produce this
response from the hearer – its utterance counts as an attempt to
elicit certain information.

It is important to note, however, that even if no answer is
forthcoming, it is possible that the act was still a question – the
effect is not necessary for the utterance to count as an *attempt*
to elicit the information. We would say, 'I asked him, but he
didn't answer my question. He was evasive'. Similarly, Brenda
still would have accused Arthur even if Arthur did not construe
what she said as an accusation. He simply would not have
understood. She could say, 'I accused him of getting me pregnant but the clod didn't understand.' An alternative view, however, might require uptake of the intended effect for the act to
be fully performed and we might say, 'I *tried* to ask that question or make that accusation but it didn't work.' This would be
equivalent to the situation of someone lifting away and the
window not budging. ' "What is X doing?" He's *trying* to open
the window.'

The concepts of illocutionary and perlocutionary force jointly
describe two related parts of the overall intentionality of verbal

action. The former, the immediate act which the speaker intends to perform, can be the means to certain intended consequences, its perlocutionary uptake, and that is why the speaker performed the act at all. The illocutionary act may be separate from its effects, however, and can be performed or at least 'tried', irrespective of whether the intended effect is produced or not. Indeed, unpredictable, unwanted effects can be produced instead. X may inadvertently smash the still-unopened window by trying to open it.

So we have seen that a speech act may be described in three different ways. Figure 10.2 illustrates this for Brenda's utterance and suggests how the descriptions fit together to jointly characterize her verbal action.

Illocutionary	Locutionary	Perlocutionary	
Brenda *intends* to convey to Arthur that he has done something reprehensible. She reasons that she must utter S to produce this effect in this context	Utters Sentence	Arthur perceives that Brenda intends to convey that he has done something reprehensible	intended *uptake*
		Arthur is surprised, becomes evasive, etc.	unintended effects

Figure 10.2 The three aspects jointly describe Brenda's speech act

Now consider the practical business of how both the hearer and the analyst might approach an utterance. Clearly, the central problem for both is to determine as precisely as possible exactly what illocutionary act the speaker intended to perform. Some perlocutionary effects of the act might be unintended and are, in any case, unpredictable, but the act which the speaker intended to perform ought to be decidable on the assumption that speakers usually want their hearers to undetstand the 'point' of what they say.

Felicity conditions

It turns out that the task of interpreting speech acts is made somewhat easier by the fact that many illocutionary acts recur and we have names for them. They are social institutions. Thus, we have names for acts such as accuse, promise, greet, request, command, congratulate, state, warn and so on. One of the major contributions of the philosopher John Searle in his classic study *Speech Acts* (1969) was to work out the rules for the performance of various illocutionary acts. These rules are sometimes called the **felicity conditions** of the act. Unless the conditions are satisfied, the utterance cannot be an instance of that particular illocutionary act. From the decoding point of view, then, when we observe an utterance we must check the context to see if the felicity conditions for the act are satisfied. If they are, then it is arguably, but not necessarily, that act, and we have inferred what the speaker possibly intended to convey in performing his utterance.

Accusations. To illustrate the nature of felicity conditions, let us attempt to work them out for the illocutionary act of accusing. What are the conditions which must be satisfied for an utterance to count as an accusation? (This is not one of the acts which Searle analysed.) Consider what sort of content or state of affairs need be involved. It can be any act, state or event which the speaker believes is bad, such as 'I'm pregnant'. But, in addition, the speaker must believe that the hearer, the individual he is accusing, is responsible for the act, state or event which is bad or reprehensible. Brenda makes explicit that these felicity conditions are satisfied when she says, 'And it's your fault'. The word 'fault' entails both responsibility and reprehensibility. The essential condition, without which the act cannot be an accusation, is that the utterance counts as an undertaking that the hearer is responsible for the bad act, state or event.

Now let us briefly look at some felicity conditions which Searle (1969: 66) proposes for the illocutionary acts of requesting and questioning. These are two extremely important illocutions to which we will be referring again later.

Requests. What conditions have to be satisfied if an utterance is to count as a request to the hearer to do something? In the first place, the act in question must be a future act of the hearer, and also the speaker must believe that the hearer is able to do it. There would be no sense in asking someone to do something I do not believe they can do, or asking them to do it in the past. The speaker must also be sincere and want the hearer to do the act. If I do not sincerely want the hearer to do it, I am not *really* requesting that he do it (whatever else I might be doing).

Finally and essentially, the utterance must count as an attempt to get the hearer to do the act. That must be the speaker's intention in uttering it.

Questions. Questions are related to requests – they are requests for information. The essential condition which must be satisfied if an utterance is to be a question is that it 'counts as an attempt by the speaker to get this information' from the hearer (Searle, 1969: 66). Again, the attempt must be sincere. The speaker must want the information. And also, the speaker must not already know the answer. To ask a question felicitously, the speaker does not have certain specific pieces of information and he sincerely attempts to elicit this information from the hearer.

Searle's rules for illocutionary acts can be considered as rules for very general 'language games' in Wittgenstein's sense. One characteristic of discourse which makes the game metaphor apt is that the players each assume that the other is following the rules, just as they are themselves.

The use of language, like a game, is an essentially cooperative activity. Thus, a speaker who intends to question or accuse or request some action of a hearer must at least believe he is using language in such a way that the hearer, because he knows the rules, is able to discern that intention in what is said. If a speaker wants an utterance to count as a given act, he must make sure that the 'felicity conditions' for that act are satisfied. Likewise, to discern that act, the hearer will have to see that those same 'felicity conditions' are satisfied in the context. Does the speaker really presuppose that the state of affairs is bad? Does the speaker sincerely think I am responsible for the state of affairs? Has the speaker, in other words, followed the rules of the 'language game' of accusing? Following the rules in fact constitutes the game.

Direct and indirect speech acts

The hearer is confronted with the speaker's utterance. He must figure out what act the speaker intended to perform. One thing he has to go on is the linguistic form of the utterance. So we can ask whether there are overt and unambiguous markers of a given illocutionary force in the linguistic form itself, such that if that form is used, and the 'felicity conditions' are satisfied, the utterance counts as a performance of the act in question. The short answer to this is that sometimes it does, and sometimes it does not. Let us consider this further.

The most transparent way to signal an illocutionary force is to use a **performative verb**. These are verbs such as 'order', 'promise', 'accuse', 'pledge', 'urge', 'baptize' and so on. Austin (1962) noticed that these verbs have a very peculiar property. If they are uttered in a declarative sentence with the subject 'I' and the object 'you', and are also in the present tense – for example, 'I accuse you of getting me pregnant' – then the utterance counts as an actual performance of the act itself, if the felicity conditions are also satisfied. This device is of very little use to the analyst, however, since speakers are only rarely that transparent.

Next, we can ask whether the **grammatical mood** is perhaps a device which indicates illocutionary force. The answer here is more complicated. English has four grammatical moods, the **declarative**, the **interrogative**, the **imperative** and the **exclamative**, and traditionally the meaning of each mood has been associated with a particular illocutionary force. So, for example, it has often been said that the meaning intrinsic in putting a sentence in the interrogative mood is to signal that the speaker is 'asking a question'. Figure 10.3 illustrates the grammatical moods and their illocutionary meanings.

The problem with this approach (if we leave out the exclamative) is that the moods do not unambiguously signal these illocutionary forces. If one considers any one illocutionary force, in fact it can be conveyed by any of the moods. Conversely, any one of the moods can convey many and various illocutionary forces. There are further problems with the declarative in that it appears to be used in the normal expression of most illocutionary forces. If the declarative mood incorrigibly means 'I state to you that ... ', then in performing virtually any act I am simultaneously stating something as well. Thus, Brenda would be stating that 'It's your fault' as well as simultaneously accusing Arthur in her utterance.

To demonstate that a single act can be performed using any grammatical mood, consider the case of requesting someone to do something. This has been studied quite intensively. There are six distinct ways of requesting, as illustrated in Figure 10.4. I have arranged these on a scale of **illocutionary opacity** in which the act intended gets progressively more opaque, moving from the first, the performative, to the last in which the very act

Mood	Illocutionary force	Example
Declarative	*state, assert, declare* (speaker intends to convey that he believes the sentence is true)	I'm pregnant,
Interrogative	*question*	Am I pregnant? Who is pregnant?
Imperative	*request, command*	Boil some water.
Exclamative	*exclaim* (speaker expresses surprise, shock, delight etc. at the situation to which the sentence refers)	What a beautiful baby!

Figure 10.3 Mood meanings

which is being requested is not even mentioned. The meanings are glossed in brackets following the examples where necessary.

One solution to this problem has been proposed by Searle (1975). This is his theory of **indirect speech acts**. Searle assumes that because of its form, a given sentence incorrigibly conveys an illocutionary force, the relation of mood to act being that displayed in Figure 10.3. So, if I utter a grammatical interrogative, whatever else I may be doing, I am in the first instance asking a question. If that question is defective in that its felicity conditions are not satisfied, or, indeed, even if the question is quite felicitously performed, the speaker might be intending the utterance to primarily count as something else. That is, he is performing another further speech act as well as the one directly signalled by the linguistic form. We will call this latter act the **direct illocutionary act**, and the former, the one not overtly marked in the linguistic form, the **indirect illocutionary act**. It is arguable that grammatical moods do *not* convey any one illocutionary act in all instances of their use, but have a more restricted mood meaning compatible with many acts, and it has been so argued in Downes (1977), Hudson (1975) and Gazdar

1 **Performatives**
   I order you to eat.
   I request that you eat.

2 **Imperatives**
   Eat your lunch.
   You eat your lunch now.
   Let's have lunch.

3 **Peremptory declaratives**
   You will eat your lunch this instant. (eat your lunch)
   This bar will close at 11.00 sharp tonight. (close the bar at 11.00 sharp)

4 **Requests**
   Can ⎤
   Could ⎬ you come now? (come now)
   Will ⎟
   Would ⎦

5 **Interrogatives and declaratives which explicitly contain the act which is requested**
   When are you coming home? (come home)
   Are the letters typed yet? (type the letters)
   You're the man who can fix my radio. (fix my radio)
   This bar needs cleaning. (clean the bar)

6 **Sentences in which the act requested is not explicitly mentioned**
   This house is a mess. (clean the house)
   You'll die of lung cancer. (don't light that cigarette)

   I'm cold. ⎤ (close the windows, door
   You look cold. ⎬ etc. or turn on the heater
   How did it get so cold in here? ⎦ etc.)

   Your water is lovely and hot now. (get into the bath)
   She got married yesterday.
   She looked ever so nice. (consider getting married to me)

Figure 10.4 Ways of requesting

(1979). For simplicity's sake, however, I will accept Searle's theory here.

Now let us consider an example of an indirect speech act as defined by Searle. Look at Arthur's reply to Doreen's request that they consider getting married, repeated here for convenience.

Doreen: She got married yesterday. She looked ever so nice.
Arthur: What was the bloke like, could yer smell the drink?

Let us assume that Doreen, in fact, intends to perform one of a small number of illocutionary acts such as 'requesting they consider getting married', or 'broaching the topic of marriage', or 'suggesting they consider, or talk about, getting married'.

Arthur's reply in this case could arguably be the following indirect speech act. He has uttered two grammatical interrogatives. These signal that he is performing the act of questioning. But, furthermore, it is arguable that Arthur also intends by his latter question to convey that he *refuses* her request. He does not want to talk about getting married. Thus, his utterance is also a refusal. In our terminology, Arthur's direct speech act is questioning, his indirect speech act is refusing. Figure 10.5 illustrates this analysis of the exchange.

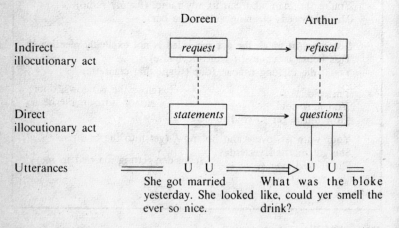

Figure 10.5 Indirect speech acts

The next task is to explain the connection between the direct and indirect illocutionary forces in each case. What is the mechanism connecting Arthur's question and his refusal, or Doreen's statement and her request? How are we to interpret the dotted lines in Figure 10.5? This is an absolutely central problem in understanding discourse.

The clue to this is that my interpretation in Figure 10.5 could be wrong. For example, the reader may have been rebelling at my interpretation of this exchange all along. One could argue that it is equally plausible that Doreen merely intended to convey that she believed the sentences she uttered were true. In other words, she merely stated them. Arthur, the argument could continue, is simply replying to her statement in terms which could be paraphrased: 'She may have looked nice, but he must have been drunk to get married.' In other words, he is stating, 'Marriage isn't a state a rational man will enter into,' and that's all. I agree that this is a possible interpretation. I would, however, *argue* that my analysis in Figure 10.5 is very plausible indeed, and to do so I would display the chain of inferences which I have constructed in this context to connect Doreen's statements with her indirect request, and Arthur's questions with his indirect refusal of the request.

The crucial point is that the connection between direct and indirect acts is in terms of inferencing. And the inferencing itself is dependent on the conversational context of the utterance.

The Cooperative principle and its maxims

So we must *infer* the indirect act. According to Searle (1975), our starting point in this task can be the linguistic form of the utterance. When we utter a sentence it is always in one of the grammatical moods displayed in Figure 10.3. The mood chosen conveys the speaker's direct illocutionary act. This interacts with context and background knowledge to make it possible for the hearer to infer the indirect illocutionary act which the speaker intended to convey. In other words, reasoning out the indirectly conveyed force of the utterance is another example of the kind of inferences we draw in context, with which we are already familiar from Chapter 9. We saw how an utterance, its context, and background knowledge working together allowed us to derive *new* contextual implications from an utterance. This was possible because of the 'principle of relevance', as that notion was defined by Sperber and Wilson (1982).

The seminal work on reasoning in conversational contexts has been that of H. Paul Grice. In his William James Lectures at Harvard in 1968, he provided a first framework for a theory of utterances in context. (Such a theory is called a **pragmatic** theory, to distinguish it from a semantic or a syntactic theory.) Part of Grice's lectures were subsequently published under the title *Logic and Conversation* (1975). Sperber and Wilson's principle of relevance is built on the basis of Grice's theory. His theory also figures crucially in Searle's (1975) view of indirect speech acts. So let us sketch out some of Grice's main ideas and relate them to both these topics.

We have already emphasized that conversation is a cooperative activity. In other words, people cooperate with each other when they talk, just as they do in any other shared activity. This greatly facilitates the coordination necessary to achieve their aim. Dancing is a very good example of such a jointly achieved aim. In order to 'bring off' the dance successfully, each partner assumes that the other reliably will follow the required steps and movements. Conversation is a similar mutual activity.

It is possible, therefore, to set up a **cooperative principle** such that participants can assume of each other that in general they obey the principle: 'Make your conversational contribution such as is required, at the stage at which it occurs, by the accepted purpose or direction of the talk exchange in which you are engaged' (Grice, 1975: 45). More specifically, Grice argues that participants can assume of each other that they are obeying certain **maxims**, which follow from the cooperative principle. (I will simplify here and not go into all the details.) The maxims are:

QUANTITY: *Don't provide more or less information than is required for the current purposes of the exchange.*

QUALITY: *Speak the truth.*

RELATION: *Be relevant.*

MANNER: *Be clear.*

So when we engage in a conversation with someone, we can assume that they are cooperating to sustain our joint activity; more specifically, that they are trying to follow these maxims.

Now let us see what happens to the maxims in the course of an exchange. Consider this example (Grice, 1975: 51):

A: Smith doesn't seem to have a girlfriend these days.
B: He has been paying a lot of visits to New York lately.

Participants work under the assumption that each is observing the maxims. If this is the case, then we have to assume that B's remark is somehow relevant to what A uttered. In order to preserve this assumption we infer the proposition, 'Smith has, or may have, a girlfriend in New York.'

Grice calls this kind of inference a **conversational implicature**, and we can say that B **implicates** the proposition just mentioned. An implicature, therefore, is an inference generated in the course of a conversation in order to preserve the assumption that participants are obeying the maxims. We produce and interpret implicatures over and against the overriding assumption that we are both trying to speak the truth, be relevant, avoid obscurity and so on.

What happens when a maxim is violated or flouted? We do a rescue operation by way of an implicature. We rescue the maxim by reasoning out the 'point' of the violation. Ah, we say, he was being relevant after all. We just have to work somewhat harder to discover what he intended to convey in flouting or violating the maxim. Consider this example (Grice, 1975: 53):

A: X is a fine friend.

Imagine a context in which both A and his interlocuter know that X has done something terrible to A – for example, betrayed one of A's secrets. In such a situation A has 'flouted' the maxim of quality. He has not spoken the truth. In this case, A will be implicating something by virtue of having flouted the maxim. The hearer's job is to work out the implicature. As Grice points out, the most obvious candidate in this case is that A is implicating the contradictory of what he says. That is, he is ironically conveying something that he *does* believe is true, that 'X is a rotten friend'.

In summary, then, participants assume that the cooperative principle and its maxims are being obeyed. A conversational implicature is a proposition which makes it possible to preserve this assumption, even when it is apparently violated or flouted. It was violated or flouted for a reason, to convey a 'point'.

It is quite obvious that 'conversational implicatures' are close relatives of Sperber and Wilson's 'contextual implications' which we discussed in Chapter 9. (From now on, I will use Grice's term.) The two classes are not exactly the same because Sperber and Wilson's arises directly from their definition of relevance, which is more explicit than Grice's rather informal usage and differs from it somewhat. In Grice (1975), the notion of relevance is left to our intuitions. And the maxim to 'Be relevant' is merely one among others.

For Sperber and Wilson, however, relevance becomes the key notion for their theory of comprehension. As we saw above, they attempt to define this notion and are quite explicit about what it is for a proposition to be relevant to a hearer (see page 281 above). Based on this definition, they argued that comprehension is governed solely by the principle of relevance; that the speaker tries to express the proposition which is the most relevant to the hearer. This is the one that will generate the maximum number of inferences with the least relative processing effort. It will be these inferences that the speaker is intending to convey. For Wilson and Sperber (1981), this is a unitary principle governing comprehension. The other maxims, in fact, follow from the principle of relevance. It is not within the scope of this book to discuss these two pragmatic theories in detail or choose between them. Needless to say, however, the theories have consequences which are different in important ways. Not least among these is that Wilson and Sperber's definition of relevance narrows down the very large number of implications available from an utterance to a subset (those produced by the principle of relevance) and claims it is those which the speaker intends to convey.

Inferring an indirect speech act

How does all of this figure in the interpretation of indirect speech acts? *If a speaker implicates that the felicity conditions for some illocutionary act are satisfied, then these can figure as premises in an argument that the speaker intends to perform that particular speech act.* That is, the most relevant interpretation of the utterance to the hearer is that the speaker intended to perform such and such an illocutionary act or acts. It is through doing '*Gricean*' *inferencing* that the hearer achieves perlocutionary 'uptake' of the speaker's intentions in those cases where the speech act is indirectly conveyed.

This needs to be illustrated with a concrete example. Let us look again at the exchange between Arthur and Doreen in Figure 10.5. We will concentrate on Arthur's utterance. Consider what happens when a remark appears to be irrelevant to what went before in a conversation. Remember we are always constrained to make our remarks relevant. And Arthur says, "What was the bloke like, could yer smell the drink?"

The Direct Act. Arthur has uttered two grammatical interrogatives. In Figure 10.3, we suggested that the mood meaning of this form conveys that the speaker is asking a question. He is seeking information of Doreen. Now is this a felicitous question or not? Are the felicity conditions on questions satisfied?

To answer this, we look to the context and the background knowledge. But we look at these in relation to the detailed form of the language which Arthur uses. There is nothing problematic in the first clause. But look at the second interrogative! The form of this clause is such that in this context Arthur quietly implicates that he believes that 'the bloke is or had been drinking', and merely asks Doreen if she could smell the results of this on him or not. It is a 'loaded' question. Arthur has no way of knowing whether or not the bloke had been drinking. And, in the context of the bloke's wedding, where the bride looked 'ever so nice', it *seems* an *irrelevant* aspect of the groom about which to ask Doreen.

We have to conclude, I think, that in all likelihood Arthur is neither sincere nor intending his utterance to count as a question. He is, we conclude, intending to convey something else. (Note that he could still be doing this even if the question were felicitous. Defectiveness of the direct act is not a necessary condition for the utterance to convey an indirect act, although direct acts often are infelicitous.)

The Indirect Act. Our immediate reaction is to look for the connection between what he says and what Doreen has just said. Thus, the deviation between the requirement to be relevant and the seeming irrelevance of the remark forces us to make inferences. These serve to connect the remark to the context and decide what Arthur intended to convey. We perform the same kind of inferencing which we examined in the last chapter under the control of the principle of relevance. I will just sketch out the reasoning informally.

Arthur implicates, given what Doreen has just said, that the bloke must have been drunk or he would not have got married. Given the meaning of the word 'drunk', which includes the inference that its subject is intoxicated or overcome with liquor and therefore not capable of acting in a fully rational way, Arthur further implicates that he believes that you would have to be impaired in this way to get married. It would be a very foolish and irrational man who would get married. Background knowledge tells us that, in general, people don't want to behave in foolish and irrational ways. Now, if we grant, as I argued above, that Doreen has just requested of Arthur that they consider, or at least talk about, getting married, it is easy to see how Arthur intends his utterance indirectly to refuse those requests. He implicates the felicity conditions of a refusal. Nobody in full possession of their faculties would consider getting married. Therefore, he intends his utterance to count as an unwillingness to entertain that proposition.

We have shown that implicatures are crucial in constructing the arguments that connect direct and indirect illocutionary forces. It is inferences of this sort that fill in the dotted lines connecting the directly and indirectly conveyed acts in Figure 10.5. Inferences of the same kind also account for the fact, displayed in Figure 10.4, that a single illocutionary act − for example, the act of requesting − can be conveyed by any sentence type. In the more indirect or seemingly opaque ways of requesting, (3–6 in Figure 10.4), the illocutionary act is inferred in context, following Gricean principles. (There have been attempts to account for these relations without using Grice explicitly; see, for example, Labov and Fanshel, 1977.)

Discourse analysis: an example

Now that we have described the machinery, let us try to apply it to the analysis of texts. For the remainder of this chapter, I will analyse texts and attempt to illustrate how the issues we have discussed offer a methodology which can be used in **discourse analysis**. Discourse analysis has to be based on pragmatic theory. Conversely, analysis of texts will allow us to make a number of important points of theory.

Just as there are different ways of conceptualizing what participants are doing in conversational exchanges, accordingly there are different possibilities for analysis. Let us look at two of these.

Conversation, in one sense, is the process by which we affect each other's beliefs. Each participant could be thought of as having a **commitment slate**, as this term was defined on page 274 above. These commitment slates are sets of propositions which represent what each participant believes at any point in the conversation. By virtue of what he says, implies and implicates, we gain a picture of what he believes at each turn – what he is committed to at that point for the purposes of this particular conversation. At each turn, we have seen that the speaker is constrained to make his contribution maximally relevant to the hearer. Each speaker's utterance, in other words, is required to generate the maximum of new information in the hearer's slate. Therefore, each utterance adds propositions to the hearer's slate. These are precisely the propositions which the speaker intended to convey. This gives us a method of analysis. We could proceed in terms of the representation of the beliefs of participants. We could then represent the additions and cancellations in the set of propositions that take place as a result of each utterance in the developing conversation.

Conversation, in another sense, is a process by which each participant performs intentional actions upon the other. Understanding is in essence the perception of the speaker's intention. When his intention in performing the utterance is perceived, this is the successful accomplishment of his action. One point of this chapter, however, is that the perception of what act the speaker intends is logically dependent on the hearer's perception of what the speaker believes. The belief analysis is prior to the action analysis. In the preceding section, I showed that we must understand what Arthur 'implicated' in order to deduce from this what illocutionary act he was performing – that he was refusing her request. The principle of relevance, however, guarantees us the maximum of intended implications from which to deduce the actions which the speaker intended to perform. And speech act theory gives us the means to represent conversation in terms of illocutionary acts.

So we have two interdependent methods for the analysis of texts: one in terms of the manipulation of sets of beliefs, the other in terms of the representation of actions which follow from those beliefs. In the following I will illustrate the speech act analysis.

Brenda has accused Arthur of, getting her pregnant. Their conversation continues. Later, Arthur says:

1 Arthur: How do you know it's mine?
2 Brenda: Why don't you want to take the blame? You're backing out now.
3 Arthur: What blame? There's no blame on me. I just want to know whether it's mine or not. It's not bound to be.

Let us see how this conversation works. On the face of it, Arthur asks a question. Brenda answers with another question and makes a statement. Then Arthur asks a question and makes three statements. These are all *direct* illocutionary acts. Now let us move on to those acts which are indirectly conveyed.

In Figure 10.6, I have schematized an analysis of this text in speech act terms, labelling both the direct and indirect acts. As before, the dotted lines represent the inferences which connect the two kinds. In this example, I leave it to the reader to try to work out the implicatures and the deductions from them that led me to this analysis. If your interpretation differs from mine, and you can spell out the inferential routes to your conclusions, then this will make an important point about discourse. That is, it is never possible to say absolutely for *certain* that a speaker intended to convey a specific proposition or perform a given act. There is always an element of *risk* in interpretation where inferencing in context is involved.

In Figure 10.6, I have said that Arthur's first utterance indirectly enacts a denial of Brenda's original accusation that her pregnancy is his fault. Given the context, I believe that Arthur's utterance is maximally relevant if I take it to implicate such things as 'only if I'm the father am I at fault, and therefore responsible', from which an act of denial can be inferred. But, given that we cannot guarantee that any two people share exactly the same background knowledge or perception of context, then I admit to a lack of determinacy in interpretation. The analyst is very much in the position of a participant in this respect, with the added problem that the utterance was not framed with the speaker's assessment of his knowledge of the context in mind.

Another tack is to see how Brenda took Arthur's utterance. Brenda's reply in 2, in fact, interprets Arthur's question as a denial of her original accusation. Replies such as Brenda's pro-

Utterances

Arthur
How do you know it's mine?

Brenda
Why don't you want to take the blame? What blame? You're backing out now.

Arthur
What blame? There's no blame on me. I just want to know whether it's mine or not. It's not bound to be.

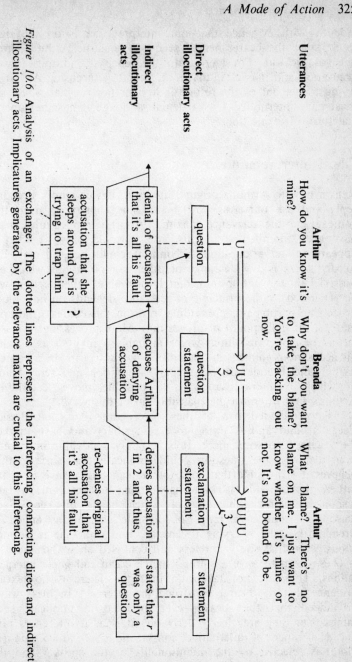

Direct illocutionary acts

Indirect illocutionary acts

Figure 10.6 Analysis of an exchange: The dotted lines represent the inferencing connecting direct and indirect illocutionary acts. Implicatures generated by the relevance maxim are crucial to this inferencing.

vide us with evidence that our interpretation is on the right track, since the hearer herself seems to construe Arthur's utterance as we did. Consider again the felicity conditions for an accusation and it is clear that in 2, Brenda is accusing Arthur of trying to get out of the responsibility for her pregnancy. So she must have interpreted 1 as a denial, although it has the superficial form of a question.

Ghost interpretations

Return now to Arthur's original question. Let us ignore Brenda's reply and ask ourselves how 1 *could* be construed, given this context and the relevance maxim. First, no implicatures might have been intended – in this case 1 would only be what it appears to be, a question. Second, it could be a denial. But thirdly, there is a wide range of other interpretations which are possible, though not so immediately derivable. Whether they will be generated by the principle of relevance depends on how much processing participants are willing to do in this context (the original 'set' of the amount of processing). More processing reveals a virtual nest of propositions which arguably point to 1 as a group of accusations aimed at Brenda. Now since in this context Arthur and Brenda are playing an 'accusation and reply' game in which counteraccusation is a possible move, could not Arthur's first utterance be plausibly taken this way?

I have included two of these in Figure 10.6 (that Brenda sleeps around and is trying to trap Arthur) and have marked them with a question mark. It is certainly a possible interpretation. That is, the question could implicate that since Arthur believes it is possible that some other man might have been the father, that Brenda is knowingly trying to get him to take responsibility for something of which he is innocent. Such reasoning produces a range of possible accusations aimed at Brenda: that she is trying to ensnare him; that she is promiscuous; even that she is careless and confused about her facts.

These seem to have a status which we can call **ghost interpretations**. They are not taken up in reply. There is no textual evidence that the hearer construed the utterance in these ways, or indeed that the speaker ever intended to implicate such things. Yet they are clearly derivable. It is as if inferences produced a range of alternative conversations of which one (or more) is selected by the intentionality of the speaker and the perception and replies of the hearer, and are thus made into the actual conversation.

One cannot help being reminded of the notion in quantum physics that quantum particles are indeterminate in their behaviour, only collapsing into a determinate reality when observed. Like quantum phenomenon in physics, the possible meaning of an utterance in conversation is indeterminate. We can only argue that a given construal is highly probable in a given context; we cannot guarantee that it was either intended or perceived.

Use of indeterminacy

Tactics in conversation can use this indeterminacy. So in 3, Arthur's reply to Brenda, he exploits the fact that 1 could be either a straightforward question or a denial of Brenda's earlier accusation. He reinstates his rejection of her original accusation and also rejects her new accusation in 2, 'Why don't you want to take the blame?'

He asserts that he is blameless. This means that he does not accept the 'fault' imposed by her original accusation and that, furthermore, since there is no blame attached to his possible paternity, he could hardly be attempting to avoid it. But simultaneously he denies her denial interpretation of his utterance, 1, by pointing to the question interpretation, 'I just want to know whether it's mine or not.' He was merely asking a question. Indeterminacy of interpretation is often exploited by the rules of politeness. Since 1 could be simply what it superficially is, a question, any other interpretation is, in principle, deniable. This means that we can convey unpleasant things, which might deface our hearers, under the convention that they were not conveyed at all. And if we are brought to task for such intentions, since they are inexplicit, they can be denied. In this example, the reader is left to decide about Arthur's sincerity.

Discourse analysis: a second example

Let us now turn to another text for a second example of discourse analysis based on direct and indirect illocutionary acts. The whole text is given in Figure 10.7. This gives us the context and participants. What I want to do, however, is focus on one

Arthur and Brenda are afraid that Brenda's husband, Jack, may have seen them together in one of their surreptitious meetings. Jack is, at present, drinking in a working man's club, so Arthur decides to make an appearance in order that there should be no suspicion that Brenda and he have been together.

He goes into the club, where men are drinking or playing darts. He greets two of them, Albert and Tom, a union organizer.

1	ARTHUR:	*Hey, Albert!*
2	ALBERT:	*Good evening, Arthur.*
3	ARTHUR:	*Hello, Tom*
4	TOM:	*How do, Arthur.* (voice from off screen)

Arthur moves on to the bar to buy a beer from the barman, Charlie.

5	ARTHUR:	*Come on, Charlie, give us a pint.*

Jack is sitting in the club room, alone at a table.

6	ARTHUR:	*Hello, Jack.*
7	JACK:	*Hello, Arthur.*
8	ARTHUR:	*What are you drinking?*
9	JACK:	*Oh ta, I'll have a mild.*
10	ARTHUR:	*Mild and a mild, please, Charlie.*

11	ARTHUR:	*When's the next strike then, Tom?*

Charlie pulls two beers for Arthur.

12	TOM:	*There's nothing to strike about yet, lad.*
13		*I expect you're too busy with young women for that, anyway.*
14	ARTHUR:	*No, not me, I spend my time with the bookies.*

He picks up the beers and goes over to Jack's table.

15	TOM:	*I believe yer!*

Figure 10.7 The 'strike' text

utterance and really tease out the intentionality behind it. This is when Arthur says to Tom, 'When's the next strike then, Tom?'

My main theoretical point in this analysis will be to show that an utterance characteristically realizes more than one illocutionary act. This is another way of saying that there is a *complex of intentionality* in the performance of a single utterance.

Our initial problem with utterance 11 is similar to the problem we faced with Arthur's first utterance to Brenda earlier on. The grammatical form is interrogative. But is this utterance simply a question, or is it an indirect speech act of some kind? Simply in terms of its linguistic form, the utterance presupposes that there is going to be a strike at some future time, and requests that Tom supply the information as to when that strike will be. The form also presupposes, by virtue of 'next', that there have been strikes in the past.

There are very good reasons for supposing that this utterance is not a sincere question. In terms of Searle's felicity conditions on questioning, mentioned earlier, it neither 'counts as an attempt by the speaker to get this information', nor does 'the speaker (sincerely) want this information'. Some of the reasons are overtly available from the context of the utterance. Thus Arthur is physically rather distant from Tom, and he makes no move to enter Tom's personal space. He glances at Tom only very briefly while uttering, and immediately lowers his eyes and engages himself in the purchase of his drinks. In fact, he walks away from the encounter during utterance 14, to join Jack as pre-arranged in utterances 8 and 9. Furthermore, his interrogative has an intonation which often signals that this form is not being used to ask a question (see Sag and Liberman, 1975). In other words, there are ample 'cues' that the question is defective.

But there are other reasons to think this utterance is not intended as a question. One is my judgement as to Arthur's personality and interests, given my previous experience of his talk. Another is the specific linguistic form he chooses to use. Contrast 11 and 11a:

11 When's the next strike then, Tom?
11a When's the strike then, Tom?

'Next' clearly makes an important contribution to the meaning of Arthur's utterance, perhaps in something like the following way. When I ask the time of a strike, I implicate that I believe that this is a relevant question; that there are reasons for us both to assume that a strike is likely soon, and I want to know when. In this case, I would use the form '*the* strike' which, by virtue of 'the', presupposes the existence, in the universe of discourse, of the strike. By contrast, when Arthur uses the form 'next', we can ask what the relevance is of him doing so. In the absence of any information from context that a strike is likely, it could implicate that Arthur's only reason for assuming a question about the time of strikes is relevant at all, is that there has been a strike, or strikes, in the past. This changes the question, because Arthur is indicating that he has no serious assumptions about the immediate relevance of his question regarding time. He does not believe a strike is imminent. Therefore his specific question about its timing is not relevant as a question, and is not a serious request for information.

Be that as it may, we are faced with the question: if Arthur's utterance is not a sincere question, then what illocutionary act might he be performing?

Figure 10.8 displays the illocutionary acts in the exchange. I conclude that 11 is simultaneously *a defective question*, *a recognition*, *a compliment* (perhaps defective), *a challenge*, and what is termed an act of **phatic communion**. In this case, in contrast with the previous examples, I have concluded that it is plausible that *a single utterance was intended to convey more than one illocutionary force*. In this I follow Labov and Fanshel (1977). I will explain the reasoning involved in deriving each of these indirect illocutionary forces in turn.

Social recognition? If 11 is not a felicitous question, what might it be? What did Arthur intend Tom to conclude he was doing?

We might say that Arthur is simply greeting Tom in a roundabout way. Searle has pointed out that a greeting need not have any specific kind of content, but must essentially count as a 'courteous recognition' of the hearer. It would be quite plausible to greet a man who was, say, characteristically interested in strikes by asking him about his interest as an act of courtesy. The problem here is that once participants have exchanged greetings, then the act is not repeatable. Try greeting again someone with whom you have just exchanged greetings and you will see what I mean. Tom and Arthur have successfully greeted each other in 3 and 4.

The solution to the problem that this is like a greeting but cannot be a greeting is that very often there are sets of closely related illocutionary acts which have certain features in common,

Arthur's utterance	Tom's utterance	
When's the next strike then, Tom?	There's nothing to strike about yet, lad. I expect you're too busy with young women for that, anyway.	
Question as to time of strike	*Answer* no reason for strike	**Direct** (inferences not dependent on context)
Recognition that Tom is active in the union	*Recognition* that Arthur is successful with women	**Indirect** (inferences dependent on context)
Compliment that Tom is active in the union	*Compliment* that Arthur is successful with women	
Challenge (a) that Tom is 'past it' (b) is wasting his time	*Challenge* that Arthur is 'young' and 'silly' and not serious about important issues	
Phatic social relationship established	*Phatic* social relationship established	

Figure 10.8 Illocutionary forces in an exchange

but differ in other respects. Thus, Searle has termed all those acts in which speakers try to get hearers to do something, 'directives' which might include, say, requests and orders. Similarly, we often attempt in our utterances (whatever else we may be trying to do) to include some recognition of the social identity of the hearer. We intend to convey only that we *recognize* some important social attribute which he or she has, or the social relationship we assume we have with them. For example, in the course of a talk with our friendly local bank manager, or our boss, we often intend to include recognitions that he has those roles, whatever else we intend to convey.

The boxes below show explicitly how two distinct recognitions can be inferred from Arthur's utterance. The inferences depend on the interaction of the meaning of 11, the context, and Grice's principles. These show explicitly the relation between the meaning of the actual sentence and an indirectly conveyed act which it is used to perform.

There are a range of other possible interpretations of Arthur's intention above and beyond that of being an act of recognition. I would argue that these are plausible. But I would not argue that a hearer, even in this specific context, would have to take Arthur's remark in the following ways. Consider whether the following are ghost interpretations or not!

Compliment? Arthur implicates that Tom has some privileged access to, or special interest in the time of the next strike; for example, Tom is a shop steward or is otherwise active in the union. If Arthur also believes, and assumes Tom also believes, that having this information or social attributes is an admirable property of Tom, then Arthur may intend to convey to Tom that he admires this property. But this is the essential condition for complimenting Tom.

That the mirror image of this act is also possible demonstrates the importance of background knowledge in construing an utterance. Thus, if Arthur believed that being active in the union was not admirable, and if Tom believed that Arthur might believe this, then it could just as easily be construed as a criticism of Tom's union activity, or even an accusation that Tom habitually fomented strikes. This is highly implausible in this case. But that is not because of the linguistic form and what it means, but because of what we assume, based on our background knowledge, about Arthur and Tom.

Challenge? There is a sense, however, in which Arthur might be intending to do something other than criticize Tom. There is possibly a kind of good-humoured aggressiveness in Arthur's remark. Such aggressiveness would be consistent with his personality. In this case, Arthur might be seen as possibly conveying a **challenge** such as: 'Tom, you are wasting your time on union affairs when it could be spent in such admirable pursuits as wine, women and song, possibly because you're "past it" or

Recognition that Tom is active in the union	Recognition that Arthur and Tom are equal and solidary
1. Arthur has questioned Tom as to when the next strike will occur.	1. Arthur has addressed Tom by his first name only.
2. Tom assumes, because of the relevance maxim, that Arthur's utterance has some relevant point.	2. Since Arthur could not have used Tom's name at all, or chosen some other form of address, Tom can assume that this choice has some relevant point.
3. The conversational setting is not such as to indicate an interest in whether there is to be a strike.	3. The use of first name conveys that the speaker and the one so addressed are equal and solidary.
4. Therefore, Arthur's utterance is probably not just a question. What is it?	4. *Therefore, Arthur intends, probably, to convey to Tom that he recognizes himself and Tom as equal and solidary.*
5. In asking the question, Arthur presupposes that Tom has the information necessary to answer the question, information that Arthur doesn't have. Therefore, Arthur is implicating that Tom has privileged access to, or special interest in, such information (e.g. Tom is a shop steward or is active in union affairs).	
6. *Therefore, Arthur intends, probably, to convey to Tom that he recognises that Tom is a shop steward or is active or interested in union affairs.*	

because you are insufficiently cynical.' I leave it to the reader to work out the reasoning involved in these interpretations.

A phatic act? Malinowski first noted that a good deal of human talk seems to exist merely for its own sake, and not to serve any further communicative function. In these cases the intention of the speaker is only to *create* a social relationship by virtue of speaking. 'Talking about the weather' is the classical example of this sort of talk, which Malinowski labelled 'phatic communion'. Notice that this labels an illocutionary act, a phatic act, for which we have no common name as we do for requesting, promising or accusing.

Could Arthur's utterance be a phatic act? The reasoning would go like this:

---

1. Arthur has asked Tom when the next strike will occur.

2. Tom can derive a number of indirectly conveyed acts from this utterance.

3. However, the only act required in this conversational setting is a courteous recognition of Tom's presence and this has already been achieved by the exchange of greetings in 3 and 4.

4. The conversational setting is such that Arthur is under *no* obligation to convey anything further to Tom, yet he has done so. What is the relevance of extra information?

5. *Arthur intended to constitute a social relationship between himself and Tom by virtue of the utterance itself.*

A schema

Figure 10.9 gives us a way of informally representing Arthur's utterance and the illocutionary forces it conveys. It is adapted from the format used by Labov and Fanshel (1977). The range of illocutionary acts is represented by A on the speaker's side of the utterance, and by α on the hearer's side. The dotted arrows represent the inferencing that connects the utterance with the

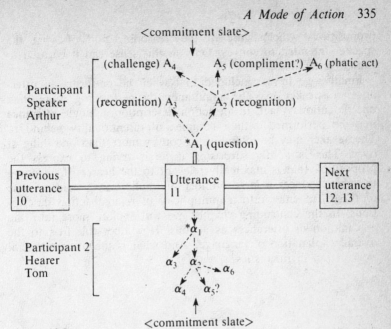

Figure 10.9

actions it is being used to perform. Defective acts are starred, and dubious assignments are marked by a question mark. The propositions in the commitment slates contain the beliefs from which the action descriptions are inferred.

In this chapter, we have looked at utterances as illocutionary acts. We have studied the way in which indirect speech acts are inferred from the linguistic form of utterances, combined with context and background knowledge. We have seen that the description of utterances in illocutionary terms, when this is indirectly conveyed, is derived from conversational implicatures. These serve as premises for the conclusion that the speaker intended to perform a certain act: of accusing, questioning, recognizing, and so on.

The interpretation of action, therefore, depends on belief. This tells us that background knowledge, of the sort we studied in Chapter 9, and the rules which govern the actions in language games, which we studied in Chapter 8, *only figure in discourse analysis as part of the process of inference by which we construe utterances*. This is also true of contextual 'cues', speech event types and so on. In other words, context can be viewed as propositions which figure in the 'reasoning out' of what the speaker intended to convey. Only in this sense can it be used to explain utterances.

Finally, we have concluded that when he performs an utterance, a speaker may be simultaneously performing more than one illocutionary act. In an action description, a single utterance may be performed with a complex of intentionality behind it. The speaker may be intending to convey more than one thing at once. This is hardly surprising if he is trying to express the proposition that is maximally relevant to the hearer. If, in doing this, he produces a large number of implications, at least some of these can enter into a multiplicity of related action descriptions. In the concluding chapter, we will explore more fully the explanation of utterances as actions. How does this fit into the overall explanation of language? And what is the place of social explanation in linguistics?

11. *Language and Social Explanation*

Where, finally, does linguistics stand as a science? Does it belong to the natural sciences, with biology, or to the social sciences? ... Behind the apparent lawlessness of social phenomenon there is a regularity of configuration and tendency which is just as real as the regularity of physical processes ... though it is a regularity of infinitely less apparent rigidity and of another mode of apprehension on our part. Language is primarily a cultural or social product and must be understood as such. Its regularity and formal development rest on considerations of a biological and psychological nature to be sure. But this regularity and our underlying unconsciousness of its typical forms do not make linguistics a mere adjunct of either biology or psychology.

Sapir (1929)

When we do an analysis of an utterance as we just did for Arthur's 'When's the next strike then, Tom?', in which sense can we be said to have explained the utterance? In Chapter 10, I offered a theory of discourse based on the idea that utterances are actions. Our theory gives us an account of Arthur's actions. It says that his utterance was probably the performance of a set of illocutionary acts. And it explains how we, and the hearer, could arrive at this set. It adds the proviso that, given different background knowledge, alternative interpretations are possible. We can never be sure we have the correct analysis. Is this a satisfactory explanation of Arthur's utterance? Indeed, what kind of explanation is it?

Two kinds of social explanation

The topic of this chapter is the contrast between different kinds of explanation of language. We will look at the different types of explanation that have been used or mentioned in this book, their relationships with one another, and their role in linguistics. We can define linguistics for this purpose as all the various theories we have which try to explain aspects of the phenomenon of language.

To begin, let us distinguish between two approaches to social explanation. The first type is the attempt to develop an *empirical theory* which will predict and explain large-scale patterns in social behaviour. The second and contrasting type involves the *interpretation of the intentional actions* of an individual.

In earlier chapters, when we examined variation in accents, we offered explanations of the first type. We explored aspects of a theory of linguistic variability and change. Let's see what we mean by an empirical theory in this case. We start with a body of well-defined facts which we want to explain. Our facts were the regularities in behaviour which we discovered. Groups used the variants in regular ways. The theory consists of a set of statements which make generalizations about these facts. From these statements we ought to be able both to predict and explain the data. The statements of the theory are of different types and relate to the facts in different ways. But, taken together, they ought to offer an explanation of why the facts are the way they are.

Consider one kind of statement we offered. We correlated average index scores with social factors. The social factors – for example, class and style – were the independent variables, and the index scores the dependent variables. The two variables showed regular co-variation. This allowed us to make general statements which we presented in graph form by means of sociolinguistic structure diagrams. On one level, we already have an explanation for the facts. Thus, we could say that social class and style explain variation. The argument goes, for example, that social class, if style is held constant, predicts average linguistic scores for a population.

Of course, the set of statements in the theory gets much more complex and absract than this. And it is then that we get more revealing explanations of the facts. Thus, we get the general statement that Labov's 'hypercorrect' pattern occurs (see page 142 above). It, in turn, is explained in terms of the involvement of the variable in linguistic change initiated by the highest social class. These statements, in turn, are corroborated by the pattern of the variable in real and apparent time. Further statements, which correlate hypercorrect behaviour with linguistic insecurity and upward social mobility, further explain the regular behaviour which the scores reveal.

The relation of statement to data is the empirical side of the phrase 'empirical theory'. No matter how deeply embedded in the theory a statement is, we have to be able to deduce the *observable facts* from it. For it to be empirical, the theory has to be able to pass the test of observation. If it does not predict the observed facts, then it stands refuted, and will have to be revised or replaced. In sociolinguistics, the facts are the observed regularities in index scores in a population. The facts themselves are quite abstract and can only be observed using the methods of investigation discussed in Chapter 4. These are the facts which the theory must ultimately explain.

It is fairly clear that studies of variability based on Labov's quantitative paradigm attempt to be contributions to an empirical theory of the sort we have just described. A sociolinguistic theory attempts to explain linguistic variability in social terms. The type of social explanation which is employed – empirical theorizing – is based on the model of explanation used in the natural sciences. If we ask *why* a variant occurs with such and such a frequency, in such and such a distribution, our answer is *because* it is in the process of change, and has been introduced by the highest class, and so on.

Now contrast this with the way we explained Arthur's utterance. It is a radically different sort of explanation. For one thing, there is no attempt to account for linguistic facts by correlating them with social facts. The utterance is not a dependent variable. We do not say that Arthur performed this utterance *because* of general determining features of the situation. So, our explanation was not predictive. In fact, I believe it would be impossible to propose a theory which would predict that Arthur would say, 'When's the next strike then, Tom?', even statistically. Our explanation makes no generalizations in this sense. This is because we were trying to explain Arthur's utterance in terms of the illocutionary acts he intended to perform. We have no way of theoretically predicting people's intentions; whether, for example, they intend their utterances to count as questions, recognitions, accusations or compliments, and so on. We also said that alternative interpretations were possible, that there was some 'risk' in our explanation.

It follows from this indeterminacy and this lack of predictive power that our explanation is not refutable by observation in the normal way. Indeed, the sort of fact involved is not even observable. Arthur's utterance can be observed, but the sort of act he intended it to be taken as cannot be observed. If I said, 'He accused Tom of being an agitator', mere observation of his utterance could not refute my claim. If you rightly wanted to dispute my interpretation, you would have to refer to Arthur's beliefs, and these are equally unobservable. So what kind of explanation are we offering, when we describe utterances in intentional terms?

Teleological explanation

In order to discuss this, we need to delve into issues which are typically of concern to philosophers. However, they are also very important in linguistics. The mere fact that studies in variation and discourse analysis use such different methods show this. The first area we must look at is the philosophy of action and its explanation. Later on, I will try to relate this to other kinds of explanation in both science and social science. The issues involved are very complex, and in a book like this we can only deal with things in the barest outline.

Let us see what we are doing when we give an account of a speaker's action in terms of his intention. What I am going to say here is based on the views of the philosopher G.H. von Wright whose book *Explanation and Understanding* (1971), is a major treatment of the problem of explaining action within the social sciences. (For a series of articles which relate to von Wright's work in this area see Manninen and Tuomela, 1976.)

Von Wright distinguishes two main traditions in the history of scientific method, that of **causal** and that of **teleological explanation**. Such traditions provide differing conditions on what we are to expect from a scientific explanation. Most of us are familiar, at least in a rough way, with causal explanations in the natural sciences. Indeed, causal explanation has such prestige, due to its success in explaining the physical world, that it is popularly viewed as the only valid sort of scientific explanation. (However, there are many different kinds of explanation which we offer and accept in everyday life – reflect for a moment on the many different ways you commonly use the words 'why' and 'because' in ordinary talk.) The kind of deductive theory we discussed above and illustrated from Labov's paradigm shows how models of explanation based on the methods of the physical sciences are commonly used to explain social phenomenon. Later, we will look at some differences between natural and social science, when deductive theories and methods are used in the two different domains.

It can be argued, as von Wright does, that teleological explanation provides a more adequate account of human action. In a teleological explanation, an action is explained by saying it was performed in order that a specific object or goal be achieved. In a causal explanation we say, 'This happened, *because* that had occurred.' In a teleological explanation we say, 'This happened, *in order that* that should occur' (von Wright, 1971: 83).

So we can give a causal account in answer to the question, 'Why did the window open?' – someone applied physical pressure to it. But this is very different from the appropriate answer to the question, 'Why did that man open the window?' A teleological explanation is that he opened it in order to cool the room.

Now to the crucial part of the argument. If the connection between the inner aspect of action, various mental states and events, and the basic act is not causal, what is it? According to von Wright, the connection is inferential.

Practical inference and teleological explanation

Intention and action are connected by the **practical inference**. The simplest version of this schema is:

	A intends to bring about *p*.
Premisses	A believes that he cannot bring about *p* unless he brings about *q*.
Conclusion	Therefore, A sets himself to bring about *q*.

Inferences of this form provide a connection between the volitional-cognitive complex behind a basic act, and the act itself. The connection is purely logical. It is not causal, in the sense that 'causal' is used in dealing with physical connectedness between events – that is, an empirical connection which can be stated as a law. The role of causation in action explanations is one of the thorniest issues in this area of philosophy. We cannot explore the issues more fully here, but for both sides of the argument see, Davidson (1980), Manninen and Tuomela (1976), Macdonald and Pettit (1981: esp. 80ff), von Wright (1971: 96ff).

Let's go through the practical inferences involved in the action of cooling the room. Say I intend to cool the room. I believe I cannot bring this about unless I open the window. This produces a second intention and so I now further intend to open the window. I further believe I cannot bring this about unless I apply upward muscular pressure to the window. Therefore, I set about doing this. The action involves reasoning. It is a rational act. The practical inference is the form which this reasoning takes.

Now imagine that someone else is watching me. How would he go about *explaining* my action? A description of my basic act, though true, is certainly not a satisfactory description of what I did. The evidence for his explanation is the observation of the basic act and its results. To say 'why' I performed the act, in the intentional sense of 'why', he has to work backwards from the action to the intention. He constructs an argument, which starts from his observation of the basic act, and concludes with his assessment of my intention. He has constructed a teleological explanation of the action.

So the observer who wishes to explain an action constructs a teleological explanation which is the agent's (the man who performed the action) practical inference '*turned upside down*' (von Wright, 1971: 96). He reconstructs the agent's reasoning. This gives him an answer to the 'why' question in terms of the agent's intention to bring about the object of that intention, his goal in acting.

Teleology and speech acts

The mere fact that we can appropriately label utterances as speech acts tells us that teleological explanation is also applicable to verbal behaviour. All along we have said that utterances are activities. To what degree can they be analysed in the same way as other kinds of intentional human action? In Figure 11.1, I have compared an analysis of 'opening the window', with the structure of Brenda's utterance, 'I'm pregnant. Good and proper this time and it's your fault.'

There are clear similarities between the two types of act. They

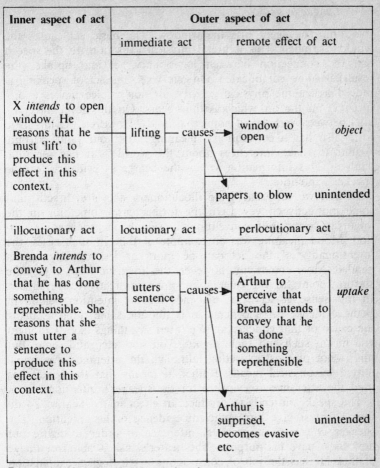

Inner aspect of act	Outer aspect of act	
	immediate act	remote effect of act
X *intends* to open window. He reasons that he must 'lift' to produce this effect in this context.	lifting —causes→	window to open *object*
		↘ papers to blow unintended
illocutionary act	locutionary act	perlocutionary act
Brenda *intends* to convey to Arthur that he has done something reprehensible. She reasons that she must utter a sentence to produce this effect in this context.	utters sentence —causes→	Arthur to perceive that Brenda intends to convey that he has done something reprehensible *uptake*
		↘ Arthur is surprised, unintended becomes evasive etc.

Figure 11.1 Verbal and nonverbal action

both have an inner aspect and an outer aspect. The illocutionary description of the speech act is equivalent to the intentional description of the nonverbal act. The locutionary description of Brenda's utterance parallels the basic act in the other type. Both have objects of intention. For the speech act this is the perlocutionary uptake. And both can also have other unintended effects.

However, the similarity is not exact. A striking difference is that the communicative act is directed towards a hearer. The object of the speaker's intention is to produce within the hearer a perception of this very intention to convey whatever it is he wishes to convey. It is to bring about this object that he performs the act.

Another difference is the means the speaker uses to achieve

this aim. The agent lifts the window. The basic act causes the window to open. This is literal physical causation. In the speech act, the connection between locutionary act and uptake (the result) is more complicated. On one level, the act of speaking is indeed a genuine physical activity. Brenda's voice makes a disturbance in the air which Arthur hears. On this level, the parallel between verbal and nonverbal holds. However, the linguistic form also has a conventional meaning. 'It's your fault' permits Arthur to make inferences about the world – it has semantic content. This information serves the hearer as evidence for the speaker's intention.

Earlier, we saw that some illocutionary acts are directly and some indirectly conveyed. In the former case, something in the linguistic form itself conventionally signals the speaker's intention. Mood meaning was an example of this. In such cases, the intentionality of the act can be more or less directly apprehended. More commonly, however, the linguistic form is just the starting point for the calculation of an indirectly conveyed act. In this sense, it serves as evidence for the intention behind it. Being evidence for a conclusion is not the same thing as being the cause of that conclusion. We often say things like, 'I thought you meant such and such, *because* you said such and such.' But this is not physical causation, although the utterance was transmitted by physical means. Rather, it means that the hearer has used the utterance as evidence for the speaker's intentions.

The speaker intends to produce an effect in the hearer. To do this, he must give him sufficient evidence of his intention. The speaker constructs a practical inference in order to figure out how to achieve his purpose. The hearer's task is a mirror image of this. He has the job of constructing a teleological explanation of the speaker's utterance. If his teleological explanation matches the speaker's practical inference, then he has understood the speaker's utterance. He asks 'why' the speaker uttered those words with those meanings, and his conclusion is what the speaker intended to convey. Figure 11.2 illustrates this relationship. It says that the way in which we understand speech acts is the same as the way in which we understand any form of intentional behaviour.

Let us explore some of the consequences of this last statement. Just as the hearer constructs a teleological explanation of an utterance, so can an observer of the exchange. He is roughly in the same position as an observer of a nonverbal act. He tries to reconstruct the intentionality from the evidence of the outer

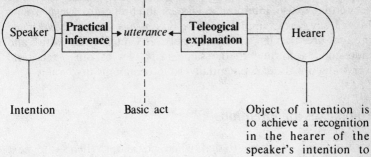

Figure 11.2 The pairing of practical inference and teleological explanation in the interpretation of utterances

aspect of the act. We are in this position when we do discourse analysis. This was our method in the last chapter. When we interpret utterances as illocutionary acts, we are constructing teleological explanations of the speaker's behaviour. We were offering explanations of this sort for Arthur's utterance, 'When's the next strike then, Tom?'

There is another important consequence of the fact that we understand different kinds of intentional behaviour in the same way. In Figure 11.1 the nonverbal act of opening the window, although intentional, was not a communicative act. But can nonverbal actions be communicative in the same way as speech acts? The answer is clearly yes. Consider gestures, for example. We could easily add a third box to Figure 11.1 which gave an analysis of the act of beckoning. Like verbal acts, acts such as waving, nodding, winking, various postures and so on have conventional or imitative meanings, and can be understood as conveying messages. But that is not all. As Malinowski said, utterances are interwoven with practical activities. And many activities are performed upon people, just as utterances are. Say someone gives me a kiss, or punches me on the nose. These are intentional acts like opening the window, and therefore to understand them I must give them teleological explanations. There are two classes of teleology to which I can assign them. I can interpret them as performed in order to bring about a certain outcome, like making me do something. But, intertwined with this, we normally also interpret a kiss as intending to *convey* something. I say, for example, that the kiss *meant* that we have made up and are friends. Utterance acts are interwoven with, and understood according to the same principles as other acts, and everything we do can potentially have communicative value.

Complexes of intentions

We noted in Chapter 10 that when he said, 'When's the next strike then, Tom?', Arthur was performing more than one action at the same time. The single utterances was simultaneously doing a number of jobs.

It turns out that this is a characteristic of the intentions behind any sort of action. And complexes of intentionality can have structure of various kinds. A second intention may follow from a first intention. Think again about the window-opening activity. Let us assume that the agent intends, first, to cool the room. Practical reasoning leads him to the conclusion that, in order to do this, he must open the window. This generates a second intention. The agent now intends to open the window. Practical reasoning leads him from this to the muscular activity involved, and so he sets himself to do it. The point here is that the **primary intention**, to cool the room, generates a **secondary intention**, to open the window. Thus, we characteristically get intentions arranged in chains, the one following from the other (Kim, 1976).

Multiplicity of intentions of this sort was pointed out by Anscombe (1957: 37ff). We can get as many answers to the 'why' question as there are separate intentional descriptions of the action. We saw how a primary intention can generate another secondary intention to do what is sufficient to bring about the first intention. There are also intentions which are *conditional* on the action required to bring about another prior intention. For example, say I intend to go to a conference in London on 12 June. In order to do this, I need to travel from Norwich to London by that date. This generates a chain of secondary intentions. I must go to the station, buy a ticket, etc. Now, say my mother lives near London. My first intention can generate another intention to visit my parent before going on to the conference. This is a **conditional intention** (Kim, 1976). The intention to visit my mother is conditional on my other, prior intention to attend the conference.

So, on 11 June, I perform the action of purchasing a train ticket in Norwich. This has behind it a complex of intentionality which might be described by a scheme such as,

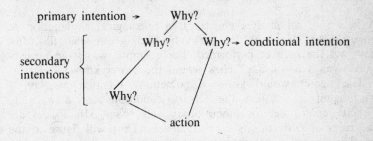

This is precisely the kind of complex of intentions we need to describe the intentionality of an utterance. Normally, if we ask 'why' a speaker performed an utterance, we get a complex of teleological answers each of which concludes, 'The speaker intends, probably, to convey that ...'

Multiplicity of intentions has been implicit in much of what we have said about utterances in previous chapters. Thus, we saw in Chapter 8 how initial exchanges perform greetings while they at the same time serve to identify participants. This was typical of many metaconversational acts. Questions, for example, could be used not only to elicit information but to select the next speaker. In Chapter 7, we saw how any utterance could also be viewed as an act of identity. In Chapter 10, we teased out a complex of intentions from Arthur's utterance to Tom. In this last example, the various illocutionary acts form a complex of primary, secondary and conditional intentions. Say we assume that the phatic act is primary, perhaps motivated by the requirements of politeness. Arthur's practical inference would be that one way sufficient to bring this about is to produce a sentence which shows that he recognizes Tom's social identity and conveys that they are equal and solidary. However, conditional on this, he can also, in passing, challenge Tom's values in an aggressive but playful way. He reasons that asking a question, insincerely, about the next strike, using Tom's first name, etc. ought to be able to achieve these aims, given the context and the rule of relevance. In analysis, we construct teleological explanations to try and get at these intentions. We ask 'why' questions about each detail of the form the utterance takes, see what implicatures are generated, and deduce from them the acts Arthur probably intended to perform.

The role of rules

A hearer or an analyst constructs a teleological explanation of an utterance. He does this partly by finding out what illocutionary act the speaker performed. For example, was it an accusation? Was it a warning? How would the hearer know?

The hearer would know if something counted as, say, a warning if it satisfied the felicity conditions for a warning. Felicity conditions for illocutionary acts (page 310 above) are the rules or conventions for verbal acts. They will figure in the speaker's practical inferences as the conditions which have to be satisfied if he is going to bring off the act he intends to perform. So he must shape his utterance in such a way as to convey to the hearer that the essential condition on the act is satisfied. He can implicate that he believes that the felicity conditions for the act are satisfied. This will lead the hearer to the correct teleological explanation.

Note that the construction of teleological explanations for utterances is greatly facilitated by the fact that illocutionary acts are rule-governed – language games in Wittgenstein's terms. When someone reports that someone warned them, or accused them, we immediately know what the speaker's intention was. We can paraphrase it by stating the essential conditions of the act. *The names we have for illocutionary acts are 'packaged up' teleological explanations of action made available by our lexicon. They are conventional ways of assigning intentional descriptions to utterances, a repertoire of language games.*

But the set of teleological explanations of utterances is larger than the set of illocutionary acts for which we have names, or clear conventional rules. This means that a method of discourse analysis which simply assigned speech act labels to utterances (accuse, warn, state, compliment etc.) would be very misleading. A more revealing methodology is to construct teleological explanations for utterances. Each explanation will conclude, 'Therefore, the speaker intends, probably, to convey' etc. It will be obvious if this is the essential condition for a familiar act, one for which we have a name.

But very often it will not be. Consider how explicitly we can work out the rules for a highly conventional act such as a judge passing sentence or a jury delivering a verdict. Contrast this with 'phatic communion', which is an act for which, before Malinowski, we had no name. Earlier on, I described the sort of 'pseudo-question' common in the classroom. This is clearly rule governed and conventional, but again there is no name for it. And think back to Robeson's testimony before HUAC. I used the word 'accusation' for Arens's utterances. But I was not totally happy with that label. What is going on is quite specific to HUAC and, perhaps, other related things like show trials, purges or smear campaigns. The intentionality behind the utterance is complex. It is performed not only upon Robeson but upon the public. The intention might be characterized as an attempt publicly to invalidate, or attach stigma, to the witness. The public, and not Robeson, is where the object of this intention resides. There is a wide range of intentional acts which have no common names. A teleological analysis of utterances allows the analyst explicitly to work out the intentionality and the social knowledge on which his interpretation depends. He can 'gloss' the utterance even in the absence of a common name for the speaker's action.

Summary so far

Let us now look back and summarize where we have got to in looking at social explanations of language. Broadly speaking, we have distinguished two main types:

(1) Empirical theories modelled on the methods of the natural sciences.
(2) Teleological explanations of action.

The first type explains language as aggregate behaviour. The second type explains language as intentional action. This chapter so far has been mainly concerned with the latter. Some people distinguish a third general type of explanation, namely, the explication of the social rules or conventions which constitute social actions. Felicity conditions are linguistic examples of this kind of rule. However, I have viewed this third type as subsumed into the second. The rules or conventions are prerequisites for explanations in terms of speaker's intentions. We saw above how an understanding of a speaker's knowledge and belief was prior to an understanding of his intentions.

I have explained the teleological or intentional approach in terms of von Wright's (1971) work in the philosophy of action, as it developed after Wittgenstein. However, intentionally oriented approaches to the understanding of both language and society also have arisen in other traditions and have a long intellectual history both in philosophy and in the social sciences. For a discussion of the intellectual background, see Giddens (1976).

As a matter of daily life, everybody assigns intentional descriptions to actions. This is our normal everyday way of understanding action, both our own and other people's. It is something that every child acquires in the process of growing up. He learns, from his society, how to use the language of intention and action, and this makes the social world intelligible to him. For example, he learns to tell an unintentional merely reflex action from actions which spring from wants, beliefs and intentions. He realizes that intentional acts are done in order to achieve specific objects. He learns the vocabulary necessary to describe what people do in these terms. In other words, teleological explanation is not exotic. We do it every day.

This kind of explanation makes certain assumptions. The most important assumption is that agents are *rational* in their attitudes and behaviour. The belief that people are rational agents is presupposed by teleological explanations because the connection between the inner states (wants, beliefs, intentions) and the outer aspects of acting is a logical one. To explain the observed act, we work back through the reasoning to the inner states 'behind' it. To do this in everyday life we assume that your reasoning is the same as my reasoning. In other words, calculability requires the assumption of rationality.

The method of teleological explanation in social science makes this everyday approach to action explicit. The analyst's interpretation takes the same form as everyday understanding. However, the explicitness itself leads to insights about what people are doing and why they are doing it at a level of self-consciousness beyond that we normally have in daily life. For example, Schegloff's analysis of how people identify themselves in telephone conversations, or our own analysis of the complex of intentions behind Arthur's utterance, go beyond our normal everyday use of teleological explanations. This makes it a valid form of social explanation. We gain insight into how the actions work.

Scientific and social explanation

This method is very different from the model of explanation we observed in Labov's paradigm of sociolinguistic research. In that case, the aim was to develop an empirical theory which could predict and explain variability in language, and which, in principle, could be refuted by observation.

The central question which preoccupies the philosophy of social explanation is whether or not the regularities which are exhibited by social behaviour can be explained in this way. That is, does scientific explanation work for aggregate human phenomenon? There are those, such as von Wright (1971) or Winch (1958) who argue either that it cannot, or that interpretative methods provide more revealing accounts in history and social science. Popper (1957), on the other hand, maintains that social explanations can be, with certain reservations, both theoretical and empirical. For a discussion of these issues, see Ryan (1970). This is perhaps the most complex issue that has arisen in this book. But we need to consider it to see if our study of variability and our theory of discourse can meet at all. What I will do is outline a position, and see what implications it has for the explanation of language.

Empirical theories in social science, such as Labov's, are based on the model of explanation used in natural science. Theories in natural science are theories of aspects of the physical world. At the beginning of this chapter we mentioned some features of a normal scientific theory. It is a set of explicit hypotheses which explain and predict facts. It has deductive rigour – the facts can be deduced from the statements of the theory. It is refutable. The predictions which it makes must not be falsified by observation. If they are, and there is no alternative explanation of why this should be so from common sense or a secondary theory, then the hypothesis must be either revised or abandoned. Agreement of observation with prediction corroborates the theory.

Let us see how the explanation of a particular event works. There are three parts: the event to be explained, a set of initial conditions, and a **covering law**, which is part of the scientific theory. The law explains the event by saying that if the initial conditions obtain, then this is sufficient to bring about the event.

Here is an example of a covering law from Popper (1957: 25). 'For light of any given wavelength, the smaller is the aperture through which a light ray passes, the greater is the angle of diffraction.'

Now say we want to explain an event – we observe an increase in the angle of diffraction of a light ray. If we take the covering law and combine it with the initial condition that someone 'has decreased the width of the aperture through which the ray is passing, we can deduce our observation. It follows from the covering law, given the initial conditions.

Covering laws in the natural sciences are causal physical laws. They state a causal relationship between the initial conditions and the event we want to explain. The initial conditions are the causal antecedents of the event – sufficient to cause it to occur and be observed. So scientific explanations are causal explanations of why things happen the way they do. But what do we mean by 'causal' here? We mean simply that as a matter of fact, if the antecedents occur, then the event in question always occurs. This could logically be otherwise; it happens this way because that is the way the world works.

Can this method of explanation be applied to the study of social regularities? Empirical theories of variability, for example, do yield explanations of the data. We saw this earlier in the chapter. There are a series of well-known difficulties, however, which have to do with the statistical nature of the phenomenon, difficulties of observation and prediction, and consequent worries about the refutability of theories in social science. But a plausible case can be made for unity of method in natural and social science (Popper, 1957: 130ff; Ryan, 1970).

Let us grant this. But are we really happy to view the statements of our social theory as causal explanations? Are there sociological or sociolinguistic laws? In practice, we often use the word 'cause' in these cases. For example, an economist might say that an increase in the money supply causes an increase in inflation. Similarly, we might say that if a variable is in the process of linguistic change initiated by the highest status group in the community, this causes a hypercorrect pattern in the index scores of the second highest status group. We are using the word 'cause' here to refer to a much looser but still factual connection between terms in our theory – just as the natural scientist does. This is a connection between events which the theory predicts, which could be otherwise. To call this a causal explanation seems quite appropriate (Ryan, 1970; Macdonald and Pettit, 1981).

But there is a difference between natural and social scientific theories at this point. Earlier on, I described covering laws in natural science as causal *physical* laws. All natural sciences are, by definition, theories of matter. They are explaining different aspects of the same thing. From this follows the unity of science. A scientist can descend a ladder of levels in the way he describes the organization of the material world. Any scientific law can ultimately be reduced to statements of physics (although there are doubts about this for the biological sciences). Say we are doing chemistry. We assume that the terms in our theory, for example the term 'molecule', can be understood in terms of the constructs of physics.

However, as I argued in Chapter 4, the social scientist cannot do this. There are properties at the level of social organization that are intrinsic to the interactions between human beings in groups. These are social facts which can only be expressed in social terms.

Now, granted that human beings are a part of nature, one obvious way to try to reinterpret social facts would be in terms of individual psychology. This would be an obvious way down the ladder of matter. Individuals have certain intrinsic psychological capacities: memory, perception, the ability to do computations and manipulate symbols, and so on. However, we argued in Chapter 4 that causal patterns exist at the social level which are not explainable in terms of the psychological properties of the individual. To put them in psychological terms we would need some such unacceptable concept as a 'group mind'. This is simply to say that the sum is greater than the parts. (I used the term 'weakly causal' to refer to these looser causal explanations we find in the social sciences, and 'strongly causal' to refer to the causal physical laws of the natural sciences.)

Expressive and explanatory autonomy

So we have two valid kinds of social explanation. Using methods modelled on natural science, we offer weakly causal accounts of sociolinguistic patterns. By contrast, using teleological explanations modelled on the way we understand action in everyday life, we gain insight into the speech acts which constitute discourse. Shall ever the twain meet?

In order to link the two kinds of explanation, we need first to look at a distinction made by Macdonald and Pettit (1981: 115ff) between the **expressive** and **explanatory autonomy** of institutions. The term 'institutions' here refers to social groups and their practices. Here is a rough and ready account of their ideas.

Say we have a set of terms to refer to some entities in a given area of experience. Examples of such terms might be 'class', 'style', and 'social network'. If this set of terms allows us to give expression to truths which cannot be expressed without those terms, then the entity in question is expressively autonomous. The referring terms make possible the expression of truths which we could not state without referring to those entities. Macdonald and Pettit argue convincingly that institutions are expressively autonomous. It is hard to see, for example, how one could express the truths in a sociolinguistic structure graph without reference to class and style. The pattern of variability is just not visible from the point of view of the individual.

Now let us contrast this with explanatory autonomy. Imagine this time we have two contrasting sets of terms that refer to different things. For example, an institutional and an intentional vocabulary:

institutional: *class, style, social network*, etc.
intentional: *speaker, attitude, intention, action*, etc.

In a sociolinguistic structure diagram we explained events by referring to things like class and style. If we *can* explain the same event in individualist terms, then institutions like class and style do not have explanatory autonomy. That is, these concepts only have explanatory autonomy if we *cannot* also explain the same events by referring to the attitudes and intentions of individual speakers.

In other words, the collective patterns revealed by using terms like class or social network may be expressively autonomous and reveal truths that cannot otherwise be put into words. At the same time, they may not be explanatorily autonomous. We may be able to explain the same events in terms of the attitudes and intentions of individual speakers.

The importance of Macdonald and Pettit's case for social science is the claim (which they argue convincingly) that institutions are expressively, but *not* explanatorily autonomous. They can always also be accounted for in teleological terms.

If this is true, then the twain shall meet. *We ought to be able to explain the large-scale patterns revealed by Labov's sociolinguistics in terms of the intentional account of discourse developed in the second part of the book.*

Sociolinguistic patterns and individual intentionality

Can aggregate scores for sociolinguistic variables also be explained in terms of the attitudes and intentions of individual speakers? I think they can. In fact, we were on our way to doing this earlier in the book.

We began by studying the social distribution of linguistic variables. Striking correlations emerged from this kind of investigation. Variants were regularly distributed according to various dimensions of social structure.

In Chapter 7 we moved from the social to the individual. Social distribution could be accounted for in terms of norms of pronunciation within a community. Because of these norms, variants had 'social meanings' – they stood for certain social identities and values. The uniformity of speakers' attitudes to variants revealed their awareness of both norms and meanings. This was more regular than their actual pronunciations. But clearly, to speak one way or another means something in social terms. With LePage's notion of an act of identity (page 229 above) these meanings informed individual speech acts. Each speaker's every utterance 'placed' him in terms of his degree of affiliation to the identities available in the community, and encoded in its norms. Each utterance claims a social identity. The act of identity, therefore, adds another dimension to the complex of intentionality behind an utterance.

The outcome of uniformity of norm and meaning (reflected in speakers' attitudes to varieties) is that individual speakers' intentions are realized in more or less regular ways throughout the community. We observe regularity in the social distribution of linguistic variables. The structure we observe reflects speakers' differing positions in relation to the norms which come about for social and historical reasons. But we are able to account for the collective patterns in terms of individual attitudes, intentions and actions.

We can conclude that two kinds of social explanation are both necessary for an understanding of variation. The Labov paradigm reveals the pattern. The teleological tells us why individuals should act in such a way as to produce the pattern.

An hypothesis: implicature and social meaning

We can, perhaps, tie sociolinguistic patterns even more closely with discourse and our account of speakers' intentions. In earlier chapters, the notion of social meaning was very important. This was the meaning conveyed by the *way* something was said. We can perhaps reinterpret social meaning in terms of Grice's concept of implicature.

An implicature arises when the use of a particular form of words conveys something which is not part of what has actually been *said*, nor entailed by what has been said. An implicature makes no contribution to whether the sentence is true or false. Now Grice (1975) distinguishes different kinds of implicature (for a discussion see Levinson, 1983: 126ff; Gazdar, 1979: 37ff). Only two of these need concern us here. The first type are the conversational implicatures which we studied in Chapter 10. They were generated in context by the speaker's apparent violation of the cooperative principle and its maxims. The second kind are **conventional implicatures**. These are also conveyed in spite of not being part of what the speaker actually *said*, and also make no contribution to whether his sentence is true or false. They differ in being attached by convention to particular linguistic forms.

Our claim here is that the use of sociolinguistic variants conventionally implicates a speaker's affiliation with particular groups within the community. For example, think of 'When's the next strike then, Tom?' pronounced in a variety of different accents. In each case, the speaker has said exactly the same thing. Each utterance of the sentence would be true or false under exactly the same conditions. Each utterance has the same entailments. Nevertheless, each utterance conveys something different by virtue of the accent in which it was pronounced. By producing different values of the variable features available, each speaker conventionally implicates, at least, a claim to a different social identity. We also saw that speakers can alter their pronunciation of variable features. A speaker, for example, can increase or decrease the frequency with which he produces a constricted *r* variant or he can code-switch between separate dialects or languages. In different contexts and between people in different relationships the use of one variant rather than the other would be considered appropriate. For example, between people who were equal and solidary the use of their mutual vernacular would signal this relationship. Such norms of appropriateness depend on the meanings conventionally associated with each form.

But such norms can also be violated. In this case, the hearer looks to the Gricean maxims. He can ask, what is the relevance of the speaker producing such an unexpected frequency for this variable feature in this context? We are supposedly equal and solidary – why has he switched away from our common vernacular? In other words, speakers can use choice of variant or changes in frequency to produce the other kind of implicature. They can *conversationally implicate* propositions by their use of variants. The argument is that changes in variables over and against what is expected within the conversation raise questions of relevance in Grice's sense just as they do on the other levels of language. Therefore, they can produce conversational implicatures.

This might give us a way to look at the origin of sound changes. Labov (1974: 253ff) has argued that three factors motivate a sound change. These are identity, solidarity and the strengthening of the force of expression. Let us look at this third factor. Say a given vowel height or a given frequency for a variable conventionally implicates a social identity. It can also, therefore, be used to convey solidarity with those of the same identity. Now say for some reason an individual wants to emphasize his identity or his solidarity. He can do this by violating the maxim of quantity – he can produce a higher frequency or a more open vowel than normal. He conversationally implicates that his affiliation with the group and its values is very strong in this context. He has increased the force of his expression for communicative purposes. In a community, such implicatures would keep pushing the norm of pronunciation further along in the direction of change.

Recasting social meaning in terms of Grice's theory further integrates our two ways of investigating language in social terms. It suggests a mechanism through which the intentional use of language in acts of identity systematically employs variability for communicative ends.

The psychological and the social

We have looked at social explanation of language. How does it relate to the dominant Chomskyan paradigm within linguistics? What is the appropriate boundary between the psychological and the social as far as the language is concerned?

As we saw earlier, Chomsky's conception of language is both psychological and universalistic. Its object of inquiry is knowledge of language. By this is meant the unconsciously known set of principles which are common to all languages.

The syntactic and other universals stated in linguistic theory specify these principles and therefore tell us the sort of system a language is. The universals are the way they are because they are intrinsic properties of the human mind – they reflect the mental equipment with which every normal human being is born. We are all 'preprogrammed' to know in advance what counts as a human language. This is what makes it possible for a child to acquire so rapidly and naturally any language to which he is exposed.

Chomsky (1980) points out that his is a psychological and ultimately a biological view of language. The statements which characterize knowledge of language in this universal sense should be referrable to statements of biology – to the actual physical structures that realize our knowledge and which are part of the biological make-up of our species.

However, because these physical structures cannot be investigated directly, the linguist must proceed in an indirect and abstract way. He does have evidence for knowledge of language in various domains. A speaker can make intuitive judgements, for example, in the domain of syntax, about grammaticality or the relations of one sentence to another. A grammar will explain and predict these judgements and thus characterize this knowledge. As I pointed out in Chapter 4, the judgements of any *individual* native speaker will do. We are after universal features which are biologically given. In principle, each speaker is the same with respect to these features. So variations between speakers or contexts is irrelevant to the investigation.

In a famous sentence, Chomsky (1965: 3) says, 'Linguistic theory is concerned primarily with an ideal speaker-listener, in a completely homogenous speech community, who knows its language perfectly and is unaffected by . . . grammatically irrelevant conditions.' The intuitive judgements which the theory explains are not about what the speaker actually utters. They are judgements about what sentences belong in the language or not. Chomsky makes a sharp distinction between knowledge of a language (**competence**), and the actual use to which the knowledge is put (**performance**). Grammars, both universal and particular, are theories of knowledge not of use. Their objects are sentences, not utterances. It is assumed that competence is prior to performance, both in behaviour and methodologically. First, we characterize the knowledge, then how it is put to use.

The distinction between knowledge and use defines the relationship between psychological and social explanation of language. It ought to be fairly clear that, in Chomsky's terms, everything we have discussed in this book are aspects of a theory of performance. Variability and language change, to the extent they are socially explicable, convention, speech acts and individual intentionality, the inferencing involved in comprehension, are all features of the way language is used, not knowledge of language.

We have come to this distinction between knowledge and use from the opposite direction to Chomsky – after exploring social explanations of language. We must ask ourselves, 'Does this distinction define the correct boundary between psychological and social/teleological explanations as far as language is concerned?'

Chomsky's paradigm runs into two related types of difficulty at this point. The first has to do with inextricability. In Chapter 9, we saw that Quine argued that it was impossible to distinguish between beliefs held because of the properties of sentences and beliefs held about the world. There was no clear-cut distinction between 'knowledge of language' and 'knowledge of the world', between meaning and background knowledge. If this is the case, it would be impossible to have a semantic theory separable from a theory of knowledge in general. Its subject matter could not be clearly defined.

There is a similar problem with syntax – the central concern of Chomsky's theory. The objects to be explained are native speakers' judgements about sentences. But are such judgements really extricable from the pervasive variability within a language, features due to the process of change, attitudes to language, or, most problematically, from properties of utterances and utterance interpretation? Can the data of a syntactic theory be well defined? Is knowledge of syntax distinguishable from the knowledge we bring to bear in producing and comprehending utterances? Are the intuitive judgements of a speaker reliable? If the answers to these questions is 'no', then linguistic theory is unempirical and insulated from falsification. Any counterexample which might refute a proposal can be explained away as performance – some irrelevant fluctuation or feature of discourse. For a discussion of these and related issues see Labov (1971, 1975), Sampson (1975).

The second difficulty goes even more to the heart of the matter. Say we proposed, for some basic syntactic property, that it was the way it was because of the way language is used in discourse. We are claiming that syntactic structure is explicable in terms of communicative function. Such proposals are usually termed **functional explanations**. In this case, social explanation, it is claimed, penetrates to the very centre of the language system.

Within Chomsky's paradigm we cannot have social explanations of knowledge of language in the intrinsic biologically given sense described above. We cannot have social explanations of competence. This is a matter of definition.

Let us imagine we have got a good social explanation for some feature of language. Now extend the idea of competence or knowledge of language in Chomsky's sense to include knowledge which is of a social kind. Let us say native speakers know rules governing variability – that variable rules are part of intrinsic competence. But we cannot do this. The reason is that the rules governing variability state facts which only emerge as properties of group behaviour. The facts cannot be expressed in any other way. This means that they are not ultimately explicable, in principle, as properties of individual psychology, nor as features of human biology. They cannot be reduced from the social, via the psychological, to the biological. So they cannot be part of the knowledge of language in Chomsky's sense.

Now say we can explain some feature of language structure in terms of Grice's pragmatic theory. Can we say that this would explain part of our knowledge of language? No, we cannot. A main point of this chapter has been the deep similarity in the way in which we understand utterances and other kinds of intentional acts. Both involve practical reasoning and teleological explanation. This in turn relies on the assumption of rationality – that people are rational agents. Likewise Grice's maxims merely formulate the assumptions people make about how each other will talk if they are rational and they want to communicate. The reasoning generated in both cases is the same. Although these abilities are probably universal and reflect the structure of our minds, they are not specifically linguistic abilities. Therefore, they are not part of knowledge of language.

Similarly for conventions. Throughout the book we have seen how convention serves us in the solution of coordination problems. Likewise, convention is a crucial part of our ability to make symbols and develop rules for actions. Social rules are, on the whole, conventional rules. Although the ability to follow rules and understand conventions is clearly a capacity of our species, it is equally clearly not confined to linguistic behaviour.

Therefore, it cannot be part of the knowledge of language which Chomsky is after.

For Chomsky, therefore, there must be universal biologically given properties of language which are not susceptible to explanation in social terms. (This is not true for Saussure, however, whose concept of *langue* both resides in individual minds and is also a social fact.)

Discourse and syntax

This is why functional explanations are important for linguistics. If major properties of language can be explained as products of human abilities which are not specifically linguistic abilities, then the domain of competence in Chomsky's theory shrinks accordingly.

Functional views of language can be either strong or weak. The strongest possible claim would be that all language structure has evolved to serve communicative ends. Language function determines language structure. There are other weaker claims which could be made. For example, one could argue that although there is a basic framework of language structure which is biologically given, this is fairly restricted. It interacts in interesting ways with other very general properties of sentences which exist because they are used to perform utterances in communicative acts. In this case one would be offering a teleological account of language structure.

In Downes (1977) I attempted to give such an alternative account of the English imperative construction. There are also very persuasive functional explanations for sentence relatedness, see page 209 above. This is one type of pervasive variation in which two or more stable grammatical structures can be used to say the same thing in different ways. The existence of pairs such as,

The vicar killed the *shark*
The shark was killed by the *vicar*

can be viewed as a resource of language motivated in discourse terms – what M.A.K. Halliday has termed the textual function of language (Halliday, 1967/8, 1970; Firbas, 1964). There has recently been an increase of interest in the explanation of syntax in functional terms. See, for example, Grossman *et al.* (1975),

Givón (1979), Sankoff and Brown (1976) and, for a critical discussion, Morgan (1982).

Conclusion

In Figure 11.3, I have sketched out the kinds of explanation required in the description of language. The necessity of the different kinds of explanation reflects the complexity of human beings. People can be truly described in different ways.

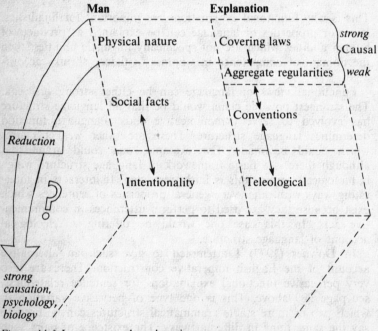

Figure 11.3 Language and explanation types

A human being is obviously part of nature. Accordingly, the properties of that amazingly complex organization of matter which we all are must be explained in physical terms. The properties of the mind can be investigated indirectly, and behaviour studied experimentally. We can assume that at least some of these properties are the result of the structures of the brain and nervous system. Since we are part of the causal systems of the physical world, human phenomenon is susceptible to causal physical explanation.

But people are also intrinsically social. Aggregate regularities of behaviour emerge from the social group. On our view, there are autonomous social facts. Accordingly, there are social laws or hypotheses similar to those in natural science (for a list, see Popper, 1957: 62). Social facts exist only at the inter-personal level of human organization. They are regular enough to be susceptible to causal social explanations which are expressively autonomous. Although individual psychological (and biologically given) abilities make it possible for us to behave in such regular ways, the regular ways in which we *do* behave are not predictable just from the abilities themselves nor explicable in those terms. There is a question mark in Figure 11.3 on any programme of the reduction of social facts.

But each individual also acts in an intentional way. We act in order to bring about the objects of our intentions. In both everyday life and in social science we offer teleological explanations for actions, including our utterances. This is central to both self-understanding and the understanding of others. Again, that we are able to reason and to explain in this way is made possible and constrained by our intrinsic abilities, but how we reason and explain in a given instance is neither predictable from nor explicable wholly in terms of the abilities themselves.

The teleological relates to the social, the individual to the collective, in a complicated interdependence. Practical reasoning and teleological explanation presuppose individual beliefs and assumptions – including the assumption of rationality. (To say we are rational is only to say that we assume we can construct teleological explanations of our own and other's actions; that what we do is intelligible.) But an individual's network of beliefs and attitudes is shaped by the social, by what others believe. Most social action is rule following. It depends on convention in order to be done and interpreted. Conventions are cases which depend on mutual uniformity of belief. You have to know the rules in order to play the game. Regularities of attitude and belief make it the case that each individual's intentional acts taken together with those of his fellows exhibit the regularities we observe as social facts.

And yet when we interpret an act or utterance, we can conclude that the individual intended to do and convey something new. We can arrive at this teleological explanation because of the assumption that he is behaving the way all other individuals behave, and against a background of common belief.

So man exists on all these levels simultaneously. Language, the central human phenomenon, has features from all the levels. It is an intentional activity; it is a conventional activity; it is a social fact; it is a universal product of our physical nature. This is what makes linguistics so exciting and so important.

References

ABELSON, R. (1973), 'The structure of belief systems', in *Computer Models of Thought and Language*, R.C. Schank and K.M. Colby (eds.), San Francisco: W.H. Freeman and Company.

AITCHISON, J. (1981), *Language Change: Progress or Decay?*, London: Fontana Paperbacks.

ANSCOMBE, G.E.M., (1957), *Intention*, Oxford: Basil Blackwell.

ANSHEN, F. (1975), 'Varied objections to various variable rules', in *Analyzing Variation in Language*, Papers from the Second Colloquium on New Ways of Analyzing Variation, R.W. Fasold and R.W. Shuy (eds.), Washington, DC: Georgetown University Press.

AUSTIN, J. (1962), *How to Do Things with Words*, The William James Lectures, 1955, Oxford: Clarendon Press.

BAILEY, B. (1965), 'Towards a new perspective in Negro English dialectology', in Wolfram and Clarke (1971).

BAILEY, B. (1966), *Jamaican Creole Syntax: a transformational approach*, Cambridge: Cambridge University Press.

BAILEY, C-J. (1973), *Variation and Linguistic Theory*, Arlington, Virginia: Center For Applied Linguistics.

BAILEY, C-J. and MAROLDT, K. (1977), 'The French lineage of English', in *Langues en contact-Pidgins-Creoles-Languages in Contact*, J.M. Meisel (ed.), Tübingen: TBL Verlag Gunter Narr.

BAUGH, J. (1980), 'A reexamination of the Black English copula', in *Locating Language in Time and Space*, W. Labov (ed.), London: Academic Press.

BAUMAN, R. and SHERZER, J. (eds.) (1974), *Explorations in the Ethnography of Speaking*, Cambridge: Cambridge University Press.

BENTLEY, E. (ed.) (1972), *Thirty Years of Treason: excerpts from hearings before the House Committee on Un-American Activities, 1938–1968*, London: Thames and Hudson.

BERGER, M. (1980), 'New York City and the antebellum South:

the maritime connection', in *Perspectives on American English*, J.L. Dillard (ed.), The Hague: Mouton Publishers.

BICKERTON, D. (1971), 'Inherent variability and variable rules', *Foundations of Language* 7, 457–92.

BICKERTON, D. (1973), 'The nature of a creole continuum', *Language* 49, 640–69.

BLOCH, B. (1939), 'Postvocalic *r* in New England speech, a study in American Dialect Geography' in *Readings in American Dialectology*, H.B. Allen and G.N. Underwood (eds.), New York: Appleton-Century-Crofts, 1971.

BLOM, J-P. and GUMPERZ, J. (1972), 'Social meaning in linguistic structures: code-switching in Norway', in Gumperz and Hymes (1972).

BLOOMFIELD, L. (1933), *Language*, London: George Allen and Unwin.

BOBROW, D. and COLLINS, A. (eds.) (1975), *Representation and Understanding*, London: Academic Press.

BODEN, M. (1977), *Artificial Intelligence and Natural Man*, Hassocks: Harvester Press.

BOISSEVAIN, J. (1974), *Friends of Friends: networks, manipulators and coalitions*, Oxford: Basil Blackwell.

BOTT, E. (1971), *Family and Social Network: roles, norms, and external relationships in ordinary urban families*, London: Tavistock.

BRADLEY, R. and SWARTZ, N. (1979), *Possible Worlds*, Oxford: Basil Blackwell.

BRONSTEIN, A. (1960), *The Pronunciation of American English*, New York: Appleton-Century-Crofts.

BROWN, P. and LEVINSON, S. (1978), 'Universals in language usage: politeness phenomenon', in *Questions and Politeness*, Cambridge Papers in Social Anthropology 8, E.N. Goody (ed.), Cambridge: Cambridge University Press.

BROWN, R. and FORD, M. (1961), 'Address in american english', in Laver and Hutcheson, (1972).

BROWN, R. and GILMAN, A. (1960), ' The pronouns of power and solidarity', in Laver and Hutcheson, (1972).

CAUDWELL, G. (1982), 'Anglo-Quebec on the verge of its history', *Language and Society* 8, 3–6, Ottawa: Office of the Commissioner of Official Languages.

CHAMBERS, J. and TRUDGILL, P. (1980), *Dialectology*, Cambridge: Cambridge University Press.

CHOMSKY, N. (1957), *Syntactic Structures*, The Hague: Mouton.

CHOMSKY, N. (1965), *Aspects of the Theory of Syntax*, Cambridge, Massachusetts: The MIT Press.

CHOMSKY, N. (1980), *Rules and Representations*, Oxford: Basil Blackwell.

CLARK, H. and MARSHALL, C. (1981), 'Definite reference and mutual knowledge', in *Elements of Discourse Understanding*, A.K. Joshi, B.L. Webber and I. Sag (eds.), Cambridge: Cambridge University Press.

DARNELL, R. (ed.) (1971), *Linguistic Diversity in Canadian Society*, Edmonton, Alberta, and Champaign, Illinois: Linguistic Research Inc..

DAVIDSON, D. (1980), *Essays on Actions and Events*, Oxford: Clarendon Press.

DENISON, N. (1972), 'Some observations on language variety and plurilingualism', in Pride and Holmes (1972).

DILLARD, J. (ed.), (1975) *Perspectives on Black English*, The Hague: Mouton.

DORIAN, N. (1973), 'Grammatical change in a dying dialect', *Language* **49**, 413–38.

DOWNES, W. (1977), 'The imperative and pragmatics', *Journal of Linguistics* **13**, 77–97.

DREYFUS, H. (1972), *What Computers Can't do*, New York: Harper and Row.

DURKHEIM, E. (1938), *The Rules of Sociological Method*, G.E. Catlin (ed.), translated by S.A. Solovay and J.H. Mueller, New York: The Free Press, Macmillan, 1964 (8th edition).

FASOLD, R. (1969), 'Tense and the form *be* in Black English', *Language* **45**, 763–76.

FASOLD, R. (1970), 'Two models of socially significant linguistic variation', *Language* **46**, 551–63.

FASOLD, R. (1972), *Tense Marking in Black English*, Arlington, Virginia: Center for Applied Linguistics.

FASOLD, R. (1975), 'The Bailey wave model: a dynamic quantitative paradigm', in *Analyzing Variation in Language*, Papers from the Second Colloquium on New Ways of Analyzing Variation, R.W. Fasold and R.W. Shuy (eds.), Washington DC: Georgetown University Press.

FERGUSON, C. (1959), 'Diglossia', *Word* **15**, 325–40.

FERGUSON, C. (1970) 'The role of Arabic in Ethiopia, a sociolinguistic perspective', in Pride and Holmes (1972).

FIRBAS, J. (1964), 'On defining the theme in functional sentence analysis', *Travaux Linguistiques de Prague* **1**, 267–80.

FIRTH, J.R. (1950), 'Personality and language in society', in J.R.

Firth, *Papers in Linguistics 1934–1951*, London: Oxford University Press.

FIRTH, J.R. (1951), 'Modes of meaning', in J.R. Firth, *Papers in Linguistics 1934–1951*, London: Oxford University Press.

FIRTH, J.R. (1957), 'A synopsis of linguistic theory', in *Selected Papers of J.R. Firth 1952–59*, F. Palmer (ed.), London: Longmans.

FISCHER, J. (1958), 'Social influences in the choice of a linguistic variant', *Word* **14**, 47–56.

FISHMAN, J. (1971), 'The relationship between micro- and macro- sociolinguistics in the study of who speaks what language to whom and when', in Pride and Holmes (1972).

FISHMAN, J. (1972), *The Sociology of Language*, Rowley, Massachusetts: Newbury House.

FOSTER, M. (1982), 'Canada's first languages', *Language and Society* **7**, 7–16, Ottawa: Office of the Commissioner of Official Languages.

FRAKE, C. (1975), 'How to enter a Yakan house', in Sanches and Blount (1975), also in Frake (1980).

FRAKE, C. (1969), ' "Struck by speech": The Yakan concept of litigation', in Gumperz and Hymes (1972).

FRAKE, C. (1980), *Language and Cultural Description*, essays selected and introduced by A.S. Dil, Stanford: Stanford University Press.

FRASER, C. and SCHERER, K. (eds.) (1982), *Advances in the Social Psychology of Language*, Cambridge: Cambridge University Press.

GARFINKEL, H. (1967), *Studies in Ethnomethodology*, Englewood Cliffs, New Jersey: Prentice-Hall.

GAZDAR, G. (1979), *Pragmatics*, London: Academic Press.

GAZDAR, G. (1981), 'Speech act assignment', in *Elements of Discourse Understanding*, A.K. Joshi, B.L. Webber and I. Sag (eds.), Cambridge: Cambridge University Press.

GAZDAR, G. and GOOD, (1982), 'On a notion of relevance', in Smith (1982).

GEERTZ, C. (1960), 'Linguistic etiquette', excerpt from C. Geertz, *The Religion of Java*, Glencoe, Illinois: The Free Press, in Pride and Holmes (1972).

GIDDENS, A. (1976), *New Rules of Sociological Method: A Positive Critique of Interpretative Sociologies*, London: Hutchinson.

GILES, H. (1970), 'Evaluative reactions to accents', *Educational Review* **22**, 211–27.

GILES, H. (1971), 'Patterns of evaluation in reactions to RP, South Welsh and Somerset Accented Speech', *British Journal of Social and Clinical Psychology* **10**, 280–81.

GILES, H. (ed.) (1977), *Language, Ethnicity and Intergroup Relations*, New York: Academic Press.

GILES, H. (1980), 'Accommodation theory: some new directions', in *York Papers in Linguistics 9, Festschrift R.B. LePage*, M.W.S. de Silva (ed.), York: Department of Language, University of York.

GILES, H. and POWESLAND, P. (1975), *Speech Style and Social Evaluation*, London: Academic Press.

GILES, H. and RYAN, E. (1982), 'Prolegomena for developing a social psychological theory of language attitudes', in Ryan and Giles (1982).

GIMSON, A.C. (1962), *An Introduction to the Pronunciation of English*, London: Edward Arnold.

GIVÓN, T. (ed.) (1979), *Syntax and Semantics*, Volume 12, *Discourse and Syntax*, London: Academic Press.

GOFFMAN, E. (1955), 'On face-work: an analysis of ritual elements in social interaction', in Laver and Hutcheson (1972).

GOFFMAN, E. (1967), *Interaction Ritual*, New York: Doubleday.

GREGORY, M. (1967), 'Aspects of varieties differentiation', *Journal of Linguistics* **3**, 177–98.

GRICE, H.P. (1975), 'Logic and conversation', in *Syntax and Semantics*, Volume 3, *Speech Acts*, P. Cole and J. Morgan (eds.), London: Academic Press.

GRICE, H.P. and STRAWSON, P. (1956), 'In defense of a dogma', in *Readings in The Philosophy of Language*, J. Rosenberg and C. Travis (eds.), Englewood Cliffs: Prentice-Hall, 1971.

GROSSMAN, R., SAN, L. and VANCE, T. (eds.) (1975), *Papers from the Parasession on Functionalism*, Chicago: Chicago Linguistic Society.

GUMPERZ, J. (1975), 'Foreword' to Sanches and Blount (1975).

GUMPERZ, J. and HYMES, D. (1972), *Directions in Sociolinguistics*, New York: Holt, Rinehart and Winston.

GUY, G. (1980), 'Variation in the group and the individual: the case of final stop deletion', in *Locating Language in Time and Space*, W. Labov (ed.), New York: Academic Press.

HALLIDAY, M., McINTOSH, A. and STREVENS, P. (1964), *The Linguistic Sciences and Language Teaching*, London: Longmans; 'The users and uses of language', reprinted in *Readings in the Sociology of Language*, J. Fishman (ed.), The Hague: Mouton, 1968.

HALLIDAY, M. (1967/1968), 'Notes on transitivity and theme in English', *Journal of Linguistics* **3**, 37–81, 199–244, and *Journal of Linguistics* **4**, 179–215.

HALLIDAY, M. (1970), 'Language structure and language Function', in *New Horizons in Linguistics*, J. Lyons (ed.), Harmondsworth, Penguin Books.

HAMBLIN, C. (1971), 'Mathematical models of dialogue', *Theoria* **37**, 130–55.

HANCOCK, I. (1977), 'Appendix: repertory of pidgin and creole languages', in *Pidgin and Creole Linguistics*, A. Valdman (ed.), Bloomington: Indiana University Press.

HAUGEN, E. (1967), 'Semicommunication: the language gap in Scandinavia', in *Explorations in Sociolinguistics*, S. Lieberson (ed.), The Hague: Mouton.

HAUGEN, E. (1968), 'Schizoglossia and the linguistic norm', in *Georgetown University Round Table Selected Papers on Linguistics*, R. O'Brien (ed.), Washington DC: Georgetown University Press.

HILL, A. (1940), 'Early loss of [r] before dentals', *Publications of the Modern Language Association* **55**, 308–21, reprinted in Williamson and Burke (1971).

HINTIKKA, J. (1962), *Knowledge and Belief*, Ithaca, NY: Cornell University Press.

HOCKETT, C. (1958), *A Course in Modern Linguistics*, New York: Macmillan.

HUDSON, R. (1975), 'The meaning of questions', *Language* **51**, 1–31.

HUGHES, A. and TRUDGILL, P. (1979), *English Accents and Dialects*, London: Edward Arnold.

HYMES, D. (1962), 'The ethnography of speaking', in *Readings in the Sociology of Language*, J. Fishman (ed.), The Hague: Mouton, 1968.

HYMES, D. (1964), 'Introduction: toward ethnographies of communication', in *The Ethnography of Communication*, J. Gumperz and D. Hymes (eds.), *American Anthropologist* **66**, 6, part II, 1–34.

HYMES, D. (1972), 'Models of the interaction of language and social life', in Gumperz and Hymes (1972).

JESPERSON, O. (1954), *A Modern English Grammar on Historical Principles*, Part I, *Sounds and Spellings*, London: George Allen and Unwin.

KARTTUNEN L. and PETERS, S. (1979), 'Conventional implicature', in *Syntax and Semantics*, Volume II, *Presupposition*, C.-K. Oh and D. Dineen (eds.), London: Academic Press.

KENNY, A. (1973), *Wittgenstein*, Harmondsworth: Penguin Books.

KIM, J. (1976), 'Intention and practical inference,' in Manninen and Tuomela (1976).

KLEIN, A.M. (1948), 'Montreal', stanza IV, in *The Rocking Chair and other Poems*, Toronto: The Ryerson Press.

KURATH, H. (1965), 'Some aspects of Atlantic seaboard English considered in their connection with British English', in Williamson and Burke (1971).

LABOV, W. (1963), 'The social motivation of a sound change', *Word* **19**, 273–309, reprinted in Labov (1972).

LABOV, W. (1966), *The Social Stratification of English in New York City*, Washington, DC: Center for Applied Linguistics.

LABOV, W. (1967), 'The effect of social mobility on linguistic behaviour', in *Explorations in Sociolinguistics*, S. Lieberson (ed.), The Hague: Mouton; also in Williamson and Burke (1971).

LABOV, W. (1971), 'Methodology', in *A Survey of Linguistic Science*, W.O. Dingwall (ed.), Linguistics Program, University of Maryland.

LABOV, W. (1972), *Sociolinguistic Patterns*, Philadelphia: University of Pennsylvania Press.

LABOV, W. (1972a), *Language in the Inner City*, Philadelphia: University of Pennsylvania Press.

LABOV, W. (1974), 'Linguistic change as a form of communication', in *Human Communication: Theoretical Explorations*, A. Silverstein (ed.), Hillsdale, New Jersey: Lawrence Erlbaum Associates.

LABOV, W. (1975), 'Empirical foundations of linguistic theory', in *The Scope of American Linguistics*, R. Austerlitz (ed.), Lisse: The Peter de Ridder Press.

LABOV, W. (1980), 'The social origins of sound change', in *Locating Language in Time and Space*, W. Labov (ed.), London: Academic Press.

LABOV, W., COHEN, P., ROBINS, C. and LEWIS, J., (1968) *A Study of the Non-standard English of Negro and Puerto Rican Speakers in New York City*. Report on Co-operative Research Project 3288. New York: Columbia University.

LABOV, W. and FANSHEL D. (1977), *Therapeutic Discourse*, London: Academic Press.

LAFERRIERE, M. (1979), 'Ethnicity in phonological variation and change', *Language* **55**, 603–17.

LAKOFF, R. (1972), 'Language in context', *Language* **48**, 907–27.

LAMBERT, W. (1967), 'A social psychology of bilingualism', in Pride and Holmes (1972).

LAVER, J. and HUTCHESON, S. (eds.) (1972), *Communication in Face to Face Interaction*, Harmondsworth, Penguin Books.

LEPAGE, R. (1980), 'Projection, focussing, diffusion', in *York Papers in Linguistics 9, Festschrift R.B. LePage*, M.W.S. DeSilva (ed.), York: Department of Language, University of York.

LEVINE, L. and CROCKETT, H. (1966), 'Speech variations in a piedmont community', in *Explorations in Sociolinguistics*, S. Lieberson (ed.), Bloomington: Indiana University, and the Hague: Mouton; also in Williamson and Burke (1971).

LEVINSON, S. (1983), *Pragmatics*, Cambridge: Cambridge University Press.

LEWIS, D. (1969), *Convention*, Cambridge, Mass.: Harvard University Press.

LIEBERSON, S. (1965), 'Bilingualism in Montreal: a demographic analysis', *American Journal of Sociology* **71**, 10–25; also in Lieberson (1981).

LIEBERSON, S. (1970), *Language and Ethnic Relations in Canada*, New York: Wiley.

LIEBERSON, S. (1970a), 'Linguistic and ethnic segregation in Montreal', in *International Days of Sociolinguistics*. Second International Congress of Social Sciences of the Luigi Sturzo Institute. Rome: Luigi Sturzo Institute; also in Lieberson (1981).

LIEBERSON, S. (1981), *Language Diversity and Language Contact*, selected by A.S. Dil, Stanford: Stanford University Press.

LIGHTFOOT, D. (1979), *Principles of Diachronic Syntax*, Cambridge: Cambridge University Press.

MACDONALD, G. and PETTIT, P. (1981), *Semantics and Social Science*, London: Routledge and Kegan Paul.

MALINOWSKI, B. (1923), 'The problem of meaning in primitive languages', Supplement I to C.K. Ogden and I.A. Richards, *The Meaning of Meaning*, London: Kegan Paul, Trench, Trubner and Co., 1945 (7th edition).

MANNINEN, J. and TUOMELA, R. (eds.) (1976), *Essays on Explanation and Understanding*, Synthese Library 72, Dordrecht, Holland: D. Reidel.

MCDAVID, R. (1947), 'Postvocalic -r in South Carolina: a social analysis', in *Language in Culture and Society*, D. Hymes (ed.), New York: Harper and Row, 1966.

MCDAVID, R. (1975), 'The urbanization of American English', in R. McDavid, *Varieties of American English*, Palo Alto: Stanford University Press, 1980.

MCDAVID, R. and O'CAIN, R. (1977), 'Southern Standards revisited', in Shores and Hines (1977).

MENCKEN, H.L. (1919), *The American Language*, New York: Alfred A. Knopf, 1980, 4th edition.

METZING, D. (ed.) (1980), *Frame Conceptions and Text Understanding*, Berlin: de Gruyter.

MILROY, J. and MILROY, L. (1978), 'Belfast: change and variation in an urban vernacular', in Trudgill (1978).

MILROY, L. (1980), *Language and Social Networks*, Oxford: Basil Blackwell.

MILROY, L. and MARGRAIN, S. (1980), 'Vernacular language loyalty and social network', *Language in Society* **9**, 43–70.

MINSKY, M. (1975), 'A framework for representing knowledge', in *The Psychology of Computer Vision*, P. H. Winston (ed.), New York: McGraw-Hill.

MITCHELL-KERNAN, C. (1972), 'Signifying and marking: two Afro-American speech acts', in Gumperz and Hymes (1972).

MORGAN, J.L. (1982), 'Discourse theory and the independence of sentence grammar', in *Analyzing Discourse: Talk and Text*, D. Tannen (ed.), Georgetown University Round Table on Languages and Linguistics 1981, Washington, DC: Georgetown University Press.

PARSLOW, R. (1971), 'The pronunciation of English in Boston, Massachusetts: vowels and consonants', in Williamson and Burke (1971).

PARSONS, T. (1951), *The Social System*, Glencoe, Illinois: The Free Press.

PELLOWE J. and JONES, V. (1978), 'On intonational variability in Tyneside speech', in Trudgill (1978).

POMERANTZ, A. (1978), 'Compliment responses: notes on the co-operation of multiple constraints', in *Studies in the Organization of Conversational Interaction*, J. Schenkein (ed.), London: Academic Press.

POPPER, K. (1957), *The Poverty of Historicism*, London: Routledge and Kegan Paul.

PUTNAM, H. (1962), 'The analytic and the synthetic', in *Readings in the Philosophy of Language*, J. Rosenberg and C. Travis (eds.), Englewood Cliffs, New Jersey: Prentice-Hall.

PUTNAM, H. (1970), 'Is semantics possible?', *Metaphilosophy* **1**, 187–201.

PUTNAM, H. (1975), 'The meaning of "meaning"', in *Minnesota Studies in the Philosophy of Science*, Volume 7, K. Gunderson (ed.), Minneapolis: University of Minnesota Press.

QUINE, W. (1953), *From a Logical Point of View*, New York: Harper Torchbooks.

QUINE, W. (1953), 'Two dogmas of empiricism', in Quine (1953).

QUINE, W. (1960), *Word and Object*, Cambridge, Massachusetts: The MIT Press.

ROBINS, R. (1971), 'Malinowski, Firth, and the context of situation', in *Social Anthropology and Language*, E. Ardener (ed.), London: Tavistock Publications.

ROMAINE, S. (1978), 'Postvocalic /r/ in Scottish English: sound change in progress', in Trudgill (1978).

ROMAINE, S. (1982), *Socio-historical Linguistics*, Cambridge: Cambridge University Press.

RYAN, A. (1970), *The Philosophy of the Social Sciences*, London: The Macmillan Press.

RYAN, E. and GILES, H. (1982), *Attitudes towards Language Variation*, London: Edward Arnold.

SACKS, H. SCHEGLOFF, E. and JEFFERSON, G. (1974), 'A simplest systematics for the organization of turn-taking for conversation', *Language* **50**, 696–735.

SAG, I. and LIBERMAN, M. (1975), 'The intonational disambiguation of indirect speech acts', *Papers from the 11th Regional Meeting Chicago Linguistic Society*, R. Grossman, L. San, and T. Vance (eds.), 487–97.

SANCHES, M. and BLOUNT, B. (eds.), (1975), *Sociocultural Dimensions of Language Use*, New York: Academic Press.

SANKOFF, D. and ROUSSEAU, P. (1979), 'Categorical contexts and variable rules', in *Papers from the Scandinavian Symposium on Syntactic Variation*, S. Jacobson (ed.), Stockholm: Almqvist and Wiksell.

SANKOFF, G. (1971), 'Language use in multilingual societies: some alternative approaches', in Pride and Holmes (1972).

SANKOFF, G. (1974), 'A quantitative paradigm for the study of communicative competence', in Bauman and Sherzer (1974).

SANKOFF, G. and BROWN, P. (1976) 'The origins of syntax in discourse', *Language* **52**, 631–66.

SAMPSON, G. (1975), *The Form of Language*, London: Weidenfeld and Nicolson.

SAPIR, E. (1929), 'The status of linguistics as a science', *Language* 5, 207–14.

SAPIR, E. (1949), *Selected Writings of Edward Sapir in Language, Culture, and Personality*, D. Mandelbaum (ed.), Berkeley: University of California Press.

SAUSSURE, F. de, (1915/1959), *Cours de linguistique generale*, Paris: Payot 1915. English translation by W. Baskin, *Course in General Linguistics*, New York: The Philosophical Library, 1959; London: Fontana, 1974.

SAWYER, J. (1959), 'The speech of San Antonio, Texas', in Williamson and Burke (1971).

SCHANK, R. and ABELSON, R. (1977), *Scripts, Plans, Goals and Understanding*, Hillsdale, New Jersey: Laurence Erlbaum Associates.

SCHEGLOFF, E. (1968), 'Sequencing in conversational openings', *American Anthropologist* 70–6, reprinted in Gumperz and Hymes (1972).

SCHEGLOFF, E. (1979), 'Identification and recognition in telephone conversation openings', in *Everyday Language: Studies in Ethnomethodology*, G. Psathas (ed.), New York: Irvington Publishers.

SCHEGLOFF, E., JEFFERSON, G. and SACKS, H. (1977), 'The preference for self-correction in the organization of repair in conversation', *Language* 53, 361–82.

SCHEGLOFF, E. and SACKS, H. (1973), 'Opening up closings', in Turner (1974).

SCHIFFER, S. (1972), *Meaning*, Oxford: Clarendon Press.

SEARLE, J. (1969), *Speech Acts*, Cambridge: Cambridge University Press.

SEARLE, J. (1975), 'Indirect speech acts', in *Syntax and Semantics*, Volume 3, *Speech Acts*, P. Cole and J. Morgan (eds.), New York: Academic Press.

SEARLE, J. (1980), 'The background of meaning', in *Speech Act Theory and Pragmatics*, J. Searle, F. Kiefer and M. Bierwisch (eds.) Dordrecht, Holland: D. Reidel.

SHORES, D. and HINES, C. (1977), *Papers in Language Variation*, Alabama: University of Alabama Press.

SILLITOE, A. (1961), *Saturday Night and Sunday Morning*, screenplay adapted from his novel by Alan Sillitoe, film directed by Karel Reisz, in *Masterworks of the British Cinema*, introduction by J.R. Taylor. London: Lorrimer Publishing.

SINCLAIR J. and COULTHARD, M. (1975), *Towards an Analysis of Discourse*, London: Oxford University Press.

SMITH, N. (1982), *Mutual Knowledge*, London: Academic Press.

SMITH, N. and WILSON, D. (1979), *Modern Linguistics*, Harmondsworth: Penguin Books.

SPERBER, D. and WILSON, D. (1982), 'Mutual knowledge and relevance in theories of comprehension', in Smith (1982).

STALNAKER, R. (1978), 'Assertion', in *Syntax and Semantics* Volume 9, *Pragmatics*, P. Cole (ed.), London: Academic Press.

STEPHENSON, E. (1977), 'The beginnings of the loss of postvocalic /r/ in North Carolina', in Shores and Hines (1977).

STEWART, W.A. (1967) 'Sociolinguistic Factors in the history of American negro dialects', in Wolfram and Clarke (1971).

STEWART, W.A. (1968), 'The functional distribution of creole and French in Haiti', in *Georgetown University Round Table Selected Papers on Linguistics 1961–1965*, R. O'Brien (ed.), Washington, DC: Georgetown University Press.

STEWART, W.A. (1968a), 'Continuity and change in American negro dialects', in Wolfram and Clarke (1971).

THAKERAR, J., GILES, H. and CHESHIRE, J. (1982), 'Psychological and linguistic parameters of speech accommodation theory', in Fraser and Scherer (1982).

TRUDGILL, P. (1972), 'Sex, covert prestige and linguistic change in the urban British English of Norwich', *Language in Society* **1**, 215–46.

TRUDGILL, P. (1974), *The Social Differentiation of English in Norwich* , Cambridge: Cambridge University Press.

TRUDGILL, P. (1974a), 'Linguistic change and diffusion: description and explanation in sociolinguistic dialect geography', *Language in Society* **2**, 215–46.

TRUDGILL, P. (ed.) (1978), *Sociolinguistic Patterns in British English*, London: Edward Arnold.

TURNER, L. (1945), 'Notes on the sounds and vocabulary of Gullah', in Williamson and Burke (1971).

TURNER, L. (1948), 'Problems confronting the investigation of Gullah', in Wolfram and Clarke (1971).

TURNER, R. (ed.) (1974), *Ethnomethodology*, Harmondsworth: Penguin Books.

URION, C. (1971), 'Canadian English and Canadian French', in Darnell (1971).

VAN DIJK, T. (1977), *Text and Context. Explorations in The Semantics and Pragmatics of Discourse*, London: Longman.

VON WRIGHT, G. (1971), *Explanation and Understanding*, Ithaca, New York: Cornell University Press.

WALLACE, R. and WOLF, A. (1980), *Contemporary Sociological Theory*, Englewood Cliffs, New Jersey: Prentice-Hall.

WEINREICH, U. (1964), *Languages in Contact*, The Hague: Mouton.

WEINREICH, U., LABOV, W. and HERZOG, M. (1968), 'Empirical foundations for a theory of language change', in *Directions for Historical Linguistics*, W.P. Lehmann and Y. Malkiel (eds.), Austin: University of Texas Press.

WELLS, J. (1982), *Accents of English*, Volume 1, *An Introduction*: Volume 2, *The British Isles*; Volume 3, *Beyond the British Isles*, Cambridge: Cambridge University Press.

WHITNEY, W. (1875), *The Life and Growth of Language* (Documenta Semiotica, Serie 1. Linguistik) Hildesheim: Olms, 1970, Facsimile, originally published London: King, 1875.

WILLIAMS, R.M. (1968), 'The concept of norms', in *International Encyclopedia of the Social Sciences*, Volume 11, D.L. Sills (ed.), London: Crowell, Collier and Macmillan.

WILLIAMSON, J. and BURKE, V. (eds.) (1971), *A Various Language: Perspectives on American Dialects*, New York: Holt, Rinehart and Winston.

WILSON, B. (ed.) (1970), *Rationality*, Oxford: Basil Blackwell.

WILSON, D. and SPERBER, D. (1981), 'On Grice's theory of conversation', in *Conversation and Discourse*, P. Werth (ed.), London: Croom Helm.

WINCH, P. (1958), *The Idea of a Social Science and its Relation to Philosophy*, London: Routledge and Kegan Paul.

WINOGRAD, T. (1972), *Understanding Natural Language*, Edinburgh: Edinburgh University Press.

WITTGENSTEIN, L. (1953), *Philosophical Investigations*, translated by G.E.M. Anscombe, Oxford: Basil Blackwell.

WOLFRAM, W. (1969), *A Sociolinguistic Description of Detroit Negro Speech*, Washington, DC: Center for Applied Linguistics.

WOLFRAM, W. (1971), 'Black-White speech differences revisited', in Wolfram and Clarke (1971).

WOLFRAM, W. (1974), 'The relationship of white southern speech to vernacular Black English', *Language* **50**, 498–527.

WOLFRAM, W. and CHRISTIAN, D. (1976), *Appalachian Speech*, Washington, DC: Center for Applied Linguistics.

WOLFRAM, W. and CLARKE, N. (eds.) (1971), *Black-White Speech Relationships*, Washington, DC: Center for Applied Linguistics.

WOODWARD, F.L. (1973), *Some Sayings of the Buddha*,

According to the Pali Canon, translated by F.L. Woodward, London: Oxford University Press.

WYLD, H. (1920), *A History of Modern Colloquial English*, Oxford: Basil Blackwell.

Index